The Forgotten Neighborhood:

Site of an Early Skirmish
in the War on Poverty

by
Ludwig L. Geismar
and
Jane Krisberg

The Scarecrow Press, Inc.
Metuchen, N. J.   1967

Copyright 1967 by
Ludwig L. Geismar
and Jane Krisberg

L. C. Card No. 67-12067

Preface

At the close of the action phase of the New Haven Neighborhood Improvement Project, the co-directors were faced with the task of reporting on this community venture. A comprehensive report on a social action--research project does not necessarily merit publication as a book; often the topical nature or highly specialized subject matter of such a report calls for a more restricted publication format. Our decision to use book form flowed from the conviction that an extended narrative would be of value to those engaged in combating poverty and deprivation. The writers want to share with their fellow social workers and with social scientists, community planners, and board members of social agencies and community action projects, their experience in carrying out a program of professional intervention in a poverty-stricken neighborhood. We hope that the story of what we did, our successes and failures, will contribute to the nationwide effort against human poverty and deprivation.

Our work would not have been possible without the cooperation and participation of the families who lived in the Farnam Courts Housing Project. We are especially mindful of the trust implicit in their wholehearted cooperation; to help us with some of our studies, they unhesitatingly furnished data on intimate details of their lives. We acknowledge our debt to them and voice our admiration for their courage and fortitude; the project has left the area, but their struggle against poverty goes on.

The Neighborhood Improvement Project (NIP) was made possible by grants from the New Haven Foundation and the National Institute of Mental Health (MH-00510). In his capacity as Group Work Secretary and subsequently Executive Secretary of the Community Council of Greater New Haven, Mr. Frank Harris provided key leadership. He planned, promoted, encouraged and guided the

3

project. It was his original vision of what constituted a multi-phasic action program, his untiring energy, and his ability to mobilize the community that brought the project to realization.

We wish to thank Mrs. R. Samuel Howe, who served as chairman of a series of pre-NIP planning committees and as chairman of the NIP Advisory Committee of the Community Council. During the five-year period that saw NIP go from the drafting stage through maturity to termination, she persevered as an ardent community worker and supporter.

Among the several agencies which participated, at one time or another, in the casework treatment phase, we wish to give particular acknowledgment to the Family Service Association of New Haven and its Executive Director, John Nichols. Mr. Nichols, a member of the pre-NIP planning committee, not only insured his agency's participation for the duration of the project but also provided additional staff when the need arose. Other Family Service staff members to whom we are indebted are Mrs. Ruth Janowicz, Case Supervisor; Miss Ruth MacIlroy, Supervisor; Michael Miller and Ross McCarthy, caseworkers. Special thanks go to another caseworker, Mrs. Janet Kiphuth. Her admirable staying power made her an active associate throughout the life of NIP, and one of her cases furnished the base for the description of intensive services elaborated in Chapter 6. We also wish to acknowledge the work of Miss Kay Starr, school social worker, who was associated with the project for three years as a part-time caseworker. Her time was allocated by the New Haven Board of Education through Dr. Estelle Feldman, Director of the Division of School Social Workers.

Special thanks go to Mr. William DeGeorge, Executive Director of Farnam Neighborhood House, who bore the major responsibility for initiating and conducting the children's group work program during the first two years of the project.

Many individuals served at one time or another on the core NIP staff. As a group they worked unreservedly and displayed unusual devotion. Their ingenuity, inventiveness, flexibility and energy, plus their sensitive response to the needs of the treatment

4

population, were essential to the implementation of this project.

For four years Mrs. Joyce Watson served in many capacities, but her principal role was research assistant. Her help was invaluable in both planning and carrying out the Neighborhood Indices Study. In addition, she helped to train and supervise research interviewers and she carried the responsibility for collecting and collating data on several other studies. In ways too numerous to mention, she was an esteemed colleague and friend. Mrs. Marie Donchian served for three years on our staff, first as administrative assistant and then as research assistant. In addition, her fluency in Spanish led to her recruitment as interpreter in an emergency. From this beginning, her other talents and capabilities led to her assumption of casework duties with the Spanish-speaking families for one year; during this time she filled with notable effectiveness one of the service gaps affecting the Puerto Rican population.

Miss Jemma Plummer and Miss Anne Marie Azarro, who served principally as secretaries, performed many other services, which aided considerably in maintaining good will between staff and treatment population.

Major responsibility for the success of the group work and recreation programs lies with the two directors. Mr. Tom Flood carried on the work with older children and youth. The nursery program was developed and directed by Mrs. Edith Woodard, who served as Adult Program Director and also supervised some community organization programs. We are further indebted to Mrs. Woodard for her help in the writing of this book; a valuable rough draft of her written reports has been used in Chapter 7.

Contributing further to the success of the group work program were Mrs. Phoebe Granshaw and Mrs. Virginia Calestro (Nursery); Mrs. Rose Zemel (Senior Citizens; Young Mother's Club); Mrs. Lillian Dimow (Arts and Crafts). The enormous good will, imagination and creativity which these women brought to the task of devising programs to meet special needs deserve special tribute; none of them received more than token monetary compensation for their long, hard hours of work day and night. We also would like to acknowledge the contribution made by a large number

5

of student volunteers from Yale University and the Southern State College who served as group leaders.

We want to thank Miss Diane Lacey, a full-time affiliate with the multi-problem family treatment work for three years. Mrs. Cynthia Reller contributed notably as the Farnam Courts caseworker.

Dr. Margaret Wheeler, NIP Research Associate for eighteen months, compiled the data and prepared the rought draft used in the major portion of Chapters 1 through 4.

We owe much to Mrs. Shirley Geismar, who took major responsibility for organizing and editing the material, and to Mrs. Leah Verri, who typed the manuscript.

L. L. G.

J. K.

Table of Contents

Tables

8

9

Introduction

This is a book about a deprived neighborhood and the efforts made in its behalf by the social work sector of the community. Farnam Courts is a small, low-income housing project located in New Haven, Connecticut. To reduce the human deprivation found there, the Neighborhood Improvement Project (NIP) was formed. It was sponsored by the community, with financial support coming from both the community and the Federal Government. NIP can best be described as a planned professional intervention to help a socially disadvantaged population. This volume contains documentation of the planning, the establishment and the operation of the Neighborhood Improvement Project, plus an evaluation of its performance.

Since the termination of this project, the slogan "War on Poverty" has gained currency. For the first time since the Depression, the government has incorporated into its official statements the belief that the whole nation shares in the responsibility for poverty and deprivation in the United States. Beyond that, Congress has passed the Economic Opportunity Act of 1964, aimed at mobilizing the financial and human resources of the nation to combat poverty. This act, a billion-dollar piece of legislation, is nonetheless insufficient to substantially alleviate poverty in the United States. Its main significance lies in its potential for sparking new programs and for creating greater public support of measures aimed at eliminating economic and social deprivation.

The reasoning that underlies many of the anti-poverty programs represents a breakthrough in official thinking and action on the subject of poverty, a shift in emphasis from the individual to the system. No longer are the poor seen as carrying exclusively the blame for their wretched condition; society is held in a large measure responsible for their fate. Human rehabilitation, which once stressed changing the behavior of the poor, now puts increas-

10

ing emphasis on changing the job situation, the schools, the health and welfare systems, and the neighborhood. The earlier tendency to view the functioning of deprived people mainly in terms of adjustment and motivation has given way to the more comprehensive view that the socially handicapped are the product of interacting social, economic and psychological forces. As a result, anti-poverty projects are emphasizing new educational approaches, job retraining, employment, social and recreational activities.

The NIP program represents a form of intervention midway between the individual-centered approach of the 1930's and the broad social approach that has many adherents in the 1960's. Advocates of professional intervention in the lives of the socially handicapped often show a strong preference for one strategy or the other. The planners and policy makers of NIP confronted this issue with a caution made necessary by a lack of precise knowledge on the causation of social malfunctioning. In choosing as a basis for programming the widely accepted but vague model of multiple causation, we were faced with the task of assessing the relative importance of various factors contributing to individual and family functioning. We attempted to do this on a case by case basis. A more comprehensive and systematic inquiry would have been a task beyond the mandate of the project.

The Neighborhood Improvement Project was conceived before the "War on Poverty" was proclaimed. The community's concern with juvenile delinquency was the immediate incentive for establishing this pilot project in a low-income housing project. Multi-problem families in this neighborhood were seen as the target population; action and research were to be aimed at them on the assumption that such families are the prime seedbed of juvenile delinquency. As the project moved from the planning to the implementing phase, however, it became increasingly clear that juvenile delinquency in the area--as recorded by the police and the courts--was interwoven with more than family malfunctioning. Also intricately involved were economic deprivation, unemployment, the lack of educational and occupational opportunities, the inadequacy of health facilities and services, and the absence of social and recreational

11

outlets. We soon realized that the project could not limit itself to dealing with just the delinquent or the multi-problem family but had to broaden its scope to include all the people of Farnam Courts, the neighborhood in which they lived, and the larger community of which they were members.

We would not wish to create the impression that these observations represent any new or unique findings. Social work and the social sciences have long been aware of the relationships among poverty, lack of opportunity and problematic behavior. Our discovery was a more particular one, directly related to our seeking ways of reducing delinquency, family disorganization and deprivation. As we began to pinpoint the multi-problem families in the Courts and develop casework services for them, we became overwhelmingly aware of the inadequacy of such services. They would do little to keep children from acting out their frustrated impulses caused by lack of play activity, to help mothers escape household tedium for a few moments of recreation or sociability, or to enable senior citizens to break through the isolation of old age. Above all, these services would not offer wage earners the opportunity of acquiring occupational skills and gainful employment. The family-centered casework services we were planning, important though they appeared to be as a means of reaching families and helping them cope with their problems, left untouched a part of life that accounted for much of the misery and deprivation of the residents.

Thus, almost from the beginning it seemed clear that we would have to broaden our focus. During our first weeks in the neighborhood we learned that although the multi-problem family can be operationally defined and can be selected for service on the basis of that definition, many families not meeting that definition were, in fact, on the verge of multi-problem functioning. Although we had no way of predicting whether they would become subjects for the treatment group, a number of more adequately functioning families did move into the multi-problem group from time to time.

Thus it appeared imperative to make casework services available to all families in Farnam Courts who were in need of

12

help, which we did early during the operation of NIP. Over one-third of the population, not judged as multi-problem, availed themselves of the services, which devoted as much effort toward modifying the clients' surroundings as toward changing their behavior. (The term "surroundings" designates such factors as the practices of health clinics, the policies of the Housing Authority, the high interest charges of merchants, and others.)

But casework, no matter how broadly conceived, clearly was not enough. The housing project, because of urban renewal, was becoming ever more detached from the larger community. The tenants spent most of their time in the project. They had negative feelings about their neighborhood, which over the years had become increasingly marked by physical neglect, tenant apathy, social inactivity, and deviant behavior. The Neighborhood Improvement Project responded by developing a program of activities designed to increase recreational opportunities, to enhance social skills and to promote the education of residents. It was hoped that these activities would have a positive impact upon neighborhood life and eventually lead to an improvement of the neighborhood image. These theoretical assumptions, plus many trial and error operations, shaped the emerging group work and recreational program.

The activities described above and covered in detail in succeeding chapters left largely untouched the area of economic opportunities and practices. Few would disagree that this is a key area of social functioning in a deprived population and that continued economic deprivation among the people would limit our chances to effect change or movement in the population. However, social research at this point is far from conclusive on the relationship between economic structure and family life, and the precise limitations of operating in an economic status quo--the year 1959 left few alternatives--were largely a matter of conjecture. On the other hand, beginning research evidence suggested--although it could not confirm--that there was a reciprocal interaction between intra-familial functioning and economic behavior. Social work intervention did not offer the possibility of modifying the economic system, but it could aid people to function better economically by helping them

13

to exercise their full potential or by gaining concessions from the system. The latter applied especially to cases in which intervention brought about more flexibility on the part of public assistance agencies in response to economic need, as will be documented in Chapter 6.

One of the striking characteristics of Farnam Courts was its remoteness from the mainstream of the community. Socially and economically secluded since the early days of its existence, the housing project was at the beginning of the 1960's experiencing physical isolation as a result of freeway construction and urban renewal. The Courts had truly become a forgotten neighborhood. Thus a central theme in our work with the Farnam Courts tenants was their integration into the larger community. Integration meant the diminution of the residents' state of alienation and a greater sharing in the ideas, activities, values and assets of the larger community. Here again we were under no illusion. Our mandate for program and service contained no provision for increasing material affluence. Yet our endeavor was guided by the belief that professional reaching-out to break the barrier of isolation, and imaginative programming based on people's needs, could serve as a beginning step in the complex process of integration. We viewed the activities of the project not as the ultimate means but as an important link in a chain of measures aimed at the rehabilitation of low-income populations. Our previous work with multi-problem families had taught us that the socially handicapped often have a limited capacity for availing themselves of economic opportunities, and so we saw our attempts at social integration as an essential technique for increasing that capacity.

In short, the Neighborhood Improvement Project constituted community-sponsored and professionally directed intervention in the lives of a deprived population. The nature of this intervention was dictated initially by the needs as we perceived them, but subsequently discovered needs often reshaped our services. In spite of the availability of behavioral science knowledge and perceptive practitioners, need often remains latent in character, becoming manifest only in response to given stimuli, such as new programs or activi-

ties. The Neighborhood Improvement Project, because of its small
size and simple structure, afforded a rich opportunity to introduce
new stimuli. It could test new ways and techniques in working with
deprived populations, without the risk inherent in large, structured,
experimental programs. Smallness in our case meant person-to-
person contact and program flexibility, both of which made it per-
missible to try and fail. Indeed, some of our failures constituted
the most important learning experiences for staff and clients alike.

In reporting on the experiences that made up the Neighborhood Improvement Project, nothing would please us more than to be
able to produce a detailed account backed by figures, systematic observations, and precise measurement of results. This is an ideal
yet to be attained in a community action project. Our research set
out to assess systematically the best established or most measurable phases of the action project. The least tested phases received
less systematic documentation. Minutes of meetings, attendance
rosters, and narrative reports by group leaders necessarily served
as the basis of much of our report.

This book begins with a description of Farnam Courts and
its population, with special emphasis on the character of the people
and the problems faced by this small community. A short history
of the neighborhood is also included, in order to illuminate the
forces of change which have shaped the neighborhood's present character. Subsequent chapters are devoted to the subject of professional intervention. The problems of social rehabilitation in New Haven
are discussed within the context of political developments and social
change in this university city. The specific issues which led the
community to support a pilot project in Farnam Courts, and the
process of planning and carrying out a social work program, are
reviewed in detail.

This volume, then, represents a distillation of experience
gained in the search for a limited, yet appropriate program for a
low-income population. Intensive casework with the thirty most disorganized families is described and evaluated by means of an experimental control study. The newly developed role of the general-
ist neighborhood social worker with a large variety of functions is

15

analyzed. The issue of trained versus untrained workers is discussed. Programming for diverse age groups is examined critically. Finally, the authors have tried to answer the obvious question; namely, what lessons were learned in the Neighborhood Improvement Project.

As we stated earlier, this project was not launched at the most propitious time. Like a number of other attempts in the 1950's to help socially handicapped populations, the Neighborhood Improvement Project lacked the broad base support enjoyed by later endeavors. On the other hand, NIP is able to summarize its experience at a time when the nation in general and the welfare community in particular are in greatest need of knowledge about methods and programs for an effective war on poverty. It is our hope that the present volume will contribute to the systematic development of such knowledge.

Chapter 1
The Setting

In the south-central portion of New Haven, hemmed in by the main line of the New Haven Railroad, the sidings along the banks of the Mill River, and the industrial zone around the waterfront, there lies a flat, triangular area known to the average New Havener only as one of several factory and slum areas that border the main business district. The average city resident seldom has reason to visit this section. His knowledge of the area is, in all probability, limited to what he can see from the highway or the railroad as he enters or leaves the city.

Five years ago these fleeting glimpses would have revealed decaying houses, dilapidated factories, and garbage-strewn streets swarming with children at play. Today many of the houses, factories and people are gone. In their place are blocks of empty lots overgrown with weeds and strewn with rubble. The pound of pile drivers and the roar of bulldozers echo as new factories go up and Interstate Highway 91 pushes through. Annoyance at the traffic diversions caused by construction is possibly the only emotion felt by the average citizen as he passes through. To the tenant of Farnam Courts, however, these changes represent radical modifications affecting almost all aspects of his life, for this housing development, the setting for our action-research project, is tucked away in a corner of the triangle.

The nature of the area in which Farnam Courts is located, now known as the Wooster Square Redevelopment Area, is for the most part a result of its ecology and the role it has played in New Haven history. For the past 150 years it has served as a point of initial settlement for urban immigrants and, to a much lesser degree, as a low-rent haven for the very poor.

For many years after the founding of the New Haven colony, the area was part of a colonial settler's land grant and was utilized

17

for farming. In 1824, six acres of land were acquired for an addition to the famous New Haven system of greens and it became
known as the Lower Green, or Wooster Park. By 1850 it had become opulent, exclusive Wooster Square, ringed by the mansions of
wealthy descendants of colonial families and the more successful
pre-Civil War immigrants. During this early period New Haven appears to have been little more than a small, quiet, college town.[1]

During the 1830's the railroads reached New Haven and
stretched beyond the city to Hartford and New London. Their
tracks and rights-of-way formed the hypotenuse of the northern and
western boundaries of the triangle, cutting the area off from the
rest of the city and limiting the direction of development. A few
factories along the waterfront had constituted the oldest industrial
section of the city; now manufacturing expanded to the north. European immigrants, who had begun to arrive in New Haven at about
this time, were attracted to the area in ever-increasing numbers--
lured by the cheap housing to be found on the fringes of an industrial district.

The wave of industrialization which swept southern New England from about 1815 to the end of the Civil War left its mark on
New Haven, so that by the end of the nineteenth century the city
had changed almost beyond recognition. From a population of about
5,000 people in 1810, New Haven doubled its size by 1830 and
reached 40,000 by 1860.

One of the earliest specific references to this area as a suburban adjunct to the growing city occurs in Robert A. Warner's
New Haven Negroes. On a "Reference Map for Early Negro New
Haven, 1810-1850,"[2] the area is shown as being "beyond the thick-
ly-settled areas of New Haven in 1850."

The low status of the area is clearly discernible from
Warner's text:[3]

> As a whole the Negroes of New Haven in 1860 were
> at the bottom of the occupational scale...(They) lived
> in segregated sections of the town, or among the poor
> and degraded white families...Vice close to their homes
> was a menace which Negroes were unable to avoid...
> (Negroes) were forced to find shelter in disreputable
> neighborhoods and to pay high prices for poor quarters...

> The dwellings were badly constructed and cheap...
> Some were sheds and outbuildings which had become
> useless or unsightly in town and had been dragged to the
> outskirts and set up for cheap rental...In this region
> which was growing up to factories, and being settled
> by immigrants, Negroes continued to live throughout
> this generation... Most of the colored people escaped
> that section for regions less disreputable.

The early Negro community thus set a movement pattern for
the area that has continued to the present day: a retreat to other
parts of the city in the face of pressures from more recently arrived immigrants and encroaching factories. From the very beginning those who left carried with them, as did the early Negroes,
the firm belief that they were leaving a deteriorating area--a slum
that had become unendurable--and that they were going to a better
life in a better part of town.

After the exodus of the early Negro community, the area
seemed to have been left largely to the new Irish immigrants and
the older Yankee families still clustered around Wooster Square.
Other nationalities followed the Irish, who were the first European
immigrants to arrive. New Haven as a whole, and the triangle in
particular, became a popular destination for immigrants. By the
end of the Civil War the days of Wooster Square as an exclusive
residential area were numbered. By 1890 the Italians were becoming so numerous that for the next sixty years, until after World
War II, the area was known as "Little Italy."

Maurice R. Davie, a Yale sociologist, surveyed the city of
New Haven for a study that he published in 1937.[4] The following
excerpt from Davie's work provides some statistics on the composition of the area during the late thirties:[5]

Area 4. (This area contains Farnam Courts.)

> With 7.5% of the city's population, Area 4 has 22.8%
> of the Italians, who constitute its largest element.
> Native-born Americans comprise less than 5%. Roman
> Catholicism is the religion of 95%. Two-, three-, and
> multi-family dwellings of low valuation predominate.
> About one third of the area is devoted to commercial
> and industrial use. Half of the heads of families gain-
> fully employed are laborers and 30% are artisans.
> Family income in 90% of cases is below $1500.00.
> The juvenile delinquency rate is the second highest in

the city...three times its expectancy. The dependency
rate is the third highest...almost twice its expectancy.

The Farnam Courts housing development, which was opened
in 1942, covered two city blocks in the northernmost corner of the
triangle. It was an attractive place, with white picket fences and
large plots of grass between the buildings. Since the project was
near the local Italian "Urban Village,"[6] it was considered a highly
desirable place to live. Hundreds of people queued up at the project
office when it opened, waiting impatiently to make application for
apartments.

But the triangle, which had seen so many different peoples
come and go, was not to remain static for long. During World War
II New Haven, like many other northern industrial cities, began to
receive a new wave of immigration. The newcomers were not Euro-
peans, however, but southern Negroes coming north to work in the
factories. After the war this migration not only continued but was
accelerated, augmented in recent years by a similar but much
smaller influx of Puerto Ricans.

City officials became increasingly aware of the deterioration
which had overtaken many of the older sections of New Haven. In
1953 they announced a vast program designed to rehabilitate these
rundown areas, and the triangle area containing Farnam Courts appeared high on the list. The Wooster Square Redevelopment Project came into being in 1958, and it dealt a final blow to the Italian "Urban Village" within its borders. The community had been losing
population gradually for some time as second and third generation
Italians moved to the suburbs. But now the trickle became a flood
as the bulldozers appeared and began their demolition work. The
landlords of the area, faced with emptying tenements, were only too
glad to give temporary shelter to the many desperate Negro families
who could not find accommodations elsewhere. As a result, in the
past fifty years the Negro population of Ward 12, in which Farnam
Courts is located, has increased almost fiftyfold while the total population of the ward decreased 51.46%.[7]

With the exception of the twenty years during which Wooster
Square proper enjoyed its reputation as an exclusive residential dis-

trict, the triangle has remained one of the most depressed areas in
New Haven, an isolated, deteriorated slum inhabited by the most recently arrived, most economically and socially deprived immigrants.
A city report written in September, 1963, stated: "Wooster Square
...Just a few short years ago the same area contained one of the
worst industrial slums in New England. From the end of World
War II to the time that redevelopment started, more than 100 people
had lost their lives in factory fires in Wooster Square (redevelopment area)."[8]

Farnam Courts, unfortunately, probably will remain a forgotten, deprived community despite redevelopment. Its future in-
habitants are to be completely cut off from other residential areas
by Interstate 91. They will be a tiny island of three hundred families marooned in a far corner of Wooster Square Industrial Park.
That they have already been forgotten is clear from that 1963 report:
"The Wooster Square Industrial Park is to be separated from the
residential area of the neighborhood by Interstate 91, now under construction. The new expressway will not only serve as a buffer between homes and factories, but will also give these new plants quick,
efficient access to their major market areas."[9]

As a result of both the history of the triangle and the current plans for the area east of Interstate 91, Farnam Courts is no
longer a desirable place to live. An air of desolation hangs over
the project as, one by one, the surrounding streets have been closed
off by the construction. Even the through traffic, which once
brought with it at least the feeling of being part of the life of the
city, has stopped. It was this inevitable isolation, plus the clear
evidence of social and economic deprivation, that led to the selection of Farnam Courts for our action-research project.

Notes

1. Edward E. Atwater (ed.).   History of the City of
   New Haven to the Present Time (New York, W.
   W. Munsell, 1887). p. 450.

2. Robert A. Warner.   New Haven Negroes: A Social
   History (New Haven, Yale University Press, 1940).
   p. 28.

3. Ibid., pp. 26-31.

4. Maurice R. Davie. "The Pattern of Urban Growth,"
   Studies in the Science of Society, George P. Mur-
   dock (ed.) (New Haven, Yale University Press,
   1937), pp. 133-162.

5. Ibid., p. 147.

6. "Urban Village" is a phrase coined by Herbert J.
   Gans to describe the Italian community in the west
   end of Boston. Herbert J. Gans, The Urban Villagers: Group and Class in the Life of American-
   Italians, (New York, The Free Press of Glencoe,
   1962).

7. United States Bureau of the Census. Fifteenth Census
   of the United States: 1930 Population, Vol. III, Part
   I, Table 23, p. 365. United States Bureau of the
   Census, U.S. Censuses of Population and Housing:
   1960. Final Report P.H.C. (1)-102, Table P-1, pp.
   15-20.

8. City of New Haven. Your City: A Progress Report,
   1963 Report of the City of New Haven (New Haven,
   New Haven Register, Sunday, September 15, 1963),
   p. 31.

9. Ibid., p. 32.

Chapter 2
The People

During the four years of NIP intervention in Farnam Courts,
social workers amassed a host of observations concerning the attitudes, values, and behavior patterns of the residents. These observations led the team to adopt a theoretical approach like that used by
Walter B. Miller, Herbert Gans, Thomas Gladwin and other researchers who have worked with lower-class populations: namely,
that the residents of the Courts are members of a "definite subculture," a long-established cultural system widely shared by lower-
class people in urban, industrial settings. Miller stresses the fact
that this is a subculture with a distinct integrity of its own; it is
not to be thought of merely as a defective, pathological, or dysfunc-
tional deviation from the middle-class culture shared by the majority in our society.[1]

Since this book is not meant to be a detailed cultural monograph, it will not be possible to discuss life in Farnam Courts in
very great detail. Our description will be restricted to the general
patterns of behavior of this social group, with some indication of
how these patterns differ from those observed in the middle class.
We have borrowed extensively from the writings of the researchers
cited above and other sociologists and cultural anthropologists working in the same field.

Farnam Courts, in its own small way, continued to play the
traditional Wooster Square role in New Haven life--that of a mixed
area of initial settlement for poor immigrants. Forty-nine percent
of its 300 units are occupied by white families, 41% by Negroes,
and 10% by Puerto Ricans.[2] Of the whites, 58% are of Italian extraction and the rest are of British-Yankee, Irish, Polish, German,
Greek, Ukrainian, French, Hungarian or Portuguese descent.[3] A
survey of the Courts in 1961 revealed that most of the adult resi-

dents belonged to families that were relatively new to New Haven.
Of the heads of white families, 14% were first-generation Americans and 78% were second generation; of the Negro family heads, a
substantial number were born in the South; all of the Puerto Rican
family heads were born in Puerto Rico.[4]

Despite this superficial evidence of diversity, the people of
Farnam Courts have much in common. An application of Hollingshead's Index of Social Position, based on occupational, residential
and educational criteria, reveals that, almost without exception,
residents in the project may be assigned to Hollingshead's Class V
or Warner's Lower Class.[5] Adults in the Courts have a median of
8.0 grades of schooling completed as compared with a median of
10.6 grades for New Haven residents as a whole.[6] Employed tenants hold the following types of unskilled jobs: factory worker,
truck driver, porter, peddler, domestic, maintenance man, and
hospital, laundry or retail store employee.[7] Farnam Courts families had a median annual income of $2,729 in 1963, of which a con-
siderable portion was some form of public assistance. In comparison, the 1960 census indicated that the median annual income for all
New Haven families was $6,620 and for Negro New Haven families
it was $4,554.[8]

The data and observations presented here describe a population and a way of life by no means restricted to Farnam Courts.
Table 16 in Chapter 15 indicates that the people of this project are
typical of those living in other New Haven Housing Authority low-
income housing projects. The data we collected are strikingly similar to those gathered by Hollingshead and Redlich for Class V people
in New Haven as a whole;[9] Myers and Roberts have also cited generation figures similar to ours for Class V whites in New Haven.[10]

The primary unit in lower-class society is, as in other
social groups, the family. The class position of an individual affects his intra-familial experiences even as it affects the beliefs he
holds, the way he behaves and the roles he plays. In the middle
and upper classes, the typical "nuclear family" of father-mother-
children can meet many of the social, economic and emotional needs
of its members. Because this type of family is extremely flexible,

it has great value for upwardly mobile individuals in a rapidly
changing, urban, industrial society. On the other hand, it is handicapped in dealing with emergencies and, at a close to subsistence
level, it cannot properly meet all the needs of its members. In
agricultural societies the "extended family," one which is multi-gen-
erational and unilateral (matrilineal or patrilineal) in lineage, is a
functional unit. It is a social group to which even young children
may make a significant economic contribution and one that meets
all the needs of its members.

The urban, industrial, lower-class family falls somewhere
between these two types. The deprived conditions under which these
families live pose many almost insoluble problems. The unskilled,
poorly educated worker usually finds himself employed in a non-
unionized job requiring heavy physical labor and long hours; piece-
work or hourly wages on a "no work, no pay" basis is customary.
His job situation is frequently unstable and he has come to expect
this. He may lose time from work due to illness or injury, may
suffer recurrent periods of under-employment or seasonal unemployment, may even see the sudden elimination of his job due to automation or the dissolution of a marginal company. In times of
trouble it is a common practice to move in with family or take in
less fortunate relatives. Consequently, the typical urban, industrial
form of the lower-class family has been called an "expanded family"
rather than an extended or nuclear one. Like the extended family,
it often consists of three or more generations under one roof, but
its composition is dictated more by the exigencies of the situation
than by unilateral family relationships.[11] In Farnam Courts 7.5%
of all families are of the expanded type, despite New Haven Housing
Authority policies designed to prevent the taking in of non-nuclear
relatives except in cases of dire emergency.[12] (Normally about 20-
25% of lower-class urban families in New Haven fall into this category.)[13]

The functioning of the typical Farnam Courts family also differs from that of the middle-class family. Spouses feel that each
partner has certain clearly defined familial roles to play, and their
attendant duties and responsibilities are sharply differentiated. The

woman is responsible for everything concerning the home and children; it is her duty to keep the family together and functioning.
Housekeeping, child care, discipline are all considered woman's
work and the man takes little interest and feels little responsibility.
His role is mainly that of breadwinner; he is responsible for bringing home "enough money for the wife to run the house." What he
does with the rest of his money, his spare time, his friends, or
his job is considered to be his own business, and the wife does not
interfere. There is little real communication between spouses, and
each partner feels much closer to his or her own relatives and
friends. Husbands and wives appear to come together mostly for
sexual reasons; unlike middle-class spouses, they give each other
very little emotional support or companionship and seldom help out
with problems arising outside their individual areas of responsibility.

As a result, the marriage bond in the lower class is considerably more fragile than that of the middle class. Since little mutual support is expected or given, this type of union might best be
described as "organized separateness" rather than "togetherness."
It is a highly functional pattern of behavior, a response to economic
uncertainty, a poor health level and deprivation. When accident, ill
health, mental illness or sudden death strikes, the surviving partner
must often carry on alone.

Among severely deprived people disaster often takes the form
of mental illness. In 1958 Hollingshead compared the general population in New Haven in each social class with the number of psychiatric patients in each class. His survey revealed that the percentage of patients under treatment for psychiatric disorders who belonged to Class V was more than double the percentage of Class V
individuals in the general population--140% higher among lower-class
men and 75% higher among lower-class women.[14]

Alcoholism, drug addiction, psychoses, and various types of
hysterical reactions are the more serious disorders, but there are
many less drastic reactions to deprivation that can cause family
crisis and affect the level of functioning. For example, a husband
overburdened with economic responsibilities may desert his family;

a husband or wife may eject an unstable or alcoholic partner, feeling that he or she can manage better alone. There are many such reasons why lower-class women are often left to raise their children alone in what becomes a matrifocal or mother-centered family, one in which the male parent is either absent or transient, or remains in a peripheral position. According to Gans, in a society where "male instability is widespread, the woman becomes the dominant member of the family, and she may live with a number of men in the hope of finding a stable mate."[15] In Farnam Courts only 52% of all families with children have both parents present; the remainder are mother-centered. Actually, some 56% of all families in the project show a configuration other than the typical nuclear pattern, and 35% of all children are being raised in such non-nuclear families.[16]

Regardless of family composition, the lower-class mother is usually so busy and harassed that she has little time to spend with her children; keeping house for a large family in close quarters on an inadequate income is a never-ending chore. Money is a constant worry. Most families have no backlog of savings, and major household items must be purchased on the installment plan. Stretching the paycheck to cover the rent, children's clothes, furniture payments, etc., is a perpetual problem, overhung by the threat of eviction or repossession.

Further problems are created by the fact that this is the only social group in our society in which a man in his twenties has reached an economic plateau. The male income curve rises until about the age of 25, remains level until about 55, and then declines steadily until the man must go on relief or qualify for old age assistance.[17] Unskilled hard labor requires youth, strength and health; the older man who cannot maintain the pace loses his job to someone younger. When the father is unemployed or out of the home, the mother must be prepared to work. Older children learn to look after the younger ones when their mother is busy, and girls begin at an early age to play the role of "little mother" to their younger siblings.

Children are raised according to adult standards, with little

attempt to understand their reactions and needs in terms of child
psychology or development.   Grownups seldom make any concessions
to the child's point of view, nor do they understand that he might
have emotional as well as physical requirements.   Verbal chastise-
ment and physical punishment are the main forms of discipline.
Parents do not deliberately and consciously teach their children, as
middle-class parents do.   They tend, rather, to react suddenly with
yells, slaps and ridicule when the behavior of the young bursts the
limits of endurance.   Controls are imposed on a child to bring peace
and quiet out of bedlam, not to mold his personality.   Lower-class
adults do tell their children how to behave, hoping to be heeded, but
there the responsibility ends--whether the children take such advice
is strictly their own affair.   Consequently, these parents do not feel
as much guilt as do middle-class parents when their children get into trouble.   It can also be observed that although the child may be
loved and accepted by his parents, he is shown little overt affection.
There is a general lack of real communication between the generations.   Certainly, children are not made the center of family life,
and this may possibly be the basis for the middle-class belief that
lower-class parents "ignore" or "neglect" their children.   This is
rather a case of cultural difference, the lower-class family being an
adult-centered rather than a child-centered or adult-directed child-
centered unit as in the middle class.[18]

The lower-class family produces children who learn early in
life to look out for themselves.   These children do not expect their
parents to help with problems and seldom ask them for aid, relying
on siblings or, more likely, peers.   Most Farnam Courts youngsters
give the impression of being mature for their age and almost ag-
gressively self-reliant.   Parents are often heard encouraging a
child to "stick up for your rights" and "get what's yours"--by force
if necessary.   This often results in an atmosphere of bickering and
fighting in the home, at school and in outside groups.

When necessary, even young children are expected to dress
themselves, prepare their own meals, get themselves off to school,
and put themselves to bed.   From a middle-class point of view,
standards of cleanliness and nutrition may leave something to be

desired, but many children cope successfully with the situation. If
the family is in great difficulties, the siblings give each other
warmth and support. A group of such self-reliant children with a
stick-together attitude is capable of tolerating a great deal of deprivation and apparent neglect. One such example was found recently in Farnam Courts, when the father of a large family of six children was hospitalized due to alcoholism. The run-down mother,
not yet thirty years of age, was left to struggle with family problems alone in addition to caring for a new baby. The three oldest
children promptly made themselves responsible for the younger ones,
caring for them, preparing them for school, and seeing to it that
they got there safely and on time.

The independent Farnam Courts child begins very early to
move out of his home, seeking friendship and recreation in the
streets and building his own peer group from among neighborhood
children, his relatives or schoolmates. The peer group, which after the family is the next social grouping to which the individual belongs, is composed of friends who are the same sex, roughly the
same age, and at the same relative position in the human life cycle.
This sexually-segregated, age-graded clique is the most important
and most influential social group to which the Farnam Courts child
ever belongs. In fact, the lower class has been described by Gans
as a peer-group society, whereas the middle class might be referred to as a family-oriented society.[19] Miller states that in the
lower class the peer group is "the major psychic focus and reference group for those over twelve or thirteen."[20] A most interesting point is made by Gans, who indicates that dependency and conformity to group values are considerably stronger drives than independence and individualism.[21]

Most members of peer-group society have a small circle of
friends with whom they spend their free time. There is little personal reticence in such a group. The thoughts, acts and desires of
one's friends are matters of prime importance; any behavior that
would tend to take the individual out of the group or cause the group
to reject him is promptly suppressed. Gans refers to peer-group
society, therefore, as a person-oriented society in which the com-

mon values of the group take precedence over most other goals in life.[22]

The person-oriented peer group and the family provide most of the social experiences of the lower-class child. There are a limited number of roles in his narrow social milieu, and this fact, combined with the adult-centered character of his family life, has a profound effect upon his personality development. Gans has indicated that lower-class society does not provide the individual with models or training that can assist him in developing empathy. Using George Herbert Mead's concept of the self, he goes on to say that an individual who cannot empathize is handicapped in developing a clear-cut self-image, which in turn makes it extremely difficult for him to feel at ease with strangers or in unfamiliar social situations.[23] When a person raised in this manner finds himself in such a situation he either retreats from it or attempts to restructure it in familiar, reciprocal or peer-group terms. The latter choice is seldom successful and the individual may be badly hurt by outsiders who do not understand peer-group ways--an occurrence that only reinforces his belief that the outside world is to be avoided as much as possible.

For example, the social workers in Farnam Courts became quite accustomed to being treated as personal friends. They were showered with invitations for casual visits or dinner, asked to meet the relatives or to have coffee with the neighbors. The women would tell the worker that they confided in her because she was a friend whom they could trust. They would often attempt to include the worker in their personal network of individuals who would be helped in time of need and who were obliged, in return, to reciprocate when trouble arose. If aid for some emergency was not immediately extended by the worker--usually because bureaucratic mills grind slowly--the client would say, "You let me down when I needed help. You're not a real friend." In such cases, the worker clearly had failed to fulfill peer-group expectations.

This kind of peer-group reliance is not found in the middle class where, as Gans points out, the tendency is to strive for individually achievable goals, goals which relate to future social, eco-

nomic and occupational success with concomitant upward mobility.[24]
In goal-oriented society, a conflict between the individual's career
aspirations and the group is settled by rejecting the group and not
the career. The individual then searches for more compatible
friends, while his personal goals remain unchanged. It is this pattern, and the fact that he has been raised by empathizing parents
in a child-centered family and has participated in a much broader
social environment, that help him to learn to empathize and play
different roles. According to Gans, the middle-class person is
capable of developing a much more clear-cut self-image, so that a
strange situation involving new people will hold far fewer terrors.[25]

It is true that the outside world and its institutions are
feared and, to a large extent, have been rejected by tenants in the
project; Farnam Courts residents choose to retreat, spending most
of their lives in close intimacy with a very small number of people.
Their sense of neighborhood and community is similarly restricted.
The word "neighborhood" in Farnam Courts means "my building,"
or "down at my end," while the word "community" evokes such responses as "the whole project," or "the Courts." Everything beyond the confines of the project (except for a few stores) is part of
the outside world. The people in the project do not think of themselves as part of the Wooster Square area or neighborhood, and
most of them will not make the journey to the Conte School and
Community Center, which is less than a mile away on the other side
of Interstate 91.

When excursions into the outside world must be made--to the
doctor, the clinic, the welfare office--many residents are uncom-
fortable with and bewildered by the formality of the situation. They
will sit for hours in the emergency room of the hospital without notifying the desk clerk that they are there. They will get lost in the
maze of hospital corridors, fail to find the clinic to which they were
to report, and yet fear to ask directions from anyone. Many are
so unnerved by the experience that they do not keep further appointments; they use hospitals, clinics, doctors and dentists only in cases
of dire emergency.

This social group knows very little of New Haven. Although

the outside world is the source of needed jobs and income, it is
viewed as a place of exploitation and unhappiness, very unpleasant
and forbidding.   The people in Farnam Courts are so isolated--by
their comparatively recent arrival in New Haven, by their location
in a project tucked away amid the factories, by their lack of contact with communications media other than television, and by their
own tendency to retreat from anything which threatens group values
--that they are almost outside our social system.   They are, in
fact, quite unfamiliar with the social structure and social functioning of their city.   An examination of data from Chapter IV of Hollingshead and Redlich illustrates this point in a slightly different
way.   Ninety-three percent of Class I respondents knew there were
social classes in New Haven and were able to place themselves cor-
rectly in the hierarchy.   Fifty-four percent of Class II respondents
also could do so, along with 52% from Class III and 66% from Class
IV, but only 18% of the respondents from Class V possessed such
knowledge.[26]   Lower-class people simply do not think that the community at large has anything to do with them, and they are not accustomed to ranking their own position relative to others on such an
externally imposed framework.   Moreover, their low status makes
this knowledge thoroughly unrewarding.

Whatever the reason, the general lower-class pattern ranges
from uncertainty through antagonism to withdrawal from the institutions of the outside world--the school, the church, the settlement
house, the "Y," the police, the Juvenile Court, the hospital, the
Social Security and welfare offices, and most clubs and formal organizations.   Officials and workers of these institutions are also
suspect; they are likely to be avoided or met with suspicion and
even hostility.   This attitude of suspicion, combined with ignorance
of the outside world, often causes overburdened individuals looking
for escape to take the geographical way out.   It is, of course, no
solution at all to move from one lower-class enclave to another, os-
tensibly looking for a new start or a better job.

Running away from problems rather than trying to find a solution is an all too common pattern.   Some families in trouble never
think of asking the outside world for aid; others, having asked, are

unable to endure the necessary formalities. In their new location
they often find the situation no better; furthermore the move has
disrupted their children's education. Officials of the Travelers'
Aid Society in New Haven have noted that many newcomers to the
city used geographical migration as a problem-saving device.[27]

Lower-class people feel most secure and relaxed within the
familiar confines of peer-group society; Gans has observed that the
lower-class individual's personality seems to function most completely in this setting.[28] The Farnam Courts world is normally
warm, loud and vital, but an immediate change occurs when a
stranger comes into the project. Faces become impassive; the
residents withdraw, stare silently or go about their business quietly. Gone are the noise and bustling confusion. Interest and curiosity are shown only covertly, by the flutter of curtains or by dart-
ing glances as the outsider passes by.

Most of the women's free time is spent in watching television or casual visiting back and forth. They seldom leave the project. Women's peer groups in Farnam Courts contain fewer relatives and more neighbors than is usual in lower-class society, since
few tenants have relatives living in the project. The women feel
that their lives are a humdrum round of household chores. Their
knowledge of the outside world is so limited, moreover, that they
believe all women are caught in a narrow boring trap. They moved
directly from the role of daughter to that of wife and mother without ever giving their marriage or their future much thought. The
typical pattern is to marry early. Many marriages are performed
in spite of family objections and many others are forced because of
pregnancy. There seems to have been a romantic belief that marriage would provide an escape from the drabness of life.[29] The re-
alities of marriage and the arrival of children soon cause this dream
to fade, however, and most women in the Courts now look back on
their teens as the best time of their lives. Watching television,
gossiping, even fighting with the neighbors serve the women residents as safety valves, providing moments of forgetfulness or excitement to relieve the monotony.

The strict separation of family functions and their fear of the

outside world tend to keep Farnam Courts women project-bound even
when opportunities to go out present themselves.   Their relationship
to the schools suffers as a result.   School authorities have stated,
for example, that attempts to interest the women of the project in
the Parent-Teachers Association of the neighborhood elementary
school have usually met with failure.   When the mothers were asked
why they did not join, they expressed such fears as not having the
right clothes, of not feeling at home there, of being snubbed by the
exclusive clique rumored to control the PTA.   In addition, most
parents are not familiar enough with the curriculum or well enough
educated to help children with homework.   Consequently, although
they want their children to remain in school and be successful in
order to learn "good behavior" and qualify for better jobs later in
life, they are unable to give any real help.   It is no wonder, then,
that they feel school is the child's affair; they will visit the school
only when summoned, and then in fearful expectation of trouble.

Similar fears and rationalizations operate to prevent Farnam
Courts women from joining outside clubs and organizations.   Although they encourage their children to participate in outside activities, they remain in the project, using most of their time and energy in the constant struggle to bring a measure of order, security
and stability into their uncertain world.   Gans has pointed out that
the lower-class woman's striving toward stability and order brings
her much closer than other members of her group to the middle-
class values.[30]

A very different set of values, fostered by male peer groups,
is adhered to by the majority of lower-class men.   Their attitudes,
beliefs and behavior undoubtedly have been molded by the kinds of
jobs that used to be available to unskilled, poorly-educated men.
Rolling back the frontier, fighting America's wars and border skir-
mishes, lumbering, mining, old-time railroading, even unmecha-
nized farming, were occupations requiring men with particular qualities.   Miller has observed that such jobs required combinations of
physical strength, endurance, and manual dexterity; they called for
the ability to work well with other men, to adapt quickly to emergencies, to face danger with courage, and to withstand long spells

of boredom between periods of excitement and emergency.[31] Most
importantly, these jobs did not require a very high level of education or prior technical training, for most of the needed skills were
acquired on the job.

Obviously, there was a far greater need in the past for such
men than there is at present. In recent years, only World War II
and the Korean War have created situations requiring such men in
large numbers. In modern American industrial cities such as New
Haven, they still can find jobs as construction workers; as moving
men; as molders in foundries; as factory workers in such medium
and heavy industries as firearms, hardware, rubber, paper cartons,
and meat packing; and as drivers or loaders. Since World War II,
however, all these occupations--the traditional ones mentioned in
the preceding paragraph as well as the more recent vocations noted
above--have undergone drastic constriction. Furthermore, the number of jobs of this kind will undoubtedly continue to shrink because
of automation. Unfortunately, cultural patterns and human behavior
are unable to change as rapidly as has our postwar economy. Gans
has pointed out that lower-class culture is continuing to produce a
type of man who finds it increasingly difficult to survive in modern
society.[22]

There is a school of thought, typified by Paul Goodman, that
believes juvenile delinquency to be a protest against the unwillingness of adults to grant teenagers a viable function in society.[33]
The recent rise in adult delinquency may be attributable in part to
a similar social protest--this time from men who find themselves
in an increasingly expendable position in our society.

The typical lower-class male, then, is a man who would be
ideally suited to a warlike or pioneer life. He is often aggressive,
self-centered and given to the physical expression of emotion; he
tends to be, as Hollingshead puts it, "hostile to formal institutional
controls."[34] Most of these characteristics appear to have their
origin in the adult-centered family and its child-rearing methods.
In the day-to-day routine of living in an industrial city--where middle-class values of stability and conformity predominate and exciting
crises seldom occur--he tends to become restless; he is unable or

unwilling to suffer dull routine for too long without a break.

Male peer groups appear to exhibit interest in activities best described as a searching for excitement--"action-seeking," Gans calls it.[35] The men of Farnam Courts often reject such things as job loyalty, striving for promotion, upgrading skills through further education, and belonging to outside community organizations. A job is considered merely a means to an end; it is thought of as a broad valley of dull routine between sharp peaks of excitement with the peer group. These peaks of action are remembered and talked about by the participants in later years as the high points of their lives.

Today's lower-class male can no longer find excitement by fighting the enemy, the Indians or the elements. Consequently, many men turn to drinking, shooting dice, playing the numbers, philandering, or "going out on the town." The fact that most of these activities cannot be pursued with impunity in our society may add to the excitement, but may also add to the individual's police record. This episodic type of life is led by most lower-class men to a greater or lesser degree.[36] It usually goes unnoticed by the community at large, since it may consist of little more than a "Saturday night on the town with the boys." For a few, however, action-seeking may interfere with their ability to hold a steady job, or it may lead to the acquisition of a criminal record, making it difficult for them to find employment. There may even be a drift downhill to alcoholism or to the status of unemployable.

Because of their strong desire for family and economic stability, most lower-class women might be classified, along with the middle class, as seekers of routine.[37] As a result, lower-class men view their women with ambivalence, as objects of sexual exploitation and excitement on one hand, and as sources of complaints and interference with action-seeking on the other. Relations between the sexes are tenuous at best. Peer-group relationships and their own family ties tend to pull lower-class spouses apart, whereas in the middle class, family structure and social relationships tend to bring couples closer together.[38] Children being raised in a lower-class social milieu soon discover that the organized separateness of family life is reinforced by the peer groups and their attitudes toward the opposite sex.

Many lower-class men live episodic lives in their youth and marry late; others return to the episodic way of life between bouts of domesticity with one or more women. Still others never marry at all but drift through life having only casual, transitory affairs with women. The women show a similar wide range of attitudes. Some patiently put up with male action-seeking on the grounds that a certain amount of such behavior is normal. Many others threaten to do something about their husbands without having any real intentions of carrying out the threat, since they believe all men behave similarly. Still others regard men as shiftless, troublemaking, undependable weaklings whose "sweet talk" is not to be trusted. If a man's action-seeking behavior becomes too threatening to family stability, some women will eject or desert him, thus bringing into existence new matrifocal or expanded households. Many have gone through this pattern several times in their search for a dependable man. Miller describes lower-class relations between the sexes as a pattern consisting of a mother-centered family and a marginal male. [39] In extreme cases this may become serial monogamy. Miller stresses that the term "broken home" ought not to be used to describe the mother-centered family with the marginal male. He points out that the word "broken" implies the expectation of a male parent who would be present in the household and involved in the support and raising of children. In most of these mother-centered units there is little expectation, despite frequently expressed hope, of such male involvement. [40]

Farnam Courts youngsters seem to come alive when they are with their gang. Separated from the peer group--at home, in the classroom, in the outside world--they tend to be quiet, retiring and somewhat passive, but as soon as school or the workday is over, they brighten visibly. As they grow older they spend less and less time with their families and increasing amounts of the day and night with the gang. For adults, the break in an otherwise dull routine comes on the weekend. For the children, there is a small peak at the end of every school day, plus a mountain top of excitement and enjoyment every weekend and all summer long.

Boys are allowed more and earlier freedom than girls, who
are supervised more closely and who are needed to help in the
home.   By adolescence, however, neither sex spends much time
with the family.   They get together with the gang to "horse around,
shoot the breeze, and kill time"--a pattern of intermittent, informal,
peer-group socializing that continues all their lives.   The teen years
are picked as the best of their entire lives not only by the women,
as we have mentioned before, but also by lower-class males.

Teenage male peer groups are seen by Miller as playing a
recognizable part in the sexual role development of lower-class boys
in conjunction with the female-based household.[41]   Since an esti-
mated 25-40% of lower-class households are mother-centered,[42]
many boys grow up without a consistent male model or object of
identification to assist them in learning adult male role behavior.
Teenage boys, therefore, turn to the peer group and adopt the gang
code, which stresses the following: intragroup loyalty, justice,
trust and cooperation; duplicity aimed at outsmarting each other and
the outside world; quick repartee, toughness and courage; and avoidance of appearing "soft" or exhibiting "sissy" behavior.   The attitudes toward women, jobs and the outside world that are approved
by this subculture also are learned through peer-group membership.   Experience rather than education is valued as the only way
to get ahead.   Upward mobility is seen as the result of luck rather
than as the outcome of the long, slow process of education and application to the job.

Miller describes how membership in peer-group society channels attitudes:

> An individual born and raised in a lower-class cultural
> milieu derives his basic perceptions and values from
> that milieu...During most of his waking hours he moves
> in a social milieu peopled with others like himself, and
> when he touches on the fringes of the middle-class world
> --on his job, in school, through a movie or television
> program--it appears remote and substantially irrelevant
> to him and his concerns.   A lower-class boy can under-
> go a forced exposure to the sentiments and concerns of
> middle-class schoolteachers for ten years of his life with-
> out really investing much of himself in the experience.

Even while in class, his mind and heart are out on the
corner with the boys, a corner where academic achievement is of little consequence and confers no status. And
he marks time until he is sixteen, when he can leave
school and push the difficult ten-year interlude out of his
consciousness as rapidly as possible. [43]

Since the lower-class population of New Haven is not nearly
as deprived as some population segments in New York and other
large cities, the behavior of teen-age male peer groups in New
Haven shows many differences from the patterns observed in Harlem or on the West Side of New York City. Farnam Courts boys
have more extensive contacts with the outside world, and their rejection and fear of it are less marked. They have not turned inward to the extent of having a strictly defined territory to defend
against rival gangs, nor do they "run with" organized auxiliary
girls' gangs. Much time is spent, rather, in looking for opportunities to develop their skills and sharpen their wits. As a result,
teen-age male peer groups in Farnam Courts, lured on by their
search for action and excitement, range much farther afield than
most of the other residents. Miller has observed that the skills
learned in such gangs are very much like those needed by an infan-
try squad in combat. [44]

For the teen-age boy in the Courts, the need for action and
the search for a "lucky break" seem to be tied almost exclusively
to sports. Some groups have become known as "basketball hounds"
or "baseball hounds." Boys will scour the whole of New Haven
looking for opportunities to enter a team in a league or for a chance
to play in a pickup game. The many professional players who
"have gotten the breaks," have been discovered and sent on their
way to fame and fortune, are idolized and their careers are followed
with great interest. However, organized competitive athletics are
not always available, and other types of action are sometimes sought.

Teen-age girls venture into the outside world far more than
do their mothers, but they are limited in their action-seeking by
parental supervision and responsibility for an appreciable amount of
the housework. These duties are viewed as a means of affording
some relief to a busy mother and also as training for the only fu-

ture role they see for themselves--that of wife and mother. Girls'
groups in Farnam Courts spend most of their free time hanging
around the entry-ways, setting each other's hair, talking about
clothes and boys. Excursions to the outside world often take the
form of window-shopping expeditions downtown, and many hours are
spent wandering through such stores as Woolworth's, Grant's or
Kresge's. As they grow older, most turn for excitement to boys'
groups and social activities. Some of the girls' groups in Farnam
Courts are known as "dance hounds" because they tour the city looking for Y, school or settlement house dances to attend. When they
get a little older they begin to frequent commercial dance halls and
places of entertainment such as the Savin Rock Amusement Park.

Dating, in the middle-class sense of a couple spending the
evening together alone or in company with other couples, is almost
nonexistent. Lower-class teen-age dating patterns here might almost be described as "parallel dating." In Farnam Courts, for example, dances are attended by both male and female teen-age peer
groups. But each group arrives separately and stays together most
of the night, the girls dancing with each other while the boys lounge
around watching them. Each side taunts the boy and girl who are
brave enough to dance together; only a couple with a very serious
relationship can withstand this teasing. When the dance is over the
peer groups repair separately to the same place for "cokes" and
hamburgers, where a further exchange of banter winds up the evening.

Dating in the middle-class sense is done only by the few
with a serious attachment and then almost clandestinely, after the
peer groups have broken up at the end of the evening. As a result,
these teen-agers are not nearly as adept at heterosexual social relationships as are members of the middle class. Most couples actually spend very little time alone together before marriage, and
this may possibly contribute to the lack of significant communication
between spouses.

Most mothers in adult-directed families begin to treat their
daughters as equals and establish peer relationships with them as
soon as they enter their teens. This pattern, coupled with the lim-

ited number of social roles in peer-group society, might account for
the fact that very few girls have any picture of themselves as independent working women, either living alone in later life or waiting
for the right man to marry. As soon as they feel they have out-
grown the role of daughter, most hasten to exchange it for the role
of wife and mother. Since the men they marry usually have followed
the male pattern of "knocking around" for a while, the age difference between husband and wife is apt to be considerable. A Farnam Courts survey on age difference between spouses revealed some
marriages with thirty years between ages, and an average difference
of over five years. [45]

          Sociologists have said that no social group can long retain a
value system which does not stand the test of reality. [46] Lower-
class peer-group society is no exception to this. Its social beliefs
apparently have arisen as a result of long experience with the outside world and its ways. For example, most members of this
group have no real conviction that it is within their power to better
their lot. They see all institutions and officials of the outside world
as instruments of exploitation and hostility. As Gladwin has stated:
"They recognize that what they do today may have consequence for
themselves tomorrow. But they also recognize that what someone
else may do to them or about them may be much more important
in determining what their tomorrow may be like than anything they
do themselves today. It is therefore unrealistic and futile to plan
for the future, and anything pleasurable should be done now. The
chance may never come again. "[47]

          This pattern of behavior has become known in social work
parlance as "the inability to delay gratification. " It might be more
aptly described as a belief in external control with a consequent lack
of future-time perspective. This is a commonly held belief throughout the world. In our society today, the belief in external control
and the lack of personal power still remains strong, especially
among rural and minority groups as well as in the urban, industrial lower class.

          Before going on to the multi-problem family, it might be
well to review the attitudes, values and behavior patterns of func-

tional families in lower-class society.   Typical lower-class culture
as seen in Farnam Courts might be summarized as follows:

Family: An expanded and/or matrifocal pattern is found,
with a psychologically peripheral male associated in what may become, in extreme cases, serial monogamy.   There is an organized
separateness of function and a lack of real communication between
spouses.   Family and peer group ties are stronger than the marital bond.   There is a comparatively large age difference between
spouses, since women tend to marry young and men do not.

Child-raising patterns: The family is adult-centered and
parents use a great deal of impulsive physical discipline.   They do
not aim for methods that would produce motivation, perseverance,
powers of sustained concentration, or emotional self-control in their
children.   Their fear of the outside world is communicated to the
children.   Mothers tend to establish peer relationships with the older children, especially daughters.

Society: The peer group is the most important psychic focus
for all adults in this community.   Its social environment is marked
by face-to-face relationships, a paucity of social roles, limited social demands on the individual, a code of group loyalty, and social
controls centered within the group.   There is a commonly shared
non-school language pattern, and a distinctive manner of dress and
deportment.   Inability to verbalize or use the language patterns of
outsiders gives the appearance of secretiveness or retardation when
judged by middle-class standards.   Group ways force conformity to
a non-upwardly mobile orientation, a lack of job loyalty or career
interest, a fatalistic attitude toward life and the future, and a belief in the importance of taking pleasures when they come.

Socio-economic patterns: As a group they are unskilled, or
semi-skilled at best.   They are poorly educated and socially marginal.   Income is low, with the earning curve leveling off after age
25 and declining steeply after 55.   Many are comparative newcomers
to the city, most being either first or second-generation continental
Americans.

Attitudes toward the outside world: Attitudes of fear, withdrawal, powerlessness and anti-intellectualism are seen, with a

consequent reluctance to accept the formal controls, institutions, facilities or aid of the outside world.   There is a turning inward to the peer-group society and a fear of becoming conspicuous to out-siders and thereby being singled out for exploitation.

Personality and values: The society is oriented toward the present and toward the peer group.   Individuals are given to the physical expression of emotion and have a short attention span. Ac-tion-seeking to various degrees, they cannot tolerate many formal institutional controls.   They are unable to empathize with others, thus have no clear-cut self-image of themselves as separate from the group.   They generally lack the self-control to learn new roles while remaining in the group, or to leave the group for the outside world and its ways.   Tension is expressed in acting-out behavior against other individuals and the larger society.   Life is felt to be beyond the control of the individual; consequently, there is a fatalis-tic attitude toward life and the future.

Typical lower-class culture might be viewed in general terms as a response to continued poverty, economic instability, exploita-tion and deprivation.   Although to middle-class eyes it may appear chaotic, the culture has definite functional patterns.   The expanded and/or mother-centered family, the peripheral male, the absence of identification with work or career, the fatalism, the retreat from the outside world into the tight, warm world of the peer group--all these behavior patterns have a survival value in a severely deprived environment.   As Gans has pointed out, other segments of our so-ciety have positive or approach responses to opportunities and depri-vations, but the lower class has a withdrawal response because its members encounter far fewer opportunities and much more depriva-tion. [48]   There seems to be a level beyond which any further in-crease in the amount of deprivation becomes more than even this defended society can bear; it results in an increase in familial and personal disintegration.

The protective, retreating pattern of the lower class makes it practically impossible for individuals, alone and unaided, to take the initiative and to seize opportunities if and when they occur. Consequently, if improvement or change in their way of life is de-

sired, the outside world must come to them. And it must be done
in a form that they can understand, without attempting to eliminate,
remold or disrupt the elements in their culture that are positive
and functional.

     Since lower-class patterns of behavior are integrated into an
on-going, functional culture, it is our contention that change cannot
be effected simply by an alteration in physical environment. Those
who believe that pulling down and redeveloping the slums will automatically cause this segment of society to remodel themselves and
leap happily into the middle class are, in our opinion, misguided.
This certainly did not happen to the people who moved into Farnam
Courts.

     It is our belief that this subculture is not a rebellious, patho-
logical, deviant or delinquent version of middle-class culture but is,
rather, a functional way of life that is probably far older than middle-class culture as we know it. If this statement is valid, it follows that cultural change cannot be accomplished quickly, certainly
not by substituting new housing for old. Miller points out that cultural change can come about only through the development of dras-
tically new patterns of welfare spending. Up to now our money has
largely been funnelled into efforts aimed at protecting the community
at large from the effects of lower-class behavior patterns, instead
of toward finding solutions tailored to the needs of the lower-class
population.[49] While we have described the functionality of lower-
class behavior, we would not characterize it as optimally useful in
promoting the welfare of this segment of the population. To say
that given patterns of behavior facilitate survival under adverse conditions and that they make possible the retention of a modicum of
mental health is not to overlook the fact that this behavior carries
many handicapping aspects. Understanding the reasons for existing
ways of thinking and behaving does not mean viewing them as opti-
mum methods for coping with problematic situations.

     Catherine S. Chilman, in a monograph on child rearing in
low-income families,[50] states that "...while understanding and accepting the sub-cultural patterns more characteristic of the very
poor, it should be quite appropriate to recognize that a number of

these patterns tend to operate to the disadvantage of many of them. "[51] Examples of disadvantageous patterns include apathetic and fatalistic attitudes toward life, and an anti-intellectual bias,[52] both of which have been described earlier.

In working with deprived populations we must avoid imposing our own, usually middle-class, values and goals. Those who set out to ameliorate poverty must view both the system and the client population as objectively as possible.

The intervener must remember that any attempt at change must take into account the functional relationship between the goals and orientation of people and the system under which they live. While the need for change in the entire economic and social system cannot be overemphasized, the behavior of the people within the system cannot be treated as a constant. A workable philosophy of intervention should, therefore, stress the reciprocal relationship between behavior and system.

A strategy of change must be guided by the question of feasibility. Is it possible to change both behavior and system? In answering this question, first consideration must be given to the factors of timing and the availability of resources. Secondly, bearing in mind the reciprocity of system and behavior, objective conditions must be studied to determine where the greater effort should be concentrated. The mutual adaptation of system and behavior must become a major concern of the intervener.

The effect of the economic and social system upon human behavior is obvious. Nonetheless, we are of the opinion that attempts at effecting behavioral changes may accomplish two things: make lower-class life somewhat more bearable under present conditions and contribute toward the implementation of system change.[53]

The first goal, that of making life more bearable, is not the same as advocating that the status quo be retained. It is, rather, a recognition of the necessity of taking whatever measures are needed to improve the situation of the poor when system change-- for whatever reasons--does not proceed at a desirable pace. Where modification of some aspects of lower-class behavior can contribute to immediate improvement, such attempts appear justifiable to us.

On the other hand, where system change is taking place, the lower class itself may turn out to be a retarding factor. Most lower-class people are distrustful of existing social institutions; many of them, by virtue of their fatalistic attitudes, are resistant to change. In this case, effective intervention might be aimed at the second goal, contributing toward the implementation of system change. This would be carried out by attempting to modify some of the "poverty syndromes," to use Chilman's descriptive phrase. The handicapping traits of the poor result from many behavioral factors --inadequate socialization, poor relationships, delinquent family structure--as well as economic and social deprivation. So it would be futile to anticipate that system change, without accompanying behavioral change, could solve all the problems of the lower class.[54]

Chilman favors application of a differential diagnosis in planning programs for groups as well as for individuals[55]--a diagnosis that may focus on the individual and the group or on the system. The NIP program focused on behavioral changes by means of services to individuals, families and groups. We also attempted to provide supplemental environmental changes where these, for reasons beyond our control, were slow in coming.

The implications of the above formulations were weighed by planners and staff of the Neighborhood Improvement Project. Intervention aimed at improving the lot of a deprived population would have to build on the strengths of existing life patterns and would have to seek modifications in functioning consistent with these patterns. The family and the peer group would have to be the prime focuses of intervention. Programming for services would have to be addressed to the needs and aspirations of the people. The literature cited here could provide valuable guidelines, but our specific pattern of intervention could come only from actual work with the people of Farnam Courts. With limited information available, we developed our program by utilizing at times that old and effective technique of knowledge-building: learning by trial and error.

Notes

1. Walter B. Miller. "Implications of Urban Lower-Class Culture for Social Work," Social Service Review, Vol. 33(3):219-236, 1959.

2. Preliminary forms used in preparing Public Housing Authority Form 1245, Conn. 4-4, Quarter ending June 30, 1963.

3. Ibid; plus analysis of surnames.

4. Farnam Courts Housing Office, Tenants' files; Raw data from Ludwig L. Geismar and Michael A. LaSorte, The Multi-Problem Family: A Conceptual Analysis and Exploration in Early Identification (New York, Association Press, 1964).

5. PHA Form 1245, op.cit.; Raw data from Geismar and La Sorte, op. cit.; Jerome K. Myers, "Ecological Survey of New Haven and Suburban Towns, 1950" (Unpublished materials); August B. Hollingshead and Frederick C. Redlich, Social Class and Mental Illness (New York, John Wiley and Sons, 1958). pp. 114-135; W. Lloyd Warner and Paul S. Lunt, The Social Life of a Modern Community (New Haven, Yale University Press, 1941) pp. 444-450.

6. Raw data from Geismar and LaSorte, op.cit.; United States Bureau of the Census, 18th Census of the United States: 1960 Population, Vol. 8D, Table 103, pp. 205-206.

7. Tenants' files, op. cit.

8. PHA Form 1245, op. cit.; 18th Census, op.cit. Vol. 8D, Table 139, p. 401, and Table 143, p. 411.

9. Hollingshead and Redlich, loc. cit.

10. Jerome K. Myers and Bertram H. Roberts. Family and Class Dynamics in Mental Illness. (New York, John Wiley and Sons, 1959). p. 51.

11. The phrase "expanded family" was coined by Donald Pitkin, in "Land Tenure and Farm Organization in an Italian Village" (Unpublished Doctoral Dissertation, Harvard University, Cambridge, 1954). p. 114.

12. Tenants' files, op.cit.

13. Hollingshead and Redlich, op. cit., p. 124.

14. Ibid., p. 200.

15. Herbert J. Gans. Social and Physical Planning for the Elimination of Urban Poverty, 1962. Institute for Urban Studies, University of Pennsylvania, Philadelphia. (mimeographed) p. 9.

16. Tenants' files, op.cit.

17. Hollingshead and Redlich, op. cit., p. 116.

18. Herbert J. Gans. The Urban Villagers. (New York, The Free Press of Glencoe, 1962). p. 54.

19. Ibid., pp. 237-248.

20. Miller, op. cit., pp. 228-229.

21. Gans, op. cit., pp. 80-101.

22. Ibid.

23. Ibid.

24. Ibid.

25. Ibid.

26. Hollingshead and Redlich, op. cit., pp. 66-135. Data cited are assembled from "Status Awareness" paragraphs for each class in Chapter IV.

27. Ruby Elwell, rough draft for grant proposal, New Haven Travellers' Aid Society. (New Haven, New Haven Travellers' Aid Society, 1964) (mimeographed).

28. Gans, op. cit., p. 40.

29. Geismar and La Sorte, op. cit., p. 149.

30. Gans, loc. cit.

31. Miller, op. cit., p. 227.

32. Gans, op. cit., p. 268.

33. Paul Goodman. Growing Up Absurd. (New York, Random House, 1960).

34. Hollingshead and Redlich, op. cit., p. 134.

35. Gans, op. cit., p. 28.

36. Nelson N. Foote. "Concept and Method in the Study of Human Development," in Muzafer Sherif and M.O. Wilson, eds., Emergent Problems in Social Psychology. (Norman, University of Oklahoma Press, 1957). pp. 29-53.

37. Gans, op. cit., p. 39

38. Walter B. Miller. "Lower-Class Culture as a Generating Milieu of Gang Delinquency," Journal of Social Issues, Vol. 14, No. 3, pp. 5-19, p. 14, 1959.

39. Miller. "Implications of Lower-Class Culture for Social Work," op. cit., p. 225.

40. Ibid., p. 226.

41. Ibid., p. 228.

42. United States Bureau of the Census. 18th Census of the United States, 1960: Population.

43. Miller. "Implications..." loc. cit., Vol. 14, No. 3, p. 223.

44. Ibid.

45. Statistics of New Haven Housing Authority.

46. Gans, op. cit., p. 167

47. Thomas F. Gladwin. "The Anthropologist's View of Poverty," The Social Welfare Forum. Paper presented at the National Conference on Social Welfare, Minneapolis, May 14-19, 1961 (mimeographed), p. 8.

48. Gans, op. cit., pp. 267-268.

49. Ibid., p. 221.

50. Catherine S. Chilman. "Child Rearing Monograph," Washington, Welfare Administration, Dept. of Health, Education and Welfare, June 3, 1965. (unpublished)

51. Ibid., Chapter IX, pp. 98-99.

52. Ibid., pp. 53, 97.

53. Marxist philosophy would tend to view the two as contradictory. We concede that they might be incompatible under conditions where, because of a revolutionary attitude on the part of local leadership and the population, even temporary accommodation would delay social

change.   Farnam Courts, by contrast, presented a situation in which local leadership was virtually absent and the prevalent state of mind could best be characterized as one of apathy and helplessness in the face of severe deprivation.

54. Chilman, op. cit., p. 96.

55. Ibid.

Chapter 3
From Physical to Social Renewal

At the end of World War II the specific problems that were
to lead New Haven to consider a program of planned social action
still lay dormant. As everyday life returned to normal, people enjoyed America's postwar boom. Salaries were high, factories
hummed, and there were increasing amounts of consumer goods
available. By 1950, however, there began to prevail in the city a
feeling that all was not well. The population had increased only
23% since 1910--from 133,000 to 164,000--although there had been
predictions in 1910 of 400,000 citizens by 1950, an increase of
300%. The city had stopped growing right in the middle of the national boom that followed World War I. Civic building had ceased
at about the same time; the last hotel had been built in 1912, and
the newest downtown office building had been erected in the mid-
twenties. Eighty percent of the schools had been built around the
time of World War I; four schools dated back to the Civil War.

The economic picture was equally depressing. As Harper's
Magazine put it, New Haven was "quietly rotting on the vine."[1]
New industries were not locating in the city, and many long-established factories were closing--some going out of business, others
moving to different parts of the country. Lack of expansion space,
dilapidated buildings, and an inadequate highway and street network
hampered the operations of many city firms.

In the early forties political and business leaders, aware of
the severity of the problem, established a City Planning Commission and hired professional planners to draw up recommendations.
Unfortunately, nothing materialized. Maurice E. Rotival, a noted
French town planner then on the Yale University faculty, spent many
months speaking before civic groups, trying without success to
arouse public interest in his plan for a rejuvenated city. He left

51

in 1944 to join the Free French Army, and there the matter rested until the close of World War II.[2]

From this disappointing beginning New Haven became--only ten years later--a leader in the field of urban renewal and the conservation of human resources. The city moved boldly, first toward large-scale physical renewal and then toward the social renewal exemplified by the Neighborhood Improvement Project.

This type of large-scale social change can best be understood if we examine it with the aid of conceptual tools provided by Lippitt, Watson, and Westley in their book, The Dynamics of Planned Change.[3] In theory, they say, a city is a social system charged with the function of creating a favorable milieu for certain kinds of economic social and cultural activities. To this end, every city must provide the goods and services needed by its human components and by the various sub-parts of the system. (The sub-parts are groups, interacting and interrelating, that are made up of citizens who act in concert. Such sub-parts may be informal interest groups, geographical or neighborhood units, political subdivisions or social strata, to mention a few.) In satisfying the needs of its citizens and sub-parts, a city develops its own distinctive structural pattern of interrelationships and operations and its own traditional problem-solving procedures.

Lippitt and his associates theorize that planned social change in cities may come about in any one of several ways:[4] (1) the normal community growth and development process may be effective enough to enable the city to solve each new problem as it arises; (2) external changes may help solve the system's internal problems without the necessity of direct action; (3) the system may solve its problems by moving to a new location where its established methods of organization, operation and problem-solving will continue to work; (4) the system may recognize that it is in trouble and call for help from an outside source; or (5) change may come about through the intervention of an individual, inside or outside the system, who sees a need, formulates solutions, and takes the initiative in establishing a helping relationship with the troubled system. If the individual and his ideas are approved, he might then be appointed the system's agent of change.

Arriving at this stage may prove a difficult process. The
hidden indices of trouble must first be widely publicized, in order
to arouse public awareness. Then there must be engendered a feeling of hope--a belief that action, if taken, can lead to success.
Next, the citizens, as potential "clients" of this volunteering agent,
must be able to assess his diagnosis and decide whether his recommendations are valid. The final step is the most crucial. Having
come to know each other, the community and the agent of change
must decide to work together. The success of the whole program
apparently depends heavily on the quality and workability of this relationship.[5]

As Lippitt, Watson and Westley point out, change agents must
decide whether their clients' difficulties are external or internal.
Mayor Richard C. Lee, New Haven's leading change agent, apparently had decided that the city's problem was largely internal. After
taking office in 1953, his actions indicated that he saw two main
difficulties--a breakdown in internal communications and a faulty internal distribution of power. The changes he brought about in these
two areas are described in the following pages. As a result of his
analysis, a promise was made during a political campaign to form
a Citizens Action Commission to investigate the causes of and find
remedies for the city's decline. Mayor Lee envisioned an organization that would provide maximum citizen participation in an overall
program of urban renewal and redevelopment. Its members were
to be influential, non-partisan citizens from various social, economic and occupational strata. They would work closely with public officials, carrying on an active publicity campaign to create a strong
public opinion.[6]

Nine months of careful planning were necessary to set the
CAC in motion. In that period the mayor's ability to interest representative, influential citizens was crucial. First he recruited
men affiliated with the most powerful interests in New Haven to
serve on the CAC's twenty-man Executive Committee. They included the presidents of a bank, of a utility company, of Yale University, of the railroad, and of the six largest manufacturing firms

in the city; the Dean of the Yale Law School; and leaders of three
of the most powerful unions.   These men met once a month in the
mayor's office, acting as his "Citizens Cabinet" or "New Haven's
Board of Directors. " Six subcommittees were formed, with a total
membership of about six hundred individuals, chosen from various
social levels for their leadership and ability to influence public
opinion.   The subcommittees were to gather information, consult experts, and formulate possible solutions.   If approved by the executive committee, the plans would be given to the appropriate agency
for implementation; they would be widely publicized and closely supervised while being enacted.

  To avoid the taint of political bias, the New Haven Foundation was asked to provide financial support.   An active publicity
campaign was started.   The CAC's first chairman once said: "The
CAC is so representative of the citizens of New Haven that if anyone throws a rock at the CAC they are bound to hit one of their
own. "[7]   The Commission gained widespread public approval--the
first step, guided by the change agent, toward the establishment of
better communications among the various sub-parts of the city.
Men and women who would never have had occasion to meet were
drawn together through their service on the Commission.

  This accomplishment was not, however, unaccompanied by
strife.   There were, and still are, people in the city who firmly
believed that the CAC was being used by an ambitious politician at
the expense of a city that did not really need his drastic remedies.
The proposed reforms ran counter to many vested interests.   They
could not, however, muster enough strength at the polls to block
Mayor Lee, who has proved so popular that he has been returned
to office five times since his initial election in 1953.

  In our opinion it matters little whether the CAC or the may-
or planned the change program.   There is evidence of independent
Commission work in certain areas.   But the important fact is that
the program enjoyed the prestige of CAC sponsorship and thus
gained the approval of the average citizen.

  During this period Mayor Lee also began to correct what he
saw as New Haven's other main problem--the inefficient administra-

tive apparatus. After visiting every municipal installation and department, he made administrative changes aimed both at reducing personnel and improving departmental efficiency. Modern methods and equipment were brought in and skilled personnel were hired, allowing a cutback in city payrolls. A new bookkeeping system was installed; the fire and police services were centralized and given an up-to-date radar system; modern equipment was acquired to speed up road repairs; a central switchboard for all city departments was set up at City Hall. A new traffic expert was hired whose decisions were supported by the administration, making it impossible to fix traffic tickets as in the past. A Redevelopment Coordinator was appointed to supervise all redevelopment activities in the city; surprisingly, he was given authority to make decisions.

The six CAC subcommittees were Industrial and Harbor Development; Central Business District, Traffic and Parking; Housing; Metropolitan Approach; Education; Health, Welfare, Recreation and Human Values. Each was to recommend solutions to problems in its area of concern. It was at this stage, with the activated subsystems beginning to operate with increasing independence, that the responsibility for planned social change was transferred from the executive. The process was an attempt to redistribute power, not by overturning the power structure but by mobilizing existing passive elements. The mayor's success in this attempt was due directly to his political skill and popularity.

In the beginning, change in New Haven was oriented toward physical urban renewal, with business and industry carrying the main burden of the program. Slum clearance was high on the list of priorities. Deteriorated housing in the inner city gave way to stores, office buildings and factories. The displaced population was relocated, either in the newly established public housing projects or in low-rent housing in other areas. Commercial and industrial redevelopment were felt to be the key to New Haven revival.

Our interest in the city's urban renewal was confined largely to the plans and activities that affected the health and welfare of the people, especially those most socially and economically deprived. This particular aspect was assigned to the Subcommittee on Health,

Welfare, Recreation, and Human Values; the Neighborhood Improvement Project was one of the end products of this group's endeavors.

The establishment of this subcommittee showed that the may-
or and his collaborators were aware of social problems, but an
overall examination of urban renewal activities substantiated the impression that social renewal initially was assigned a very minor role
in the city's rejuvenation.[8] The low priority given health and welfare action reflects both the climate of opinion in the United States
in the early 1950's and also the attitudes of CAC leaders, who were
not recruited from social service ranks.

In 1954 the subcommittee on human values received a nine-
point directive, covering such points as the formation of a Human
Relations Commission, the study of problems of the aging, and improvement of the conditions of neglected and handicapped children.[9]
Several small groups were formed to study these problems; one of
these was the Committee on Juvenile Delinquency, composed of fifteen people: the Police Commissioner, the Chief of Police, and two
judges from the city courts; the Superintendent of Schools and the
chairman of the PTA Council; two clergymen, a doctor, a psychologist, and several representatives of public and voluntary social
agencies. The committee's first task was to interview workers in
agencies handling problem children; its members also traveled about
the city observing the actual conditions under which these youngsters
lived.

The problem of juvenile delinquency attracted the subcommittee's special attention, for it represented a threat to the security
and stability of society and the well-being of those in positions of
leadership. The planners represented the segment of the community that would lose most were juvenile delinquency to remain un-
checked; they naturally viewed delinquency prevention and control as
the one activity that could substantially improve both the image of
the community and the welfare of its citizens.

During the fifties, official thinking on the subject of juvenile
delinquency followed the popular assumption that young offenders, as
well as dope addicts, criminals, prostitutes, etc., were products
of the slums. Those who guided New Haven's redevelopment were

convinced that a change in the physical environment would eliminate
the social problems as well as the deprivations of the slum dwellers.
The city took special pride in the fact that "whole streets which
symbolized helplessness, despair, poverty, and crime were going to
disappear and with them would go the flop-houses, the pool halls,
the junk yards, and the flea markets."[10]

Throughout the nation, the largest portion of budgets allocated for combating juvenile delinquency went to programs designed
to protect the rest of the population. The delinquent's behavior was
considered deviant and pathological; this prevalent attitude was shown
by the title of a luncheon address before the Human Values Subcommittee in 1957: "Juvenile Delinquency--Challenge and Menace." It
was a sign of the times that the Committee on Juvenile Delinquency
contained a comparatively large number of persons involved with
law enforcement. It was also typical that the position of coordinator, one who would work with all public and voluntary agencies in a
concerted community attack on youth problems, went in 1957 to a
policeman.

The Committee on Juvenile Delinquency presented its first
report in January, 1955.[11] It recommended that certain projects
be undertaken and that changes be instituted in the structure and
function of some city departments. Among other things, the report
called for:

1. Earlier recognition and treatment of juvenile delinquency.

2. More publicity.

3. Greater liaison between the agencies involved, both public
   and private.

4. A social service cross-indexing system to promote better
   liaison and prevent duplication of services and funds.

5. A survey of service gaps in each area of town.

6. A change in the philosophy and organization of the police
   and the courts with respect to their handling of youthful offenders.

7. A check on the handling of repeaters in state institutions
   and also in juvenile court, where they comprised 28%
   of all cases.

8. The establishment of a single court to handle all family
   problems.

9. The establishment of community centers in the schools, with attached group workers.

10. The cessation of building large public housing complexes, and the construction of a larger number of small units instead.

11. Assignment to each public housing project of a social worker who would work independently of any agency, to serve as a general practitioner for the residents.

12. A more aggressive approach to casework.

At a later date, the Committee on Juvenile Delinquency recommended that the mayor appoint a coordinator. The post was given to Sergeant (now Lieutenant) Biagio De Lieto and proved to be an outstanding appointment, for he was a sensitive, capable, highly intelligent official who welcomed the help and suggestions of all interested individuals.

Frank Harris, then Director of Group Work and Recreation for the Community Council of Greater New Haven, responded to the sergeant's request for help and was appointed a consultant to the Juvenile Delinquency Committee. This marked the formal entrance of the welfare community into the program; from then on, the prime agent of change was the Community Council, as represented by Frank Harris. Consequently, unlike communities where the advice of trained social work personnel goes unheeded, New Haven allowed social welfare thinking to share in molding plans for social action.

Frank Harris attributes much of the progress of New Haven's program of social renewal to the questioning atmosphere in which this phase of planning took place. There was an open-minded search for answers and a willingness to consider new ideas; these factors, along with the exposure afforded by continual publicity, guaranteed a fair hearing to any suggested programs or innovations.

One of the documents studied by the Committee on Juvenile Delinquency was prepared by John Nichols, Executive Secretary of the Family Service Agency of New Haven, for the Council of Social Agencies. Among other things, Mr. Nichols wrote:

> The family service field has long known that a strong tie exists between disturbed family relationships...and unstable family living, which results in civil or criminal action...The family service organizations throughout the country have proved to their own satisfaction that

> constructive help and important family services can be
> offered to these families if sufficient time, money and
> opportunity are provided. This type of family...has come
> to be known as a multi-problem family.
>
> The New York City Youth Board discovered last year that
> less than 1% of that city's families...produced 75% of all
> its juvenile delinquents....It seems very likely that there
> is a similar group in almost every community, including
> New Haven.
>
> The St. Paul, Minnesota Family Centered Project...
> pointed up also that these families have been known at
> one time or another to an average of nine social agen-
> cies...many have been known...because of financial prob-
> lems or had been in conflict with society for as long as
> 18 years....After three years of operating an intensive
> community project, aimed at social treatment and reha-
> bilitation of these families, the researchers have come
> up with positive findings....End results...have been
> changes in policies of many agencies which become more
> family-focused and less focused on individuals, and bet-
> ter relationships among all agencies involved in the project.
>
> We believe that an effective social work program with
> multi-problem families is essential if we are to get at
> the root of sociological ills and we feel that our com-
> munity must be made aware of these implications....
> We request the Council of Social Agencies...to explore
> the need for more adequate services to multi-problem
> families in New Haven. [12]

The committee studied recent research projects throughout
the country. After four months Sergeant De Lieto submitted a progress report to Mayor Lee and the CAC, outlining a ten-point plan of
action that would "involve all social and city agencies in a broad
concerted attack" on juvenile delinquency. [13] The report reiterated
the need for increased coordination among city departments, for
greater cooperation among the various public and voluntary agencies,
for direct liaison between the Committee on Juvenile Delinquency and
city departments dealing specifically with juveniles. It called for an
inventory of recreational programs and facilities, and a study of
juvenile delinquency rates in the city as a whole and in renewal
areas specifically. Two programs--Wheel-Disc Marking and Car-
Key Campaign--were suggested to deter the common first offenses
of hub-cap and car thefts; a Bicycle Loan Program was recom-

mended, along with a Youth Program sponsored by the Fire Department and the Boy Scouts.   High School Teen-Age Councils were
proposed, also "floating" group workers for gangs, and "detached"
social workers who would function in housing projects or community
house settings.

Item Number Seven of the report proposed the following:

An experimental Neighborhood Saturation Program, with
the neighborhood selected on the basis of high juvenile
delinquency rate, sub-standard housing, broken homes,
plus insufficient school, recreational and social services.
Once chosen, the coordinated services of all public and
voluntary agencies would be concentrated in that locale
long enough to demonstrate whether or not the approach
proved effective. [14]

The report contained only three suggestions (Disc-Marking,
Car-Key, and Bicycle Loan Program) aimed at treating symptoms
of juvenile delinquency.   It concentrated instead on a coordinated
attempt to get at some of the contributing factors.   After receiving
the progress report, the CAC asked the agencies, departments, or
organizations that might be involved in implementation to submit detailed suggestions, so that informed decisions could be made.

The Neighborhood Saturation Program called for the coordinated services of all public and voluntary agencies to be concentrated in a selected locale.   It seemed reasonable to Harris and
De Lieto to assume that this recommendation, if approved, probably
would be handed to the Community Council of Greater New Haven
for implementation.   Therefore, they kept the Council informed
from the very beginning, and the Council began early to study its
acceptance.   At a meeting of the Casework Division of the Council,
early in 1958, Frank Harris presented a report, [15] using as background material the writings of Bradley Buell.   Harris mentioned
Buell's theory that disordered behavior might stem from a separate
and recognizable group of families exhibiting a high degree of disorganization, but having also far greater rehabilitative potential than
was once expected; very few social services were brought to bear
upon these families unless they were specifically brought to the attention of an agency.   Although the goal of most agencies was prevention, it was Buell's contention that little had actually been ac-

complished in that area because most attempts had been segmented and episodic in nature (in answer to a specific crisis) rather than community-wide and continuous. Harris then turned specifically to the proposed neighborhood program:[16]

> The casework division ought, therefore, to have a tre-
> mendous stake in a neighborhood saturation project. If
> a small-scale saturation project is initiated it will be a
> concrete demonstration to New Haven of what can be done
> at the neighborhood level. It is quite likely that Case-
> work Division cooperation will be required to provide staff
> without additional funds until the neighborhood program
> can be undertaken. If a demonstration proves to be valu-
> able, it is possible that Federal funds may become avail-
> able. It is recognized that the neighborhood saturation
> program would cost money and would require the com-
> bined forces of Federal and local governments as well as
> public and voluntary agencies to make it effective. Such
> a project would be jointly sponsored by the Municipality,
> through one of its departments, and the Community Coun-
> cil.

He then named the four city areas having the highest delinquency rates, examining each in terms of community services and
geographical makeup. The ideal pilot area had to be compact in
nature and suffer from a lack of services, so that effects of a research program could be clearly demonstrated and assessed. Three
of the areas did not meet these requirements; the fourth, Farnam
Courts, was deemed the most suitable:

> It is a deteriorating area slated for redevelopment; it
> suffers from a lack of community services, and it con-
> tains a Public Housing complex, called Farnam Courts,
> in which 300 families reside. In addition, the families
> living in Farnam Courts will undoubtedly benefit from
> additional supporting services to see them through the
> upsets of redevelopment.

The items in Sergeant De Lieto's report dealing with increased coordination, an inventory of recreation and delinquency
rates, and specific temptation-reducing programs were accepted and
given to the appropriate agencies for implementation. The concept
of a neighborhood project was agreed upon, while the proposals for
gang workers, detached social workers, and teen-age councils were
held in abeyance for possible coordination with the Farnam Courts
effort. As had been expected, it was suggested to the Board of

Directors of the Community Council of Social Agencies on February 25, 1958, that the Neighborhood Saturation Project be administered and supervised by the board.

To examine the scope and feasibility of the project, a Temporary Committee on Neighborhood Saturation was set up by the Community Council. From this point, planning was in the hands of trained professionals collaborating with interested laymen from the welfare community. The committee was composed of thirty members, representing most of the public and voluntary agencies belonging to the council. With the exception of the Coordinator of Youth Activities, Sgt. De Lieto, members of the law enforcement community were no longer involved; laymen played the crucial roles. Under the chairmanship of Mrs. Samuel Howe, the committee undertook to examine the "saturation approach" in other communities, to determine its validity and its applicability in New Haven. The group also gathered specific data on Farnam Courts families by searching through a two months' caseload file of appropriate public and voluntary agencies, and by obtaining lists of families considered multiproblem from schools, neighborhood agencies, the Visiting Nurses Association and the Housing Authority.[17] With a master list and a sober evaluation of the saturation approach, the Temporary Committee hoped to establish the need for the project, delineate the extent of the problem, and recommend a course of action to the council. The council would decide whether to undertake the Farnam Courts pilot project and whether to attempt the type of saturation program, focused primarily on the family, suggested in John Nichol's letter.

Frank Harris reminded the Temporary Committee that the CAC Committee on Juvenile Delinquency had conceived of the project as a three-pronged offensive:

1. Neighborhood organizations--the development of local leadership and responsibility to produce needed change and improvement.

2. The provision of needed health, group work, recreational and casework services for the whole area.

3. A family-centered casework concentration dealing intensively with the multi-problem family.

He also pointed out that the council was not being asked to operate the program but merely to sponsor and coordinate it; additional personnel, if needed, would be recruited from outside the council staff. Although all types of agencies were to be involved in this family-focused project, it was hoped that one agency would assume primary responsibility. All agencies would contribute qualified caseworkers, who would continue work with families already known to them and accept new cases according to their specific areas of competence.

For financing, Mr. Harris suggested that the New Haven Foundation be asked to underwrite a two-year demonstration; local funds could continue the program if it proved successful. While the Temporary Committee was to explore financial possibilities, it was not to negotiate. The question arose of possible interference accompanying city financial support, should it be granted. The Executive Director of the CAC gave assurance that the Redevelopment Agency could turn over the project to the council by means of a subcontract; this, if properly drawn, would serve as protection from municipal interference in the program.

The Temporary Committee began its evaluation of the saturation approach by reviewing pertinent projects in other communities, by informing themselves of the latest development in reaching-out social work practice, and by importing experts to discuss the problems that might arise. The committee soon realized that the word "saturation" was too sweeping a term for the planned project and it was quietly dropped.

A variety of reaching-out projects was then in operation around the country, from which advice and information could be gained. Some were limited to casework, some had a group work phase followed by casework, some were composed of group work services only. There were projects designed to reach multi-problem families, and others aimed at particular groups--juvenile delinquents, street gangs, etc. Most of the projects served either a large geographic area or a certain population group dispersed throughout the city. Detailed information was gathered from projects in Pittsburgh; San Mateo, California; Boston; St. Paul, Minne-

sota; Minneapolis; and Chicago. From a study of the literature,
the committee concluded that the reaching-out approach had demonstrated some degree of usefulness in dealing with certain types of
clients. In retrospect one can see that the committee was influenced by the material it had received; it decided to substitute for
"saturation project" a "reaching-out" casework approach, as it would
be embodied in a small neighborhood project, using simultaneously
the three major methods of social work--casework, group work, and
community organization.

Before it could gather specific data on the multi-problem
families residing in and around the Farnam Courts Housing Project,
the committee had to define its criteria for selection. It was finally decided to choose families known to a number of agencies over a
long period of time, who had school-age children known to the police
and the Juvenile Court, and who had the reputation of being unable
or unwilling to accept previously offered help. Fifty-one names
were provided by the schools, the Housing Authority, and the Farnam Neighborhood House. When these names were checked against
the files of key agencies, it was found that thirty-six families were
known to four or more agencies, twenty were known to five agencies, and twelve were known to seven, eight or nine agencies.
Some cases were opened as early as 1932, while many went back to
the forties. Agency records indicated innumerable openings and clos-
ings for these families; the contacts usually were of short duration.
From this analysis it appeared that thirty to thirty-five families, or
approximately 10 to 12% of the households in Farnam Courts, might
be classed as multi-problem.

From the study came a strongly worded resolution in April,
1958, stating that "a concerted all-out effort... is not only feasible
but mandatory, and should be undertaken under the auspices of the
Council..."[18] While noting the difficulties that might arise because
of prior agency commitments, the Temporary Committee on Neighborhood Saturation urged the immediate start of a two or three-year
project, with possible financial support from the New Haven Foundation, and a full-time director free of local agency affiliation. The
Board accepted these recommendations and put the actual organiza-

tion and conduct of the project in the hands of an Advisory Committee. Mrs. Howe remained as chairman, thereby providing the necessary continuity of interest and coordination.

During the summer of 1958, the project acquired a name--
the Neighborhood Improvement Project--and the committee continued
to consult with directors of other reaching-out projects and with the
faculty of a nearby school of social work. Possible sources of funds
were checked, a tentative table of organization was drawn up, and
brief instructions for NIP's future director were made out. Local
welfare agencies, both public and voluntary, were canvassed to determine the extent of participation that could be expected.

NIP was well on its way, an outcome of the Human Values
Sub-Committee's interest in juvenile delinquency and its preoccupa-
tion with questions of societal security and stability. The early program of the Committee on Juvenile Delinquency had put greater
stress on delinquency identification and control than on prevention
and rehabilitation. But the introduction of social welfare professionals into the Committee on Juvenile Delinquency had resulted in
a significant shift in focus. The primary object of community action became family and neighborhood disorganization, of which the
young delinquent was considered only a symptom. Members of the
Committee on Neighborhood Saturation, which was heavily staffed by
social welfare professionals, felt that treatment, to be most effective, would have to be addressed to the entire family and, to a
lesser extent, the whole neighborhood rather than to the individual.

Without entering into a lengthy defense of this theory, we
wish to point out that the structure and goals of the Neighborhood
Improvement Project, as envisaged by the Temporary Committee,
reflected thinking that was widely accepted and expressed in the literature of the 1950's. NIP was to be not a broad, community-wide
program, but a small, geographically focused demonstration project.
Financing had not yet been assured, and the leaders of the committee were relying on member agencies for future personnel contributions.

Notes

1. Harper's Magazine. "Lee of New Haven," 215(1289):
    37, October, 1957.

2. Ibid., p. 38.

3. Ronald Lippitt, Jeanne Watson and Bruce Westley.
    The Dynamics of Planned Change. (New York, Har-
    court, Brace, 1958).

4. Ibid., pp. 9-11.

5. Ibid., pp. 129-143.

6. Annual Report of the Citizens Action Commission, New
    Haven, November, 1954, pp. 3-4 (in the files of the
    Commission).

7. Harper's Magazine, op. cit., p. 39.

8. This picture changed substantially in the 1960's with
    the creation of New Haven's Community Progress, In-
    corporated, and the investment of substantial sums
    from the Ford Foundation and the federal government
    in diverse community action projects.

9. Report to the Citizens Action Commission by the Sub-
    Committee on Human Values, New Haven, December
    1954 (in the files of the Commission).

10. Report by the Committee on Juvenile Delinquency to the
    Citizens Action Commission, New Haven, January,
    1955 (in the files of the Commission).

11. Ibid.

12. Letter from John W. Nichols, Executive Secretary Fam-
    ily Service of New Haven, January 3, 1958, to Presi-
    dent of the Board, Council of Social Agencies, New
    Haven.

13. Tentative Project Ideas. Minutes of Meeting of Citizens
    Action Committee on Juvenile Delinquency, December
    6, 1957 (in the files of the Committee).

14. Ibid.

15. Minutes of Meeting, February 3, 1958, Casework Divi-
    sion of Council of Social Agencies, New Haven, pp. 3-
    4 (in the files of the Council).

16. Ibid., pp. 2-4.

17. Minutes of Meeting, Temporary Committee on Neighbor-
     hood Saturation, Council of Social Agencies, New Haven,
     March 10, 1958 (in the files of the Council).

18. Minutes of Meeting, April 22, 1958, Board of Directors,
     Council of Social Agencies, New Haven (in the files of
     the Council).

Chapter 4
The Pilot-Project Stage

Change was the keynote in New Haven during the late 1950's. The Community Council had moved quickly, reflecting the political atmosphere current in the city. From the time in December, 1957, when the possibility of a neighborhood saturation project was first mentioned, to the beginning of NIP in August, 1959, only twenty-one months had elapsed. Similar endeavors had taken much longer. In the case of the St. Paul Family-Centered Project, six to seven years elapsed between the first suggestions and the beginning of action.

In New Haven, the decision to move quickly created problems that became apparent only as the project unfolded. Certain matters had to be left for later consideration. It was impossible in the allotted time to indoctrinate agencies in the philosophy, aims and procedures of the new project; consideration of methods of continuing the project after the demonstration period was also postponed. The Planning Committee, occupied with the mechanics of setting up and operating the demonstration phase of the project, decided that the task of cultivating the interest and support of the welfare community would be put off until actual work with clients began.

The Beginnings of Casework

NIP was launched with financial support from the New Haven Foundation and with contributions of service from some of the city agencies. Miss Jane Krisberg, a social worker who had served six years with the New York City Youth Board Casework Treatment Unit, was hired as full-time director. She was assisted by a secretary who doubled as research analyst. The instructions of the Council and NIP Advisory Board were broad and without formal directives; it was expected that the director would develop the necessary procedures as the work progressed. This allowed considerable freedom in planning; the director did, however, frequently consult with the council staff, receiving from them continuing support and a great deal of technical assistance.

NIP's first annual report gave an indication of the work done in the pilot project, listing the following goals considered preliminary to establishing a casework program:[1]

1. Establish a more precise definition of the multi-problem family.

2. Establish criteria to be used in the selection of the multi-problem families to receive NIP's services.

3. Select the families to receive treatment.

4. Write referrral summaries on the families selected for treatment.

5. Orient agency personnel assigned to NIP in the methods and techniques of NIP's treatment and research through regular seminars.

6. Assign a full caseload to allotted workers.

7. Orient community agencies to the purpose and scope of NIP.

8. Establish a reporting system, and maintain a file of data from key community agencies as a means of identifying additional cases in the event of attrition in the active treatment load.

The problem of defining "multi-problem family" came first. Although NIP had used the term in planning sessions and discussions, a clear working definition had not yet been developed. The definition that finally evolved was the result of collaboration between the director and the technical subcommittee of the NIP Advisory Committee. (This subcommittee consisted of executives and supervisors of the New Haven agencies most directly concerned with the treatment of multi-problem families: the City Welfare Department, the State Welfare Department, the Family Service Agency, the Visiting Nurse Association, and the Secretary of Family and Child Services for the Community Council.) Adapting the definitions used by the St. Paul Family-Centered Project and the New York City Youth Board, the NIP developed this definition to suit its own requirements:

A multi-problem family is one in which disorganized

social functioning is present to such a degree that it
adversely affects the following: 1) individual behavior,
2) relationships within the family, 3) relationships outside the family group, particularly in the neighborhood
and community-at-large, and 4) the ability to perform
"instrumental" functions--tasks concerned with those economic, health and household practices necessary to maintain the family as a physical unit.

The emphasis was on the way in which these essential functions were being performed rather than on who performed them. A
multi-problem family, then, was one in which essential family functions were being performed so badly that the welfare of the family
and community was seriously threatened or actually endangered. A
more refined definition within this conceptual framework and ration-
ale may be found in Geismar and La Sorte. [2]

In choosing the first families for treatment, the NIP had to
use indices much cruder than those in the above definition. From
this broad, preliminary selection, the multi-problem cases would be
extracted by diagnostic evaluation and research measurement. Potential treatment cases had to meet the following conditions: 1) The
family had to be living in Farnam Courts, with school-age children
in "clear and present danger;[3] 2) it had to be known to at least
three health or welfare agencies in New Haven, [4] 3) it had to have,
in the director's opinion, problems in the areas of functioning mentioned above sufficient in number and severity to warrant the appel-
lation "multi-problem;" and 4) it was necessary for the family to be
judged "unable or unwilling to accept help in the past."

The stipulation that the family had to live in Farnam Courts
was added when the rapidity of redevelopment in the area led to the
abandonment of many buildings outside the housing project.

The term "children in clear and present danger" was used
loosely as a selection criterion, since it was hoped preventive treatment could be given those children who had not yet been brought before a court but who might still be judged to be in potential danger.
There was a deliberate attempt to avoid official indices such as the
Juvenile Court adjudications of delinquency or neglect. We preferred
to use data gathered informally from schools, the Visiting Nurse
Association, the Housing Authority and the Settlement House.

Our selection was arbitrarily limited to families having children between the ages of five and sixteen. While this excluded families with only pre-school children, it was deemed necessary because of the difficulty in these cases of documenting "clear and present danger" from agency records. Families with children over sixteen were not selected for the intensive treatment program because we wished to concentrate our services on family units containing children who would continue to live at home for several years.

In order to identify the Farnam Courts families that might be classified as multi-problem, it was necessary to document the existence of a wide range of family problems and establish some method of rating their seriousness. Since the best and most up-to-date family records were kept by the agencies the families frequented, it was decided to use these case records as the basis for diagnosis.

The last stipulation for preliminary selection called for an inability or unwillingness to accept help; NIP defined this to mean a family with a recent record of several serious problems and, in the opinion of the reporting agencies, one that had been unresponsive, uncooperative, or had shown a history of no progress.

Since a survey done in 1958 to show the need for a project was out-of-date and contained insufficient data, another was made in September, 1959, based on the above selection criteria. We began with the names of 300 families residing in Farnam Courts. The families without school-age children were eliminated, and the remaining 143 families were checked through the files of all major health, welfare, and correctional agencies in New Haven. This was a complicated and tedious task, since the New Haven Social Service Exchange had been discontinued some years before. The work was divided by agreement between NIP's director and the agencies.

It took approximately six weeks to complete the survey, which revealed fifty "multi-agency" families with school-age children. The following table groups these families according to their number of agency contacts:

Table 1
Number of Contacts for Multi-Agency Families

Number of Agency Contacts	Number of Families
10 or more	2
9	1
8	3
7	7
6	9
5	10
4	9
3	9
	50 total

The detailed case records of these fifty families were used to identify those considered multi-problem under the NIP's definition. All multi-problem families turned out to have three or more agency contacts, but not all multi-agency families could be classified as multi-problem. For example, a family that had had eight contacts with six different agencies did not merit inclusion in NIP as a multi-problem family. Although the family members had recent serious problems, case records failed to uncover any evidence of disorganization, or inability to perform essential family functions. Three of the top twenty families, with six or more agency contacts, and ten of those with three or more contacts, were rejected on similar grounds. Our examination showed that about twenty percent of the multi-agency families were not also multi-problem. In general, however, the number of agency contacts was correlated with the designation of "multi-problem."

The director decided to include in the selection procedure primarily those family incidents occurring within eighteen months prior to the activation of NIP on August 1, 1959. She felt that the inclusion of older items from the records would weaken the case for intervention at this later date and would make it more difficult for the worker to gain entry into the family. Feelings of hostility and rejection might be aroused in the family if a worker were to offer help with old problems that were no longer acute.

Miss Krisberg also attempted to adhere to the facts in the records, excluding judgments, impressions or opinions that were not substantiated. The following excerpt from a case report shows the kind of information desired:

Basis of Concern:

Both parents are mentally subnormal, extremely un-stable, and given to uncontrolled emotional outbursts. Their entire married life has been characterized by repeated brawling, fist fights, separations and reunions too numerous to count. The children have been placed several times, are physically neglected, thin, pale, and undernourished. Mrs. J. has fought fiercely to get the children back each time they have been placed.... It is questionable whether the children should remain with the parents and a current evaluation of the total situation is needed.

That both these young parents were mentally subnormal was substantiated by their school records and by reports of psychologi-cal examinations done by courts and clinics. Their marital strife, which involved violent physical fights resulting in arrests, was fully documented in court records. The poor condition of the children was confirmed in their health records. The statement that Mrs. J. "fought fiercely" to get her children back after placement was based on the fact that she had attacked an agency worker and was put un-der a court order to undergo psychiatric examination.

When the facts culled from a family's case records pointed to a need for intervention, the director compiled a detailed family case history. The fifty families were ranked in order according to the severity of their problems. After eliminating the families that could not be termed multi-problem or that had moved away from Farnam Courts, NIP was left with thirty-five potential or actual multi-problem cases. The diagnostic information available on them was then measured against the St. Paul Scale of Family Functioning (the quantitive picture obtained will be given in a subsequent chap-ter.) These thirty-five families, the initial treatment group for the intensive casework service operation, were to be the target of the reaching-out approach that the project hoped to effectively demon-strate. During the course of the project a total of forty-five cases received these services.

Since information was gathered from a number of sources, it became imperative to assemble the available data in an organized, structured form. This would give a clear picture of total family functioning and make it easier to present evidence for intervention. Agency records are notable for their variety. Some are highly structured, with paragraph headings identifying the subject matter; others are written in a loose narrative style. To eliminate this diversity, responsibility for the entire intake process--record reading, data selection, structuring of reports, and record writing--was assumed by NIP's staff. This made for far greater consistency than if each agency had written its own reports. The compilation was done by the NIP director and the casework associate, using the St. Paul Profile of Family Functioning [5] as the format for documentation. The Profile of Family Functioning, a research instrument that was designed to serve also as a casework tool, was used from the beginning to structure casework data. The resulting outline, known in NIP as the screening-in report, was given to the workers assigned to the case. In addition to structuring data, this arrangement had the additional advantage of training workers in the NIP form and manner of assembling information.

Rather than set up a new and separate agency to administer the intensive casework phase, the NIP intended to make maximum use of personnel from existing agencies that were already dealing with the multi-problem family in New Haven. These agencies were asked to select a staff worker to become a member of a coordinated team under the overall supervision of NIP's director. Agency executives agreed that a skilled, experienced worker, holding a master's degree from an accredited school of social work, was required; they agreed also that the worker should voluntarily accept the assignment to NIP. An informal selection process operated in each agency in addition to volunteering, for each executive necessarily made some preliminary judgments about which worker should be offered the chance to work with NIP. In addition, the executive's choice was governed by the agency facts of life: the staff situation and the budget. When the selections were finally made, it was

found to our disappointment that all casework participants, with one
exception, were part-time team members, saddled with a dual set
of responsibilities and loyalties.

Supervision of the individual caseworkers was the responsibility of their respective agencies. The NIP Director ran weekly
seminars for the caseworkers, which were designed to teach the
philosophy of intensive reaching-out casework and to ensure consistent application of the NIP casework methods and techniques. At
these seminars answers to common work problems were sought and
the workers were provided guidance in carrying out research objectives. Stress was placed on integrating the casework program with
the other project phases that made up total service to the residents
of Farnam Courts. The director attempted at these weekly meetings
to develop an esprit de corps and to assuage the natural anxieties
of her workers, who were involved with unfamiliar methods and techniques and a different type of client.

The Casework Notebook of the St. Paul Family-Centered Project was used to teach the philosophy and methods of intensive,
reaching-out casework with multi-problem families.[6] Since this approach was new to all, and very few had experienced concentrated
contact with multi-problem clients, the workers needed help in re-
adjusting their concepts of treatment and in setting more limited
goals for themselves.

NIP's casework seminars, begun in December, 1959, continued throughout most of the life of the project. They were the
means by which workers were instructed, during the early months
of the project, in the reaching-out approach and the necessity for
directness in client relationships. Workers were advised of the necessity for persistent, regular, continuous home visits and of the
need for actively involving all immediate or extended family members related to the family's basic problems. Great stress was
placed upon the need to reach out and pursue the client for as long
as there was any hope of accomplishment. The workers were taught
the necessity of openness or directness, of informing the family fully
about NIP and its aims. These seminars prepared workers to share
the information they had obtained about the family's problem areas;

to state how they got that information; to state whom they represented and why they had come; to solicit the family's views on the problems presented; to inquire about other problems, which might seem more urgent to family members; and to specify how they could be of help to the family.

The need for a limited or "protected" caseload in the treatment of multi-problem families is well understood by most social workers, and accordingly the limit for one worker originally was set at fifteen cases. When inception of the research phase brought added responsibilities and requirements, twelve cases were determined to be a full caseload. To adhere to this limit, the NIP had either to obtain more workers or reduce the total number of cases to be treated. The latter course was taken, since the number of workers from existing agencies was fixed by a budget allocation of $13,000 worth of worker services from the participating agencies. Prior budget commitments and staff shortages in these agencies limited the amount of time that could be given to NIP. Our workers, with one exception, were part-time team members. These factors, plus the restricted caseload per worker, severely limited the number of cases that NIP was able to handle during the life of the project.

The starting team consisted of four workers representing four different agencies. Two were assigned to NIP on a half-time basis and two on a one-fifth-time basis, which was equivalent to one and two-fifths workers. Table 2 below shows our position in December, 1959, when we began assigning cases. Table 3 gives an indication of the nature of the family problems confronting these part-time workers; the items mentioned illustrate why multi-problem families require a great investment of worker time and effort. [7]

The four workers assigned to NIP represented a much more limited casework potential than had been originally planned. With a projected caseload of 35 to 45 multi-problem families, the equivalent of four full-time workers was the minimum requirement. Faced with the choice of waiting for improved conditions or starting inadequately and working toward expansion, NIP decided to begin at once.

Problems in administration and the division of responsibility

Table 2

Time Donations and Caseloads of
Participating Agencies

Agency	Time Donated	Caseload
Family Service Agency of New Haven	1/2	6
Diocesan Bureau of Social Service	1/2	6
Psychiatric Out-Patient Clinic, Grace-New Haven Hospital	1/5	2
New Haven Board of Education, Division of School Social Workers	1/5	2
Total:	1 2/5 workers	16 cases

Table   3

Facts about the First 16 Families
Selected for Treatment

Homes with both parents present	11
Homes with mother only present	5
Families receiving relief	12
Families with serious health problems	7
Families with adult delinquency: (Multiple arrests for assault, non-support, theft, breach of peace, fraud, etc.)	10
Total number of children (average per family: 4.6)	73
Number of school-age children	57
Children with serious school problems	31
Instances of adjudicated juvenile delinquency	27
Instances of youth contacts with Juvenile Youth Bureau	38
Number of children in correctional institutions	5

can occur under dual supervision of workers.   NIP caseworkers
were supervised in their own agencies; they also attended seminars
given by the NIP Director.   To avoid confusion and keep the administrative lines as clear as possible, monthly meetings between
agency supervisors and the Director were held.   At these sessions,

the participants discussed the philosophy and purposes of NIP, the
casework methods and techniques which were being taught to assigned workers, and the nature of the research instrument, with
guidelines for its use. Supervisors were asked for suggestions
about the possible use and refinement of the instrument in their own
agencies. The Director proposed ways in which the supervisors
might promote NIP treatment objectives, and she also shared with
those present the problems and reactions of the workers that were
being discussed in the workers' seminars.

Conferences were also held with the administrators of all
agencies involved with NIP treatment families. These meetings
were designed to clarify areas of responsibility and mutual relations,
and to explore the means whereby needed information could be obtained. The Director also arranged a series of meetings with the
staffs of community agencies and institutions, in order to acquaint
them with the goals and methods of NIP. In this manner the project planners attempted to coordinate all the participating elements.

The NIP staff was aware that extra cases might be needed in
the future, because of attrition. Since multi-problem families have
periods of relative stability between "blow-ups," the Farnam Courts
families already known to three or more agencies might well dis-
play problematic functioning in the future, even though they had not
qualified for help during the screening period. Consequently family
histories for those near the bottom of the priority list were compiled, for possible future use. With this added precaution, it was
felt that the casework portion of the NIP program was safely under-
way.

Starting the Group Work Program

Farnam Courts had been selected as the site for NIP because
the area suffered from a lack of health, welfare, and recreational
services and facilities. Since there was a pressing need for recreational services for school-age children, it was decided that this program would be given priority in the group work phase of the project.

The Planning Committee had determined that recreational

services would be handled by the Farnam Neighborhood House (FNH), a nearby settlement house with a long history of service to area residents. The director of FNH had agreed to contribute the settlement house facilities, as well as his own services and those of two staff members on a part-time basis. There was also a supplementary budget allotment, which made it possible for him to hire four part-time group leaders to assist in the program.

The first step in the group work program was to assess the areas of greatest need and formulate new programs accordingly. It was deemed necessary to establish liaison with existing group work resources, especially those that could serve the Farnam Courts population, and to encourage residents to make greater use of those facilities. Regular meetings were scheduled with the group work staff to deal with work problems, to coordinate program with the casework phase, and to give in-service training. A system of recording attendance was set up. Detailed reports of behavior problems were to be collected from the group workers, which could be used in establishing the need for casework treatment or other services.

The target group of seven to thirteen-year-old youngsters were to be offered a varied program of activities: intramural sports, arts and crafts, games, field trips, special parties, dances for the older age groups, etc. It was planned to begin the program at Farnam Courts but to get the children over to FNH as soon as possible, introducing them to greater use of other community recreational resources.

In October 1959, the group work phase was instituted when the supervisory staff of FNH and part-time leaders began organizing the children into groups, on their home grounds. At first all activities were held in the Administration Building at Farnam Courts; then the children were occasionally taken to the Neighborhood House, as if they were on a field trip. The response was immediate and overwhelming. By December there were twelve NIP club groups, meeting every week and with a total membership of 175. Before NIP's arrival less than thirty children from the Courts were known to FNH personnel--and this figure included Fresh Air Fund scholar-

ship campers. The NIP-sponsored activities rapidly filled Farnam
Neighborhood House to capacity, occupying every open time period
and facility.   Some children even lied about their ages in order to
qualify for more than one group. Older children began frequenting
Farnam Neighborhood House on their own; the staff noticed an appreciable increase in the number of Farnam Courts children using
the gymnasium and game rooms and attending FNH's regularly scheduled field trips and dances.

The FNH director and supervisory staff discussed program
needs with the NIP director at weekly meetings, offering a great
deal of information on the behavior and adjustment of Farnam Courts
children.   Frequently a leader would catch intimations of difficulty
in a child's group behavior; such data, when passed on, made it possible for the casework staff to begin early assistance.   One NIP
caseworker, for example, was able to utilize information obtained
in this fashion to get a complete medical and psychological work-up
started on a seriously disturbed child, whose parent had evaded the
task for two years.

First Attempts at Community Organization

Community organization was seen as the final part of the
three-pronged intervention effort, as important as casework or group
work services.   The first step in mobilizing the community was to
revive the tenants' council.   Next there had to be an assessment of
the interests and needs of the population, so that appropriate tenants'
council programs could be planned.   The third step was to explore
appropriate resources in the community at large in order to make
suitable services available, and to encourage the Courts population
to make full use of them.

Reactivating the council proved difficult.   Prior to 1958 the
Hamilton Neighborhood Council had served a large part of the triangle; it had drawn its membership from people who lived, worked
or showed interest in the area.   Redevelopment, with the consequent loss of a large percentage of the population, had probably
contributed to the council's demise, and during the early stages of
NIP's planning there was no functioning neighborhood council in the

area. Frank Harris, then Secretary of Group Work and Recreation
for the Community Council, decided that some advance organization
in the area--before NIP officially began operations--might prove useful. Mustering a few key people--among them the Housing Project
manager and social worker, the director of the local settlement
house, the elementary school principal and the school guidance
counsellor--Mr. Harris and his associates were able to interest
thirty to fifty Farnam Courts tenants and fifteen or so other residents in "doing something" for their neighborhood. Under the strong
leadership of the key community activists, this informally constituted group began, in February 1958, to move rapidly into action.
Intra-mural ball teams and dances were established for teen-agers;
bingo was organized for adults. Small fees were charged at enter-
tainments and refreshments were sold, in order to build up a treasury for expenses and equipment. Committees of tenants were put
to work on a local library, the acquisition of play-area equipment,
baby-sitting services, a children's study club, and a Senior Citizen's
Club.

It was an integrated group from the first. The white majority was more heavily represented, but there was good attendance by
Negroes. Both segments had a few articulate, aggressive, sophisticated individuals who acted as self-appointed spokesmen; most of the
members were quiet, passive individuals who seemed willing to accept specific tasks and responsibilities when delegated to them.

In the fall of 1958, when the group had been operating for over
six months, one of the leaders suggested a more formal structure.
Consequently, officers were elected, bylaws adopted, and the Farnam Courts Tenants' Council was incorporated as the Farnam Courts
Community Council. Leadership remained in the hands of the original racial spokesmen, each supported by a small, active clique.
Then attendance began slowly to drop off--from an early average of
twenty-six to a later one of about fourteen. This did not seem unusual, since most organizations have a small corps of hard-working
doers and a larger body of passive members. But soon the situation became more complicated.

Both men in key leadership positions--one Italian-American

and the other Negro--might be characterized as upwardly mobile.
The white leader, though in poor health and economically dependent,
had a number of political connections in the community and showed
good organizational ability.   The Negro was a lay minister, intelligent and articulate.   Both men revealed a great need to exercise
power and they were prone to use it without inhibition.   They had
led the drive for independence, writing the bylaws, organizing the
election and incorporating the group.   The Negro held the office of
president; the white man was treasurer.

Professional sponsors of the Tenants' Council viewed the for-
malization favorably, and the two men worked together reasonably
well so long as Frank Harris, the Housing Manager, and the Neighborhood House director guided their activities.   Trouble began after
incorporation, when the professionals were relegated to lesser roles.
A sharp division on goals and priorities split the leaders;   accusations and counter-accusations, chiefly about the misuse of money,
flew through the neighborhood.   The active members split along ra-
cial-ethnic lines; as the conflict deepened the white treasurer refused to relinquish any funds for use by the group.   In retaliation
he was read out of office on an action initiated by the Negro president.   At the same time the teen-age dances began to take on racial
overtones, and the threat of violence loomed over this activity.   The
City Housing director decided to put a moratorium on the dances at
the end of the school year.

We cannot state definitely the reasons for the failure of the
independent Farnam Courts Community Council.   However, on the
basis of later observations and interviews with tenants, we reached
the tentative conclusion that it is most difficult to have successful
peer leadership in a severely deprived population.   The people of
Farnam Courts had little experience in organizing, and no opportunity to work for the realization of collective goals.   Their whole
focus of life was on the present.   When a chance for initiating action arose, the bulk of the people stood on the sidelines, watching
incredulously.   The very few with leadership skill, often acquired
within a context of socially deviant behavior, quickly moved to take
over, experience having taught them that identification with a parti-

san cause is a quick road to success. They used power less subtly than do leaders of the middle class. They learned that scapegoating (often of a socially inferior group) is a means of enhancing one's own position in one's own group. Deprivation and frustration, of course, are the natural breeding grounds for the type of scapegoating activity that took place in Farnam Courts in the fall and winter of 1958.

Only the inner group of activists were involved in this conflict, which first divided and then brought the Farnam Courts Community Council to an end. The bulk of the members--shy, inarticulate and passive--watched the process from the sidelines and then withdrew. In later conversations they confessed that they had never understood the issues of the struggle and that they were unable to follow the continuous wrangle over procedure that had finally alienated them.

While the passivity shown by most of the tenants may represent a response pattern characteristic of the lower class, we are inclined to theorize that living in low-income public housing discourages social action. The provision of the Federal Housing Authority that sets a ceiling on tenants' income has served to remove from the projects the upwardly mobile families, who might have been a source of local leadership. The income limitation has tended to homogenize the tenant population by bestowing tenure of residence upon those least likely to overcome their economic and social handicaps. A large number of families in public housing are without a male head, and an increasing number of residents are members of the most deprived minority groups.

Housing project rules, which allow tenants no voice in management, have discouraged grass-roots organization and social action. Occasionally, a resourceful housing manager has overcome the limitations of federal or local regulations--Farnam Courts has had such managers in the past--but in general the housing regulations and the growing management responsibilities of the housing administrators have been an effective barrier to the growth of community organizational activity. Thus, public housing is a most unlikely setting for the development of social action experience and skills. The passivity of the majority of Farnam Courts tenants in the face of efforts to create a local council can, therefore, also be seen as a response to the conditions imposed by their environment.

Such was the state of affairs when NIP came into being with a mandate to reactivate the Farnam Courts Community Council. A newsletter was sent to all residents in September, 1959, explaining NIP and its purposes, giving recognition to the past successful activities of the Tenants' Council, and inviting the public to a meeting with the NIP Director to consider a future program. The meeting attracted a few of the outspoken clique leaders and a larger number of the rank and file. It became immediately apparent that there was a power struggle taking place, which the white group would probably win by force of numbers. Actually the whites succeeded only by sheer staying power. Neither faction openly vetoed a program suggested by the other but reduced all discussion to a wrangle over minute details; reconciliation was obviously impossible. On one point, however, there was agreement: the NIP director should be responsible for the treasury and for running the program. By the third meeting only five or six of the militant white women remained, so that plans for neighborhood organization had to be abandoned for the time being.

An attempt was made to elicit community response through a series of meetings devoted to subjects of specific interest to the Courts population--various aspects of the school program and the effect of redevelopment upon the neighborhood. These meetings were fairly well attended at first and elicited a lively response. But attendance soon fell off and the meetings became an obviously insufficient method for building and supporting a community program.

The immediate problem remained: what kind of program could be offered? An intensive home-visiting campaign was conducted to solicit the views of the fifty residents who had been members of the previous tenants' group. From these visits it became clear that almost all the Negroes, and some of the whites too, harbored intense resentment against the small group of aggressive white women who had taken a hand in every activity and had vigorously tried to exclude others. Withdrawal, suspiciousness and fear of retaliation were never more in evidence than during this survey. It took the utmost persuasion, along with repeated reassurances of confidentiality, to get doors opened wide enough to allow conversation. Most interviews began with, "I'm not interested in anything connected with that (the previous Council)," or, "I don't want to talk about it." The survey showed an almost unanimous opinion: local leadership had been negative and divisive, people simply had to "get along better," "they" (the aggressive group of women) should not be allowed to "take over everything." When asked for concrete program suggestions, a number of women stated that they had enjoyed bingo, the only adult recreation offered, but had been alienated by the women who ran it. Those questioned seemed unable, however, to mention a specific activity they wanted NIP to offer. When provided with a list of possibilities, fifteen to twenty women indicated interest in a sewing class. This interest seemed worthwhile pursuing and a class was started, which met on the project grounds once a week for ten weeks with an instructor from the Board of Education Adult Education Department.

The popular appeal of bingo could not be ignored, nor could the clamor for it from the small band of women who had dominated previous activities. Sewing was evidently too passive for them, for these women shunned the class. All were middle-aged, with children in their teens, and ran neat and orderly homes. They were desperately in need of some concrete and physical project in which to pour their boundless energy and managerial talent. They loved all the chores connected with running a bingo game--shopping for prizes, setting up equipment and chairs, selling refreshments, calling out numbers and awarding the prizes. While bingo did not seem to be a particularly appropriate starting point, it had the advantage of being an obvious and immediate way to attract a relatively large group of adults with whom the staff could get better acquainted.

We took care, though, to neutralize the negative aspects when we reorganized the game, curbing the antagonism caused by the clique while at the same time making constructive use of their drive. Attendance gradually rose from about twenty to an average of about thirty-five, with a noticeable increase in Negro players.

To gain this modest success the following changes were made: all
profit-making was eliminated by reducing the admission price and
offering free refreshments; a ceiling of four cards per player was
established (in the past a few more affluent players had purchased
as many as twelve cards, causing a very narrow distribution of
prizes); job responsibilities were spread among more people, chos-
en by the NIP staff; a half-hour recess for refreshments and socializing was instituted; and a number of attractive door prizes were
awarded each game night. With the presence of a staff member
who greeted and talked with everyone while supervising the routine,
bingo became a pleasant social occasion. For many homebound women with young children, it provided their one chance for a night
out.

Bingo served several useful purposes. It was a small but
widely reported demonstration of our ability to hold a negative power
group in check. It gave us the opportunity to closely relate to this
aggressive group and to introduce them to a new form of role playing, which antagonized less and still brought desired results.
Though at first these women tried in every possible way to wrest
control from NIP they had to acknowledge the program's success.
Their pet activity flourished; they were given recognition for their
contributions; although curbed, they were continued in important positions. But the most important result of this popular evening activity was the chance it gave the NIP staff to become acquainted with
more Courts residents.

Bingo, together with four general meetings and the small sewing class, was all that could be accomplished that first year in the
community organization phase of NIP. Because of the emotions generated by the failure of the tenants' council, as well as the lack of
a community organization worker because of budget limitations, we
restricted community organization activities to continued exploration
of tenants' needs.

Setting Up the Research Program

Until September, 1959, there was uncertainty about the research plan. It had been decided to model NIP's casework phase

on the St. Paul Family-Centered Project, but no actual research design had been formulated. It was Frank Harris, newly appointed Executive Director of the Community Council, who suggested that Ludwig Geismar, former research director of the St. Paul project, be consulted before final plans were made. Fortunately Dr. Geismar was willing to serve as Research Consultant for NIP.

It became apparent that NIP's research effort would be severely limited in scope because of its small budget. However, a modest research plan was possible, one which would furnish a means of measuring NIP's casework endeavor and which would also be valuable as an application of the St. Paul outcome study.

Expanding to an Action-Research Project

It was the inadequacy of this projected research plan, more than any other factor, that spurred the staff and the Advisory Committee to seek additional sources of funds. Ludwig Geismar, the new consultant, who was also a faculty member of the Rutgers Graduate School of Social Work, collaborated with Miss Krisberg in drawing up a project to be submitted to the National Institute of Mental Health for possible financial support. The project, Geismar and Krisberg believed, would need a strong research base to qualify for federal financing.

At this point it is worth recalling that the Neighborhood Improvement Project arose from a community endeavor designed to deal with juvenile delinquency and its corollaries, social deprivation and family disorganization. NIP emerged as a tentative program that reflected the planners' set of action priorities, priorities that followed the then current trend of seeking solutions to social problems by providing intensive services to socially handicapped families. The planners of NIP saw casework to multi-problem families, and group work and community organization services to the neighborhood, as effective ways of reducing the incidence of juvenile delinquency in the area. The design for action was severely limited, however, by the meager financial resources, consisting mainly of $23,000 in funds from the New Haven Foundation and contributions from some agencies in the form of workers released for project participation. In such a constricted financial situation, the planners could do no more than formulate a pilot study. The choice of Farnam Courts, a neighborhood of only three hundred households, reflected planning aimed largely at demonstration rather than at significantly reducing the incidence of problem behavior. A demonstration project requires a research program to evaluate the effectiveness of the approach chosen, but here again the Planning Committee was handicapped by lack of resources.

If funds could be obtained from the Federal Government, an adequate research plan could be developed, which would yield information on process as well as outcome, and service components of the project could be expanded as well. During the late fall and early winter of 1959, while multi-problem families were being screened for the NIP treatment service, the Geismar-Krisberg plan for an expanded multi-service operation was drawn up. It was approved by the NIP Advisory Council and the Board of Directors of the New Haven Council of Social Agencies. Submitted to the National Institute of Mental Health in February, 1960, it was granted financial support in July of that year. The starting date for the expanded NIP program was set for September 1, 1960.

The following excerpts from the NIP's proposal to the NIMH give the essence of the modified plan for the operation of the Neighborhood Improvement Project:

PROPOSED PLAN

A.   Specific Aims

> A study of the incidence of juvenile delinquency in New Haven revealed that the Farnam Courts Housing Project, a low-cost federally supported project, was one of the three areas of highest delinquency in the city. The community's determination to deal with this problem led to the formulation of a plan to concentrate social services in one of the high delinquency neighborhoods. The Farnam Courts Housing Project was chosen because its geographical compactness made the introduction of services feasible, and the size of the population, three hundred families, made a diversified program possible.
>
> The aims of the new program, the Neighborhood Improvement Project (NIP), are the reduction and eventual prevention of family disorganization. The Project will attempt to carry out these aims by providing the following kinds of service:

1. Treatment of family disorganization and its correlates, adult disordered behavior and juvenile delinquency. We offer a three-pronged treatment plan:

   a. Institute intensified, reaching-out casework treat-
      ment to the most disorganized, multi-problem
      families with children "in clear and present dan-
      ger," i.e., where the immediate physical and/or
      emotional welfare of the children is being threatened
      to the extent that the community assumes a clear-
      cut responsibility to intervene.

   b. Establish and carry out a group work and recrea-
      tional program geared to reach all age groups of
      the population, the program to take place on the
      grounds of the housing project.

   c. Act as coordinator between the neighborhood popu-
      lation and the community resources in such areas
      as health, economic dependency, rehabilitation, and
      education, for the fuller utilization of these serv-
      ices. This involves making agencies aware of popu-
      lation needs, working with them to strengthen serv-
      ices and to fill gaps, educating and enabling the popu-
      lation to use the resources appropriate to their needs.

2. Evaluation of changes resulting from services given by
   doing a detailed analysis of treatment techniques. To
   accomplish this we propose:

   a. To carry out a study of social functioning and changes
      in social functioning of the multi-problem families in
      the area. This evaluation will use the Profile and
      Scale of Family Functioning, [8] instruments developed
      by the Family-Centered Project of St. Paul, Minne-
      sota, which have been tested for reliability and scal-
      ability and recommend themselves for use in other
      communities. At the same time, we propose to eval-
      uate changes in social functioning in a control group
      of multi-problem families outside the Farnam Courts
      Housing Project, who are receiving only conventional
      services. The same instruments would be applied to
      these families to measure movement or change in so-
      cial functioning.

   b. To do a detailed analysis of casework treatment
      methods and to correlate these with movement. To
      this end, a Treatment Log designed to document
      methods of family-centered treatment has been de-
      veloped and is being tested by a pilot research pro-
      ject currently under way in the Farnam Courts Hous-
      ing Project.

    c. To study the effects of the services given as re-
flected by incidence of juvenile delinquency, adult
disordered behavior, public assistance, and formal
social participation, by comparing the changes found
in Farnam Courts with those which take place in
two other housing projects during the same period.

    3. To do a study aimed at the early identification of multi-
problem families. A comparison will be made between
disorganized and stable families from the same socio-
economic group in the Farnam Courts Housing Project.

B. Significance

Repeated studies have shown that the seriously disorganized
multi-problem families provide a disproportionate number of
children who are juvenile delinquents.[9,10] Conventional methods of dealing with this problem have been confined to a segmented approach, such as child guidance, vocational counseling, recreational programs, etc. It is widely recognized that
the social functioning of the family is one of a number of determinants in the behavior of children. Very little has been
done to deal with the problems of juvenile delinquency by using
a total family-oriented approach. In the few instances where
a family-centered approach has been used, it has been limited
primarily to giving intensive casework services only.

We propose to deal with the problem of juvenile delinquency
by using a multi-dimensional approach to the seriously disorganized family. Our program of services takes into account the family in its various roles in the neighborhood and
the community at large, and its special needs in these roles.
We postulate that this broader treatment approach, which is
quite unique in the United States, will express itself in significant changes in social functioning in the disorganized families and lessen social disorganization in the neighborhood as a
whole.

Positive results in this project may be seen to suggest a new
pattern for treatment to be used by this and other communities trying to cope with the problem of family disorganization
and juvenile delinquency.

C. Method of Procedure

    1. Treatment

        a. Casework. In order to select the multi-problem
families who would be receiving intensive reaching-
out casework services, a survey of the three hundred families in the Farnam Courts Housing Project
was made. This resulted in a master list of 143
families with children 5-16 years of age, which was

cleared through the files of all major health, welfare and correctional agencies. The records of the families known to the largest number of agencies within the past eighteen months were read. A selection of those families to be treated was made on the basis of: (1) their having children with socially deviant behavior; (2) their having a multiplicity of serious problems in one or more areas such as health, economic dependency, social adjustment; and (3) their having been unable or unwilling to use treatment in the past. A total of fifty such families were identified.

The plan is to give intensive family-centered treatment by the method detailed in the Casework Notebook of the Family-Centered Project of St. Paul, Minnesota. (A copy is appended.) Techniques include persistent reaching-out by the use of regular, continuous home-visit interviews, active involvement of all immediate or extended family members who have any relationship to the basic problems, having the family caseworker act as a coordinator of total family treatment among all resources brought to bear on the situation.

The casework staff will be composed of a team assigned by their respective agencies for the duration of the Neighborhood Improvement Project. They will retain their affiliation with their parent agencies, which will supply worker supervision. Regular weekly seminars for the caseworkers will be conducted by the NIP Director, to guide them in the method of treatment. Concurrent meetings between the supervisors and the NIP Director will serve to keep the supervisors oriented to the method and objectives of the Project.

NIP plans to offer treatment for a period of three years. With a projected caseload of fifty families it is anticipated that a total number of seventy-five families may be treated during this time. Such a service program calls for the equivalent of four full-time caseworkers. The experience of other similar projects has shown that the worker-caseload ratio must be kept between 1:12 to 15 maximum, to insure the most effective coverage and treatment possible with such seriously disorganized families.

b. Group Work and Recreation. A survey of the neighborhood revealed an acute shortage of recreational resources for both children and adults. Furthermore, the residents of the Farnam Courts Housing Project were found not to avail themselves of those few re-

sources in the general vicinity. The absence of
youth activities was most apparent, as shown by
the large number of children roaming without purpose through the court grounds, halls, and nearby
streets. In addition there was a considerable
amount of mischievous and/or destructive activity,
such as defacing buildings, littering halls, digging
up shrubs and grass, breaking fences, etc. It is
proposed to inaugurate a recreational and group work
program which will reach out to and give leadership
to all the different age groups of the population according to the special needs of those age groups.

The plan calls for a staff of part-time workers who
will carry out the program under the overall direction and supervision of a group work director. The
director will be responsible for program and supervision of a part-time staff qualified to work with
adults. In addition to carrying on activities already
in existence, a program to cover as yet unmet needs
will be instituted. There is present need for new
activities to cover a number of age groups not now
being reached, such as pre-school children, young
mothers, young married couples, older teenagers
(16-20 years of age), and a large aged population
(60-87 years of age).

c.   Coordination of Services. There is a need to do
continuing interpretation to community resources as
to the nature of the NIP services and the specific
needs of the population served. In turn, the services which can be rendered the population need to
be brought to the notice of the families so as to insure their fullest use of these. In this work it can
reasonably be anticipated that there will be uncovered
service gaps which need to be filled. The staff of
NIP in its coordinating role can bring the knowledge
of these gaps to the community. This work will be
centralized in a professional social worker with training and experience in community organization. It is
proposed that the group work director be selected
with a view toward assuming this overall responsibility.

2.   Evaluating Changes

a.   The need for evaluating a demonstration project which
is clearly of an experimental nature is usually taken
for granted. In the case of the plan for extending
services to residents of Farnam Courts outlined above,
we feel fortunate in being able to utilize an already
tested instrument of evaluation. The Profile of Family Functioning, an instrument designed to document
the nature of social functioning in families and to

measure changes in such functioning, represents the
fruit of a two-year research investment made by
the Family-Centered Project of St. Paul, Minnesota.
Simplification of the instrument mainly for evaluative
rather than diagnostic purposes, using various techniques of scalogram analysis, has already been done
jointly by the School of Social Work and the Department of Sociology at Rutgers, The State University
of New Jersey.

It is proposed to apply the Profile of Family Functioning, which serves as a diagnostic casework tool
as well as an instrument of research evaluation, to
all the multi-problem families in Farnam Courts
selected for family-centered treatment. The evaluation is to be done at the beginning of treatment, at
semi-yearly intervals (to establish a trend), and at
case closing.

A modified version of the Profile called Scale of
Family Functioning (highly correlated with the complete Profile), whose information can be abstracted
from the full profile or can be obtained independently, will be administered to a control group of multi-
problem New Haven families not receiving special
services of the kind offered by NIP. A comparison
of changes in social functioning registered by the
Scale of Family Functioning in families in Farnam
Courts, with changes in the control group families
should help answer the question of whether significant changes were brought about as a result of the
experimental program offered to the multi-problem
families of NIP.

b.   A basic question which must be raised in a program
     of treatment as broad as the one contemplated here
     is: what particular techniques of treatment were
     found to be useful in helping the multi-problem fam-
     ily? An answer to this question, it is hoped, will
     be forthcoming by a detailed study of treatment meth-
     od in relation to changes in social functioning as reg-
     istered by the Profile of Family Functioning.

     A study of method of treatment will be undertaken
     by means of a structured Treatment Log designed
     to allow the worker to document techniques and con-
     tent of treatment on a week-by-week basis. The
     Treatment Log was developed in a pilot research
     project with multi-problem families under the guid-
     ance of Dr. L.L. Geismar, Associate Professor,
     Graduate School of Social Work, Rutgers University.
     The Log is presently being tested in the field by
     three New Haven social workers. A beginning effort

in correlating treatment with movement in multi-
problem families was made in the St. Paul Family-
Centered Project.[11] The present plan represents
an extension of that effort.

c. The Neighborhood Improvement Project plans to extend concentrated services to the most disorganized
families as well as to all other residents of Farnam
Courts on the basis of the assessed needs of the residents, the families, and the neighborhood as a whole.
It is assumed that the overall program carried on
over a three-year period will result in an improvement of the well-being of this community. Such improvement, we postulate, will express itself in several crude indices of neighborhood functioning as can
be obtained from official community statistics. We
suggest a study in the rates of the indices given below and their comparison with the rates in two other
low-cost housing projects not receiving special services, as a way of evaluating the results of the plan
in the total project neighborhood:

Juvenile delinquency (official adjudicates)
Police contacts with minors
Adult crime and other officially reported dis-
    ordered behavior
Public assistance figures
Participation of residents in neighborhood
    centers, clubs, and other public social
    and recreational activities.

3. Study Aimed at the Early Identification of
Multi-Problem Families

The ultimate solution to the problem of family disorganization rests upon prevention. Prevention in turn pre-
supposes knowledge about causation. While the present
plan does not contemplate a full-fledged causation study,
which would have to be longitudinal in nature, it seeks
to discover background factors in family functioning which
will help in the early identification of problem families.
Such a study would rely mainly upon detailed cross-sectional analysis of multi-problem and non-problem families
and on a focussed longitudinal comparison between disorganized and relatively stable families in the same socio-
economic group. The cross-sectional study would utilize
the Profile of Family Functioning and seek to isolate factors in the present social functioning of families which
are associated with multi-problem behavior. The limited
longitudinal study would seek to isolate background factors
which can be studied post facto and are assumed to be
correlated with family disorganization.

By following the exploration in this area done by the
St. Paul Family-Centered Project,[12] we propose to
focus the longitudinal study upon the following factors
seen as being possibly related to multi-problem functioning:

> Agency registrations on the parents of the heads of
> families residing in Farnam Courts
> Broken homes among the parents of the heads of
> families in Farnam Courts
> Early agency registrations of the families served
> by NIP
> Time span between marriage of parents and first
> agency registration of the family[13]
> Time span between marriage of parents and first
> application for public assistance
> Delinquent behavior of parents prior to marriage
> and immediately following marriage
> Emotional disorders of parents prior to and immedi-
> ately following marriage
> Extreme marital conflict immediately following
> marriage

All of these background factors are based on information which can be obtained from local health and welfare
agencies, the police department and the courts. To the
extent that it will be possible to isolate factors in the
early functioning of family members which are highly
correlated with multi-problem behavior at the time of
NIP operations, a predictive index could be developed
which would aid in the early identification of family disorganization and multi-problem functioning.

The research functions listed under sections C2 and C3
will be carried out under the direction of a research director and two research associates. The research staff
will perform all tasks of data collection, analysis, and
interpretation. The present plan envisages treatment
services extending over a three-year period. The fourth
year of operation will be devoted to writing up the experiences of the service program, analyzing data and presenting the findings, and preparing material for publication.

This plan, submitted at the beginning of 1960, was carried
through with only minor modifications. These were mainly of two
kinds: (1) Program elaborations that were brought about by newly
uncovered needs or by the discovery, in the process of program
implementation, of methods of intervention not previously considered.
Examples of such program elaborations are the neighborhood caseworker and the pre-school program for both English-speaking and

Spanish-speaking children. (2) Program abridgments made necessary by unanticipated changes in the research-action setting. The
multi-agency team approach to treatment, for instance, had to be
modified when the bulk of the casework agencies withdrew within
two years of joining the project. The result was a restricted
agency alliance rather than the community-wide effort originally
anticipated (see Chapter 12, "Work with the Community").

The various phases of the program, as outlined in the original proposal or as modified in the process of implementation, are
described in the present volume, with the exception of the study
aimed at the early identification of multi-problem families (item
C3 in the proposal). This research was reported in Chapters 4 and
5 of the previously published volume, Understanding the Multi-Problem Family. [14] A comprehensive theoretical statement, serving
as a basis for the measurement of change in family functioning reported here, is also contained in the earlier book.

Notes

1. Annual Report to the New Haven Foundation by the
   Neighborhood Improvement Project, New Haven, June
   1960, p. 1 (in the files of the Council of Social Agencies, New Haven.)

2. Geismar and La Sorte, op. cit., pp. 74-90.

3. This concept, used by the Family-Centered Project,
   refers to a situation where the physical and/or emotional welfare of the child is threatened to the point
   where the community has a right to intervene. See
   Alice Overton and Katherine H. Tinker, Casework
   Notebook (St. Paul, Minn., Family-Centered Project,
   1959), pp. 5-10.

4. This also was a preliminary selection criterion.

5. L. L. Geismar and Beverly Ayres, Measuring Family
   Functioning (St. Paul, Minn., Family-Centered Project,
   1960).

6. Alice Overton and Katherine H. Tinker, Casework
   Notebook (St. Paul, Minn., Family-Centered Project,
   1959).

7. Annual Report to the New Haven Foundation, loc. cit.

8. L. L. Geismar and Beverly Ayres, Measuring Family
    Functioning: Manual on a Method for Evaluating So-
    cial Functioning of Disorganized Families, The Family-
    Centered Project, St. Paul, Minn., awaiting publica-
    tion. [The monograph was published in 1960, subse-
    quent to the drafting of the proposal reproduced here.]

9. Ralph W. Whelan. Interim Report on Delinquency Pre-
    vention and Control. (New York, New York City
    Youth Board), p. 12.

10. L. L. Geismar and Beverly Ayres. Families in Trouble
    (St. Paul, Minn., Family-Centered Project, 1958),
    pp. 87-91.

11. L. L. Geismar and Beverly Ayres. Patterns of Change
    in Problem Families (St. Paul, Minn., Family-Cen-
    tered Project, July, 1959), pp. 23-28.

12. L. L. Geismar and Beverly Ayres. Families in Trouble
    (St. Paul, Minn., Family-Centered Project, 1958), pp.
    53-76.

13. Found to be negatively and significantly related in the
    St. Paul study.

14. Geismar and La Sorte, op. cit.

Chapter 5
Social Characteristics of the
Multi-Problem Families

Up to this point our attention has centered largely on the people of Farnam Courts and on the efforts of the community to help them. The residents of the Courts have been described as a lower-class population whose way of life, given the limited economic and social opportunities available, can be termed functional and endowed with survival values.

Studies have shown that the bulk of families residing in low-income areas function quite adequately in meeting the basic needs of family members, providing a sense of identification with the group, and operating within the law. Nevertheless, lower-class neighborhoods such as Farnam Courts contain a disproportionately large number of multi-problem families. As mentioned earlier, between 10 and 15 percent of the households in Farnam Courts could be characterized as multi-problem. These families, with their delinquent children, became the chief focus of the community effort at social rehabilitation. Elsewhere, we have sought to define the multi-problem family conceptually,[1] and in a later chapter of the present book we present case materials to illustrate typical behavior patterns of the multi-problem family. This chapter concentrates upon the structural characteristics of these families, particularly those distinguishing them from other lower-class families.

In a prior book, also the result of the Neighborhood Improvement Project experience,[2] we compared stable families with disorganized or multi-problem lower-class families. By using retrospective data we came to the conclusion that early in the family life cycle there already exist differences between the two types of families. However, these differences are largely in the realm of attitudes and expectations rather than in readily apparent social charac-

teristics. Even later in the family life cycle, when the multi-problem family has become more clearly differentiated, differences between the two appear to be more pronounced in behavior rather than
in demographic make-up.

Systematic information on the subject remains sparse because
comparative studies based on representative samples are lacking.
The present analysis will examine structural differences between
multi-problem and better functioning families by comparing the thirty seriously disorganized families treated in NIP with the thirty-
nine stable families also included in NIP.[3] Comparable data for the
two populations are available in some dimensions but not in others.
On a few factors a comparison of NIP cases with the total Farnam
Courts population will provide additional information on differences
between multi-problem and other families. Data from two St. Paul
studies and one New York study of multi-problem families[4] will also be drawn upon, in order to illustrate similarities and differences
from one community to another.

Is the multi-problem family more likely to belong to a lower
status minority group, particularly the Negro group? This question
has often been asked, and since multi-problem behavior is to a
large measure a product of lower-class existence, it would not seem
surprising to find a high proportion of Negroes in the multi-problem
category, heavily represented as they are among low-income groups.
A more meaningful question would be, are there proportionately
more Negroes among the multi-problem families than is justified by
their representation among the low-income population?

The Farnam Courts data answer negatively; the percentage of
Negroes among the problem families was very similar (37%) to that
of Negro families in the population of the Courts (35%) in 1960. The
overall impression gained from such geographically diverse studies
as the Youth Board Project in New York City, the Family-Centered
Project of St. Paul, and the Area Development Project of Vancouver,
British Columbia, is that ethnic composition among disorganized
families follows closely the modal ethnic pattern in lower-class
areas.

The Farnam Courts data do show a difference in family size

between disorganized and more stable families. The average size
of the families in treatment was 5.67, whereas in Farnam Courts
as a whole the average number per household (which included some
one and two-person units) was only 3.83. St. Paul Problem families numbered 5.9 persons on the average.[5] The mean number of
children in the treatment group was 4.1, whereas the 39 stable
Farnam Courts families had only 3.2 children on the average.[6] St.
Paul multi-problem families had a mean number of 4.4 children,
while the Youth Board study reported a median of 5.5 children per
case.[7]

        In the New Haven early identification study the observation
had been made that multi-problem families were younger than stable
ones in the same socio-economic category.[8] The NIP treatment
group was found to be younger than the Courts' population as a
whole (72% of individuals in treatment families were under age 21
whereas 56% in the total neighborhood were below that age). This
striking difference was in part a function of the treatment selection
process, which omitted families without dependent children.[9] Median ages of male and female heads of families were similar in New
Haven and St. Paul families (men 41 and 43 years and women 36
and 38 years, respectively), and the median ages of children (New
Haven 8.5, St. Paul 9 years) were but half a year apart. In the
treatment cases the median duration of marriage in two-parent families was sixteen years, compared with nineteen years in the stable
families. Until longitudinal analysis of family development supplies
contrary evidence, we are inclined to adhere to our hypothesis
stated elsewhere[10] that severe family disorganization is related to
earlier (but not the earliest) life-cycle stages.

        Multi-problem families are larger, but their income is
smaller. The per capita median income was only $603 a year for
the NIP treatment families, as against $823 for all residents in
Farnam Courts. In 1963, 77% of the treatment cases had received
some form of public assistance, compared with 57% of all families
in the Courts. Only six Farnam Courts multi-problem families
(20%) had husbands who were regularly employed; all employment
was of an unskilled or semi-skilled nature.

Family composition is not a sharply distinguishing characteristic of multi-problem families. In thirteen (43%) of the treatment families both parents were in the home, while in two families
(7%) the father was only intermittently present. In the remaining
fifteen families (50%), there had been five separations, three deser-
tions, two divorces, two deaths, two prolonged absences resulting
from jail sentences, and one instance where no one father had ever
been present, the biological family being the result of transient sexual experiences. A comparable proportion of St. Paul families
(45%)[11] and New York Youth Board families (50%)[12] were reported
to have fathers out of the home. In the sample of thirty-nine stable
Farnam Courts families, twenty-three (59%) had a male head. By
contrast, the City of New Haven as a whole had less than 18% one-
parent homes,[13] but this statistic made no reference to class differences. It would appear that the one-parent family is a phenomenon
characteristic of the lower-class as a whole, rather than one that
separates the multi-problem family from the lower-class family in
general.

The early identification study yielded a positive correlation
between family disorganization and the discrepancy in age between
husband and wife.[14] The treatment families, which overlapped to
a large extent the Low Functioning Group of the early identification
study, showed a median age discrepancy of five years, as against
3.75 years for the thirty-nine stable families. The latter group
contained only two families (5%) where the age difference between
husband and wife exceeded eight years, in sharp contrast to the NIP
caseload where nine out of twenty-nine families (information was
lacking on one case), or 31%, revealed such a large age discrepancy.

Data on formal education of parents revealed no pronounced
differences between malfunctioning and well-functioning families in
the early identification study.[15] The NIP treatment cases were
found to be headed by parents whose median level of education (men
slightly below eight years, women eight years of schooling) was
close to the general level of Farnam Courts (8.5 years).[16] By
contrast, the median number of years of school completed for the

city of New Haven was eleven years,[17] indicating that education is
just one more factor separating the lower class from the rest of the
population but doing little to differentiate between stable and multi-
problem low-income families.

Among psycho-social factors which characterize the multi-
problem family, those of intelligence and level of psychological adjustment are of special interest because of their theoretical causal
nexus to family functioning. It is hard to imagine that the mental
performance of family members, particularly of the parents, is not
an influential factor in shaping the character of family life. Yet not
a single study known to us had produced reliable information on intelligence and psychological behavior of heads of multi-problem
families. Obstacles cited for the failure to procure these important
data include the difficulty of getting the families to submit to psychological testing and the cost of carrying out a testing program.
It is questionable whether there is enough systematic evidence to
prove that families cannot be readily involved in standardized testing. The problem of cost, especially where it involves the use of
trained psychologists, cannot be denied, but cost must not be allowed to remain a barrier to the procurement of essential knowledge
in the quest to reduce family disorganization.

A comparison of stable and malfunctioning lower-class families produced little evidence that personality disorders differentiate
clearly between the two groups,[18] although the value of this comparison was limited by the absence of standardized data. The thirty
NIP treatment cases, because of the absence of systematic psychiatric consultation, yielded no data on diagnosed mental illness.[19]
The St. Paul research, which did have the benefit of such consultation, listed eleven families (11%)--including twelve individuals--as
being afflicted by psychosis and two families as having members
suffering from character disorders.[20] No lower-class nonmulti-
problem families were available against which to compare these
rates, and questions can be raised as to whether the rate of 1,504
per 100,000 population cited by Hollingshead and Redlich for Class
V in their New Haven study[21] can serve as a basis for comparison.
As a crude comparison, the St. Paul multi-problem rate, when con-

verted on a per capita basis (2,000 per 100,000), is not strikingly different from that cited here for a Class V population.

In the St. Paul study, twenty-two families (22%), comprising thirty individuals, were identified as being afflicted with mental deficiency or retardation. The NIP data showed nine families (involving twelve adults) where one or both parents were mentally retarded, as evidenced by past or present institutionalization or psychological testing by an agency other than NIP. Furthermore, there were fifteen families (involving twenty-four children) in which one or more children had been diagnosed as mentally retarded, as indicated by placement in special classes and/or submarginal intellectual performance related to low I.Q. An unduplicated count of NIP treatment families showed that mental retardation affected eighteen families (60%) and thirty-six individuals. This appears to be a high rate for any population,[22] even if we take into account the class bias inherent in intelligence testing.

The various paper and pencil I.Q. tests given in American schools are, of course, only of limited value for inter-class comparisons, because these tests are heavily biased in favor of the middle class. Even nonverbal performance tests like the Pintner General Ability are conceived and developed in a cultural context that is less familiar to immigrant and slum children than to the offspring of the middle-class population. Here another question may be posed. Granted the limitations of the I.Q. test score, what differences does it reveal between stable and multi-problem lower-class families?

The early identification study reported in Understanding the Multi-Problem Family offers an opportunity to extend the comparisons between disorganized and stable families to the area of mental retardation, at least with respect to children. I.Q. test performances in grade school and high school were found to be sufficiently consistent over a period of several years to make it possible to use the most recent test--usually given within a three-year period--as a rough indicator of subnormal intelligence. It should be remembered that whatever the limitations of the I.Q. test score, they applied equally to the stable and problem families, all of whom came from comparable social, economic, and ethnic backgrounds.

From the thirty NIP treatment families we obtained individual and group test scores on fifty-four school-age children. The thirty-nine stable families contained forty-one children for whom such scores were available. Of the NIP children, twenty-four or 44% made scores of 75 or less, placing them below what is generally considered the lower limit of borderline intelligence. Of the stable families, eleven or 27% scored 75 or less. Thus, while the 27% retardation rate for stable lower-class families may contain a subcultural bias, the 44% rate for the multi-problem families (same subcultural group) is substantially higher than that for the children from stable families. It would have been helpful, of course, to have had comparable data available on the parents of stable and multi-problem families. In the absence of such information we are left to speculate about the significance of a situation in which mental retardation has affected one or more persons in over half of the families in the treatment group. Is retardation a causative factor in family malfunctioning or does the latter contribute to the former? To what extent is there mutual reinforcement between the two? Research based upon valid measurement of mental capacity is urgently needed.

The extensive contact of multi-problem families with social agencies has been well documented.[23] The thirty NIP treatment cases were known to eighteen agencies, and seven of these agencies had contact with ten or more of the families. City Welfare had come to know twenty-three, while State Welfare and the Visiting Nurse Association were each acquainted with nineteen of the treatment families. Comparable data on past agency registration of the thirty-nine stable families could not be procured, but it was known that at the time of the study roughly 40 percent were maintaining contact with one of the public assistance agencies and others had received aid in the past. Both groups had had approximately the same number of agency contacts at the beginning of marriage but showed divergent rates as the families grew older. Multi-problem families used agencies more, while stable families used them less frequently[24] as time went on; but both types of family, because of their lack of financial resources, were forced to use public and private welfare services in times of need.   Thus, the extensiveness of agency contacts rather than their presence or absence may be seen as an index of family stability or disorganization.

The evidence from this limited analysis of structural characteristics does not point to any striking differences between multi-problem and more stable lower-class families.   Those differences which do exist are of small magnitude, characterizing the multi-problem family as a little larger, younger in age, more economically dependent, and slightly more fragmented than other low-income families.   The discrepancy in age between husband and wife also tends to be somewhat larger in the problem family.   No comparative data on the mental health and mental capacity of multi-problem families were available, although the incidence of mental retardation among parents and children appeared to be high.   This is an area that merits intensive inquiry, because the whole strategy of causation research as well as treatment intervention must take into account the mental capacity of family members for coping with life's problems.

By and large, the distinction between multi-problem and less problematic lower-class families is one of functioning, not structure.   This is a point which Geismar and La Sorte sought to demonstrate in their early identification study.[25]   By definition, multi-problem families differ from stable families living under similar socio-economic conditions by the way (1) their family relationships are disturbed or disrupted; (2) their relationships to relatives, neighborhood and community are marked by conflict or hostile detachment; and (3) their handling of health, economic and household matters fails to meet basic needs of family members.   The difference between the stable and multi-problem family, when evaluated systematically and plotted as a family profile, is clear-cut and consistent in all areas of functioning.[26]

It is obvious that divergent patterns of functioning have not produced clearly differentiated family structures.   Nor are there compelling theoretical reasons for assuming that the process of family disorganization should create a family that is far different in its structural characteristics from the more stable lower-class family. In spite of some beginning evidence that family malfunctioning extends from one generation to the next, it should be remembered that both stable and disorganized families function within a societal framework which sets limits to deviations from the norm. To be permitted to live in a public housing project, to be eligible for public assistance, and to raise one's children in the home all require a degree of conformity in behavior, which comes clearly under the scrutiny of the community. Thus, families in which both parents relinquish their responsibility for the children, exhibit serious behavior disorders, engage in law-violating behavior, defy basic provisions of financial eligibility, etc., are likely to find their existence as a unit terminated. The truly multi-problem family is likely to exhibit deviant functioning in many areas of family life, but in each instance the framework of the law, particularly as it applies to the highly visible lower-class family, will set the limit within which the family is able to undergo structural changes. Even the seeming predisposition toward social malfunctioning from one generation to the next, sustained by living under conditions of social deprivation, will not basically displace the boundaries within which a family must fashion its existence if it is to survive.

Any effort to differentiate between lower-class multi-problem and stable families must consider whether multi-problem families are a separate culture, or a subculture of lower-class society. A strong case has been made by anthropologists and sociologists for the belief that the impoverished share a distinctive life style or culture, which is transmitted from generation to generation.[27] This culture, it is maintained, enables the lower classes to adapt to conditions of poverty, deprivation, and lack of opportunity. Assuming as we do here the correctness of this thesis, it may be asked whether multi-problem families share in the general lower-class culture or have their own life style and value system, which helps them survive under stressful living conditions.

The bulk of the studies on this subject have compared middle-class society either with lower-class populations as a whole or with such subgroups of the lower class as chronic relief recipients.[28]

We know of no studies which have juxtaposed the life styles and
values of stable and disorganized lower-class families.   Our own
research makes no systematic inquiry into this area of knowledge,
but such data on social functioning as have been collected cast some
doubt on the tenability of any separate culture hypothesis.

    Judging from the evidence of the early identification study,[29]
the social and economic backgrounds of stable and multi-problem
lower-class families are too similar to postulate clear-cut differences between the two groups.   Factors indicative of life style--
such as ethnic origin, presence of fathers, income, and number of
children in the house--do not differentiate between the stable and
disorganized families.   It is difficult to conceive of a situation in
which a population, living dispersed among the urban lower class
and sharing its physical, social and economic environment, might
have developed a way of life and corresponding belief system much
different from its immediate neighbors.

    Differences in such values as the desirability of having chil-
dren, planning for the future, etc., do obtain, but we are inclined
to view these as personal values closely tied to the families' social
functioning rather than as collective values representing separate
life styles, traditions, and socialization processes.   The personal
values of the multi-problem families are closely related to their
failure in social functioning in such areas as marital life, child
rearing, social activities, economic practices, and others.   Their
lack of self esteem, lack of initiative, poor communication, and
distrust of others represent above all a fragmented social situation.
These traits, perhaps found only to a lesser extent throughout lower-class society, should be viewed, in the words of Harriet C. Wilson, "not as a manifestation of a specific subculture but as an index of the breakdown of a culture."[30]

    It is, of course, possible to argue about the use of an im-
precise concept like subculture.   If shared patterns of malfunctioning and a set of personal beliefs in defense of such malfunctioning
can be termed a subculture, we have no quarrel with the concept.
Use of the term subculture would become even more plausible if it
could be shown that multi-problem functioning tends to be continued

from one generation to the next. For the present, however, the
seeming absence of observable or measurable differences between
stable and disorganized families in structure, tradition, style of
life, basic values and goals suggests an understanding of the multi-
problem family in functional rather than cultural terms.

Notes

1. L. L. Geismar and Michael A. La Sorte, <u>Understanding
   the Multi-Problem Family, a Conceptual Analysis and
   Exploration in Early Identification.</u> (New York, Association Press, 1964), pp. 15-93.

2. <u>Ibid.</u>, pp. 94-171.

3. <u>Ibid.</u>

4. L. L. Geismar and Beverly Ayres. <u>Families in Trouble</u>
   (St. Paul., Family-Centered Project, 1958).

   L. L. Geismar and Beverly Ayres. <u>Patterns of Change
   in Problem Families.</u> (St. Paul, Minn., Family-
   Centered Project, 1959).

   New York City Youth Board, <u>A Study of the Characteristics of 150 Multi-Problem Families.</u> (New York, New
   York City Youth Board, 1957), (Mimeographed)

5. Geismar and Ayres. <u>Families in Trouble</u>, p. 15.

6. Geismar and La Sorte. <u>Understanding the Multi-Problem
   Family</u>, unpublished data from the early identification
   study reported in Chapters 4 and 5.

7. Geismar and Ayres. <u>Families in Trouble</u>, p. 88.

8. Geismar and La Sorte. <u>Understanding the Multi-Problem
   Family</u>, p. 170.

9. This bias is counteracted in part by the fact that families
   in which all children were below school age were also
   excluded from the treatment group.

10. <u>Ibid.</u>

11. Geismar and Ayres. <u>Families in Trouble</u>, p. 17.

12. <u>Ibid.</u>, p. 88.

13. United States Bureau of the Census, <u>18th Census of the
    United States: 1960 Population</u>, Vol. I, Pt. 8, Table 72,

pp. 8-113 ff.

14. Geismar and La Sorte. Understanding the Multi-Problem
    Family, pp. 153-154.

15. Ibid., p. 155, ff.

16. United States Bureau of the Census. 18th Census of the
    United States: 1960 Population, Vol. I, Pt. 8, Table P.
    1, pp. 16-20.

17. Ibid., Vol. I, Pt. 8, Table 103, pp. 205-206, 8D.

18. Geismar and La Sorte. Understanding the Multi-Problem
    Family, p. 179.

19. Ten percent of family heads had been in a mental insti-
    tution sometime in the past, but none were institution-
    alized at the time of treatment.

20. Geismar and Ayres. Families in Trouble, pp. 30-33.

21. August B. Hollingshead and F.C. Redlich. Social Class
    and Mental Illness. (New York, John Wiley and Sons,
    Inc., 1958), p. 230.

22. Of the 4,200,000 children born annually in the United
    States, 3 percent (126,000) will never achieve the intel-
    lect of a 12-year-old child...Richard L. Masland, Sey-
    mour B. Sarason, and Thomas Gladwin. Mental Sub-
    normality: Biological, Psychological, and Cultural Fac-
    tors (New York, Basic Books, 1958), p. 3.

23. Geismar and Ayres. Families in Trouble, pp. 73-76.

    Beverly Ayres and Joseph Lagey, A Checklist Survey of
    Multi-Problem Families in Vancouver City (Vancouver,
    B.C., Community Chest and Councils of the Greater
    Vancouver Area, 1961). (Mimeographed), pp. 25-31.

    Geismar and La Sorte. Understanding the Multi-Problem
    Family, pp. 60-64.

    Beverly Ayres. Analysis of Central Registration Bureau
    Data on One Hundred Family-Centered Project Families
    (St. Paul, Family-Centered Project, 1957). (Mimeo-
    graphed)

24. Geismar and La Sorte. Understanding the Multi-Problem
    Family, p. 63. The closing of the New Haven Social Service
    Exchange precluded a study of agency contacts up to the
    point where the families became part of the research
    program.

25.   Ibid., pp. 94-131.

26.   Ibid., p. 115.

27.   Oscar Lewis.   The Children of Sanchez (New York, Ran-
      dom House, 1961).

      Thomas Gladwin.   "The Anthropologist's View of Pover-
      ty," The Social Welfare Forum, 1961 (Columbia Univer-
      sity Press, 1961), pp. 73-86.

      Walter B. Miller.   "Implications of Urban Lower Class
      Culture for Social Work," Social Service Review, Vol.
      33, (3 September 1959), pp. 219-236.

28.   Leonard Schneiderman.   "Value Orientation Preferences
      of Chronic Relief Recipients," Social Work, Vol. 9,
      No. 3 (July 1964), pp. 13-18.

29.   Geismar and La Sorte.   Understanding the Multi-Problem
      Family, Chapters 4 and 5.

30.   Harriet C. Wilson.   Delinquency and Child Neglect
      (London, George Allen and Unwin Ltd., 1962).

Chapter 6
Intensive Services to Multi-Problem Families

This chapter will describe, chiefly by means of a case study,
the reaching-out family-centered casework services rendered to
some 45 problem-ridden families in Farnam Courts by the Neighborhood Improvement Project. The case study focuses on the E. family, one of the thirty families[1] that were treated and studied systematically during the research phase of the project. The narrative
covers the family's social functioning and the client-worker interaction over nearly three years of service. Changes in functioning are
assessed quantitatively by means of a technique known as the St.
Paul Scale of Family Functioning, whose methodology is described
elsewhere.[2] The case presentation illustrates the conversion of
qualitative data into quantitative symbols and thereby furnishes the
reader with a tangible example of the way in which the movement
study, reported in Chapter 15, was executed.

The E. family is typical of the multi-problem families in the
treatment group. Its beginning Profile of Family Functioning corresponds closely to the mean scores of social functioning of the thirty
treatment cases in the study, with four areas of predominantly instrumental behavior being slightly higher and five areas of mainly
expressive functioning being just a little lower than the group means
(see Chapter 15). In family structure, likewise, the E. family does
not differ greatly from the remainder of the multi-problem families
studied (see Chapter 5). Their movement pattern during the treatment period researched (the time during which the E. family was
treated exceeded by fourteen months the period covered by the experimental control study) places them at the top of the third, or
next to the highest quartile of change.

There are two other purposes for the detailed reporting on
the E. family. First, the case demonstrates the project's way of

111

bringing together several methods of service such as casework,
group work, recreational and educational activities, to meet the
needs of one family. Secondly, since members of the E. family
did take part in a number of NIP programs, this case shows how
the clients responded to multiple programming.

The action or service phase of the Neighborhood Improvement Project, as was stated earlier, was launched with the introduction of social casework services to the thirty most disorganized
families in the Farnam Courts housing project. Since these were
seriously deprived families, moving from crisis to crisis, with
members' lives characterized by personal and interpersonal failure,
reaching-out casework services were considered the most appropriate method of help. Later a new phase of the NIP program began
when casework services were extended to all Courts families with
problems.

In North America, social casework continues to be the preferred method of helping socially disadvantaged individuals and families in trouble; it is a form of help, using a variety of techniques,
whose goal is the improvement of the individual's psycho-social
functioning. Counselling, support, guidance, any appropriate means
of help are used.

The Neighborhood Improvement Project saw in casework the
most direct way of reaching out to those families who were experiencing serious problems. While not considered the only way--or
perhaps even the most effective way--the case-oriented approach
seemed to be a necessary part of a rehabilitative program. Multi-
problem families are, for the most part, either hostile or apathetic
toward helping agents. They are not likely to benefit from the mere
availability of better resources or services. Their attitudes and
behavior patterns become a barrier that stands between them and
social opportunity and improved functioning. To such families,
casework could serve as the mediator, striking some kind of balance between their needs and existing or evolving means of satisfying them.

Casework services to the rank and file of Farnam Courts
tenants, as opposed to the multi-problem families, may be charac-

terized as a resource for problem solving. Although the problems
varied in nature and intensity, they were generally more amenable
to solution by short-term counselling, advice and guidance, provision of resources, etc. than those of multi-problem families. One
form of casework service offered by NIP was established to satisfy
the special needs of the Puerto Ricans who could not speak English,
and thus failed to use existing community resources. A Spanish-
speaking worker, therefore, became the first prerequisite for effective service. Except for the few multi-problem families among this
group, intervention was aimed at promoting the process of acculturation by educational techniques and opportunities for social participation. The typical multi-problem family presented a more complex
pattern of problems, requiring a multi-faceted approach.

Social casework has been defined as "...a method of social
work which intervenes in the psycho-social aspect of a person's life
to improve, restore, maintain, or enhance his social functioning by
improving his role performance."[3] This broad definition covers a
vast variety of techniques applicable to a great number of social
roles.

Reaching-out, family-centered casework differs only in emphasis from the form of casework practiced in agencies in North
America and taught in graduate schools of social work. Instead of
waiting for the client to approach him, the worker actively seeks
him out. Those segments of the population--for the most part the
lower socio-economic strata--that cannot or will not avail themselves
of services on their own are most appropriately helped by this method. Again, in reaching-out casework there is greater emphasis on
environmental change. The well-documented observation that the
families' multiplicity of problems is to no small extent due to
stresses produced by the environment leads the caseworker to direct
his attention first to such issues as income, employment, housing,
neighborhood, and health problems. Therefore, intervention for the
purpose of improving a person's or family's role performance may
well begin with the identification and weighing of environmental factors as well as interpersonal and individual behavior components.
Although the caseworker must work within the framework of existing

welfare legislation and material resources, which seriously limit
the extent to which he can modify the environment, he will do everything he can to help his client by relieving stress caused by the environment. This might call for stretching existing resources or
seeking more liberal interpretations of the law by playing the role
of client advocate vis-a-vis public assistance and social control
agencies. It might require intervention at clinics and hospitals on
behalf of the client. And on occasion the worker will have to de-
vote time and effort to the creation of a needed resource.

Reaching-out casework also emphasizes the coordination of
services. The contention that the environment, and particularly the
social welfare environment, contributes or has contributed to the
family's problems leads the social worker to work with other agencies serving the client. Improved coordination of the services of
agencies already active in the case may be one of the most effective
paths toward the goal of improved client functioning.

The average multi-problem family will present a diagnostic
picture revealing deep-seated personal maladjustment, serious relationship problems, a high incidence of socially deviant behavior and
a lack of social skills. The question as to what extent these characteristics are the product of present environment or the result of
early socialization is not of immediate concern to the social worker.
His task is that of bringing environmental conditions to a tolerable
level and of attempting a modification in behavior to cope with an
improved environment. Given the average American community in
the early 1960's and the average multi-problem family of long standing, there are limits to the attainment of both of these objectives.
A radical change in social functioning as a result of services can
hardly be anticipated. However, even some improvement in family
functioning, resulting in the family's better and more focused use of
community resources, especially in a time of crisis, and a somewhat enhanced ability to meet the needs of family members, would
seem to justify a service such as the one being described here.
Realistically, such modification in social functioning would express
itself in limited gains of one or two scale steps in three or more
(out of nine) areas of family functioning.

In the pursuit of these objectives, what are the specific techniques used in reaching-out, family-centered casework? During the 1950's and the early 1960's a sizeable literature emerged on this subject.[4] The Neighborhood Improvement Project patterned its services closely after the model laid out in Alice Overton and Katherine H. Tinker's Casework Notebook.[5] We would cite these principles as being the key elements in reaching-out, family-centered casework: going out to the client rather than waiting for him to come to you; directness in dealing with clients; supportive use of authority; viewing and treating the family as a unit; having the worker act as a coordinator of services. The Neighborhood Improvement Project added another basic component: seeing the family and treating it within the context of the larger social system of which it is a part. The larger system might be a housing project, as in the case of Farnam Courts, or another kind of neighborhood or social grouping beyond the neighborhood; this system could include not only the housing environment but all types of informal and formal associations, services, institutions, and any other facility or resource with which the family interacts.

In the Farnam Courts neighborhood the caseworker had to focus his services not only on family members but also on the many groups, activities and organizations with which the family was associated. And in the case of the E. family discussed below, relatives living outside the neighborhood became an important concern in casework treatment.

Little systematic research has been done on the time span and constituent phases of family-centered treatment to multi-problem families. Some rough guidelines on the time required to close a case or to shift from intensive treatment to a more attenuated form of service are provided by action-research endeavors such as the St. Paul Family-Centered Project. The mean length of service appears to be about two years, with two-thirds of the cases receiving between 13 and 36 months of treatment.[6]

While for purposes of systematic evaluation of movement in the thirty treatment families we divided the experimental period arbitrarily into two equal units of nine months, in the E. case we

sought to identify natural phases representing differing patterns
of client-worker interaction.   The differences among the three periods we identified, each about one year in length, constituted more
a shift in modal client behavior and worker method of intervention
than a radical change in interaction from one period to the next.

Phase one was characterized by worker activity focused on
tangible problems, particularly health, and on getting the family to
use available community resources.   The worker's role as a bridge
between resource and family became crucial; throughout this treatment phase he was busy "doing for and with" the client, especially
in response to crisis situations.   In the broadest sense the social
worker engaged in a structuring of client roles in areas of concern,
and he engaged in joint role-playing, often taking the lead whenever
the client was unprepared to assume full responsibility.

Phase two, following the client's realization that worker intervention can bring positive results, was marked by a strengthening of the client-worker relationship, permitting the worker to concentrate on interpersonal problems.   There was a marked reduction
in worker-led activity around tangible problems, although the worker
continued structuring critical roles for the client.

Phase three was devoted to a systematic promotion of client
independence by encouraging him to assume greater role responsibility.   A step-by-step attenuation of worker activity, accompanied
by a testing of client capacity, led to a gradual withdrawal and
eventual termination of intensive casework services.

This presentation is a combination of selected quotations
from the record, prepared summaries, minutes of group leaders'
reports, and information gathered from conferences with various
staff members who were in contact with the family.   At the close
of each phase we have related the movement as observed from experience (contacts with the family) to the movement as measured by
the research instrument (the Profile of Family Functioning).

The case presentation is followed by a summary in which
the functioning of the E. family, as seen at the close of treatment,
is examined with regard to prospects for future adjustment.   Finally, since we found the E's to be representative of a whole group of

multi-problem families commanding attention, an attempt is made
to predict their future needs and the implications that these have
for community planning.

Screening-In Report on the E. Family

Mrs. E. - Born		10/15/18
Lowell -	"	7/6/45
Stanley -	"	4/10/49
Carla -	"	6/18/51
Debbie -	"	2/1/56

Out of home:

Sharon -	Born	12/25/32
Richard -	"	11/9/33

Basis of Concern

Mrs. E. is limited both intellectually and in her capacity to
accept the responsibility of running a house and guiding her children. She has had three different involvements with men, all of
which have proved unsatisfactory, and has moved around the country
quite a bit, trying to support her children by doing domestic work.
Until recently she had the children "farmed out" in various foster
care arrangements. Presently, the four minor children are with
her. She has been in poor health and has been unable to cope with
the various health and adjustment problems. Lowell has made a
poor school adjustment, has gotten into trouble and is a worry to
her, as are Debbie and Carla. There is danger that the children
may drift into more serious trouble, and Mrs. E. expresses eagerness to get help.

A. Family Relationship and Family Unity

1. <u>Marital Relationship:</u> Mrs. E. had two out-of-wedlock
children, the first when she was 13 years old. She subsequently
married their father (now deceased), who was physically abusive,
drank heavily, and did not support her. She separated from him
after five years and later married a soldier in the Regular Army in
1944. This relationship was evidently short; her husband was
shipped overseas, and when he returned wounded from Germany,
saw his son Lowell only once. He asked for a divorce in 1946 and
subsequently disappeared.

After a few years Mrs. E. became involved with Henry
Waters, father of Stanley, Carla, and Debbie.   They separated because Mr. Waters drank heavily, gambled, and did not work or support them regularly.   Mr. Waters now lives in the South and the
Department of Welfare is trying to arrange his contributions for
child support, which were interrupted when the family moved North.

2. Relationship between Parent and Children: Very little is
known.   Mrs. E. infers that she can't do much with the boys.   She
has been seen to be cold, harsh and very impatient with Debbie,
who demands considerable attention.

3. Relationships among Children: Nothing known.

4. Family Solidarity: There has been almost none.   All the
children have been placed for the better part of their lives in a succession of different homes.   Mrs. E. may possibly feel guilty about
this, for she has stated that moving around may be a factor in
Lowell's present maladjustment.   She seems to have a very close,
warm relationship with her married daughter, Sharon Bradley.   Her
second oldest child, Richard, is in the army, married for the second time, and stationed in the South.   Nothing is known about the
communication between Mrs. E. and this son.

B. Individual Behavior and Adjustment

1. Mrs. E. was an out-of-wedlock child whose father, John
Sutton, died before she was born.   Her mother later married Jerome Henry, whom Mrs. E. knew as her father and thought had
legally adopted her.   She used the name of Henry before her marriage, but her children's birth certificates record her maiden name
as Sutton.   (This has created a legal complication that has kept Mrs.
E. ineligible for ADC--details under E, source of income.)   Mrs.
E. lived in the rural South, completed the 4th grade in school, and
worked as a domestic in homes and in hospitals.

In November, 1957, Mrs. E. left her children with various
relatives or friends and came to New Haven, where she had received a job as a live-in domestic through an employment agency.
She came thinking job opportunities might be better and hoping to
terminate her relationship with Mr. Waters.   The placement ar-

rangements for the children fell through and in 1958 the children came to live with her. For a time she continued working in order to support them but expenses exceeded her earnings; when she became ill it became necessary for her to apply for welfare assistance.

Mrs. E. is of medium stature, graying, with a sad and worried expression. She responds almost magically to any attention or guidance; her face lights up as she humbly expresses her gratitude and apologizes for being "so much worry" to the worker. She is utterly straightforward and honest, sharing information to the best of her ability and memory.

2. Lowell was raised for the most part by his maternal grandmother in the South. He is nervous and a poor student. He was twice brought to the attention of the Juvenile Youth Bureau for tampering with parked cars and breaking school windows.

3. Stanley is reasonably well adjusted at school. However, the Neighborhood House reports a recent change in attitude--poor sportsmanship, sulking, violent reaction if he doesn't get his way. A follower in groups, he goes along with the crowd.

4. Carla is tall and somewhat overweight. With strangers she seems shy, speaks in a timid, low-voiced manner, but responds readily to attention. Recently, she has been taunted and picked on by girls in her class, so that she cried daily and refused to go to school. According to school reports, she is not bright and will be tested there soon.

5. Debbie was boarded with her maternal grandmother from the age of 7 months until June, 1958, when she joined her mother. Little else is known.

C. Care and Training of Children

1. Physical Care: What little is known or has been recently observed indicates considerable unevenness. In the past two months Mrs. E. has been ill, and dependent on whatever kindness is offered by neighbors and friends. It can be assumed that the children have had to shift for themselves. The general or normal pattern of physical care is unknown.

2. Training Methods and Emotional Care: Nothing is known except what can be inferred from the fact that the children were raised by others until 1958.

D. Social Activities

1. Informal Associations: Mrs. E. has some friends in the neighborhood and some in widely scattered areas (she placed Debbie with a friend in New York recently while she was ill). Nothing else is known.

2. Formal Associations: She has attended several tenant meetings at Farnam Courts, bringing Debbie with her. Nothing else is known.

E. Economic Practices

1. Sources and Amount of Family Income: There is a food budget of $25.20 per week from the New Haven Department of Welfare. Rent is paid automatically and medicine and clothing are allowed "as needed." Mrs. E. was referred to the State Department of Welfare for ADC consideration in June, 1959. She was found ineligible because of the mixup in her legal maiden name (see B1). To date there is no legal document establishing the relationship between Mrs. E. and the children whose mother's maiden name was Sutton. If a marriage certificate with the name of Mae Sutton could be found, the matter might be cleared up.

2. Job Situation: Not applicable at present.

2. Use of Money: Nothing known except that Mrs. E. undoubtedly has a struggle. The present allotment is not the full one designed for family needs.

F. Home and Household Practices

1. Physical Condition of Home: A 5-1/2 room Farnam Courts apartment with shabby furniture. It is interesting that in addition to a TV, there is an upright piano.

2. Housekeeping Standards: The place is cluttered, grimy, and neglected. Small attempts to brighten it are shown by gaily patterned drapes, a spray of artificial flowers in a vase, a picture on the piano. Whether Mrs. E. was a better housekeeper before her health problems set in is not known.

G.   Health Conditions and Practices

1. Health Problems: Mrs. E. was hospitalized in April, 1958, for urethral calculi; she states she has frequent backaches that she suspects are due to her kidneys.   Recently she has had difficulty in walking.   In the past month she had a virus attack for which she was treated once at home by a Department of Welfare doctor.

Carla had the flu recently.   A few days after being seen by the doctor she had a convulsion, which the doctor thought might have been the result of the high temperature; however, there is some vague family history of possible epilepsy that he thought would bear watching.   She is in need of dental care.

Debbie complains frequently of stomach pains, but has no vomiting.   The clinic doctor thought it was an attention-getting device, but Mrs. E. did not agree and is worried about her.

Lowell was tested for glasses some time ago, given a prescription, which was lost, and nothing further has been done.   He is also in need of dental care.

2. Health Practices: Not much known.   Mrs. E. is slated for a complete check-up in the Women's Medical Clinic of Grace New Haven Hospital on March 10, 1960 (made through NIP office). She also "plans" to get dental appointments arranged for the two children and make an appointment for Debbie about the stomach complaint.   Mrs. E. has not followed through on health care in the past and may need help in doing this.

Debbie is known to the well-baby clinic; her next appointment is to be in June-July, 1960.

H.   Relationship to NIP Office

Shortly after the opening of the office in September, 1959, Mrs. E. began to come to us for help and guidance.   She has come in or sent for us (when ill) six to eight times, sometimes for help with concrete problems (Carla's school, her own health), sometimes because of anxiety and worry.   She has always expressed gratitude for the smallest service or attention.

I. Use of Community Resources

Mrs. E. seems to have tried to use the resources that have
been available to her in terms of her needs. She is considered
very cooperative and scrupulously honest. Several times she has
gone to the school trying to straighten out Carla's problems.

Phase I of Treatment

At first glance, the case appears atypical. Mrs. E. is
eager for help; in fact she applied for it before we were able to
assign a worker. She seems to be alert to some problems and she
is making a genuine effort to use available resources, such as medical attention for herself. She is concerned about the children, taking Debbie to the well-baby clinic and visiting the school in regard
to Carla's troubles. Her "cooperativeness" and "honesty" are impressive; personnel in the welfare office had greatly extended themselves attempting to untangle the legal complications that made her
ineligible for Aid to Dependent Children. As a result, she began
to receive an ADC allotment about a month before the NIP worker
entered the case.

The qualitative picture of the E. family functioning began to
emerge as soon as the worker effected direct contact. Although
Mrs. E. did not seem hesitant about telling the worker her problems, the initial interviews were difficult to conduct. Sometimes
the apartment was full of the children of a sick friend; at other
times, neighbors were visiting. There were instances of "forgotten"
appointments, with Mrs. E. still in bed or taking a bath. Her
conversation was muddled; she talked incessantly, jumping from
topic to topic, breaking off sentences and skipping details. At one
visit she insisted her problems were all solved--her health was
better because of the new pills and the children were getting along
fine in school. But next time the worker found her distraught and
unkempt, the house in disorder, the children a constant source of
worry and irritation.

The worker described that interview as follows:

There was no focusing on any one thing for more than
a few minutes. Mrs. E. brought up a number of things
that were on her mind and I followed her lead.

Following her lead meant the worker's promise to arrange
dental appointments for three of the children; a suggestion that they
discuss summer camp opportunities in April when more information
would be available ("This will get them out of my hair," Mrs. E.
said); and an agreement to thoroughly discuss budgeting in the near
future. Mrs. E. admitted that she worried about receiving a large
check once a month; she also indicated anxiety about her health, at
which time the worker discussed following through on clinic appointments.

Apparently in response to the worker's interest, there was
a flurry of activity: Mrs. E. made the dental appointments and
took the children for care; she visited the school, and told the
worker she was keeping up her personal clinic visits.

In the third week of contact there was a crisis involving the
oldest child at home, described as follows by the worker:

> Mrs. E. had called me the day before to make sure I
> was coming to see her because, as she said, there was
> trouble about Lowell. I was not able to get any informa-
> tion at that time from Juvenile Court and when I arrived
> on this day I found Mrs. E. anxious, distracted, and ill-
> looking... (she) had not yet talked with the Probation Offi-
> cer and was waiting for word to appear (there). In the
> meantime all she knew came from the grandmother of one
> of the other boys implicated with Lowell in thefts from a
> store several days previously. They were held in Chil-
> dren's Building for a couple of nights. Mrs. E. was per-
> haps most upset by the fact that... she could (not) believe
> the story Lowell was telling her about how some goods
> had accidentally gotten in his pockets. I promised to be
> in touch with the Probation Officer and to explain anything
> she might not understand after her interview.

In this meeting with the worker, Mrs. E. once again hopped
from one concern to another. She worried aloud about cleaning the
apartment for the Project inspection the following day and about how
she could get her oldest son, who is in the army, to come home
and help out. Money matters troubled her; she told the worker she
spent almost all of her ADC check the day after it was received
and that after next week she would probably have to buy food on
credit. Camp and her own poor health were again touched upon in
her rambling conversation.

Mrs. E's main concern lay with her boy Lowell, and her inability to understand his behavior. The worker helped her through this period by contacting the Probation Officer, clarifying the boy's status, and arranging for a recommended physical and psychological work-up. The worker also obtained more developmental history on the boy and advised Mrs. E. on ways of coping with his present behavior. Even though her financial mismanagement and home neglect produced a chaotic state that left her exhausted and frantic, Mrs. E. was unable to respond to any guidance in these problem areas. Meanwhile she became obviously ill, exhibiting such symptoms as shortness of breath, dizziness, and an inability to focus her eyes, but she continued to insist that she was faithfully attending the clinic.

The worker had earlier gotten permission from Mrs. E. to write the clinic for a report in order to interpret medical details and had thereby established her identity as the family worker. Consequently, the clinic nurse notified the worker after Mrs. E. failed to keep all of her appointments. The worker recorded:

> I told Mrs. E. about my telephone call from the clinic and after some difficulty in pinning her down...she finally said that she won't go back to the clinic because they want to cut her up. In the meantime, however, I had received a letter from Dr. S. at the hospital and I was able to explain that it was important to return to clinic for further diagnosis before any decisions were made. I offered to take her the following Tuesday and she reluctantly accepted. (On the next visit): When we got to the subject of Mrs. E.'s clinic appointment which had been given to me for 6/14, she showed her reluctance and said she would try to be ready...I insisted that we needed to get started as soon as I arrived and be on time as instructed, and finally Mrs. E. showed her anger at me. We then engaged in a little banter and the outcome was that the date was circled on the calendar.

At the clinic the doctor explained privately to the worker that he strongly advised a hysterectomy but that a D & C (dilation and curettage) was an immediate necessity. When advised of the doctor's views, Mrs. E. gave her consent for the hysterectomy almost too quickly:

> On the way to the hospital and going home Mrs. E. talked to me about how a tooth was hurting...the clue to what would happen about the hysterectomy became clear (to me) when she told me...that the dentist last

fall had told her that her tooth needed to come out and
so she has not been back to him since. I discussed the
forthcoming surgery very little with Mrs. E. on the way
home, but told her that I would be in to see her the following morning.

The crisis now shifted to Mrs. E.'s health and the attempts
to make her continue with the prescribed medical care. Although
the worker made an appointment with her, Mrs. E. was found the
next morning leaving the apartment at the specified time, holding
her youngest child by the hand. Taken aback, she told the worker
that they were on their way to the store to buy a box of cereal.
The worker accompanied them, and when they all returned to the
apartment, there was a long talk about the proposed surgery. As
the talk progressed, Mrs. E. "admitted flatly that she had no inten-
tion of having the surgery."

> She told me with some enjoyment of having been
> in a hospital in Georgia once for her tonsils and once
> with appendicitis. Both times she had been almost on
> the operating table and then had walked out.

The worker told Mrs. E. she suspected that the D & C
would not be done.

> Mrs. E. said, "You did! How?" I told her about what
> she had said about her tooth and said the two things were
> very much the same and I thought she probably was really
> telling me that she wouldn't be operated on.

To this revelation Mrs. E. responded, "You knew before I
did." She then stated with conviction that she would have the D &
C. (The worker suspected that this resolve stemmed from her
previous experience with that type of operation, and not from newly
acquired insight.)

Meanwhile the worker hunted for sources of inexpensive camp
supplies and arranged camp checkup appointments at the clinic. The
supplies were bought by Mrs. E. with state welfare funds (she had
gotten her state worker's authorization) while the worker took the
children for the examinations.

By the worker's careful maneuvering, three children were
away at camp when Mrs. E. entered the hospital for an anticipated
two-day stay. But her stay was extended five days for further care,
meaning that Mrs. E.'s return home would coincide with the chil-

dren's arrival, and she would not have a convalescent period free
of child-care responsibility.

Then a more serious complication occurred. During the
added five-day period Mrs. E. had a convulsion, making it necessary for her to remain even longer in order to undergo a series of
tests for a suspected brain tumor. This precipitated an added crisis. Who would be responsible for the children when they returned
from camp? Neither homemaking services or foster care arrangements were available.

At this point, Mrs. E.'s daughter-in-law Shirley, 22, arrived from the South for a visit--what Mrs. E. called a "miracle."
She took back her words, however, as she elaborated on Shirley's
history. The daughter-in-law had been declared an unfit mother because of a serious drinking problem and her own child had been removed from her custody. Irresponsible, immature, and suffering
from a relapse of illness, Shirley not only ignored the E. children
but mismanaged the finances to such a degree that they were without food. However unsuited, Shirley was the only person available,
and the worker met this reality by initiating frequent visits with the
young woman. She directed her in the use of money, shopping,
meal planning, child supervision, and the establishment of some
minimal routine. The worker also had to solve some welfare grant
problems regarding the supplemental food allowance and Shirley's
status as homemaker.

The many friends Mrs. E. spoke of turned out to be a loose
network of acquaintances, who could give nothing but a few favors
in times of emergency. The woman was quite alone with her dread
of the hospital; in addition, she was plagued by almost frantic worry
about the children. One night she was intercepted in the hospital
corridor, trying to leave. Mindful of these factors, the worker
visited Mrs. E. almost daily, acting as intermediary with the staff
and bringing news and gifts from home. The increased intimacy during the enforced hospital stay brought results: Mrs. E. revealed
that Lowell's delinquency had increased, admitted to feelings of guilt
about leaving him in the care of others for so long, and supplied
the worker with many details about his past history. She also con-

fided a good deal about herself--her family and early upbringing, her three unhappy involvements with men, her past illnesses and her struggles to support the children. Throughout this history ran the theme of having been disappointed by everyone in whom she had trusted or from whom she had expected help.

Mrs. E. was finally released from the hospital, with every indication that a tumor had not developed. The worker, transporting her to the apartment, found it pathetic that the woman had had to remain an extra day because no one had come to escort her home.

For the next five weeks the worker's efforts were geared to taking Mrs. E. to the clinic, for once again she failed to go by herself. The neurological findings were negative, but she had to visit the eye clinic to clear up a minor irritation. The worker was also busy attempting to work out some system of money management that would eliminate the end-of-month deprivation and/or serious debts; helping Mrs. E. curb an over-involvement with Shirley's problems that was detrimental to her own children; and dealing with Mrs. E.'s worries about Lowell.

This first four-month period of intense worker activity was followed by the worker's vacation of one month. Although left the name of another worker, Mrs. E. made no contact. When her own worker returned, she greeted her with shyness and constraint, but showing in small ways that she had been awaiting her with pleasure. By mid-December the worker noted that Mrs. E.'s health was considerably improved and she was feeling easier about the children, all of whom had made gains in school adjustment and general behavior. When problems arose, her approach was a little more organized and she took some initiative in dealing with them. Household standards and routine were better, as was the personal hygiene of all family members. The E.'s also began to emerge from the home; the mother enrolled in the NIP sponsored sewing class and encouraged the children to participate in appropriate programs. All this indicated that the E.'s were feeling more like a family. Mrs. E. could say that although she still wanted to send the children away when she is sick, most of the time now she was glad to

have them with her. She told the worker with a good deal of
pleasure about her younger son's birthday party; significantly, only
the family was present. Mrs. E. for the first time took pride in
the accomplishments of one child or another. She also limited the
traffic of neighbors in and out of the apartment, giving more time
and concern to her own children.

The gains described above can be seen from the records of
the four to six-month period following Mrs. E.'s return from the
hospital. But Mrs. E.'s problems were by no means solved. She
continued to have her ups and downs in the form of "bad days."
On those occasions the children invariably reacted to her irritability
and there were echoes of the old cycle; yet she did manage to
weather these setbacks with fewer extremes in functioning than for-
merly.

With the fear of a serious malady eliminated, Mrs. E. resorted to her old pattern and abandoned all pretense of getting medical care for herself; she simply refused to return to the clinic.
Money difficulties continued to plague her, but she could not respond to management guidance from the worker. In spite of the
haphazard fashion in which she handled her income, each month
found her feeding the family well; nevertheless, she still grumbled
and complained endlessly about "money troubles." Lowell's problems continued to haunt her; she increasingly talked with the worker
about his "growing up," his lack of emotional stability, and her tenuous control over him.

This record material illustrates the client-worker interaction
characterizing the treatment for Phase I, the first year of contact,
when the worker took the initiative in "doing for and with" the client. With virtually no testing of the client's ability to act for himself, the worker assumed major responsibility for making collateral contacts, appointments, arrangements, etc., and insured that
family members made use of resources by personally escorting
them much of the time. For the most part, tangible problems
were given top priority. In the crucial problem of Mrs. E.'s
health, the worker was so insistent on treatment that one might view
her as the prime decision-maker in the matter. It seems reason-

able to assume that the worker's initial efforts--to meet the client
where she is and to be demonstrably helpful to her--achieved results, for Mrs. E. went along with the worker's insistence on treatment despite her aversion to medical care.

While most of the "doing" was accomplished by the worker,
there was some division of tasks with the client. Mrs. E. could
accept the relatively uncomplicated task of shopping for the camp
clothing, but only after the worker had given her information on the
welfare procedure and allowance, and the names and addresses of
appropriate stores. She quickly took the initiative in making dental
appointments for the children and starting them on treatment, but it
is more noteworthy that these coincided with her own clinic appointments. After first consulting the worker, she made a school visit
about Lowell, seeing four of his teachers; she also kept an appointment with his Probation Officer. In both of these contacts, however, she was inarticulate; unable to ask questions, she came away
dissatisfied. The report of Lowell's acceptable behavior at school,
in sharp contrast to his behavior in the community, increased her
bewilderment. She could not understand the boy and turned to the
worker for clarification and direction.

Shirley's arrival brought another treatment practice into
play: that of working with any relative or interested person whose
relationship or role has impact on the family. Shirley, too, became part of the worker's reponsibility, because of her close relationship to the E. family and also because of the results of her becoming the homemaker. Her severe limitations, immediately apparent, made it necessary for the worker to "do for and with" her
also. Even after Mrs. E.'s return home, the worker continued to
intervene. This included reluctantly acting as referee in a heated
argument between the two women over the welfare check, which was
mistakenly made out to Shirley and claimed by her although it was
intended for the entire E. family.

With someone like Mrs. E., a worker follows the time-
tested treatment approach of "starting where the client is." While
not directly working with the children, the worker follows the

mother's most obvious cues and becomes involved first in activities
related to them, such as dental care, camp plans, collateral contact with the court and schools. A worker usually reacts to this
kind of distressed and anxious client with an urgent desire to do
something quickly. This reaction is reinforced by familiarization
with the family history (screening-in report), documenting years of
inadequate functioning, and acquaintance with the client, who appears
too overwhelmed to move constructively in any direction. This evidence causes the worker to dismiss any plans of "testing" the client's ability to "do for" himself at this early stage; however, the
worker must constantly be on the alert to avoid doing anything the
client can do for himself. Occasionally a worker, responding to
the first hint of need, may go through some unnecessary motion, as
in the case of Mrs. E. and the dental appointments. However, an
immediate response almost invariably impresses the client with the
worker's good intentions, genuine interest, and ability to do something that is realistically needed at the time.

It is, of course, possible that the worker may misread the
client for a while. The client's strengths may be misjudged or
problems given wrong priorities. For instance, the E. family
worker--drawn by her own concern for the children's welfare--went
along for some time with the mother's emphasis upon the children's
problems. Through the ten weeks of contact, the worker did considerably less intervening in Mrs. E.'s health problems, although
they could be observed to be worsening and the woman mentioned
them frequently.

Mrs. E.'s health was the core of the family's current disorganization. It may be suggested that the worker should have
treated Mrs. E.'s medical fears first; we may ask, however,
whether Mrs. E. would have responded as she did if the worker
had not helped her with the children's problems first. The worker
may put forth a further defense: those problems that received attention needed attention. Mrs. E., driven by guilt feelings about
her children, was motivated to move in their behalf, although essentially it was all surface movement. With her great fear of
medical treatment and her mistrust of those in positions of respon-

sibility, it is doubtful if any other approach would have been successful.

Without full awareness, Mrs. E.'s worker began by using a principle found to be essential in treating the multi-problem family: doing something quickly. The worker who can relate his efforts closely to those problems that the client views as pressing is most effective. For when the client has been given a demonstration of the worker's ability to obtain tangible results, he will begin to consider him positively as a potential friend, someone who can be relied upon in time of need. This is the way to quickly gain the trust of the multi-problem family. "Doing something" may very often mean acting quickly to obtain financial assistance, household needs, or clothing; it may also mean directing the client through the intricate maze that precedes seeing the clinic doctor or talking to a teacher; it may mean interpreting the interview in terms that the client can understand.

Structuring the role performance of the client is one of the worker's primary techniques for achieving positive results in treating multi-problem families. The worker spells out, step by step, what is to be done and how to do it. It has been our experience that this kind of structuring, with the worker herself as a model to be imitated, allows for the kind of learning experience best suited to these families. Even so, this learning process is relatively slow. Any procedure involving many steps may require repeated demonstration before the client can manage all of them independently. Furthermore, the capacity to carry over the learning experience from one situation to another may be slow in developing. In general, the worker is required to repeat the process many times before clients can modify their performance in succeeding tasks by incorporating their learning from past experience. In addition to structuring roles and serving as a model, the worker has to help the client stretch his capabilities. It is this time-consuming procedure that lies at the heart of effective treatment with multi-problem families and that goes on throughout contact at a pace tailored to the individual client.

Quantitative Assessment of Family Functioning by the Use of the Profile of Family Functioning

In the preceding paragraphs we have used recorded material to picture the gains made in family functioning, describing the changes that were observed during the treatment process. This material can also be systematized within the framework of our evaluation method by using the Outline of Family Functioning and then comparing the profiles available prior to and at the end of twelve months of treatment.

This method of evaluation utilizes the techniques underlying the St. Paul Scale of Family Functioning. Families are evaluated on a seven-point scale ranging from adequate to inadequate functioning, in terms of a) whether laws are violated or observed, b) whether behavior contributes or is harmful to the physical, social and emotional well-being of family members, c) whether behavior is in harmony or conflict with the standards of a family's status group, and d) whether a family member's behavior is commensurate with his potential for social functioning. The conceptual scheme and the method of evaluation have been discussed elsewhere.[7] The quantitative values assigned to each family range from (1) Inadequate Functioning to (7) Adequate Functioning, with value (4) Marginal Functioning occupying a mid-position. The ratings used in quantifying the social functioning and changes in functioning of the E. case are averages of ratings given by three independent raters.

In table 4 below, by arranging the nine major categories in descending order from lowest rating (indicative of most problematic functioning) to highest (most nearly adequate), we get a more systematic picture of the changes that occurred in the E. family.

When we look at the beginning alignment of categories with regard to possible implications for treatment, we see that the first six areas, with their marginal or below marginal ratings, were sufficiently low to warrant community intervention. We can also see in the Beginning Profile that the alignment results in an even grouping of categories by threes: below marginal, marginal, and above marginal. The three categories that were most problem-

Table 4

	Profiles of the E. Family	
Category	Beginning Profile	12-Month Profile
Health Conditions and Practices	Below marginal (3)	Above marginal (5)
Family Relationships and Unity	Below marginal (3)	Marginal (4)
Economic Practices	Below marginal (3)	Below marginal (3)
Individual Behavior and Adjustment	Marginal (4)	Above marginal (5)
Home and Household Practices	Marginal (4)	Above marginal (5)
Care and Training of Children	Marginal (4)	Marginal (4)
Social Activities	Above marginal (5)	Near adequate (6)
Relationship to Worker	Above marginal (5)	Above marginal (5)
Use of Community	Above marginal (5)	Above marginal (5)

atic (below marginal) made a total movement of three scale points;
the three that fell in the middle rating (marginal) made a total
movement of two scale steps; the three that were highest moved
one scale step.   The greatest combined gain was made in the most
problematic or least adequate areas of functioning.   When we make
a closer internal examination of these three groups, we find the
greatest gain--two scale steps--was made in Health Problems and
Practices; one scale step was gained in Family Relationships and
Unity; there was no gain in the third most problematic area, Economic Practices.   In the middle group, the total combined gain was
two steps, with one scale step each gained in Individual Behavior
and Adjustment and in Home and Household Practices; no gain was
made in Care and Training of Children.   In the third group, most
nearly adequate at the beginning of treatment, the least combined
gain was made, with one scale step realized in a single category,
Social Activities.

Recalling the dramatic improvement in Mrs. E.'s health, we
are not surprised to see that the health category registered a two-
step gain.   Furthermore, considering the crucial connection between

the state of her health and other areas of family functioning, we
also are not surprised at gains in such areas as Individual Behavior
and Adjustment, Family Relationships, Home and Household Practices, and Social Activities.

In Economic Practices, there was no measurable progress.
It should be noted, however, that this area is least amenable to
radical change. As long as family income is on the welfare subsistence level, it is defined as being marginal. Consequently, the
only improvement that can be registered is an ability to manage
better. In other words, a family with a marginal income can never
achieve a rating of adequate in Economic Practices.

In the first year of contact, the treatment was aimed chiefly
at establishing some routine for family life by attending to unmet
needs; this was accomplished mainly by worker-initiated activity.
At the close of this period we were able to note that there were only three categories still at the "danger" level:

Economic Practices   Below Marginal (3)
Family Relationships and Unity Marginal   (4)
Care & Training of Children   Marginal   (4)

It is obvious that there was need for further treatment aimed
at improving functioning in these three areas. The health area also
continued to require aid, for the movement, while dramatic, was
superficial. In addition, it was essential in four of the five categories that stood at an above marginal level to test the family's
capacity to maintain this level, with hopes of achieving an even
higher level during the next treatment period. However, little lasting effect could be anticipated unless treatment shifted its focus to
interpersonal problems, particularly in such key areas as Family
Relationships and Unity, Care and Training of Children, and Individual Adjustment.

To demonstrate how the Profile could be used in treatment
as well as research, we made a realignment (Table 5) at the end
of one year of contact.

It is now possible to see how the Profile, by its very design,
lends itself for use as a treatment tool. The right hand column
gives the worker both a picture of those areas of family functioning

Table 5
E. Family Profile After One Year of Treatment

Category	Rating	
Economic Practices	Below Marginal	(3)
Family Relationships and Unity	Marginal	(4)
Care and Training of Children	Marginal	(4)
Health Conditions and Practices	Above marginal	(5)
Relationships to Worker	Above marginal	(5)
Individual Behavior and Adjustment	Above marginal	(5)
Home and Household Practices	Above marginal	(5)
Use of Community Resources	Above marginal	(5)
Social Activities	Near adequate	(6)

that need improvement and a quantitative guide of the amount of gain needed. A similar assessment at the end of the next treatment period allowed us to see its further applicability.

Phase II of Treatment

By the beginning of the second year of contact with the E. family there were fewer tangible problems requiring the worker's intervention. This treatment phase was characterized by a gradual but perceptible deepening of the client-worker relationship, making it possible to deal with interpersonal problems. The first sign of this progress was the resumption of office visits. Office visits had been introduced by the worker early in contact but had to be abandoned because of Mrs. E's health and her chaotic state of mind. Now, Mrs. E. came regularly to the worker's agency office, with a more purposeful approach. She showed clearly that she had given advance thought to the discussion and the problems to be aired, that she had considered a number of possible solutions and was seeking the worker's help in choosing the most appropriate alternative. She also began a process of self-examination, questioning her pattern of functioning--whether and how much she could change--and her way of handling the children. Moreover, she showed increased respect for their emotional needs and sought ways to improve her own performance.

While it was an achievement to arrive at a point where Mrs.

E. could look objectively at herself, she by no means carried this
out in a consistent manner. There was a striking similarity between
the way she fulfilled her household responsibilities--working with
great gusts of effort at one time and then at another time sitting
down and doing nothing--and the way she engaged in self-appraisal.
For example, in several interviews she discussed her uneven functioning, acknowledging that her "ups and downs" seriously affected
the children. However, when this discussion led to an examination
of the fitful way in which she cared for her health, Mrs. E. returned to her old pattern, either insisting that she felt well and no
longer needed medical care or giving lip service to getting care if
she should feel ill again.

Her financial management followed the same pattern. One
week she might initiate discussion; a few weeks later she adamantly closed it. This occurred with such cyclical regularity that the
worker made repeated attempts to help Mrs. E. when she indicated
motivation. To quote the record:

> Mrs. E. promised to gather all her pending bills so that
> the total financial situation could be looked at. By the
> following week, however, she made every effort to avoid
> discussion... by deflecting the conversation to other topics
> ...She signalled the end of any effort on her part by stress-
> ing the fact that she always had money left to buy food un-
> til the end of the month and this was more than many fami-
> lies she knew could do.

Mrs. E's spending pattern included lavish buying at the first
of every month, when the allotment check arrived, and impulsive
credit buying when she was tempted by door-to-door salesmen--
both common neighborhood phenomena. Her ability to "buy food 'til
the end of the month" was indeed a real achievement, for which she
justifiably received worker recognition; but throughout treatment she
never moved far from this precarious type of economy.

Mrs. E., unable to have attention focused directly upon herself, showed greater motivation in strengthening her performance
as a parent than in insisting upon her needs and rights as an individual. The worker accordingly focused treatment upon her functioning as a mother, giving her recognition for her gains and encouraging her to stretch her capabilities a bit more with each ex-

perience.

> For the most part, though limited, the gains that al-
> ready had been made were maintained...Mrs. E. seemed
> able to push herself a little more when she was not feel-
> ing well.   For instance, she got out of bed...to prepare
> lunch for the children.   I called this to her attention and
> praised her for it and she recognized that this was some-
> thing she could not have done several months before.

Developing an awareness of what she should do as a good
parent, Mrs. E. was as yet unable to always act accordingly.   At
one point she informed the worker that she thought it best to
straightforwardly tell a neighbor wishing to borrow money from her
that this would seriously deprive her own family.   Several months
later, however, Mrs. E. revealed in another context that she had
made one of the children lie when the neighbor came to the apartment, saying Mrs. E. was not at home.   This inability to follow
her own considered opinion made her vulnerable to the child's ac-
cusation that she was the one responsible for the falesehood.

There was an improvement in her relationship with her older daughter, Carla, who had been taunted about her large size both
by her mother and her schoolmates.   The child might have pro-
voked some of the attacks the other children made upon her.   In
the NIP club, for instance, Carla was thoroughly disliked.   She
wore a perpetual frown and physically attacked those who teased
her, often requiring restraint.   Mrs. E. first displayed concern for
her daughter by expressing interest in a complete physical examination.   Although still requiring the worker's intervention to make the
initial arrangement, the mother managed to accompany the girl to
a series of medical appointments, so that the checkup was completed.   She showed a growing awareness of causal relations, telling the worker that she found it difficult to help the girl follow the
doctor's dietary instructions since she too found eating an intensely
personal pleasure.   This insight seemed to help Mrs. E. accept
Carla as she was, for her habit of teasing the girl gradually disappeared.

Mrs. E's ability to complete Carla's series of clinic appointments was the first step in breaking her resistance to medical help.
A few months later another accomplishment was recorded.   Mrs.

E, arriving for an interview unable to speak because of a toothache, announced to the worker that she had already called the clinic and been told to come the following day or, if necessary, to the emergency room at once. The worker offered to take her to the hospital immediately, and Mrs. E., feeling trapped, complied. The next day she informed the worker with great pride that she not only allowed the dentist to extract the tooth, but made appointments for extensive work. She followed through for a prolonged period, although with forty percent of the appointments missed her overall attendance record was spotty.

With her increased ability to individualize the children and with more genuine concern for their welfare, Mrs. E. lost the jealousy that erupted whenever the worker paid attention to them. Direct contact could now be established with several of them. Lowell, approaching 16 and previously involved in neighborhood thefts, had been taking candy and cookies from a nearby grocery. Mrs. E. protectively concealed this from the worker and arranged to pay the grocer, who allowed the situation to continue. The mother's attitude toward the boy swung between two extremes: on the one hand, she described him as lazy, sneaky, unable to stay out of trouble; on the other, she said he was "good," earning money by cleaning halls, baby-sitting, and taking clothes to the washing machines.

Lowell, though not considered a behavior problem at school, was described as "a dreamer, uncooperative, could do better work, but just doesn't try." He was in a special ungraded class, in which he might not be able to remain because of his borderline I.Q. of 75. He read on a second grade level. In projective testing he revealed feelings of inadequacy, seeing himself as deprived, lonely, and rejected by his father. His passivity was marked; he was seclusive and withdrawn. This information was gathered by the worker at a conference with Lowell's teacher, the guidance counsellor and the psychologist, before she started contact with the boy. She, in turn, shared with the school staff pertinent information about the home situation and the direction of her treatment of the family. Ways in which the school personnel and the worker might coordinate

their efforts were arranged at this conference, and a promise given
to re-test the boy in order to determine the best possible class
placement.

Another child directly contacted by the worker was Stanley.
He came in for a good deal of uneven treatment from his mother,
although she was more openly hostile toward Lowell.   At times she
seemed to favor Stanley, but at other times she was cold and critical.   This boy was not openly a problem at school; he was a follower, easily influenced by others, and an indifferent student with
marginal grades.   In the neighborhood he was a "loner," drifting on
the periphery of group activities but not responding to overtures.
Although he did not as yet show problems as serious as his brother's,
he was in the same potential plight.   Four years younger than Lowell, he was eligible for a group therapy program conducted by the
worker's parent agency; when an opening occurred in the fall of
1961, it was possible to enlist Stanley's interest in joining the
group.   This gave the boy an opportunity to relate to a male worker
and to be helped to improve his relationship with his peers.   It was
some time before Stanley moved actively from the periphery of the
therapeutic group into a more integrated position.   Though he remained silent at meetings, there was evidence that the sessions
held great meaning for him.   He became one of the steadiest and
most faithful members in a group of boys that were notorious for
bad attendance records.

The worker, taking advantage of a visit from Mrs. E's oldest
son, Richard, talked with him about a number of family problems
that dovetailed with his own.   It was Richard that revealed Lowell's
latest thefts and his mother's attempts to conceal them.   Richard
disapproved of his mother's solution; he also expressed concern
about Lowell's apparent limitations and his poor preparation for facing a job situation.   Encouraged by the worker to show his interest,
Richard met with school personnel and arranged to keep in touch
with them about the boy's adjustment, promising to encourage Lowell by letters after the visit was over.   Sometime later when the
worker brought up the subject of Lowell's thefts, Mrs. E. dismissed it by saying she had "stopped all that" (i. e. collusion with

the grocer). Richard's involvement with the boy's problems probably led him to successfully confront his mother.

By the second summer of treatment (sixteen months) Mrs.
E. showed an ability to act independently in some practical matters.
She also demonstrated a growing capacity to plan in accordance with
a particular need. Because of Lowell's age, it was questionable
whether camp would be a meaningful experience. Without discussing
it with the worker, Mrs. E. arranged to send him south to work on
his uncle's farm. The plan was for him to draw a small allowance,
with the bulk of his wages saved for his school clothing in the fall.
Lowell enjoyed the experience; there was noticeable improvement in
his behavior when school resumed. Re-tested and found to have an
I.Q. of 59, he continued in the special class, where he got more individual attention. He showed greater effort in his schoolwork and
improved his personal appearance, as a response to the encouragement he received to stay in school.

When the worker talked with his mother about the boy's improvement, she stressed Mrs. E's contribution, pointing out how
important her support was to the boy. Mrs. E. responded by accepting his scholastic limitations and their effect upon his behavior.

A new problem arose when Lowell began to show an interest
in girls, particularly those his mother called "much older." Mrs.
E. became quite alarmed and began to question him closely; he became secretive and withdrawn. However, he confessed to the worker that he resented his mother's mistrust. It was clear in the way
he expressed this that he felt he might as well be guilty since his
mother would not believe him anyway. Mrs. E. , still limited in
her ability to sustain much self-examination or to perceive cause
and effect, was unable to change her approach and the mother-son
relationship remained poor for almost another year.

Meanwhile, other forces were having their effect. Lowell
began to show a keen interest in the NIP group work program.
Although alerted to reach out to the boy, the group workers had
found him unresponsive. Now he asked to join a group of boys interested in basketball. Tall, slim, athletically skilled, Lowell
was accepted by his peers. For a while his passivity and docile

group behavior handicapped him.   But with attention and coaching
he gradually developed assertiveness, and as he became more skillful he showed more self-confidence.   Mrs. E. found this group participation very important.   She sought out the group leader and let
him know that this was the only group Lowell ever joined; she informed him that she was very happy to see how much this experience meant to the boy.

Mrs. E's appreciation of other phases of the NIP program
had been building up over an extended period, developing concurrent-
ly with the casework process.   Her experiences in the adult educational and recreational group work program illustrate both the close
coordination of the total program, which included planned casework-
group work collaboration, and the impact of a multi-dimensional
program on the outcome of family treatment.

From the start, Mrs. E. was a loyal participant in the fort-
nightly bingo games, attending even when quite ill.   When her health
improved after surgery, she enrolled in the sewing class.   Unfortunately, the first pattern she selected was too difficult and unsuited to her large frame.   Reluctantly, Mrs. E. accepted the
teacher's suggestion that she make the dress for Carla.   To the
caseworker she indicated her unhappiness; feeling very hostile toward the girl at this time, she was not at all enthusiastic about
making a dress for her.   Her slow progress further discouraged
her.   When the caseworker shared this information with the group
leader, special attention and encouragement were given Mrs. E.
She then persisted to a degree that surprised everyone; she came
to class even when ill, making the caseworker understand that she
did this out of loyalty and respect for the teacher.   When Carla's
dress was completed, she started one for herself, this time with
enthusiasm.   She blossomed with success; she displayed such consistent good humor, native wit, and willingness to help others that
she became very popular in the class.   Two events climaxed this
experience: both Mrs. E. and Carla modeled their dresses in a
class fashion show and Mrs. E. received a certificate for the best
attendance.   Mrs. E. was so overcome with emotion at the presentation that she had to leave the room.   She subsequently sent the

certificate home for her mother to see. This was obviously her
first public recognition, and it was very meaningful to her for its
"educational" aspect.

Because of her appreciation of her own program and her
growing ability to individualize her children, she took the initiative
in seeing that her children participated in programs designed for
them. For example, she responded to the first notice of the nursery
program and enrolled Debbie immediately. She was one of only two
mothers who complied at once with the physical examination requirement.

Mrs. E. became one of the most enthusiastic and regular
participants in all the adult programs she could possibly attend.
Because of her new popularity she was accepted as an honorary
member of the Young Mothers' Club, a group for which she was not
eligible because she was over thirty-five. In groups she seemed to
exercise a subtle but noticeable influence; when there were tensions
and bickering, she acted as a peacemaker by injecting gently humor-
ous remarks that had a soothing effect. This acceptance helped
Mrs. E. develop self-confidence and poise. At a lecture with illustrated slides on the life and customs of Ghana, she asked a number of pertinent questions. When a minister told of his prison experience for participating in a Freedom Ride and appealed to the
group for support, Mrs. E. was the first one with a suggestion:
she would "give up candy and cigarettes"--a genuine sacrifice--to be
able to afford a contribution.

There was, however, one negative outcome of Mrs. E's increased popularity. Tenants made increasing demands upon her,
particularly to baby-sit. Mrs. E. had always been unable to say
no when appealed to for help. It was not long before she became
widely regarded as the neighborhood mother, constantly in charge
of a flock of children. Mothers became accustomed to leaving their
young children with her, often depositing them outside her apartment
without even letting her know, secure in the knowledge that she
would keep an eye on them and even feed them. Mrs. E. did an
extraordinarily good job in this capacity, exercising more patience
and good humor than she showed her own children. Probably she

was satisfying needs unmet by care of her own family, but there
were serious repercussions to her giving so much time and attention to the care of others.   These difficulties are illustrated by
what occurred in her relationships with her daughter-in-law Shirley
and her grandchild Thomas.

Both Shirley, separated from her husband Richard, and her
son Thomas had been intermittently sheltered in the E. home, de-
pending upon the fluctuations of Shirley's unstable arrangements
with another man.   While Mrs. E. soon put a stop to Shirley's moving in with her during these periodic crises, she assumed considerable responsibility for the feeding and care of Thomas.   This
had detrimental effects upon the household, putting additional strain
upon a marginal budget and causing Debbie, who was close to Thomas in age, to become sullen, sad and apathetic.   She had to share
her mother not only with the neighborhood children but with Thomas
as well; for months she slept in the same bed with the boy, who
was enuretic.   In varying degrees the other children also shared
Debbie's resentment.

The worker sought a resolution to this problem over an extended period of time, discussing it with Richard during the visit
mentioned earlier.   Despite the great concern that he voiced to the
worker, Richard was unable to request action from the Humane Society, because of his mother's objections.   Mrs. E. simply would
not hear of outsiders assuming what she considered a family responsibility, although the worker tried to help her consolidate her
growing awareness of cause and effect and move to a sounder course
of action.   Mrs. E. finally reached the limits of her forbearance,
feeling put upon enough to sanction a warranted and long-overdue
investigation by the Humane Society.   Her ability to take this step
followed and appeared to have been related to her successful resolution of another personal problem; both decisions illustrated the enormous growth she had made.

The other problem, long hidden from the worker, dealt with
the question of remarriage.   The worker learned of Mrs. E's new
suitor four months after he began to show interest in her.   Even
then it was not Mrs. E. who informed the worker but little Debbie,

talking about her new daddy. Mrs. E, delighted that the secret
was out, seemed eager to discuss the matter. The worker attempted to structure the discussion in the step-by-step manner that
had in the past accorded with Mrs. E's pace and capacity to examine all the factors involved. Characteristically, Mrs. E. started
by recounting the many practical obstacles to be overcome before
marriage. Both would need to obtain divorces--she, from a husband whose whereabouts was unknown; George, from a wife who
lived in another city. While she dwelt at length on these difficulties
she also indicated considerable reservations about marriage, for
George drank a great deal and had questionable companions. In addition, her conversation revealed that the children, especially the
two boys, had been showing signs of increased resentment. As in
the past, however, she did not respond to the worker's attempts to
relate their behavior to George's presence and his demands for her
attention. For about one month these doubts continued to come up
intermittently.

After the worker's vacation, which came at this time, Mrs.
E. evaded serious discussion. She kept the interviews focused on
the concrete, day-to-day matters that took up much of her time.
A number of needs arose simultaneously, primarily because school
was starting, and she once again felt overwhelmed, lapsing temporarily into a state of greater dependency. Then Mrs. E. surprised
the worker with the announcement of a plan to seek schooling for
herself, as preparation for getting a job. When the worker attempted to probe deeper, Mrs. E's reaction indicated that she was
planning to attend school in order to escape George. In this way
she would repeat her past pattern, avoiding the necessity of coming
to grips with the problem.

The worker frankly discussed what she considered a conflict
in Mrs. E's feelings toward George; as a result, the client failed
to keep the next appointment and became openly hostile. When the
worker, changing her approach, praised Mrs. E. for a series of
household and child care accomplishments, the woman responded
with a spontaneous announcement that she had broken off with George.
Her decision rested heavily on consideration of George's negative

effect upon her children and his jealousy of her care of them.
However, it was indicative of her own growth that she also gave
some consideration to her own comfort, admitting that the man was
unreliable, lied as well as drank, and acted like a selfish, over-
demanding child who would only be an added responsibility. As she
put it, he would be "all take and no give." Responding to the worker's praise, Mrs. E. was able to see, with great satisfaction, the
change she had undergone in her method of handling a bewildering
problem. In the past her only solution was to move far away and
then only after a long, painful involvement--now she had learned to
face the situation.

Over the next several months there were indications that
Mrs. E. might have incorporated what was learned from the experience with George; she struggled to control a variety of other involvements that had long had a detrimental effect. The first signs
of this were vocal expressions of resentment at being "used" by
people. She followed this by taking the long-avoided stand on her
grandchild Thomas. This occurred about six weeks after her decision about George, but this time personal considerations played the
largest part. She had been responsible for almost the total care of
Thomas. When Shirley failed to pay a small camp fee and then requested that Mrs. E. lie in court for her, Mrs. E. reached the
end of her tolerance. This seemed to prove to her that Shirley was
unfit, and she agreed to a referral to the Humane Society. Even
when this did not bring a satisfactory solution, Mrs. E. was able
to disengage herself more than ever before and to feel more comfortable when others accepted responsibility for her grandchild.
While she continued to do some baby-sitting for neighbors, she began to exercise more control on her generosity. Her family now
had the highest priority. With the worker's guidance she made a
division of home chores according to each child's ability. The children became more cooperative and a strong family feeling emerged
as members took an interest in each other and enjoyed doing things
together. On one occasion the worker, coming for a home visit,
found the whole family cheerfully engaged in cleaning and refurbish-
ing the apartment.

Despite these gains there was still unevenness in Mrs. E's performance. While at times pleased with her better ability to cope, she periodically regressed to turning the "doing" over to the worker. The worker structured these dependent episodes in such a way as to enlarge Mrs. E's responsibilities and reduce her own; it was, however, still necessary that the worker be partially involved before Mrs. E. would tolerate an examination of her dependent behavior. Discussing her refusal to take three of the children for camp physicals by herself, she expressed her ambivalence: at times she did enjoy the satisfaction stemming from demonstrated competence, but she also resented the increased burden that these responsibilities presented. While she was struggling to achieve more independence from the worker, there were still times when she felt overwhelmed, especially in the area of health. When faced with such problems she became immobilized and panic stricken; it was some time before her fears could be brought under control and in the meantime she lost ground in her struggle for increased competence.

In the intra-familial area Mrs. E. still had some way to go. There was improvement in her relationship with Lowell and Carla, with whom it was poorest. Limited in her ability to help them with maturation problems, she was at the level of perceiving intellectually what she should do but she was unable to follow through. One of her biggest difficulties was dealing with her sons; this stemmed from her opinion of males, an attitude carried over from her disappointments with men into her family relationships.

Toward the end of this treatment period the worker, going on a five-month leave of absence, told Mrs. E. of her impending departure. The woman expressed a keen sense of loss, obviously having had her feelings of dependency aroused once more. She rejected the worker's suggestion of relying on Lowell's group therapist, a worker at the same agency and with some knowledge of her situation, because she would not be able to "talk with a man." The worker concluded by encouraging her to keep the agency in mind, suggesting that the group worker might be able to make a more comfortable arrangement if the need arose.

When we reassembled the descriptive material on the second year of treatment within the framework of our evaluation outline and applied the criteria of rating family functioning, the changes became evident, as shown in Table 6 below.

Table 6

Continuing Profile of the E. Family

Category	Rating at 12 Months of Treatment		Rating after 24 Months of Treatment	
Economic Practices	Below marginal (3)		Marginal	(4)
Family Relationships and Unity	Marginal	(4)	Above marginal	(5)
Care & Training of Children	Marginal	(4)	Above marginal	(5)
Individual Behavior and Adjustment	Above marginal	(5)	Above marginal	(5)
Health Problems & Practices	Above marginal	(5)	Above marginal	(5)
Relationship to Worker	Above marginal	(5)	Near adequate	(6)
Home and Household Practices	Above marginal	(5)	Near adequate	(6)
Use of Community Resources	Above marginal	(5)	Near adequate	(6)
Social Activities	Above marginal	(5)	Near adequate	(6)

At the beginning of this period there were three categories rated marginal or below; at the close, each of these showed a gain of one scale step. Economic Practices moved from below marginal to marginal; Family Relationships and Care and Training of Children both moved from marginal to above marginal. It is evident that minimal worker attention was given to income management counselling. Even though Mrs. E. resisted help in this area, she did make an adjustment by using her own system, which worked well enough to keep the problem from becoming of prime concern. The improvement in family solidarity and some lessening of parent-child tensions were reflected by the gain in Family Relationships and Unity. The gain in Care and Training of Children was attribut-

able to the increasing concern voiced by Mrs. E. and the attention
she began to give to the children's emotional needs, although--as
noted--there were still unresolved problems as well as unevenness
in her behavior and attitudes.   Since the ratings of the main categories are derived from the total of subcategory ratings, it is possible to have a gain registered in the subcategory which is not reflected in the overall rating.   (Only main category ratings are reported here, for the sake of brevity.)   Such a situation occurred
in the main category, Individual Adjustment and Behavior.   Here the
subcategory, Older Children, registered a gain due to the improvements made by Lowell and Carla; this improvement, unfortunately,
was not enough to affect the main category rating at this point.
Since Mrs. E. remained blocked with respect to Health Problems
and Practices, the static position of the rating in this category was
to be expected.

    Real growth was shown in Mrs. E's capacity to tackle inter-
personal problems.   She moved quite far beyond the point at which
we first saw her.   That first year she perceived the worker as a
"doer" and an "enabler," and used her accordingly.   The second
year, in contrast (and more in line with what casework practice
holds to be essential for lasting treatment), she perceived the worker as a counsellor and used her to help her own patterns of behavi-
or and to improve her functioning.   This growth was reflected by
the gain of one scale step, from above marginal to near adequate,
in the category Relationship to Worker.   This year of treatment was
free of crises; although fluctuations occurred, they did not seriously
undermine the family or impede movement.   A greater sense of
well-being, felt in one way or another by all family members, was
shown by the gain of one scale step in each of three categories:
Home and Household Practices, Use of Community Resources, and
Social Activities.   All of these moved from above marginal to near
adequate.

    At the end of two years of treatment, there was only one
category at marginal level and in need of further buttressing--Eco-
nomic Practices.   However, this family had only one parent, who
was, realistically, limited, and who would be responsible for quite

some time for the care and guidance of four children. Considering
this, we concluded that there were four other areas where--although
some gains had been made--Mrs. E. had not as yet come to grips
with the problems or else lacked the depth of understanding needed
to prevent backsliding. These areas were Family Relationships and
Unity, Care and Training of Children, Individual Behavior and Adjustment, and Health Problems and Practices, all of which had
reached an above-marginal position.

Phase III of Treatment

The third and final phase of treatment was inaugurated by a
resumption of contact in the fall of 1963. It was characterized by
the increasing independence of Mrs. E., which began while the
worker was on a leave of absence. During that time Mrs. E. had
not availed herself of any help; she had managed her affairs so well
that family life was relatively calm for the longest period yet. Several children went to camp, and the entire family made a trip south
to visit relatives.

On Mrs. E.'s return she verbalized the feeling that "home
is here." Mrs. E. revealed that she had always considered herself
"the black sheep" of the family, since she was very dark while her
mother had red hair (now turning white), freckles, and very light
skin color. Significantly, Mrs. E, became ill during the visit south
and again upon her return and was forced to seek medical attention; an electrocardiogram taken in each instance gave negative findings. She was, however, unable to engage in any deeper discussion with the worker about these matters.

Some initial constraint, caused by the break in treatment,
was soon overcome, and Mrs. E. began to demonstrate a consoli-
dation of some earlier small gains. On her own, she applied a
more planned approach to the use of income, paying off debts, al-
ternating clothing purchases for the children, and attempting to curb
her installment buying. She joined a mending class sponsored by
NIP and kept the family clothing in better condition. She made
better and more consistent use of community resources, especially
the clinic and school. She used a minimum of interview time dis-

cussing these matters, merely informing the worker of what she had been doing. She also seemed able to control her panic when acute illness threatened. A referral for another neurological examination aroused momentary fear, for she confused "neurological" with "psychiatric." On another occasion she reacted fearfully when referred to the gynecologist; she suspected surgery, but responded reasonably to the worker's interpretation of the visit. She continued to be more attentive to the needs of other children than to her own. A long series of minor family ailments forced her to make frequent use of the clinics. She finally remarked to the worker that she loved going to the clinic because she felt so at home there now. One can infer that this familiarity related to the children's visits rather than her own, for Mrs. E. still forgot or confused appointments--especially those arranged for herself. But here, too, she showed improvement for she usually got another appointment, which she kept.

In the care of the children, Mrs. E. continued to have much more success with the two girls than with the boys. Though unable earlier to discuss it directly with the worker, she took the worker's advice and prepared Carla for the onset of menstruation; when it occurred the girl took it in stride. Mrs. E., a loyal PTA member, was pleased and proud with Debbie's excellent school adjustment, perhaps partially a result of her two years in the NIP nursery program. This child had by far the least problems of all the children, possibly because she was too young to have been shunted around from relative to friend to relative.

The boys presented a different picture, and Mrs. E. began to concentrate on their problems during counselling sessions. In a thoughtful self-examination about her methods of handling them, she struggled to understand their behavior and looked for ways to meet their individual needs. Lowell was still her greatest concern. A senior in high school, his demands for a variety of costly graduation items aroused her suspicions. She though he might be gambling, and she considered him a "weak" boy. When the worker initiated a realistic review of his needs, the high level of tension between mother and son was relieved for a short time. However,

Mrs. E. remained hostile toward her son; she considered him dis-
obedient, uncooperative, and bossy toward the other children.   She
complained about his late hours, fearing he might be involved with
a seductive older woman in the neighborhood.   Once when an open
quarrel broke out, the boy in a temper smashed some dishes. Mrs.
E. could not accept the idea that his subsequent behavior--vacuum-
ing his room and making friendly overtures to his siblings--signi-
fied an apology.

       Lowell, resentful of his mother's suspicions, aired his
grievances to the worker.   He told her of his job in the school
cafeteria, which he found enjoyable and handled conscientiously--but
he would not tell his mother.   The worker agreed to hold some of
his earnings for graduation expenses, for his fears that Mrs. E.
might take the money from him were not without foundation.   Although both mother and son were reluctant to make the first conciliatory move, the worker over a period of time was able to help them
achieve a relaxation of hostilities.   When Lowell--although still
harboring resentment--responded to his mother's buying him clothing by informing her of his job, she, very pleased, began putting
aside some of her own money for his graduation requirements.
The situation improved so much that the mother could speak favorably of the boy to the worker, telling of his interest in plants and
animals.   This information was shared with the school as a possible
aid in planning Lowell's future job training or employment.

       While the tensions with Lowell were at their height, Mrs.
E. revealed some problems concerning Stanley, the second son.
An energetic go-getter, he had shined shoes in the past but--teased
by his peers--switched to a paper route.   His success was praised
by his mother, but she became alarmed when the boy brought home
objects that she was sure cost more than he had earned.   He had
also broken into an abandoned building, evidently as a result of the
heckling of his brother and friends.   Although the authorities did
not bring action against him, Mrs. E. considered this a serious offense.   Finding this boy less trouble than Lowell, she was better
able to deal with him directly.   She talked with Stanley about his
break-in, and her subsequent discussion with the worker revealed

that she handled this competently. On the other hand, when the
boy earned nine dollars shoveling snow, she took five dollars from
him and distributed some of it among the other children. The worker used this incident to discuss with Mrs. E. the effect of her actions on Stanley's initiative, suggesting that both boys were at an
age where they needed to exercise some personal control over their
earnings. The point appeared to Mrs. E. to be well taken. She
eased her control, there was a noticeable improvement in their relationship, and there were no further appearances of costly objects.

Some of Mrs. E's feelings remained forbidden territory.
She would not discuss her feelings about being a Negro, although
she dropped subtle hints, such as when she described her light-
skinned mother. Another clue was that Debbie upset her very much
by wishing to be white in order to "be beautiful," accusing her
mother of being responsible for her blackness. Mrs. E. made it
clear to the worker that there could be no discussion on this subject. However, once during an interview Mrs. E. contrasted her
positive relationship to the white caseworker with the negative relationships she had had with other whites such as the landlords and
merchants that had exploited her.

The subject of sex and her relationships with men also remained closed. Some details of her past were divulged when she
was in a reminiscent mood; from these it was evident that Mrs. E.
considered all men "lazy, no good, don't want to work" types. She
did tell the worker of being raped at the age of thirteen by one of
her mother's boarders. Her marriage to this man, when she was
only fifteen, was engineered by her grandmother after Mrs. E. gave
birth to her second child. She made it very clear that the subject
was so painful she would not tolerate further discussion. During
the period that Mrs. E. was undecided about marrying George, the
worker repeatedly attempted to get her to examine her feelings and
attitudes about men. Mrs. E. would only go so far as to admit
that her relationships had included "sex;" she would not evaluate her
behavior as it affected herself or her children. A few months after
her break-up with George, Mrs. E. casually revealed that she was
maintaining a friendship with a man she had known for several

years. She continued to disparage men in general, letting the worker know she was being careful not to get "involved"--her term for having sexual relations. Not at all sure about her feelings toward her current male friend, she decided to postpone serious consideration until he got a divorce.

The worker then began to prepare Mrs. E. for the termination of NIP treatment, six months away. The process started with sessions devoted to joint stock-taking. When Mrs. E. commented on the feeling of security that her long reliance on the worker had given her, she was encouraged to examine her own growth. To her surprise, she saw that she had been doing very well on her own. The next interviews were spaced more widely; Mrs. E. was assured that after termination she could see her worker at the agency, if necessary. Interestingly enough, Mrs. E. then began to act as though she were searching for a worker substitute; in her church, particularly, she became closely attached to various workers. Some appointments were missed now, and occasionally Mrs. E. scheduled another activity at the same time. On one occasion, calling about a cancelled meeting, she left the most organized message the worker had ever received from her. She told the receptionist there was no cause for alarm, that she was breaking the appointment to attend a school play in which her children were performing. This was in sharp contrast to her behavior in the first year of treatment; then every phone call invariably meant another crisis.

In this terminal period the daughter-in-law's situation, once more acute, was brought to court. Mrs. E., although exercising more control, could not completely divorce herself from the situation. She did however take two noteworthy steps. First, she discussed with her own children why she had to help care for Thomas. They accepted her explanation, showing concern for the little boy. Secondly, Mrs. E. had a talk with Shirley, suggesting that she seek help from the family agency. In discussing the situation with the worker, Mrs. E. affirmed that her first duty was to her own children.

Lowell's graduation was attended by a proud mother, whose

more relaxed attitude had been in evidence for a number of months.
She could verbalize her feeling that he had achieved a level of maturation that called for a loosening of the tight control she had attempted to exercise. In her two final contacts with the worker,
she told of being busily engaged getting Carla ready for camp, of
making arrangements to have three of the children baptized, and of
enrolling in an adult literacy class recently launched in the community.

Table 7 below shows the categories aligned for purposes of
evaluation at the end of the third period, the final ten months of
treatment.

Table 7
Final Profile of the E. Family

Category	Rating after 24 months of treatment	Rating after 34 months of treatment
Economic Practices	Marginal (4)	Above marginal (5)
Individual Adjustment and Behavior	Above marginal (5)	Above marginal (5)
Care and Training of Children	Above marginal (5)	Near adequate (6)
Family Relationships and Unity	Above marginal (5)	Near adequate (6)
Health Conditions and Practices	Above marginal (5)	Near adequate (6)
Home and Household Practices	Near adequate (6)	Near adequate (6)
Relationship to Worker	Near adequate (6)	Adequate (7)
Use of Community Resources	Near adequate (6)	Adequate (7)
Social Activities	Near adequate (6)	Adequate (7)

By the end of treatment, Economic Practices rose to an
above marginal rating. Early in the final period Mrs. E. had begun to demonstrate better control over financial management, an
achievement she continued to maintain. With this gain all nine categories of family functioning reached a rating of above marginal or
higher. Of the four key areas that were at the above marginal
rating, only one remained at that same level, Individual Behavior

and Adjustment. Mrs. E. demonstrated individual growth in a variety of role performances--as homemaker, mother, and community member. This was not accompanied by corresponding growth in
scalable quantity for the other family members, so the overall category of Individual Adjustment and Behavior remained unchanged.
The other three categories that were rated above marginal and in
need of strengthening at the end of the previous treatment period
moved to a rating of near adequate. Among these, the gain in
Care and Training of Children was accounted for by Mrs. E's increased attention to her children's physical and emotional needs.
With the improvement in interpersonal relations and the establishment of a demonstrable family solidarity, Family Relationships and
Unity registered a gain of one scale step. The third of these categories, Health Conditions and Practices, also showed a one-step
gain. Although Mrs. E. was still somewhat resistive when her own
health was involved, she tried to overcome this tendency and followed through on personal care; moreover, she attended to the children's health problems capably.

Four categories at the beginning of this treatment period
stood at the near adequate level. One of these--Home and Household Practices--remained static. While Mrs. E. had reached this
high level in the previous period and maintained it, two weaknesses
retarded further movement. Her sociability attracted a heavy flow
of visitors, who informally dropped in at all hours. Also, her
habit of collecting clothes, household linens and useless bric-a-brac
continued to clutter up her home.

The other categories that were at the near adequate level all
moved to adequate: Relationship to Worker, Use of Community Resources and Social Activities. As described earlier in detail, Mrs.
E. reached the peak of achievement in her now adequate use of the
counselling relationship. She also reached out to and made full use
of a wide variety of community resources and social programs,
both for herself and the children.

Implications of the E. Case

When we first saw the E's, a relatively typical multi-prob-

lem family, they had just been put on a more secure income base
than they had ever known. Despite this, Mrs. E's ability to function was so poor that it was obviously impossible for her to make
even a marginal adjustment on her own. Furthermore, while she
had some knowledge of resources and was willing to use them, there
had been no alteration in the pattern of family malfunctioning. The
family had developed a mode of adaptation that probably could not
be radically modified or even altered appreciably by three years of
treatment. With the possible exception of the youngest child, all
family members had suffered years of deprivation; the effects were
so deeply ingrained that we seriously questioned whether they could
be ameliorated.

What, then, were the gains that might be attributed to our
investment? We would rank in first place the establishment of a
pattern for family life, with some healthy routine. In second place
would come Mrs. E's new ability to use help constructively. And
third in priority order would be her new knowledge of where to go
to get help when it is needed.

The E's reached this point only by a heavy reliance on a
number of props, some of which will continue to be needed. First
of all, they must have steady financial assistance, even though Mrs.
E. is interested in finding employment and might possibly benefit
from it psychologically. Putting aside the question of her capacity
to manage home, children and job simultaneously, we can conclude
from her health problems that she will probably never be financially
independent.

Then there are the two boys, who in a few years will reach
an age where they will be expected to be self-supporting. Unfortunately they are ill-equipped to become independent, both because
of their history and natural endowment. Good vocational training
will be needed in order to help them become productive adults.

The girls have also suffered years of serious deprivation.
Mrs. E., as their primary figure for identification, offers a poor
model for future patterning. Though she now wishes to help the
girls avoid her many mistakes, it is doubtful that she can satisfy
their many needs. To help her cope with all the children and to

aid in her relationship with the boys, which suffers from a negative attitude toward males, Mrs. E. will need continued counselling services. There are major gains, however, in her inclination to apply to resources for help, to recognize danger signs and act quickly, and to function with increased competence in some basic areas of family living.

The E. family is representative of a whole group of multi-problem families that despite extensive treatment will undoubtedly continue to experience crises that will once more render them dependent. It is important to be clear about the nature of the crises that beset these families, because the way in which the welfare community perceives the crises has a direct bearing on the procedures adopted to treat the problem of recurrences. The crisis-dependency nature so characteristic of multi-problem families stems from both external and internal causes. The external factors are societal conditions, generally beyond the control of the family or individual, such as limited educational opportunities, unemployment or intermittent employment, economic insecurity, ghetto living, social and economic discrimination. The internal factors are the faulty perceptions or sets of attitudes, adversely affecting their performance, that multi-problem families develop through years of deprivation. Lack of occupational and social skills, poor or incomplete education, deficient health, feelings of defeat, hopelessness and lack of power are examples of internal factors. They give rise to the appearance of apathy, resignation, or indifference, and to the practices of avoiding problems as long as possible and of withdrawing in the face of frustration.

These feelings and attitudes, in turn, give rise to modes of behavior that may be expected to operate even after treatment, for the unchanged external environment must be met again. These modes of behavior must be respected if a return to pre-treatment status is to be prevented. The following approach is an attempt to meet the specific needs of multi-problem families--needs inferred from perceived behavior:

1. Multi-problem families cannot tolerate waiting. When they apply for help, they need immediate attention. This means the

community must adopt an open-door policy that insures the availability of help when the family needs it. Treated families have been
taught to recognize need and to ask for help; however, treatment
has not changed their inability to tolerate a long wait. The argument that this results in continued or increased dependency will not
solve the problem. It has already been amply demonstrated that
failure to effectively and quickly reach these families results in an
exhorbitant cost in money and human suffering, which communities
can ill afford. Furthermore, the practice of fitting them into existing methods of service, giving no consideration to their particular modes of behavior, has also been demonstrated to be a failure.

The service they may require on a self-demand basis after
intensive treatment is in no way comparable, in quality or quantity,
to what was needed before. It might be said that they have undergone partial education as a result of treatment. They can now determine what to do and where to go. If once again confused, they
must have recourse to someone who will point out the direction to
take. They will need a treatment booster shot, and at the time the
patient--not the doctor--requests it.

2. Multi-problem families need a family-centered, coordinated approach. We link these two concepts because they are inter-
related; both need to be applied at the onset of contact. Multi-problem families, even those who have been given intensive treatment,
are poorly equipped to fit their problems to specialized functions or
services. They are apt to get discouraged and give up what seems
the bewildering process of finding the correct resource. They need
support from one agency that will take primary responsibility and
formulate a complete picture of their complex problems and needs.
These families can make full use of services only when they have
the security of a worker that they know, who listens to the whole
story and then structures the required course. This worker, whom
we may term an anchor man, may have to smooth the way, explain
complicated concepts or procedures, and give the encouragement
that is especially needed with clients who are so inarticulate. Because these clients do not volunteer important information or readily
reveal material essential for making a proper referral or treatment

plan, the family-centered approach becomes a necessity. Very often, contacts with several family members may be needed to get necessary information.

Even when referrals are accomplished, it is still necessary for one agency to remain in contact and oversee results--in effect, carry on a coordinating function. When complications arise, for whatever reasons, the coordinating agency must take the initiative in attempting to solve the difficulties. There are no winners in this situation if, in the face of legitimate need for service, the client withdraws.

3. Finally, the effectiveness of treatment to multi-problem families will depend heavily upon the existence of community-wide planning. The numerous agencies and institutions called upon to render service can operate with maximum effectiveness only when clearly understood community-wide guidelines exist and there is general support of procedures and policies. Machinery is required to insure that the responsibility for treating these families is equitably and appropriately distributed.

In summarizing our work with individuals and families, we once again stress that the expectation of completely solving their problems and thus removing them from the multi-problem category is completely unrealistic. Such a goal does not take into account the undermined base which characterizes them, or the relatively late point in family life at which treatment is given. It has been demonstrated, however, that these families may be brought to the point where crises occur less frequently, with a consequent reduction in the extreme disruption that these upheavals occasion. While these families will not entirely overcome their cyclical pattern of functioning, treatment--promptly given when requested--can help them avoid apathy and the downward spiral into total disorganization.

Notes

1. Because of client attrition (see Chapter 15) only 30 families were included in the evaluation study.

2. L. L. Geismar and Michael A. La Sorte, Understanding the Multi-Problem Family, A Conceptual Analysis and

Exploration in Early Identification. (New York, Association Press, 1964.) Chapters 2 and 3. See also
other references, dealing with the technique of measurement, cited in footnotes further on in this chapter
and in Chapter 15.

3. Werner W. Boehm. The Social Casework Method in
Social Work Education. A Project Report of the Cur-
riculum Study, Vol. X, (New York, Council on Social
Work Education, 1959) p. 44.

4. We shall cite here some of the most relevant of these
publications: Frances H. Scherz, "What is Family
Centered Casework?" Social Casework, Vol. 34, No.
8, Oct. 1953, pp. 343-349; Alice Overton, "Serving
Families Who Don't Want Help," Social Casework,
Vol. 34, No. 7, July, 1953, pp. 304-309; Elliott
Studt, "An Outline for Study of Social Authority Factors
in Casework," Social Casework, Vol. 35, No. 6, June
1954, pp. 231-238; Charlotte S. Henry, "Motivation
for Using Casework Services: Motivation in Non-Volun-
tary Clients," Social Work, Vol. 39, No. 2 and 3,
Feb.-March 1958, pp. 130-137; Berta Fantl, "Integrating Psychological Social and Cultural Factors in As-
sertive Casework," Social Casework, Vol. 3, No. 4,
October 1958, pp. 30-37; New York City Youth Board,
Reaching the Unreached, A Study of Service to Families
and Children, New York, 1958; Helen Hallinan, "Coordinating Agency Efforts in Behalf of the Hard-to-
Reach Family," Social Casework, Vol. 40, No. 1, Jan.
1959, pp. 9-17; Katherine H. Tinker, "Casework With
Hard-to-Reach Families," American Journal of Ortho-
psychiatry, Vol. 29, No. 1, Jan. 1959, pp. 165-171;
Alice Overton, "Taking Help From Our Clients," So-
cial Work, Vol. 5, No. 2, April 1960, pp. 42-50;
Violet G. Bemmels, "Seven Fighting Families," Social
Work, Vol. 5, No. 1, Jan. 1960, pp. 91-99; Janet E.
Weinandy, Families Under Stress, (Syracuse, Youth
Development Center, 1962.)

5. St. Paul, Minn., Family-Centered Project, Greater St.
Paul Community Chest and Councils, Inc., March,
1959.

6. L.L. Geismar and Beverly Ayres. Patterns of Change
in Problem Families. St. Paul, Minn., Family-Centered Project, 1959, p. 2.

7. L.L. Geismar and Beverly Ayres. Measuring Family
Functioning, A Manual on a Method for Evaluating the
Social Functioning of Disorganized Families. (St. Paul,
Minn., Family-Centered Project, 1960). See also
L.L. Geismar and Michael A. La Sorte, Understand-

ing the Multi-Problem Family. (New York, Association Press, 1964). L. L. Geismar and Beverly Ayres. "A Method for Evaluating the Social Functioning of Families Under Treatment," Social Work, Vol. 4, No. 1, 1959, pp. 102-108. L. L. Geismar, M. La Sorte, and B. Ayres. "Measuring Family Disorganization," Marriage and Family Living, Vol. 24, No. 1, 1962, pp. 51-56.

Chapter 7
An Open-Door Casework Service

From the very beginning of operations it was generally assumed by the NIP staff that there existed in Farnam Courts a population in need of casework services that was considerably larger than
the thirty to forty multi-problem families with which we were working. Several factors led us to this belief. In the first place, the
two surveys that had been conducted--the pre-NIP community study
and a later, more precise survey--had found 10 to 15 percent of
the families in Farnam Courts to be multi-problem. This constituted a considerably higher ratio than that found in total urban populations.[1] The neighborhood was, after all, composed entirely of
poverty-stricken people, a population perpetuated by the eligibility
requirements for low-cost, federally subsidized housing. The rigid
housing policy in effect at that time made it impossible for a turnover to alter the low economic status of the tenancy. Since economically deprived families have proven most vulnerable in the past,
we expected that under stress a number of these families, functioning on the margins of adequacy, would become multi-problem unless
intervention was forthcoming. We had no way of identifying the
families that were in danger of becoming multi-problem, but we
hoped that a neighborhood-wide casework service could serve as an
effective deterrent. We conceived of a service where the worker
would act as an enabler, helping families deal with problems as
they arose, guiding them to the proper resources and insuring their
adequate use before complete family disorganization could set in.

Before instituting this service, however, we initiated a variety of actions designed to show us the extent to which this larger
population needed service, the kind of service required, and the
methods we would have to use to reach this type of client.

In the first four months of the pilot program, the Director

162

met with as many of the tenants as possible. Approximately fifty
home visits were made to tenants that had been active in the pre-
NIP Tenants' Council. Twenty mothers who sporadically attended
the well-baby clinic in the Administration Building also were interviewed. Social interaction was observed monthly at the bingo
games in the social hall of the Administration Building, where thirty-
five women were regularly in attendance. Moreover, all chance
meetings with people--on the premises, in the halls, at the rent
office--were used to publicize our interest in "giving help with problems."

From these contacts there emerged a picture of a population
that had many characteristics in common with multi-problem families. The most striking was a pronounced ineptness in talking and
dealing with each other and in maintaining social relations. Frustration and hostility, whatever their sources, lay near the surface
and were frequently vented on friends. For example, one or another of a group of five women who were intimate daily companions
would frequently reveal a secret confidence loudly in public gather-
ings, to the embarrassment of her confiding friend. A feud would
ensue, each side soliciting partisans and spreading gossip about the
other, pursuing vengeance with such thoroughness that even the children were enlisted in the hate campaign.

Ineptness with "outsiders"--community representatives, service personnel, housing authority employees--was equally apparent,
and sometimes crippling because of its severity. Many minor problems were allowed to become acute because the people practiced
"avoidance," hoping that things would turn out all right by themselves. For example, important letters were left unread[2] or
shelved, with the result that damaging actions would be taken against
them. Furniture would be repossessed; fines would be levied for
late rent payments; wages would be garnisheed; litigations would be
started against them. Letters from schools, clinics or hospitals
were often ignored and appointments were repeatedly missed. Such
behavior understandably aroused ill feeling in the community.
Aware of this, the people practiced further avoidance, even when a
service such as medical care was greatly needed, because they an-

ticipated a hostile reception.

As we repeatedly met many of the same people in the course of these early explorations, picking up clear indications of their problems at the same time, we did some preliminary testing of their capacity to use referral information. Investigating their use of the services to which we had sent them, we found that these families-- like those termed multi-problem--were unable or unwilling to follow through and initiate contact with community resources, even when direction was given.

With these preliminary findings supporting our assumption about neighborhood needs, we inaugurated in September, 1960, a casework service available to any family living in the housing project, excepting the multi-problem families slated for inclusion in the experimental treatment sample. The Housing Authority was enlisted as co-sponsor and contributed 2/5 of the salary for a worker, who would receive casework supervision from the NIP staff. Hopefully, this would insure continuity within a permanently established community structure should the program prove effective. Budgetary considerations made it necessary to use an untrained worker for the position; we therefore planned to limit the type of service to be offered in accord with the expected abilities of untrained workers. Our plan was to offer the tenants information, advice and direction about resources through an easily accessible worker, who would refer only upon evidence of client motivation. Contacts were expected to be of short duration, limited to a few months at the most even in those instances where exploration revealed complicated, serious situations warranting referral for long-term counselling. The new service was widely publicized. Newsletters were sent to each tenant and explanatory letters were mailed to the various community agencies and institutions, so as to encourage referrals.

We soon found that easy accessibility, publicity, and alert, sensitive personnel were but the first steps in our program of help. They served to expose problems that had been hidden, but they did not necessarily insure the use of the services we offered.

The office of the Farnam Courts Social Worker was located just inside the main door to the Administration Building, and every

tenant had to pass it in order to pay rent or see the housing staff.
It was small and poorly ventilated; whenever possible the door was
left open. A sign on the door gave the worker's name and position. We soon found that many clients approached help of this kind
very indirectly. Those who came voluntarily would often stop by
the open door, pretending to linger for a chat while on their way to
the manager's office. After an exchange of pleasantries the worker
would explain her job, sometimes in response to a tenant's questions but often on her own initiative. When the worker would indicate her availability, the tenant would react with feigned surprise,
denying any problems, but at the same time edging into the office
to sit down "for a little rest." In most of these cases the tenant
would eventually get around to indicating that a "little problem" or
a "worry" was on his mind; in this way a service need was established. In some instances, however, the tenant would continue to
deny any need for help, parting with the remark that the worker
would be kept in mind "if something comes up." Some of these tenants did return later after thinking it over, having found a problem
for which the worker's guidance might be of help.

In the same indirect way, tenants active in the NIP programs
would air identifiable problems to the group leaders, who would interpret the social worker's job and suggest an application for help.
In some instances there would be no follow-through by the tenant,
although the same problems would be discussed at each meeting between the group leader and the tenant. Some tenants who accepted
referrals would tell the worker that they had no idea why they were
sent to her. Then they would engage again in a rambling conversation before they could respond to the worker's encouragement and
discuss any problems.

An entirely different situation was presented by those tenants
brought to our attention by concerned neighbors. These were the
ill, the aged, those who lived alone; they needed service but required a worker to initiate home visits. There were a few families
where the mother could not leave the apartment because of illness
or the presence of many very young children. In these cases, too,
we decided to take the initiative, even though many times the mother

was hesitant about asking for help.

These early experiences made us alter our original approach. We abandoned our plans for a purely "voluntary" service when we found so much need coupled with such a widespread inability to initiate application and to follow through on service. While not insisting that people accept our service, we did institute and persist in practicing a systematic, intensive, reaching-out approach. All of the "inside staff"--Housing Authority personnel, Visiting Nurses and NIP workers--were given direction in exploring problems and in determining the depth of client concern. The staff was requested to encourage tenants to get help whenever indications of problems were revealed. They were also asked to be on the alert for evidence of reluctance and to consult with the Director when they had questions about whether or how to proceed. If referrals appeared to be accepted by the tenant, the referring staff member subsequently checked on them; in those instances where the tenant did not follow through, the staff member to whom the problem had been revealed would approach the tenant to further clarify the situation. If the problem persisted and the reasons for reluctance could not be determined, either a personal introduction to the social worker or a home visit was offered. This was coupled with the explanation that here was an opportunity to talk in greater detail with a person especially equipped to help. The tenant at the same time was assured that he was free to decide whether he wanted any service.

This approach proved to be very successful in gaining the trust of tenants and in attending to numerous minor, episodic problems. An appreciable number of families with more serious, complex situations were discovered in this way; these were retained for longer periods of treatment, as will be subsequently detailed.

This change of approach--from voluntary to reaching out-- was arrived at over a period of three-and-a-half months of experimentation. Our administrative structure was such that the Director could be the central repository for the experiences of all staff members, regardless of their diverse functions. This greatly facilitated the accumulation of information about emerging patterns of behavior, expedited the sharing of this information with the staff, and allowed for program flexibility.

Information was gathered in an informal, unsystematized way from day to day. It is gratifying, therefore, in examining the records long after they were written, to find documented substantiation for the radical shift made in treatment procedure--a shift that was originally instituted on the basis of what might be called educated guesses. Case records for the period covering the first three-and-a-half months of service by the Farnam Courts social worker are analyzed in Table 8 below.

Table 8

Service by the Farnam Courts Social Worker for the First 3-1/2 Months

No. of Cases	Source of Referral
12	Self
5	NIP staff
3	Community agencies
2	Neighbors
2	Visiting Nurse Assoc.
1	Housing Authority
25	

It is significant that our open-door policy and easy accessibility brought in only twelve cases, or slightly less than half the clients, on their own initiative. In nineteen cases with a minimal contact of three full interviews, at least one follow-up home visit was required to encourage continuance of service for serious problems. It made little difference whether the family was referred or applied for help on their own; the need for follow-up home visits existed in both instances. Eight, or roughly one-third of the cases, required 50 percent or more home visits, in contacts that ran for at least eight interviews. This latter group was composed of (1) aged, ill, lone residents; (2) one-parent families where illness or many young children made it impossible for the woman to come to the office; (3) emerging multi-problem families that required on-going treatment.

These early experiences necessitated the change mentioned

earlier--namely, the introduction of an intensive, reaching-out method for the larger neighborhood population similar to the one used
with multi-problem families.

Our second change in approach stemmed from the large number
of near multi-problem families appearing in the growing caseload of the
Farnam Courts neighborhood worker, requiring her to change her service emphasis from environmental intervention to more intensive family-
centered treatment whenever indicated.

Selection and Training of Workers

In the three years that this service was offered, each year
saw a new worker in the position. Two workers with B.A. degrees
from liberal arts colleges had had about nine months' experience as
workers in public assistance agencies, while the third had completed
an undergraduate social work curriculum that included one semester
working in a juvenile court. All three workers had the following in
common: they were married women under 25 years of age; they
were able to project warmth and show concern for people; they were
especially interested in deprived people; they were energetic and
flexible, enthusiastic about the job, and with a natural flair for the
work. Strongly motivated to learn, they were aware of their limited experience and lack of training and sought and used supervision
constructively.

These women were closely supervised by professionals with
many years of experience in treating severely deprived, lower-class
families. The workers were required to write and maintain case
records, to furnish statistics and work schedules. Casework principles were taught them in supervisory conferences, using their own
case records and various reading assignments in books and periodi-
cals. In addition they attended general NIP staff meetings and the
seminars held for the workers who were carrying the experimental
multi-problem caseload. Attendance at local and regional social
welfare meetings, conferences, etc., was encouraged, and expenses
were subsidized whenever possible. (Qualitative assessment of their
work will be given in Chapter 13).

Extent to Which Service Was Used
and Length of Contacts

In all, 105 familes[3] came to the neighborhood worker for
service, either by direct application or through referral.   In Table
9 below, which shows the sources of referrals, the Housing Authority and the Visiting Nurse Association are set apart from Community Agencies.   Both operated regularly on the project premises; as
a result, they had more exposure and they were able to identify
need more quickly than other community agencies.   Furthermore,
they had a close working relationship with NIP, which expedited
consultation and referral.

Table 9

Sources of Referrals to the Neighborhood Worker

Source	Number of Cases
Self	47
NIP	25
Housing Authority Staff	10
Neighbors	9
Visiting Nurse Association	4
Community Agencies	10
	105

From Table 9 it may be seen that 55 percent of the cases were referred, the same ratio between self-initiative and referral as in the
first few months of service.   Of these referred by others, all but
ten were identified by personnel working very closely with the population.   Almost all of these cases required some reaching-out   in
order to establish contact.

Twelve cases were seen for one interview only.   During
these contacts the worker made one or more collateral contacts,
either to get information, to make a referral to a community agency,
or to pave the way for the client's return where there was a strained
client-agency relationship.   Ninety-three cases were given continued
service for periods ranging from one to thirty-six months.   Table
10 gives the distribution of cases by duration of contact.

Table 10

Distribution of Cases by
Duration of Contact

No. of Cases	Duration of Contact	Mean No. of Visits	
		Office	Home
12	1 interview	6	6
30	up to 1 month	2	1
15	1 - 2 months	4. 5	2
11	2 - 3 months	5	2. 5
15	4 - 6 months	5. 6	8. 7
13	7 - 9 months	20. 6	10
3	10 - 12 months	6. 6	30
5	13 - 24 months	30	56
1	36 months	4	70
105			

The bulk of the cases, 79 percent, received treatment for a period of not more than six months; 65 percent were treated for not
more than three months. For the total number of cases, the mean
length of contact was about three and one-half months, indicating
that our assumption about need for a relatively brief treatment
period had been fairly accurate. Furthermore, an examination of
record data indicates that there was wide use of reaching-out techniques in order to connect the population with service. For example, in the 56 cases where contact was for no more than three
months, 91 home visits and a minimum of 93 worker-initiated contacts[4] with various community agencies and institutions were required in addition to 183 office visits. Out of the 105 there were
only 26 cases (25%) that came exclusively to the office (including
six that were one-interview contacts).

Nature of the Problems

    We have not attempted to use the conventional method of dif-
ferentiating "presenting problems" from those problems uncovered
during exploration and/or on-going counselling, because our principle interest lies in the entire array of problems identified by the

worker in the process of treatment intervention.   These problems
are listed in Table 11 below.

Table 11

Distribution of 105 Problems Identified
During Treatment

Problem	Number
Financial	55
Physical Illness	30
Marital	28
Personality (adult)	23
Unemployment	20
Behavior (child)	16
Parent-child Relations	15
Child Care	14
Language	13
Homemaker Needed	11
Debts	10
Housing	10
Drinking	7
Desertion	6
Law Violations (arrests)	6
Mental Illness	6
Mental Retardation	4
Litigation	4
Non-Support	4
Child Neglect	1

As might be expected, financial problems were dominant. In
general, they were related to attempts to spread marginal incomes
over basic family needs.   There was insufficient money for medical
care, clothing, and basic household supplies; debts and rent arrears
were often chronic; homemaking services, even when desperately
needed, could not be afforded.   In an appreciable number of cases
unskilled or semi-skilled men, employed full time, could not earn
enough to cover the minimal basic needs of their families.   Another
group of financial problems was caused by seasonal employment;

there were also some cases of destitution due to desertion.   Special needs were found in a number of families already receiving
welfare assistance--the client had been unable to make a request or
the allotment had not been adjusted.   There were a few cases where
gambling or drinking had resulted in deprivation.   Another type of
difficulty was caused by the common practice of using "food money"
to cover sudden emergencies.

Financial assistance was given to thirty-five families, in
small amounts at a time.   Emergency needs in hardship cases were
covered, while continuing efforts were made to establish a more
stable arrangement with the agencies responsible for financial assistance.

While the high incidence of medical problems is related to
marginal income, other factors are also involved.   Fear, superstition, avoidance, awe of clinic and hospital procedures--all operate
to hamper good health practices.   Only a small minority of clients
were able to take advantage of information about available medical
service or follow through on a referral without the intervention of
the worker.

In a majority of the cases presenting marital conflicts there
were three or more other serious problems present.   The impact
of unemployment, under-employment, financial crisis precipitated by
illnesses, etc., was quickly reflected in the marital situation, and
it often seemed to set off a chain reaction of adverse affects on individual adjustment, parent-child relations, behavior of children,
and child care.

Problems of child care arose in a number of large families
with many young children, usually when illness of the mother and/or
several of the children occurred simultaneously.   It was not uncommon to find three or four children all needing bed care or clinic visits, while the mother was ill or convalescing, the father was in
jeopardy of losing his job if he stayed home to help, and no friends
or relatives were available to appreciably relieve the situation.   The
need for homemaking services was about equally divided between
these cases and the aged, many of whom were restricted in physical activity because of illness.   For the most part, the category of

"housing problems" referred to those situations where there was
medical reason for requiring a change of apartment--a ground-floor
unit for example.

Nature of Service Given

To help with the problems enumerated above, the following
six services were rendered by the Farnam Courts social worker:

1. Advice and Information--advising on services or resources, clarifying with the client his specific need; informing him how, where and when to avail himself of help;
   explaining what is required of him.
2. Tangible Service--taking direct action with or on behalf
   of the client to insure the use of resources.
3. Counselling--engaging in a problem-solving process based
   mainly on face-to-face, verbal, client-worker interaction,
   maintained for at least two contacts.
4. Coordination--acting as liaison to insure a unified approach and the continuity of treatment where multi-agency
   contacts exist.
5. Financial Assistance--giving the client money to immediately relieve emergency or crisis situations, or to meet
   special pressing needs not covered by existing resources.
6. Interpretation--acting as interpreter for clients who do not
   speak English.

Only twelve cases confined themselves to one service, dividing themselves equally between Advice and Information and Counselling. The six cases using Advice and Information only were of
brief duration; they were further characterized by clearly identifiable needs for which resources existed and by highly motivated clients with a capacity to follow through after receiving direction from
the worker. By contrast, the six cases who used only Counselling
were retained for an extended period of time by the Farnam Courts
worker because motivation and ability to use referral were lacking.
The bulk of the cases, 93, used a combination of two or more
kinds of service. Tangible Service was rendered in 90 cases and
Counselling in 56, in combination with several other services.

While often in conjunction with other services, the fact that Tangible
Service was necessary in 90 cases supports our early assumption
that an ineptness and/or inability to connect with resources was
prevalent.

In Table 12 below, which identifies the various resources
contacted by the worker, only the initial contact in a case, per individual resource, is recorded; usually many contacts were necessary.

Table 12
Number of Worker-Initiated Contacts

Type of Resource	No. of Contacts
Welfare Departments	77
Hospitals	34
Housing Authority	31
Voluntary Family Agencies	13
Lawyers	13
Visiting Nurse Association	12
Private Physicians	11
Domestic Relations Court	9
Credit Bureau	9
Employment Resources	7
Employers	6
Vocational Rehabilitation Center	5
Children's Placement/Treatment Facilities	5
Law Enforcement Agencies	3
Board of Education	3
Neighbors	2
Minister	1

There was a high degree of relationship between the two most problematic areas--economic and health--and those resources that were
most frequently contacted by the worker--welfare departments, hospitals, physicians and nurses.

Table 12 gives a clear picture of the services we considered
of primary importance to economically deprived families.   First
was the need for a ranking of problems in order of priorities, based

either on the client's statements or on information that the worker
could gather. Secondly, there was the need for someone who would
tell the clients what resources to use, when to use them and how.
In effect, the worker was required to structure the situation by
aligning problems and relating them concretely to resources and to
be available thereafter to bridge any gaps. Tangible Services, in
combination with Counselling or Advice and Information (as we have
defined them), was the type of aid we found most universally appropriate for the majority of deprived families treated.

With one exception, the problem of a language barrier was
confined to those families that had come from Puerto Rico. While
the total Farnam Courts population was about 10 percent Puerto Rican, the Farnam Courts treatment load had 19 Puerto Rican families, or 18 percent of the 105 families. In addition to the problems
they shared with other families, there was the problem of acculturation. Language difficulties further handicapped twelve of these families, who were without relatives or friends sufficiently fluent in English to serve as interpreters. In answer to this critical need, we
attempted casework with them for one year through the use of hired
interpreters, with obvious limitations. Subsequently an administrative and research assistant fluent in Spanish joined the staff. Though
untrained, her capabilities were such that she was able to give casework services under supervision to a caseload of six to ten Puerto
Rican families for a two-year period (see Chapter 11).

By the time the open-door casework service was instituted,
the professional staff of NIP had managed to become acquainted with
almost all the population of Farnam Courts. The identification of
30 to 40 multi-problem families and of a little over 100 families in
need of short-term treatment constituted a fair estimate of the nature and scope of the need for treatment in this neighborhood. To
the extent that we can make a case for Farnam Courts being quite
representative of other low-income housing projects (see Chapters
15 and 16), we may also claim that our estimates apply to other
deprived populations living in similar housing complexes.

The six case illustrations given below, however, are selected
not for their representativeness but because they are examples of

diverse types of problem cases calling for different modes of intervention. The cases share the characteristic of limited problemicity,
i.e. problems are confined to relatively few areas of social functioning, and key members of the family show a capacity to adapt or
modify their social roles in ways that permit the family to weather
crises and move toward improved functioning. Intervention, of short
duration compared to services given multi-problem families, was
heavily focused on work with agencies and organizations upon whom
the client was dependent. One of the first tasks of the social worker was the improvement of communication between the client and
health and welfare agencies, Housing Authority, places of employment, etc. Considerable effort was directed toward modifying the
faulty perceptions of each other's role held by both agencies and clients.

Case Illustrations

As mentioned earlier in this chapter, our basic approach was
one of reaching out to the population and encouraging them to deal
with problems as they arose by making use of the casework services available within easy reach. We expected that such an approach
would relieve immediate distress within a relatively short treatment
period in a majority of cases. As predicted, 65 percent of all
cases were in treatment for less than three months. Four cases of
brief service duration have been selected to illustrate the kinds of
problems encountered and the manner in which they were treated.

Since we had only one worker serving a large population, it
was necessary to contain the number of contacts, i.e., to limit the
degree and extent of worker involvement in a given case. Despite
this attempt to be pragmatic, once the helping process was set in
motion a force was often generated that operated against any such
arbitrary cut-off point; in the course of their interaction either the
client, the worker, or both in concert, saw factors in the situation
that justified lengthier treatment. We found that it was not possible
to strictly control the treatment cut-off point. We did find it possible in most cases, however, to control the degree or depth of
worker involvement. In particular, we discouraged the treatment of
deep-seated personality problems, a policy that in itself did not

eliminate the need for relatively long-term treatment because some families had to be carried for quite a while before they reached a "safe" point and were considered able to carry on independently. Two more cases have been selected to illustrate the complications that made more extended contact necessary. In both of them there was some improved individual functioning, although the worker focused primarily upon environmental treatment and support.

The total of six examples to be presented show the extent to which our population was familiar with social agencies. At the onset of treatment, five of the six families were active with at least one agency and had been so for a significant period of time. Although only one client in six was unfamiliar with community resources, they all showed evidence of feeling "lost," of reacting with bewilderment and fright and thus becoming inept or ineffectual.

In all the cases the worker addressed herself to the immediate problem, since our purpose was to deal with emerging problems or to contain existing ones. Treatment was begun by structuring the problems and matching them to available sources of relief. The worker invested a good deal of time in dealing with environmental problems that called for a knowledgeable person who could give instruction in the kinds of resources to use, when to use them and how. Though there was some variation in its extent, "doing for and with" the client was found to be an essential part of treatment in every case. The cases that follow are described by excerpts from the case records and by summaries of those records.

The A. Case

Mr. A. - 79 years old

Mrs. A. - 78 years old

Referral and Presenting Problem

This case was referred by the Housing Authority because of low housekeeping standards, which might lead to eviction.

Worker's Report, 3/22/61:

I made a home visit. Mr. and Mrs. A. both sweet. elderly, incapacitated people. Mrs. A. is virtually crippled by arthritis. Mr. A. has a heart condition.

I suggested to them that since it is obvious that they

must have a great deal of difficulty with the cleaning, it might be possible to have someone come in to help. They were pleased with the idea.

Summary: 3/22/61 to 4/28/61

Mrs. B., welfare worker, was contacted. When told of the situation, Mrs. B. went to the A. home to discuss the possibility of having a homemaker come in. The A's got authorization from welfare to pay a homemaker. The A's had a friend whom they wished to have for the position. Should this friend not work out, Miss C., Director of Homemaking at the Family Service Agency, has been alerted to the situation and upon notification by the A's, will assist them in getting a person to do the work. Report given to Mr. D. of Housing Authority.

The A's were fairly typical of a majority of the elderly residents, who comprised almost 10 percent of the Courts population. They were estranged or isolated from their relatives and kept themselves aloof from their immediate neighbors. Frail in health, yet undemanding, it would not occur to most of them to request help and they assumed a "make do" attitude. As our service became known to the population at large, we received many messages from neighbors informing us of aged individuals in need of medical care, homemaking services, transportation to clinics, etc. Sometimes we were alerted to the need for someone to "look in" on a regular basis, to insure that the aged infirm were managing adequately. In many instances there was voluntary apportionment of aid by neighbors, but as individual family demands arose these informal arrangements could not provide the consistent attention that was needed. The answer was to assign the responsibility to one individual, and thus coordination of neighborly aid became part of the Farnam Courts social worker's job.

The B. Case

Mrs. B. - 32 years old
Alice   - 10
Edward - 9
Daniel - 3
Carl   - 6 months

On 1/11/61 worker received a phone call from Mrs. B. requesting a home visit. Mrs. B. sounded very upset and said that she was calling worker because she had nowhere else to turn.

Presenting Problem:

Someone from the Housing Authority came to her house the previous day to inform her that neither December nor January rent was paid and she must report to the Housing office immediately. Mrs. B. had a strep throat and the doctor had told her not to go out of the house. She thought that welfare had paid the December rent and at the moment she was at a loss as to what to do.

History:

Mrs. B. had remarried one year ago. This was her second marriage. According to Mrs. B., Mr. B. had been a good worker until they were married, when he turned out to be not a worker but an alcoholic. She had three children from her first marriage and one by her second. Mr. B. gave her no money for food for her children so she went to the City Attorney. At this point Mr. B. left her. She told worker that her marriage had been a terrible mistake but if she could just get this rent situation straightened out she could relax and try to forget him. Mrs. B. was very nervous during this interview.

Financial:

Mrs. B. is receiving state aid for three of the children. Mrs. C. is the state worker. Mr. B. left the home on 12/7/60. Mrs. B. spoke to Mrs. C., who promised an increase by the beginning or middle of January. In order to have her rent paid before the state increase came through, Mrs. B. went to the City Department of Welfare. The agency promised to make a home visit the next day but never did. Mrs. B. assumed that they had paid the rent until the man from the Housing Authority informed her that neither December nor January rent was paid.

Plan:

Speak to Housing Authority, City Welfare and State Welfare in an attempt to straighten out the rent problem.

Reason for Plan:

Mrs. B. was obviously sick as were two of her children. She had been told by her doctor to stay in the house and she was too confused and worried at this point to straighten out the problem herself.

Collateral Contacts:

Housing Authority--was willing to wait a few days before starting eviction procedure.

State Welfare--Mrs. C. was out ill and her supervisor was not certain as to when the increase for rent would come through.

City Welfare--spoke to supervisor, who accepted responsibility for the December rent since the home visit promised

by the agency had never been made. She said she would,
however, negotiate with the state as to who should pay the
January rent.

Mrs. B. informed of the solution. She was very relieved.

Impressions:

Mrs. B. is a large woman, who gives the impression of
being quite pleasant. She was very upset over the rent situation. Once the problem was resolved her relief was very
evident. Mrs. B. seems to function well and from my short
observation she seemed to handle her children very well.

Closing Statement:

Mrs. B. was seen in her home on 1/11/61 and 1/16/61.
Her problem was a financial one concerning rent and an adjustment in her State Welfare allotment. While she was
sick, worker supported her in her dealings with the State
and City Welfare, but when she was well, worker felt she
was capable of taking care of her affairs herself. Case
closed.

Mrs. B.'s situation illustrates the kind of interagency problem that was not at all uncommon in New Haven and that probably
occurs in many other communities where responsibility for welfare
assistance is divided between state and local agencies. The client,
caught in the middle, is usually the individual least equipped to sort
out the issues and deal with the agencies that represent such awesome authority. In this case a third agency, the Housing Authority,
was involved; most tenants do not view the Authority benignly and
seek to avoid consulting its staff, if possible. In presenting their
own situations, the general ineptness and poor public image of these
people afford them a less than fair hearing unless an agent representing some community authority intervenes in their behalf.

The C. Case

Mr. C. - 38 years old
Mrs. C. - 32
Peter -   12
James -   8
Esther -   3

Home Visit: 9/26/61

I called at the C's to talk with Mrs. C. about Esther attending Nursery School. This was part of a project-wide
visiting campaign. I noticed that Mrs. C. was bent over
when she walked and limped considerably. I asked her what
was the matter.

Mrs. C. had fallen down the stairs about two months ago but hadn't felt any pain until the next day. Then she could not sit or walk. She went to the Emergency Room at the hospital and had kept several appointments in the orthopedic clinic. She paid $1.00 for each visit, as her income is marginal. The pain lessened after they gave her therapy treatments so she was given no return appointment, but the doctor recommended a back brace. She said she couldn't afford one so the doctor said that she should wear a tight girdle. She has tried two different ones but neither has done her any good. She was just about giving up on them when I came to call. I learned that the C's have a very low income of about $2,200 a year. Mr. C. owns a dump truck and does odd jobs; he is in business for himself. I said that if she would like I would inquire as to the possibility of obtaining a brace at less than the $50 price she had been quoted. She seemed very relieved and pleased about this.

9/28/61

I visited Mrs. C. briefly to ask her a few pertinent questions. I found that she has never received welfare assistance and that her husband is a veteran, having served eight years in the Army. I thought possibly she could obtain help from the Soldiers, Sailors and Marine Fund but this proved not possible.

9/29/61--Collateral

I called the Department of Welfare, which referred me to the Rehabilitation Center. I called there and learned that they could help Mrs. C. at no cost if she could provide information as to her low income. Mrs. C. was also to provide a prescription for the brace from the hospital and come in to be fitted for brace.

10/4/61

Home visit to Mrs. C. No one was home.

Letter sent Mrs. C. (see copy filed).

10/8/61

In response to my letter of 10/5/61 Mrs. C. in the office with Esther. The information pertaining to the brace was relayed to her. She seemed in her own reserved way to be very grateful. She said she would act upon this information right away.

Esther has come to the Nursery School the last two times and both she and her mother say she likes it a lot. Her mother said she will come on a regular basis. Case closed.

This example of the reaching-out approach showed the worker picking up an observed problem and introducing the idea of remedial action. It also demonstrated the common client character-

istic of "putting up with" a problem, once a course of treatment
has been followed as far as his limited grasp of resources allows.
It is noteworthy that the worker, with her considerably more sophisticated knowledge, had to explore three community resources before arriving at a solution.   Even then, several steps were required (proof of low income; medical prescription) before it was possible for the client to receive the medical aid.

The D. Case

Mrs. D. - 45 years old
George - 18-1/2

2/9/61

Mrs. D. came to my office of her own accord.

Presenting Problem:

Mrs. D. is receiving State Welfare assistance.   Mrs. D's
son, George, had been working for a store after school and
on Saturdays for the past three years.   A month or so ago
he gave three cartons of cigarettes to a brother of a friend
of his, expecting the boy to pay later.   The boy never paid
and the boss called him into the office and questioned him
about the cigarettes.   The management took the money from
George's pay and George quit--supposedly because he hadn't
meant to steal the cigarettes.   The problem is that Mrs. D.
needs the money he used to bring home so has asked the
welfare for an increase.   She did not tell the welfare worker
the real story of why her son is no longer working because
she does not know her, feels ashamed and terribly upset
over the whole affair and is afraid that welfare would refuse
to help her.

According to Mrs. D., George was always a good boy and
steady worker.   Then a couple of months ago he "turned bad
all of a sudden."

Mrs. D. spoke very haltingly and needed much encouragement.   She said that George is afraid to go back to work
there now because if something is missing from the store
they will blame him, even though one of the store owners
told Mrs. D. that he would be willing to take George back.

When I asked her if her son is interested in working anywhere now, she said that she didn't know.   Through direct
questioning I learned that she and her son are not on speaking terms, that George has a terrible temper, and that he is
conceited.   Mrs. D. went on to say that he comes home
from school, grabs a bite to eat and runs out with his
friends, then comes home late at night.   Mrs. D. then hur-
riedly added that he doesn't "hang around with rough boys."

Impressions:

Mrs. D. is only 45 years old but appears to be much older. She gives the impression, both physically and through her speech, of being a frail older woman. She is obviously not in control of her boy. The D's are divorced and Mr. D. has remarried. Mrs. D. seems to be on poor terms with her ex-husband. When asked if perhaps her husband might be able to help her discipline the boy, she said he would just blame her for her son's trouble.

I have the impression that this woman is frightened because of her son's trouble but that she has had trouble coping with her boy for a long time.

Plan:

Contact welfare and clarify situation. Mrs. D. is terribly upset over George's behavior and although she wants the truth out in the open she is afraid to tell State worker.

I called Mrs. B., State Welfare worker, and told her of Mrs. D's visit to my office and the true story. I explained why I was calling instead of Mrs. D. Mrs. B. said that Mrs. D. should have told her the truth but that she was glad to hear the story and she had some doubt as to their eligibility for an increase. Apparently the previous welfare worker had told Mrs. D. and George of the state law that says that working children must give 2/3 of their income to their parents. According to the welfare record both Mrs. D. and George were very upset about this news and considered it to be unfair. The State, not knowing that George had been fired, felt that he had quit so as not to have to give his mother 2/3 of his income.

On 2/13/61 Mrs. D. came to my office per appointment. I told her of my conversation with Mrs. B. and we discussed the "2/3 law." She felt it unfair so our discussion revolved around the reality of it.

Mrs. D. said that she had no money for the rest of the month so I suggested that she call her welfare worker, Mrs. B. She agreed to do so and said she would also talk to the store about her son's status. I asked her to let me know what she found out.

4/3/61

Mrs. D. returned to the office this date. She revealed that she and George have at least begun talking about his situation. She complains that her son is not working and doesn't like to go to school. She stated he stays out of school more than he goes, claiming he is sick, but later in the day goes out with his friends. Mrs. D. says George owes money to people but she doesn't know to whom or how much. He said at one point he would go back to the store to work but missed the appointment made with the management. He kept the next appointment but one partner refused to take him back. (Mrs. D. said of this uncooperative man, "Nobody can get along with him.") The only improvement in this situation is that George and Mrs. D. can discuss it.

Mrs. D. told me that sometimes the boy upsets her so much that she tells him to go to his father and live. She added that she doesn't mean it when she says it.

I had suggested that George come to see me but since he refuses to talk with me, a referral to the school guidance counsellor will be attempted. If George could get some direction toward possible jobs after graduation, both he and the family situation would be helped.

Collateral Contact:

Theodore Watson High School--I spoke to Guidance Counselor, who said that George has passing grades; he has been absent a great deal and though he has always had a poor attendance record, he has been in no trouble.

On the grounds of Mrs. D's concern she agreed to refer the case to the School Social Worker. The plan is that the worker will speak to him about his attendance and then lead into a discussion of employment and family problems.

4/15/61

Mrs. D. came to my office to inform me of the following:

1. She had received an increase from State Welfare.

2. Her son George has returned to work at the store and Welfare had been notified of this fact.

3. Mrs. D. is getting married in a few months. Her son likes the man she is going to marry, whom she describes as being very nice. He owns his own store and has given her an engagement ring. She has known him for 8 months.
Case closed.

Mrs. D's case illustrates a client dilemma and a reaction to it that we encountered frequently. She was already dependent upon a public agency when her son's behavior increased her dependency. In order to resolve her problem she had to make disclosures that she was sure would be prejudicial to her interests or, at the very least, reflect negatively upon her. She felt guilty and ashamed at the same time that she felt helpless and trapped. We found an acute fear of being "cut off" by welfare among most clients in these circumstances. While most of them were willing to accept responsibility for past infractions and attempted to subsequently modify their behavior, they were generally unable to make the necessary disclosures to agencies without an intervener to lend support and guidance.

In the case just cited, George's work record indicated that
he had some real motivation; referral to the school social worker
was an attempt to provide him with a sound source of guidance,
previously lacking.

The G. Case

Mr. G.	- 40 years old	Bob	- 6 years old
Mrs. G.	- 25	Ruth	- 5
Larry	- 8	John	- 3
Betsy	- 7	Albert	- 1
		Roy	- 1 month

10/13/60

Mrs. G. came to worker's office this date with a problem about her rent. Mr. G. has been unemployed for 16
months. Financial assistance to the family is divided between the City and State Welfare Departments, but one department has not forwarded its share of the rent for four
months. Since it was general policy of this agency to include rent in the supplementary check, worker wondered why
Mrs. G. had not been receiving this. It was Mrs. G's
feeling that a month-to-month arrangement was being used
because "they think" her husband would go to work and not
notify the Welfare Department, though maybe "they have other reasons."

Upon inquiring, worker found out that Mr. G. had been
working steadily in a foundry but had gotten "pneumonia of
the muscles" and had been advised by the doctor that he
could no longer do this type of work. "The man needs to
find light work," but had found this impossible. Mrs. G.
told worker that when she first applied for welfare, eligibility had been made contingent upon her willingness to prosecute her husband for non-support. In desperation she had
gone to the City Attorney, who was convinced that her husband had made honest efforts to locate work and by his intervention, eligibility had been established.

Worker contacted the welfare department and learned that
a departmental administrative tie-up had occurred but had
just been resolved and a check for the four months' rent arrears was now being forwarded. In the future Mrs. G.
would receive the rent allotment in her regular supplementary
check.

Mrs. G. was notified of the new plan and told what the
tie-up had been.

Summary of contacts 11/7/60 - 2/27/61

Mrs. G. seen 3 times at home. Mr. G. was seen 7
times in the office. Worker saw Mrs. G. at home, because
her large family of young children and the recent birth of

her seventh child made office visits impossible. Mr. G's
health and employment problems furnished the basis for on-
going contact. The worker noted that Mrs. G. was an
"easy-going", "good-natured" mother who, despite a very
overcrowded apartment and many responsibilities, maintained
a fine sense of humor, was an attentive mother, and had
much affection and respect for her husband. She told the
worker of Mr. G. having found employment as a dishwasher,
but even by working 7 days a week he was not able to earn
enough to support his large family and there was a continuing problem of getting the welfare supplementation that they
still needed. In addition, even this job was proving to be
too heavy for him; coming out of a steaming kitchen into the
cold to wait for buses after work was aggravating his physical condition. According to his wife, Mr. G. was sick,
nervous, anxious, and bitter about the welfare department's
attitude toward him because he had worked hard all his life,
did not shirk his responsibilities, and wanted only to be able
to support his family. With worker's help, Mrs. G. was
able to overcome Mr. G's resistance and to get his consent
to an appointment with the worker.

In the course of the next several months, after a first
meeting in the home, Mr. G. kept office appointments and
detailed his health history, which indicated the need for a
thorough medical check-up. Mr. G. was particularly resistant to this. He had had some past associations with doctors,
which to him were very unpleasant and discouraging, but he
also seemed to be riddled with fears. When he had pains in
his muscles he was frightened that he had polio; he recalled
a doctor having told him that his mother had died of rheuma-
tism and he feared that he had this and would die of it too.
Dissatisfied with going to a "city doctor" because of his feelings about welfare, he could ill afford the one visit he made
to a private doctor who did not have the special equipment
needed for a full work-up. In the meantime he continued to
make every effort to find more compatible work and became
increasingly discouraged with his lack of success.

The worker repeatedly gave Mr. G. recognition for his
efforts and his sincere desire to look after his family independently. She dealt with his misconceptions about diseases
and symptoms and allayed his fears while she worked through
the administrative complications of getting him referred to a
hospital clinic for a complete check-up, a preliminary step
needed for referring him to the Vocational Rehabilitation program that seemed indicated.

Mr. G's response is contained in the record along with
worker's impression: "Mr. G. is a quiet, soft-spoken man
who appears to be sincere. He has tried very hard to find
suitable employment. Each time he came to my office he
insisted upon my looking at his employment card. His guilt
seems to have been intensified by welfare workers asking to
see his record of visits to the employment center. He was

so helpful to and considerate of me--being on time for appointments, making and keeping appointments to agencies I referred him to, letting me know the outcome of these. He called me to report that the clinic had diagnosed his condition and was forwarding his record to the Rehabilitation Center, where he now had an appointment, which he would keep. He thanked me for all my help. Case closed.

Mrs. G. was no less harried by responsibilities than her husband, but she was more aggressive, had had more exposure to community representatives, and her experiences had been less negative than her husband's. She was, therefore, able to present the Farnam Courts worker to Mr. G. in a positive way and effect the initial home introduction. Mr. G. was, first of all, in need of someone who would listen to him seriously, in a manner clearly indicating belief. Once he perceived that the worker respected him he was able to communicate his many fears about illness, which in part kept him from getting medical attention. This unburdening indicated both the degree of his desperation and his trust in the worker. Mr. G., a huge, brawny man who had done hard labor all his life, must have found it exceedingly difficult to admit physical failure. While the worker was establishing a feeling of trust by showing respect for Mr. G. and giving him recognition for his past accomplishments, she was at the same time laying the groundwork for the steps that had to follow. As she dealt with his misconceptions about his illness, she also told him of ways of receiving treatment other than those which he had used and found unsatisfactory. By the time Mr. G's fears had been somewhat alleviated, the worker had made the necessary arrangements for an examination and Mr. G. was ready to be helped, step by step, through a series of medical and vocational appointments.

The treatment handling here is very important. The low frustration tolerance of deprived people is well known and since excessive delays and waiting lists have a very negative effect upon treatment outcome, timing becomes of utmost importance. It is difficult to hold individuals like Mr. G. in treatment if, when he is ready to go for medical care, he is confronted with a long waiting period.

Mr. G. is an excellent example of the lower-class, unskilled

man whose brawn is the only commodity he has to offer on the labor
market. (Some time after the case was closed we learned he was
illiterate.) This type of man reaches the peak of his earning power
early in life; if illness does not render him unemployable, shrinking
job opportunities because of advancing age may well do so at the
very time when his need becomes most pressing because of the
growing size of his family.

The G's illustrate a case not of family failure but of societal
failure. Mr. G. was constantly being judged by a stereotyped im-
agery, which precluded belief in his desire to work, in the reality
of his illness, and in the sincerity of his efforts to find an honor-
able, dignified solution to his problems.

The F. Case

Mr. F. - 48 years old
Mrs. F. - 42

Referral:

Mrs. F. timidly and apologetically approached the NIP
Director on the project grounds about a financial problem
and possible eviction. Mrs. F. was distressed when it was
suggested that she see the Farnam Courts social worker for
on-going help; she felt at ease with the Director, having
chatted frequently, whereas the social worker was "a stranger." When given reassurance, she was still reluctant to
take the first step of making contact but was obviously relieved when it was then suggested that the worker would be
briefed about the problem and initiate contact by making a
home visit.

12/12/61--Home Visit to Mr. and Mrs. F.

They presented as their problem the fact that they had received their first eviction notice and that they had no money
at all.

Mr. F. was laid off two weeks ago Friday. He was working part-time in a tavern for about three months. Before
that they had been on City Welfare for three or four months.
Mr. F. had been a truck driver for many years but had suffered a slipped disc in his back a year ago last August. He
had received unemployment compensation and when it ran
out, City Welfare helped them. Now he is limited to doing
only light work and must refrain from any lifting. Mr. and
Mrs. F. have been married for two years and she claims
she is unable to work because of heart trouble, though she
had "defrauded" Welfare by working two or three months in
a factory. Mr. F., while on unemployment compensation,
was contributing to the support of a daughter, age 14, by a

previous marriage.

The F's had received welfare assistance several times
for short periods over the past year but obviously were in
bad standing because of the fraud. Their own negative feeling handicapped them in dealing effectively with the agency
about their present needs, so the worker assumed responsibility for clarifying their present status. Mrs. F in particular expressed feelings that "the whole world is against
me" and gave some indication of guilt about her past, saying, "People around here call me a tramp." She indicated
that her life before marriage had not been very good but did
not elaborate.

Summary of Contact 12/15/61-5/30/62

Mr. and Mrs. F. were seen over a 5-1/2 month period
that involved 17 office visits and 5 home visits. In addition,
the worker had one or more contacts with six community
resources: two welfare departments; two employment agencies; Division of Vocational Rehabilitation; Domestic Relations Court.

The worker intervened for the F's with the Welfare Department and got them an allotment for rent and subsistence,
while employment was explored for both of them. Because
Mrs. F's contention of "heart trouble" had not been believed
by Welfare, the Farnam Courts worker expedited a medical
checkup. This was a preliminary step in exploring the
feasibility of Mrs. F's working, since the couple had no
children to prevent her from contributing to the family income.

The checkup revealed a heart condition, which required
the taking of digitalis and the necessity of rest, but permitted light work of about four hours daily. The welfare
worker expressed appreciation for this information as Mrs.
F. had been "professing a heart condition for some time."

Though conscientious in looking for work, Mr. F. continued to be unemployed and the couple was quite discouraged.
Both the F's became very nervous, with Mrs. F. suffering
from headaches. The worker helped Mr. F. in his job exploration and located some possibilities, which, however,
would not materialize for a month or so. In the meantime
she explored his health situation, learned more of his history, and encouraged and helped arrange for a checkup since
his physical limitations were such that the services of the
Vocational Rehabilitation Center might eventually be needed.

Morale picked up considerably when the worker located a
light, satisfactory job within Farnam Courts for Mrs. F, as
part-time housekeeper for an aged, ill couple. Mrs. F. was
especially pleased because she felt she was helping her husband, to whom she was quite devoted. She worried a great
deal and was most gratified to learn from the worker that
the couple were very pleased with her services.

The worker continued to act as a go-between for the F's
with the Welfare Department; because of their past history,
they continued to be under a cloud of suspicion. It was believed that they might not be reporting all present earnings
and that Mr. F. might not be sincerely seeking work. Frequent reports were given the investigator in an effort to help
distinguish past from present behavior and to modify the
couple's negative impression. Effort was made with Mrs.
F. to change her almost paranoid attitude toward the Welfare
Department by helping her see the universality of the regulations and adjust to the realistic limitations of the agency allotments. The worker's task was made more difficult by the
fact that Mrs. F's pay was part of a welfare allotment to
the aged couple; the checks so urgently needed for subsistence by the F's were often late. On one occasion money for
food was advanced to Mrs. F., who immediately repaid the
sum to NIP when she received her wages. Despite these difficulties there was evidence that the worker's support was
having a positive effect on Mrs. F. This was shown by the
fact that even when she had good reason to be angry, Mrs.
F. began to independently handle her affairs with the welfare
worker in a poised, calm and reasoned manner.

With Mr. F. the worker got a full health history, explored
resources for the medical checkup indicated and guided him
through the various stages involved in getting him placed in
an appropriate work situation. The following steps were necessary: identifying his veteran's status and getting him to
use the facilities of the Veteran's Hospital for an examination; effecting a referral to the Vocational Rehabilitation Center; seeing him through the early period of full employment
in a "sheltered" work situation with Goodwill Industries; helping him work out the problem of an equitable contribution to
his child with the Domestic Relations Court. The latter
agency assumed that Mr. F. was trying to shirk his parental
responsibility by claiming inability to work and that when finally employed he was not reporting the full amount of his income. His former wife kept a close check on him, and
once he was employed by Goodwill Industries, she told the
Court that she had "knowledge" of wages that were, in fact,
far in excess of what he was actually earning.

When Mrs. F's job terminated, the worker guided her in the
use of the State Employment Agency and worked with that
agency to find another part-time job in keeping with her physical capacity. Light work caring for a partial invalid was
located. Mrs. F. again experienced some fears about her
ability to perform but the worker was able to allay these by
pointing to her past success.

Summary:

Over a 5-1/2 month period the F's were seen jointly and individually while they were helped to deal with subsistence,

health, and employment problems about which they were
discouraged, nervous, and unable to cope.

As soon as the F's were both employed and able to maintain themselves independently, there was a marked improvement in their morale. Mrs. F. took more care with her
appearance and lost the drab look that had characterized her.

There were hints of a possible underlying personality problem and these were explored. In particular, it was widely
"reported" that Mrs. F. drank excessively. Mrs. F. admitted to the worker that she did "drink a little" and under
stress, "a little more." At one time she had been referred
to the Commission on Alcoholism but the worker learned
that she was not considered to be in need of treatment, and
at no time during this contact was there any overt evidence
of a problem in this area.

At time of closing the F's were in much better spirits; Mr.
F. had even assumed a rather cocky attitude, but he seemed
nevertheless, fairly well balanced in the new family success.
The case was closed when the F's were seen to be managing
fairly well on their own. There is the possibility that they
may not sustain their adjustment and may return for further
help. Case closed.

Brief Contact 6/26/62

Mr. A. of the Rehabilitation Center called to inquire about
Mr. F. Goodwill Industries had called him about the man,
considered a good worker and liked on the job, because he had
missed work and not notified the employer he would be out.
I visited the home and talked with Mrs. F., who stated that
her husband had had to go to court with his daughter. Mrs.
F. had called Goodwill promptly at 9:00 a.m. on both days
that Mr. F. was away from work, to explain his absence.
She had left the information with the woman who answered
the phone and had been assured that her message would get
to the proper source. When this information was given to
Mr. A. he said he had heard of such occurrences before.
He planned to give the information to the supervisor there to
insure that employees were not misjudged for absences.
Case remains closed.

This middle-aged pair had serious health and economic problems, complicated by a very poor reputation with the agency that
had to be relied upon for help. Agency reports, complemented by
broad hints from Mrs. F., indicated that they had not managed their
lives too successfully in the past. Nevertheless, there were indications of real affection between the two and healthy strivings to
better their condition--a goal they might achieve if given genuine

support and direction.

Treatment methods in this case had much in common with
those in the G. case just described. There was, first of all, a
need for the step-by-step process of lining up problems and re-
sources--in this case for two individuals rather than one. The physical limitations of both created complications that lengthened the
time required to find solutions. As in the G. case, the clients'
state of discouragement and frustration required the worker to supply a great deal of support and do a good bit of "enabling." With
the F's it was the wife who was more overtly bleak in outlook, while
with the G's it was the husband. It would seem, however, that
Mrs. F. was the stronger of the two, since Mr. F. left her the responsibility for finding a solution to their troubles. Again, as in
the G. case, modification in attitudes toward agencies and the development of client ability to deal with them were essential treatment
goals.

There was also an attitude of suspicion operating here, enter-
tained by both sides as in the G. case. This distrust was much
more entrenched in the F. case, since the welfare agency had concrete evidence of past fraud. The court shared in this suspicion of
Mr. F., making it necessary to channel considerable worker time
and energy into an effort to modify the attitudes of both court and
agency. This attempt to change the official view of the couple was
cast in the form of an on-going reporting system, notifying others
of modifications in client behavior as these occurred. The worker
concentrated upon the reality-based difficulties in the F's situation,
reporting primarily upon those factors--health and earning limita-
tions--that the clients were powerless to change.

In spite of this effort, it would be unrealistic to suggest that
the client image changed radically. This case, more clearly than
the previous one, highlights the problem facing clients who are recorded as exhibiting behavior that might be loosely termed dishonest
--behavior running the gamut from omission (not reporting all the
facts) through concealment and fraud. Once such behavior is documented, it remains a part of the permanent record--never overlooked, rarely forgiven, prejudicial to the client the next time he

asks for help. These people are usually ill-equipped to surmount the weight of their bad reputations on their own; seldom encountering a neutral attitude, they feel any effort would be worthless since so much hostility has been directed toward them by agency personnel.

In this case treatment focus, particularly for Mrs. F., who carried the burden of managing family income, was upon gaining a much clearer understanding of client and agency roles and responsibilities. Mrs. F. and the worker discussed what the agency expected from the client and the client's rights, the requirements of eligibility, and, specifically, a more effective method of conducting herself in order to maintain good agency relations.

With the agencies themselves, the worker made a conspicuous effort to neutralize the documented negative information by getting the current, positive evidence into the record. Both Mr. and Mrs. F's health pictures were established and verified, as were their sources and amounts of income. The detailed report, verified by the worker, can hardly have failed to register with the personnel of those community agencies with whom such close liaison was maintained throughout contact.

Notes

1. L. L. Geismar and Michael A. La Lorte. Understanding the Multi-Problem Family, pp. 56-59.

2. This practice was not confined to functional illiterates or to those of Puerto Rican extraction who had no reading skill in English.

3. In addition there were 29 re-opened cases, 23 of which made re-application on their own initiative. Ten among the 23 had originally been referred.

4. Represents a count of agencies with which the workers initiated contact. Many of these were contacted repeatedly.

The needs of lower-class deprived populations in general and of multi-problem families in particular, as shown by our experience, are so pervasive that no one agency can be expected to meet them all. Even multi-functional agencies would find it difficult to be so all-encompassing as to satisfy every service requirement, and certainly our own limited program, multi-dimensional though it was, proved in reality too limited to make such an attempt. At the same time, as we have described in earlier chapters, we found in our client population a widespread inability to use services constructively or to maintain working relationships once contacts were effected. As a result there was all too often a disappointing relationship between client and resource.

We addressed ourselves to these problems by requiring that all caseworkers associated with NIP act as family treatment coordinators and two-way change agents. This chapter deals with the problems we encountered and our methods of handling them, using material from the team of workers who treated the multi-problem families and from the succession of workers who treated the general Farnam Courts population.

When intervention is begun it is not possible to know the reasons for the breakdown in functioning of a particular family. What is evident is that there are pressing family needs, together with a generalized ineptness that makes it impossible to maintain a workable relationship or to make constructive use of community resources. These needs must be met quickly, not only to relieve distress but also to accelerate the formation of a positive relationship; the technique whereby one person assumes prime responsibility for the management of a family's multiple collateral contacts best meets the necessity for speed. The family worker, designated

"coordinator of treatment," takes whatever action is needed to start
the process of aid and support, bringing the client together with the
resources that can best serve his needs.   Where there has been pri-
or contact of a negative kind, success depends upon the establishment of a better climate between parties who had met before in an
atmosphere of misunderstanding and/or distrust.   Whether an impasse or a battle has resulted in the past, the client is the immediate loser.   As A. F. Philp writes, these "clients feel worthless,
hopeless and undeserving and they make others feel this way about
them.   They involve others in treating them the way they feel they
should be treated.   Families with gross social failure and bizarre
behavior both show the greatest need and call forth the punitive ele-
ment in services, thus creating conflict for the services themselves. "[1]

The family worker may have to work individually with both
client and collateral personnel in an attempt to modify mutually
negative attitudes before further confrontation.   As he deals with
agency personnel in this dual role of intervener and mediator, the
family worker encounters a whole spectrum of reactions.   On the
positive end of the scale are those collateral workers who have a
sympathetic appreciation for the client's condition and a recognition
of his inability to cope with complex agency routines and requirements.   These workers, willing to cooperate, understand the need
for one person to "enable" the client by "doing for or with" him until he learns to manage independently, and they are not defensive
about the realistic limitations of their agencies.   In the middle
stands a group of workers who are genuinely puzzled at the client's
ignorance of regulations or his inability to follow fully explained
procedures.   These workers are unaware of the fact that the client
may appear to understand while not comprehending at all.   They are,
however, reasonably receptive to interpretation and to efforts by the
intervener aimed at effecting a cooperative relationship.   On the
other end of the spectrum are those workers who exhibit a frankly
negative attitude.   They disapprove of "doing for" clients, seeing it
as a form of mollycoddling people who are consciously and deliberately remaining dependent.   The inadequacies of the client dominate

their view of the situation. Resentful of intervention, they see it
as a negative reflection upon their job performance or the functional limits of their agency.

Community acceptance of the policy of using NIP workers as
interveners and coordinators was obtained from agency administrators well in advance of the actual program. Further theoretical
understanding of what would be entailed was given to the personnel
of the various agencies through a series of meetings with the Director prior to instituting treatment. As happens, there remained
a gap between the plan and the reality. We warned our workers
that they would have to bear the major responsibility for interpreting their role, anticipating that this would become most important
as direct worker-to-worker contacts were established in giving service to a mutual client.

When taking the initiative in establishing a collateral contact,
the NIP worker was asked to set the stage for a complementary
working partnership by:

1. Explaining the purpose of this special assignment and his
   role with respect to the client and the collateral agency.
2. Sharing information that would substantiate the need for
   intervention.
3. Eliciting information regarding the collateral service, the
   client-collateral worker relationship, and the collateral
   worker's assessment of problem areas.
4. Determining an appropriate and mutually agreeable division of work.
5. Arranging for on-going communication between NIP and
   the collateral worker.

Community workers generally welcomed the intervention of
the NIP worker. Many of them realized that an inordinate amount
of time was needed to reduce impediments and enable the families
to make more effective use of services; they were keenly aware of
the fact that they were unable to make such an investment. The
NIP worker, doing just that, was able to enhance and support the
service function of the collateral agency.

When a NIP worker began his contact with a multi-problem family he could be sure of the following three facts: that there were anywhere from two to six or more collateral agencies that, curently or in the recent past, knew the family; that in a majority of these cases there was a less than satisfactory relationship; that the family needed services from these agencies. Even when not immediately indicated, it was safe for the NIP worker to assume that the need for his intervention as coordinator or expeditor or mediator would probably arise. Consequently, we informed the collateral agency workers of our involvement in a case as soon as it occurred. This courtesy was undertaken through telephone conversations for the most part, during which the NIP worker might use any number of steps from the guide mentioned above which he judged to be pertinent. If no pressing problem was in evidence, he would have, at the very least, laid the groundwork for future collaboration.

The family worker as coordinator often found it necessary to make appointments for the client or accompany him on visits to the agency or clinic. In doing this, he was taking action traditionally considered the function of the client. To justify this departure the worker had to share sufficient information about the client. Although the exchange of information among agencies has long been an established practice in social work, it has been limited by a desire to protect the confidential nature of the client-worker relationship. Consequently, the extent to which agencies share information has been a controversial subject. There seems to be a rule of thumb that uses professional status as a key criterion: agencies with trained workers tend to discourage or limit the sharing of information with agencies having predominantly untrained workers. Fear of the injudicious use of disclosed information is the cause of this situation. While there undoubtedly may be some risk, it is evident that a genuinely cooperative relationship cannot be established without reciprocity of information. The picture that exists in any given agency of this particular client group is at best fragmented; more often it is distorted and/or erroneous. As a first step the intervener must round out, balance, or correct the record by delineating strengths as well as weaknesses, identifying those client attitudes, patterns of behavior, and values that are worthy of strengthening and preserving. This cannot be done without sharing information. It is also apparent that the altered client image calls for an adjustment on the part of the collateral agency worker, a point of view which is difficult for some to accept since it is commonly held that the client must be the one to change. The role of the intervener as it affects the client, modifying negative practices and changing attitudes toward community institutions, has been readily understood and accepted. However, the role of the intervener as it affects collateral workers, attempting to modify what may be a stereotyped or erroneous image of the client, is not readily accepted either by the worker acting as intervener or by the worker being contacted. Our staff were informed that they were expected to expand their role of change agent to include collateral workers when necessary, functioning, in effect, as two-way change agents.

In practice, our workers found themselves acting most vigorously with negative collateral workers, whose attitudes were often expressed as soon as introductions were made. Fortunately, the worst fears of the NIP workers were not realized; they were not often called upon to share negative information that was not already known. Social work training and experience that stressed traditional confidentiality had blinded our workers to the fact that the lives of their clients were virtually open books. It was conspicuous malfunctioning that had brought these people to community attention in the first place. Furthermore, they were characterized by a peculiar facility for publicizing their worst attributes. Confidentiality, a basically protective measure, was not as relevant to this group as to other portions of the population. What seemed to be indicated here was a counteraction based upon communication, aimed at balancing a distorted and negative picture.

Obviously, the actions taken by the intervener must vary from case to case in order to be appropriate to specific situations. At the risk of oversimplifying the many complex variables of this client-intervener-collateral worker relationship, we will nevertheless attempt to give meaningful examples by using the alternative patterns of collateral worker response mentioned earlier in this chapter. Our

experience indicated a relationship between the degree of difficulty
our workers experienced as coordinators and the kind of attitudes
toward client and intervention held by collateral workers.

Fewer complications occurred with the collateral worker who
possessed a positive attitude, accepting the need for intervention involving both himself and the client. In some cases the problem
clearly lay with some aspect of the client's functioning. Mrs. F.,
for example, informed the worker that she had long needed to replace the broken-down bed shared by her two girls. Exploration
revealed that Mrs. F. had been instructed to submit three price
estimates, a requirement of the Department of Welfare; the AFDC
worker had said that he would complete the processing of a grant
upon receipt of these. Discussion with Mrs. F. revealed that she
had not fully understood what was expected of her. The NIP worker, through close and intensive exposure to Mrs. F., had learned
that the impression she gave was often deceptive. While she appeared to grasp instructions, she was often too anxious and worried
to pay close attention. The positive collateral worker considered
this information valuable for the useful insight it afforded him.
This oversimplified situation illustrates two points: how the intervener may furnish useful information and how the positive collateral
worker may use the information in his future work with the client.

In other such cases the problem may lie primarily in some
aspect of the collateral worker's situation--in the large caseloads of
public agencies, for instance, which cause delays in meeting needs.
A reminder from the intervener, given without recrimination but
with recognition of ever-present pressures, will move the positive
worker to take prompt action. In our experience with such workers,
we have often been asked to re-contact them after a reasonable interval, to make certain that some unforeseen complication has not
interfered with service. While some of these workers may initially
indicate reservation or even doubt about the necessity for intervention, they will give us a fair hearing, often responding to the interpretation and the shared information by doing some client "testing"
of their own. The process of alerting them stimulates a sharpening of their own observations and leads to some client reassessment.

They develop an appreciation for the enlarged picture that can result, giving more precise knowledge of client behavior in a diversity of relationships and circumstances.

Obviously, the most difficult situations NIP workers encountered were those involving the collateral workers that were negative to the intervener and/or the client. These workers let NIP personnel know that they were viewed as interfering outsiders, who were inferentially criticizing the collateral workers' performance or the latter's agency. Such workers often paraded client shortcomings before NIP coordinators, with descriptions running from "inadequate" or "undeserving" to "illegal" or "fraudulent." While some of these terms may have been correct, they were used with hostility or prejudice. These workers resorted to unnecessary delays or attempted to deny needed services that the client was eligible to receive. Clearly, the basic responsibility of the intervener is to see that the client gets the services he is entitled to. Under unfavorable circumstances there is no alternative but to discuss the issue openly with the collateral worker.

Before the intervening worker can deal with this kind of hostile situation, however, he must be in control of his own feelings. The inexperienced worker, prone to become defensive about his client, must be careful to avoid adopting a belligerent stance, which can only lead to charge and countercharge, rage and recrimination --all to the detriment of the client. For effective dealing with collateral agencies, we suggested the following to our staff:

A. Acknowledge facts. If the negative assessments or accusations are substantiated by existing records, admit them.

B. Allow and encourage the expression of negative, hostile or prejudiced feelings. This is necessary because attitudes that are causing service to be withheld can then be separated from the question of eligibility. The intervener will know just what he must deal with in his attempt to modify the collateral agency relationship to the client.

C. Correct the record. Once frank expression has given the

intervener a clear idea of the extent and degree of dis-
tortion, he must establish a corrected image through
the use of documented facts.

D. Distinguish between the past and the future. Help to the
client with a bad reputation must be guided by the reality of his current need. It may be necessary to suggest a "fresh start" or "another chance," this time
with the family worker acting as coordinator of treatment, guiding the client and helping him make appropriate use of the service.

The above approach usually makes it unnecessary to confront
the hostile worker with the fact that his attitudes are holding back
needed aid. However, the collateral worker may adamantly describe
the case as hopeless and ask the intervener just what he can possibly expect to accomplish. The worker can answer that the case
may very well turn out to be hopeless, but a new treatment approach
may bring results if the collateral agency will cooperate.

This approach did not always culminate in a quick resolution
of strongly-held differences of opinion. Sometimes there was a
need to confront collateral workers with their prejudiced attitudes.
If this had to be done, the NIP worker was instructed to be as
tactful as possible, to examine and bring under control his own feelings first. We cautioned our staff against assuming the presence of
biased or hostile attitudes. Perhaps they masked a new worker's
unfamiliarity with agency regulations--common in large public agencies where staff turnover is heavy or where flexibility of practice
is fully known only to supervisory or administrative personnel.
When necessary, we suggested conferring with a supervisor; this did
not need to imply incompetence on the part of the collateral worker
since certain responsibilities and decisions must rest with a higher
echelon.

Inter-agency problems are not, of course, confined to public
agencies. Some voluntary agencies stress client motivation and initiative, with the result that they look with disfavor upon the client
that needs an intervener to set up the contact and help him get
there. Even when an explanation is given, voluntary agency workers

will react like their colleagues in public welfare positions; even if
not openly hostile, they will oppose the action of the intervener,
feeling it reflects in some way on their ability to handle the client.

Naturally, there is no pat formula that can cover all situations. Our general rule when dealing with hostility was to protect
the client, preventing his exposure to situations that we thought
might have negative results. Whenever feasible, NIP workers were
expected to "clear the air" in advance. In emergencies this was
not always possible and clients were often exposed to negative experiences, with which the NIP worker would subsequently have to
deal.

It is almost impossible to get a client to accept such reali-
ties as responsibility for his own behavior after an encounter with
a community worker that has not properly carried out his job. The
most promising antidote is a positive experience, and this is what
the worker hopes to realize when he accompanies the client. More
often than not such an outcome may be achieved; though problems
may linger on and need continuous attention in some cases, a partial rapprochement can generally be effected. There were a few
cases where the NIP worker was treated very roughly in the client's
presence, with unanticipated positive results. The clients were at
first astonished, then reassured, at the sight of a social worker being treated in a way they had thought was reserved for them. In
those rare instances where it was necessary to approach higher administrative echelons to resolve an impasse, the clients learned
which channels were available for seeking redress and under what
circumstances it was appropriate to use them. When all else
failed--establishing a just claim to services, allowing a reasonable
time to elapse, and making a tempered effort to resolve differences
--the NIP worker was expected to exert polite but persistent pressure until needs were met.

Similar in many ways to the multi-problem families, the
families served by the Farnam Courts caseworker were reluctant to
ask for service, unsure of where they should go, inept in the use
of resources, ignorant of what would be required of them. Since
they had many of the same types of problems, we used essentially

the same approach in securing resources.

There also were what might be called quantitative differences between the two groups. For instance, most of the nonmulti-problem families were unknown to the agencies; where there had been contact, it had been of relatively short duration and/or infrequent. Furthermore these families exhibited far fewer personality problems that might adversely affect client-agency relationships. As a result these families were far less embittered or openly hostile; the agencies did not have voluminous records of family "failures" and so could assume a more benign attitude.

The greatest volume of work done for these families by the Farnam Courts workers fell in the category of determining appropriate resources, keeping clients from needless frustration in attempting tasks for which we knew they were unsuited. While many also needed "enabling" to actually begin using resources, they did not as a rule require the intensive and time-consuming work that characterized our treatment of the multi-problem families. By structuring the problems and the procedures for getting help, it was possible for a majority of these 105 families to carry through; multi-problem families, by contrast, required continuance of this approach for a considerable length of time before any capacity for independent action was developed.

In summarizing we can state that one of the most serious needs of lower-class families, badly disorganized or not, is a neighborhood-based community agent, who can insure that a satisfactory connection is established between people in need of services and the resources geared to render them. The community agent must function in a variety of roles: advisor, teacher, enabler, intervener, coordinator of treatment, expediter, supporter, and confidante. One role may be adequate in a given situation; all may sometimes be needed, particularly with multi-problem families. With both groups of families--stable or multi-problem--intermittent, recurring incidents upsetting family functioning must be expected. Deprivation and the lack of education render these people extremely vulnerable, at the same time hindering them from forming adequate coping mechanisms. These families desperately require an agent who can bridge the gap between themselves and available resources until such time as they are more economically and socially secure.

Notes

1. A. F. Philp. Family Failure. A Study of 129 Families with Multiple Problems. (London, Faber and Faber Limited, 1963), p. 284.

An integral part of the NIP program was assessment of case-work movement. Did our intervention effect measurable change in the functioning of families? To answer this question we adopted a three-part method of evaluation: (1) assembling data with the struc-tured Outline of Family Functioning; (2) applying a uniform grading system; (3) comparing treated cases with a crudely matched sample of untreated cases to which the same instrument had been applied. Of the thirty cases which received intensive, reaching-out casework treatment for a minimum of eighteen months, four cases registered no movement or negative movement. We consider these four our "failure cases" because, according to our measurement criteria, no quantifiable treatment objectives were realized as a result of our intervention.

In an effort to get at the causes of treatment failure, we subjected these four cases to further examination, looking at some of the factors bypassed by the Outline of Family Functioning. These include worker capability and training; the treatment approach used by the worker; idiosyncratic family behavior, history, problems and/or defenses that might have some bearing on the negative out-come. By first extracting the common denominators in the four cases and then briefly assessing each family individually, we have tried to arrive at some conclusions about our lack of success.

Three cases were handled by trained, experienced workers. Two of these were assigned to the same worker, who, in a total caseload of six families, realized movement with four; the third was one of a caseload of two, the other registering movement. The fourth failure case was handled by an untrained worker, who car-ried a total caseload of ten families, nine of which showed move-ment. Since all three workers proved capable of effecting measurable change, worker failure _per se_ did not account for the lack of movement.

In our search for common factors we found that all four clients denied having difficulty in coping with problems. Unlike the vast majority of our cases, they did not have at the point of entry a large number of tangible problems to which the worker could refer when faced with resistance. In two of the families, the condition of the home and physical care of the children was of very high caliber and social graces were emphasized and practiced. These high standards were not in evidence in the other two homes, but the families had independently weathered recent crises with some degree of success. This reinforced their denial of need for help at the time our worker entered the situation. All four clients were very well defended individuals, who presented a facade of capability, gave the worker no immediate indication of need for help, and found reinforcement in the reality situation.

All four families were functioning at the marginal or below marginal level in two key areas: Family Relationships and Unity, and Individual Behavior and Adjustment. There was ample documentation of seriously disturbed behavior on the part of one or more children in each of the four cases; in three families there were children that had long been in need of psychological or neurological diagnostic examinations, which the parents had failed to obtain. There was a poor parent-child relationship in all the cases, and emotionally damaging training methods had been used. On the other hand, no overt dependency was shown at the onset of treatment, and only one family exhibited the kind of disorganization for which the workers had been prepared. Consequently the workers, faced with stiff resistance, uniformly addressed themselves to the problems of the children, remaining so firmly committed to this approach that they treated the adults almost exclusively in the light of their parental roles. Furthermore, in two of the cases the children's problems were not sufficiently serious in the beginning to justify intervention.

Only one of these cases, involving severe client personality problems, presented a complexity beyond the worker's level of skill.

Yet in all four cases the workers were unable to have any impact
on the family and as a result were greatly discouraged.

The Y. Case

The Y. family was established on a weak foundation. When
she met Mr. Y., at the age of nineteen, Mrs. Y. had already
experienced a very unhappy family life. Her father was a drunkard
who physically abused her mother; he had been treated in a State
Hospital when she was a small child, and the parents had finally
been divorced. Mrs. Y. had never liked her step-father, whom she
described as being miserly and unconcerned about her welfare. She
quit high school in her third year. She had been a poor student,
but she told the worker that she left because she was not allowed
sufficient clothing to keep herself presentable.

Mr. Y. came from a family that prided itself on its respect-
able standing in the community. His father was a strict discipli-
narian, and Mr. Y. rebelled at an early age. He ran away from
home many times, quit school in the eighth grade, and joined the
Navy shortly thereafter. He had a long record of arrests for various offenses--theft, robbery, gambling. His navy record was extremely poor. Frequently A.W.O.L., he once engaged in a fight
that resulted in a drowning. Although he was not prosecuted for his
part in this affair, some psychiatric treatment was given him while
in service. His navy career ended with a dishonorable discharge.

Mr. Y. met his wife while he was in the Navy and they kept
company for about one year. When she became pregnant she forced
him into marriage by threatening to commit suicide. The union was
marked by Mr. Y's violent temper outbursts, during which he often
beat his wife. Their early marital relationship was characterized
by frequent fights, arguments, separations and reconciliations.
While her husband was still in service, Mrs. Y. had a brief extra-
marital affair that resulted in a second pregnancy. This caused increased strife, but Mr. Y. finally accepted the child and a reconciliation followed. He continued his wild outbursts and physical
abuse of his wife. He was employed intermittently as a construction worker, never being a good provider. In the 1950's he spent

about six months in a state hospital; he also was treated in a hospital for alcoholics.

Both of the Y's had relatives in better economic and social positions. The extended family came to the rescue innumerable times, giving such things as financial assistance and lawyers' fees.

In spite of this stormy history and the precarious economic and emotional base, the family appeared remarkably cohesive at the time of the worker's entry. Mrs. Y., an attractive woman with an extremely youthful, almost girlish appearance, kept an immaculate house. The six children were all handsome, well dressed, and healthy looking; five of the six had made remarkably good adjustments. In many respects, there seemed to be a healthy family solidarity. There were often expeditions to the homes of various relatives, and the family had enjoyably cooperated in such projects as painting the apartment. The parents had been successful in setting high standards of behavior for the children. The youngsters practiced good manners, and social graces were in evidence; the girls were taught home management and cooking by their mother. All of the children were encouraged to take part in healthy activities with their peers, to make use of group activities available in the immediate area, and to entertain their friends in their own home.

Two of the boys had shown anti-social behavior, but at the onset of treatment there was only one boy causing concern. Since 1956, Jerome had been involved in activities that had brought him to the attention of school authorities and the Juvenile Court. He had been a truant, had stolen from cars, panhandled from people in the downtown area, and participated in a group found throwing stones at trains. For a short while Jerome had exerted some influence on his younger brother, George, who showed signs of imitating him. However, George responded to the attention of a sensitive teacher; he had settled down in school and had made an apparently satisfactory adjustment in the period just prior to NIP contact.

Some improvement in economic security had recently occurred as a result of Mr. Y's steady employment. Mrs. Y. was a capable manager, so that at the time that the worker initiated contact, there was only one conspicuous problem that could be used

to gain entry. That problem was Jerome's behavior, plus the fact
that his diagnostic work-up, recommended by the court, had never
been completed.

The family presented a united front; accepting the worker
graciously, they were in reality extremely wary. Mr. Y. pointed
to his improved adjustment, a result of past help, and was firm in
his rejection of further assistance. Mrs. Y. suffered momentary
lapses in her defensiveness. She occasionally alluded to her concern about Mr. Y's precarious adjustment to work and his continued
drinking. She then, however, countered her fears with the claim
that he would never seek treatment or respond to it, and therefore
there was no point in pursuing the topic. At other times she
claimed that she had become adjusted to his behavior. It appeared
that she had in fact accepted him much more than in the past; she
had made some sort of accommodation that worked within certain
limitations, so that open strife was absent and the family was not
seriously malfunctioning. However, it was obvious that underlying
problems called for attention.

The worker, taking the initiative to "do with" the family,
succeeded in getting Jerome a complete psychological and physical
work-up, which eliminated the suspicion of brain damage and neurological complications. Finding his IQ to be 80, the school removed
the boy from a special class to one that could offer him more stimulation. The child continued his delinquent activity, however, and
again came to the attention of the Juvenile Court. Since the family
continued to be resistant to the worker, the case was transferred
to a male NIP worker then associated with the Juvenile Court.

Over another six-month period the second worker succeeded
in obtaining only two interviews with Mrs. Y. She alternated between expressed determination to go to the Commission on Alcoholism for help with her husband and expressions of futility because
she felt he would not respond to treatment. The boy continued his
mischief, bringing him again before the court; the offenses were not
serious, however, and he was discharged with a warning. When
the NIP worker departed after a total contact of eighteen months,
the case had to be transferred to a Juvenile Court probation officer,

not associated with NIP, for continuing supervision.

In this case there was enough support from the extended family and enough internal strength, especially in the mother, to achieve a level of family functioning sufficient to maintain good physical and mental health in most of the children. Five exhibited no serious problems and were making satisfactory adjustments in school and in the community.

The workers did not make a concerted effort to break through the family's resistance, and, as we observed earlier, committed the error of treating the adults as parents and not as individuals. Perhaps the workers did all they could in this atypical case. Although the family had a pathological history that was characteristic of a multi-problem family, it was, in fact, not one. There was the mother's strength, and long periods of support and material help from relatives. In addition, Mr. Y's father was prominent in the city government. This might have reinforced an unrealistic but strong family feeling that use of community resources might expose family skeletons to public scrutiny. NIP assistance could very well have been considered a threat to family status.

The T. Case

Mrs. T., the second oldest of eleven children, was brought up on a farm in the rural South; at thirty-five she still nourished a nostalgic, idealized picture of rural life. Her first child was born when she was fifteen and at seventeen, again pregnant, she married the father of both children. The couple came to the New York area, where serious marital problems began. Following the birth of two more children, the couple separated. Mrs. T. then had several casual and transitory relationships with other men, leading to two abortions and the birth of a fifth child.

For two years prior to NIP contact, three of Mrs. T's children had been of serious concern to the community. Two girls and a boy appeared to be suffering from gross physical neglect and were thought to have neurological, psychological, and/or psychiatric problems. Although they needed thorough checkups, Mrs. T. would not cooperate. The children's behavior was characterized by unprovoked

violence, hyperactivity, destructiveness, irrational actions. Before
the case became active the six-year-old boy had set fire to the
apartment, causing considerable damage. This was one of a long
series of complaints that the Housing Authority had against Mrs. T.
She was already considered an undesirable tenant because of the
birth of a baby extra-maritally conceived and her very poor housekeeping standards.

From the beginning, Mrs. T's attitude toward the worker
was described as negative-passive. She showed strong control of
her emotions and either denied or excused the behavioral problems
of the children. The worker considered the plight of the three children so overwhelming that she classified it as the most pressing
problem; the treatment focus was entirely child-oriented and Mrs.
T. was addressed exclusively as a parent. The emphasis was upon getting physical, medical, and psychological workups on the children; the mother continued to respond in a passive, submissive manner. At rare moments personal revelations afforded the worker
openings that she failed to fully utilize. When the worker became
aware of her one-sided approach, about seven months of treatment
had elapsed and it appeared to be too late to change. For several
more months the worker tried to reach Mrs. T. by treating her as
an individual in her own right, but there was no response and the
worker returned to the children.

Mrs. T. became pregnant again and during this period there
was a slight, temporary improvement in the client-worker relationship, with the woman sporadically accepting the worker's advice to
give attention to her own health. With this second extra-marital
pregnancy, Mrs. T. was faced with imminent eviction from the project; at this point she completely rejected the worker's offers of
help to find other housing, solving the problem in her own way by
moving away. This coincided with the worker's leave of absence,
and no worker was available for further coverage.

Mrs. T. was an exceptionally well defended client, who despite overt and deep-seated problems found it necessary to deny help
in order to maintain a facade of independence. The worker, responding to a situation where three of five children gave indications

of gross physical neglect and serious emotional damage, never over-
came her need to focus upon them.   She attempted to alleviate the
children's problems by helping Mrs. T. become a more adequate
mother.

Some workers are unable to establish a relationship with
such poor parental figures.   This worker carried six cases, four of
which showed successful treatment outcome.   It is interesting to
note that both her "failure" cases consisted of clients who would not
or could not show need for her help.

The J. Case

This was a well-documented case of adult malfunctioning.
The J's were married in 1943, when the wife was thirty-four and
the husband forty-six.   Mr. J. had had difficulty making a living
since 1946, when he became ill with pulmonary tuberculosis.   Recurrences necessitated a number of hospitalizations.   He wore a
hearing aid, and he had suffered a severe heart attack, causing him
to be under constant medical attention.   Although a chronic drinker,
he denied any problem.   During one hospitalization he was tested
and found to be mentally subnormal; the report listed him as functioning "to the best of his ability."   He had schooling to the seventh
grade; he had served in World War I and had been for many years
a merchant seaman.   He was the dominant marriage partner, making all decisions, supervising all aspects of family life, guiding his
wife and his six children, who ranged in age from fifteen to four.

Mrs. A. quit school at sixteen, when she was in the seventh
grade.   Agencies through the years had come to know her as a woman who failed to function well in most areas and roles.   Considered mentally dull, she was highly emotional and had outbursts of
loud screaming.   She depended on Mr. J. to do the cooking,
cleaning and marketing, to handle all money matters, to train the
children and take them to clinics, make school visits.   Mrs. J. repeatedly stated that such responsibilities were "too much trouble"
for her and she did not "want to be bothered" with them.   Social
workers and the Visiting Nurse labeled her ineducable, for she was
unable to follow the simplest instructions.   In 1957 she was unable

to tell a worker how many rooms there were in the apartment where she had lived for two years, or the name of her youngest child, then two years old.

Mrs. J. had complained bitterly about her husband's drinking, his physical abuse of her and of the children, his use of vile language. Vicious quarrels between the parents, with the children present and cowering, had been witnessed by agency workers. The mother had no control over the children, who ignored or mocked her, while the father ruled by severe and frequent beatings.

An unexpected picture presented itself when the NIP worker made her first visit in January, 1960. The six-and-a-half room apartment was tastefully furnished and immaculately clean. The entire family was well clothed, neat and clean, with excellent manners. Mr. J. displayed a fine sense of humor and great affability toward the worker; Mrs. J. was accepting, though she indicated no particular need of help.

As treatment progressed, the couple appeared to form an easy, trusting relationship with the worker. Mrs. J. responded by getting medical care for some neglected problems. She took more interest in her personal appearance and social activities, even developing a satisfying hobby, sewing.

Mr. J. was also seen regularly and one of the key topics for discussion was his method of punishing the children. He genially admitted both the severity of the beatings and the fact that they were not effective controls. For a few months, Mr. J. claimed that he had relinquished beatings in favor of withholding privileges and "talking things over." Gradually the worker learned from one child or another that the improvements the parents had been outlining were not really occurring. Two boys were repeatedly involved in delinquent actions, staying out late at night and committing acts of vandalism. For each action Mr. J. beat the boys severely. The oldest child, an adolescent girl, was in open rebellion, staying out late at night, defying her parents by her choice of undesirable companions, and supposedly "running around" with older men. While this steady deterioration was taking place, Mr. J's abusive outbursts and drinking increased. In addition, Mr. J. had several at-

tacks of illness, and there was medical confirmation of a severe
heart condition imperiling his life.   In the face of this the worker
found it impossible to compel Mr. J. to control his behavior with
the children.

In a series of crises arising from the behavior of the older
children, the worker saw each case through court proceedings preliminary to placement in state institutions.   During this period the
worker on many occasions attempted to find out how this family
managed so well on its welfare allotment.   About a year after contact the mystery was solved when the J's were discovered to have
received money from Social Security without reporting it to the Department of Welfare.   The fraud involved a substantial sum of over
$4,000.   Only the worker's intervention on the grounds of the man's
poor health and the need for him at home saved him from a long
jail sentence.

There was evidence that the pattern of anti-social and delinquent behavior established by the older siblings had already had
some effect on the younger children.   Two of them, who were just
beginning school, were already imitating the behavior of their broth-
ers.   All of the children were given work-ups and found to have
IQ's between 60 and 70.   Mr. J. was known to have retarded intellectual capacities and Mrs. J's school reports indicated the same.

This was a case where the responsible adults were mentally
limited and virtually uneducable; they could not modify their child-
rearing practices.   Except for the corporal punishment, which was
never witnessed by anyone but family members, the children received superior physical care.   Because of this, it was impossible
to establish a case of neglect in court and so placement could not
be made early enough to salvage the older ones and protect the
younger ones.

The failure in the J. case was largely the result of the
worker's initial inability to perceive the limits within which her intervention could proceed effectively.   She allowed herself to be
dragged from crisis to crisis, and her work was hampered by the
personality problems and mental retardation of family members.
The natural tendency of the family-centered worker to avoid or post-

pone placement of children whenever there is a chance of saving the
family as a unit was reinforced by the superficially cooperative gestures of the parents and by the difficulty of establishing a clear
case of neglect.

The W. Case

Miss W. left school after the eighth grade to work as a domestic.   In 1933 she married, but there were no children from this
union.   In 1949, divorced by her husband on the grounds of desertion, Miss W. reverted to her maiden name and insisted upon being
called "Miss."   Subsequent involvements with different men produced two daughters.   A third pregnancy, in which the child was
lost, occurred while she was involved with still another man and
living in Farnam Courts.   The relationship was common knowledge,
provoking gossip to which her children were exposed.   The fathers
of both daughters were in and out of the home repeatedly, and the
girls became confused about their parental situation.

Miss W. was very candid about the fact that she had not
wanted any children.   At the time of her first pregnancy she was
thirty-five and certain that she was incapable of bearing children.
She was hostile and indifferent to the girls, ignoring their physical
care and screaming at them for no apparent reason.   Neighbors often found the girls shabby, hungry, and frightened.

When NIP contact began, neither girl was doing badly.   The
tangible problems were of a minor nature, concerning poor housekeeping standards and periodic difficulties in managing the welfare
allotment.   Miss W. was indifferent to the physical appearance of
her girls and to their supervision and guidance.   However, the girls
were not behavior problems, doing passing work in school and getting along well with each other.

For some time Miss W. seemed guarded in her dealings
with the worker, doing a good deal of testing.   The situation was
complicated by the fact that the NIP worker assigned to her was also on the staff of the Welfare Department, administering Miss W's
grant.   Despite these handicaps, however, a superficial, outwardly
accepting relationship was formed.   The client's initial guardedness

gave way as she verbalized her feeling that she was a "bad" person, that she was "not worth much," and that she really never wanted the children but became adjusted to having them. She did not conceal the fact that she devoted little time or attention to their care and training.

There was increasing outward evidence that Miss W. felt worthless and placed herself among the outcasts of society. She boasted about her choice of companions--several prostitutes with court records, people convicted of morals charges, homosexuals that were also alcoholics or suspected drug addicts. Miss W. courted these people, invited them into her house, and gave them the run of the apartment. She told the worker that these were "dear friends" whom she would help at all costs, even if it meant eviction from the Housing Project.

Some personality deterioration seemed to be taking place during contact. Miss W. experienced increasing financial difficulties, but rejected offers of help from the worker. At the same time she enlarged her circle of undesirable companions. Despite the woman's behavior and the conditions of the home, there was actually improvement in the school adjustment of her two girls.

The worker felt in the early period of contact that Miss W's wariness was due to the worker's connection with the Welfare Department as well as NIP. Although this double affiliation terminated, the situation never improved much. There was some relationship established later when Miss W. dropped her defenses long enough to detail her great difficulty in managing her income. (She bought extravagantly and then fell back on borrowing, begging from neighbors, or asking the worker for money or clothing.) However, the client would not face her own responsibility for mismanagement; the worker could not effect any change, for Miss W. adamantly refused to modify her way of doing things.

Miss W. verbalized problems regarding her children, but when the worker attempted to help her she reverted to the same evasive tactics. Many appointments were missed and the client eluded the worker as much as possible. Miss W. seemed to have absolutely no desire to improve her own functioning or the external

situation. Although the home environment was considered potentially
dangerous to the children because of the disreputable people to whom
they were exposed, there was not sufficient evidence to support a
court case for their placement.

At the time that the NIP program was terminated the case
had reached an impasse. At a conference with the State Department
of Welfare, primary responsibility for ongoing supervision was
passed on to that agency.

The NIP worker involved in this case was untrained and inexperienced, obviously lacking the skills needed to help Miss W.
But we may question whether even a skilled worker would have dealt
successfully with this complex and problematic personality.

Summary:

We considered these four cases failures because they registered no movement when assessed quantitatively. Even when we
subjected first the workers and then the families individually to close
scrutiny we arrived at no clear-cut explanation for this treatment
failure. Of course, in all four situations an effective relationship
never existed between worker and client. On the one hand, it is
possible to say that the workers were responsible, because they employed a one-sided, child-oriented approach. They did not address
themselves sufficiently to the adults as individuals, and thus did not
foster a meaningful relationship. On the other hand, the clients
were extremely well-defended people, who completely rejected help.
This is undoubtedly significant, for few workers are so experienced
or secure that they can function in the face of sustained rejection.

The family histories were awesome in detail and very discouraging. The workers had to invest much of themselves in ardu-
ous, long-term treatment; they also had to radically adjust their
customary treatment goals, for there was little possibility of a successful outcome.

Strong client rejection, unrealistically high worker goals,
and demanding long-term treatment may in some instances bring so
much frustration and discouragement that a worker cannot overcome
his feeling of hopelessness. Furthermore, not every worker is
capable of treating every type of situation. In theory we do not ex-

pect any given worker to be able to treat all the cases he may encounter. First of all, our knowledge is still very limited; it cannot provide the understanding necessary to build a consistently high
level of skill. Furthermore, while we acknowledge the fact that incompatible personalities and temperaments may sometimes prevent
workers and clients from forming a working relationship, we usually just pay lip service to the idea. We tend to place the burden of
responsibility for the treatment impasse on the worker. Too often
when a transfer of a case to another worker is indicated, it occurs
only after a long delay, with the worker forced to feel defeat and
personal failure. We place considerable emphasis in the social
work profession upon the worker's ability to examine himself, to
search out personal factors that may interfere with his practice; but
we do not usually make it possible for him to give up a case and
remain relatively free from a sense of personal failure. From our
own experience and from observing others we have come to the conclusion that there is a tendency on the part of supervisors to suc-
cumb to workers' entreaties to be allowed "another try," to accede
to their determined desire to rise to a difficult treatment situation.
While agencies have moved over the years to a point where they can
categorize some cases as untreatable within their own particular
framework of services, the same latitude is not extended to workers.
As long as treatment demands are given priority when assignments
are made and worker suitability is given second consideration, some
worker-client incompatibility would seem inevitable and should be accepted without its present connotations of personal failure.

An example of this is furnished by the T. case. It was
clear to us relatively early in contact that the worker was having
serious difficulty relating to the client; she was overly sensitive to
the needs of the grossly neglected children and Mrs. T's undis-
guised absence of responsible feeling toward them. The worker's
dedication and determination to surmount the problem were such that
she could not relinquish the case without severe pangs of conscience.
We succumbed to her pleas, but in retrospect we take issue with
this capitulation. We now believe that the case should have been
transferred at an early point, and that we should have insured the

worker's comfortable acceptance of this necessity.

The other three failures seemed to stem from limitations inherent in the situations. In the case of the seriously pathological woman, Miss W, while it is true that the worker was unsuited in training or experience, it is equally true that in this case not even the most highly skilled worker was likely to succeed. We have seen treatment problems strikingly similar to Miss W.'s in a number of cases carried by highly trained and experienced personnel working under close psychiatric supervision. In those instances the psychiatrist suggested, more in earnest than in jest, that a "delinquent worker" would be best at working with this type of client, and still the prognosis would be guarded.

The second failure case also suggests institutional policies as a factor. The Y. family had recourse to their extended family, enabling them to cope with problems. Only one of the six children was problematic; this child's difficulties might have arisen from the needs of both parents for a delinquent child to act out some of their own unconscious anti-social drives. The mother expressed early in contact a sincere desire to have the delinquent child removed from the family and placed elsewhere, but the lack of availabile facilities kept the worker from considering this appropriate treatment plan.

In the case of the J. family, where both parents had long, documented histories of ineducability, it seems reasonable to assume that failure was not primarily due to lack of treatment skills. This family was carried in intensive treatment for three years; during that time we were unable to modify the damaging pattern of child rearing. We were not able to effect a "rescue" of the older children, nor were we able to prevent the perpetuation of delinquent patterns by the younger ones. This case would seem to be representative of a number encountered in treatment, where the failure is basically one of our society. Many localities still refuse to recognize emotional neglect as a valid reason for removing children from parental custody. In addition, there is a failure to provide the kind of substitute facilities that will furnish such children with the care and living conditions needed to help them develop into healthy adults.

Chapter 10
Work With Groups
Introduction

The terms "work with individuals and families" and "work with groups" are loose conceptual designations based upon the traditional social work divisions of casework and group work. The two methods use different techniques, or clusters of techniques, for dealing with people, but this cannot be termed a clear-cut conceptual difference. Social group work is said to utilize the group experience as the primary method of practice;[1] it should be pointed out, however, that the group experience is being used with increasing frequency in family-centered casework. Some families in the NIP program were larger than some of the special interest groups. Perhaps the most useful distinction between the two methods is the fact that work with groups is directed toward systems other than individuals, single families, or households; it is focused upon shared roles that commonly lie outside family life.

Robert D. Vinter cites three conceptions of group work service.[2] The first conception is one that emphasizes the crucial importance of small groups in maintaining a democratic society: "Central to this conception, then, are goals of social participation and democratic decentralization." The second conception holds that "an individual's development can be facilitated by training in social skills and by inculcating social values that are mediated for clients through guided group experiences." The third conception of group work stresses its use "in ameliorating the adverse conditions of individuals whose behavior is disapproved, or who have been disadvantaged by the workings of an imperfect society."[3]

The close relationship between the first two conceptions is probably best demonstrated in a low income housing project such as Farnam Courts, where the absence of social participation and demo-

cratic process is not only the result of long-term social and economic deprivation but also the product of living in an environment
that fosters dependency and discourages democratic expression. The
latter can be defined as a value-based skill, part of a larger pattern of social skills that lower-class families never have a chance
to acquire. Group work aimed at developing social skills has a
function parallel to that of the educational system.[4] Indeed, Vinter
reminds us that "at an earlier time group work was often referred
to as a mode of informal education largely focused on children and
youth."[5]

The third conception of group work is, of course, central to
service in a neighborhood such as Farnam Courts. We saw it as
the preferred method of dealing with the social and emotional problems of a population whose environment offered little security and
stimulation. The group experience was particularly appropriate in
promoting the socialization of deprived pre-schoolers, providing recreation and informal education for school children, supplying social
and aesthetic stimulation to home-bound mothers and to senior citizens living in social isolation. Our decision to work with these
groups was guided by observations we made about social relationships in the Courts long before specific group programs were designed.

The people of Farnam Courts were known to be non-users of
community resources. At times, however, problems such as serious illness, lack of income, or anti-social behavior would compel
families to contact social agencies and institutions. No similar
pressure existed, however, to force them into contact with those
resources offering group work, recreation, or educational programs.
There was no motivation to seek activities that lent purpose or direction to the use of leisure time. Thus the sphere of social relations was constricted to the narrow confines of the housing project.
As a result, the circular form of the problem became evident:
isolated from broader experiences, the people failed to develop social skills; living closely together in the Courts, they found themselves unable to get along in the intimate social climate.

Farnam Courts residents engaged in very few formal activi-

ties; the characteristic pattern of social relations was casual, informal, and accidental. This impression, gathered by extensive observation of and conversations with a wide segment of the adult
population, was verified by a systematic social participation study[6]
done in 1962, two years after the start of the NIP program. We
found that 65 percent of the female heads of households did not participate in any neighborhood or community activity. When participation in NIP groups was excluded, 82 percent of the women were
found to be inactive. The older the woman, the less likely it was
that she was a formal participant.[7] Women with husbands in the
home were somewhat more likely to engage in a formal activity.[8]
Women with children under eighteen in the home were also more
likely participants,[9] the difference presumably reflecting divergen-
cies in age more than anything else. Negro women were much more
active than white women and this relationship held true whether or
not NIP group activities were taken into account.[10]

Informal social participation was not as restricted as formal
participation and it provided an important social outlet for most of
the women. Informal participation was broken down into three categories: (1) planned, in which the woman had arranged a get-togeth-
er with relatives, friends, neighbors, or acquaintances; (2) casual,
in which the woman engaged in social interaction without a prior
plan, usually as a result of an accidental meeting or of unannounced
visiting; and (3) telephoning. Women between the ages of thirty-six
and fifty-eight had higher social participation scores[11] than younger
ones. For the older group the modal pattern of participation was
casual, whereas for the younger women it was planned. The older
the housewife the more important telephoning became as a means of
interacting with relatives, friends, and neighbors. For the total
group of women casual participation was the most common type of
interaction.[12]

Whereas women with husbands in the home engaged in more
formal participation than those without husbands, as we observed
above, the reverse was found to be true in informal social participation.[13] Women with husbands might have found it easier to leave
the home for meetings and parties and at the same time might have

been less in need of informal social stimulation.

Even though marital status related differently to the two types of social participation, formal and informal association were positively correlated for the total sample of lower-class women. Those engaging in some type of formal participation were about twice as likely to have high informal participation scores than were non-participants in formal activities. Negro women in Farnam Courts were found to be more active social participants than white women,[14] but the latter were more likely to engage in informal social interaction with relatives. This difference may have simply reflected the presence or absence of relatives in the area. Among the whites in Farnam Courts, many of Italian descent, kinship ties were found to be strong and possibly a reason for their settling in New Haven many years before. The Negroes, more recent migrants, seemed to have far fewer relatives living in the area.

Summarizing, the systematic social participation study showed that the women at the head of Farnam Courts families engaged in little formal social or recreational activity. When the NIP activities (in 1962) were discounted only one out of six women was found to be active. Older women participated much less in neighborhood and community groups than did younger ones, but by 1962 the introduction of NIP activities had served to double overall formal participation and to considerably reduce the differences between the age groups.

On an informal level women interacted throughout the day, with friends or acquaintances, neighbors and relatives, most of the contacts taking place without prior planning. There was an almost continuous grouping and regrouping taking place among the women as various chores brought them together on the grounds, near their apartment entrances, at the clothes-drying areas, and in the utility rooms. While some daytime home visiting occurred, relationships were tenuous for the most part; the participants usually maintained an attitude of wariness and mistrust. This was understandable in the light of our observations that gossip, cutting remarks, and personal taunts constituted the substance of many conversational exchanges. Other than these, the major subjects were complaints about

bad conditions in general, and lamentations over their personal lives
in particular.

Although all the residents kept their distance, the most isolated were the aged. The young and middle-aged adults found some
relief from the monotony of daily living in gossip, quarrels and
scapegoating. This constituted a form of social intercourse, however negative the after-effects. The elderly, though, exhibited an
overriding need to avoid turmoil, noise, and, above all, vigorous
physical activity. In fact, they even expressed dissatisfaction at
having to live where there were children playing or women gossiping. Many feared being bumped or jostled, being hit by balls or
bicycles. As a group, the elderly were nearly unanimous in stating
that it was unsafe to become well acquainted with neighbors; "stories" might be told that could jeopardize one's residency in the project, where superior physical facilities insured their comfort, a factor of prime importance. This self-imposed aloofness, greater than
that of any other group, left them virtually devoid of social intercourse, except for polite greetings to others on chance meetings in
the hall. Our Neighborhood Survey revealed that this pattern extended even to relatives, principally their grown children, whose
own problems and distant residences made visits a rarity.

While the children maintained groupings on a peer level during play, these bore a striking resemblance to the adult pattern.
Personal taunts, scapegoating and insults led to frequent quarrels
and pummeling matches; there were frequent regroupings and relationships were tenuous. The physical activity of these children was
characterized by a restless aimlessness. When school was out the
grounds were filled with youngsters lashing wildly about, climbing
on buildings and fences, chasing each other, or wrestling over the
few toys available. The smaller children soon were knocked down
and hurt; some of the younger tots would then retreat to dig in the
dirt plots that remained from landscaping attempts.

The games occasionally played called for vigorous running.
While ball games were popular, they were loosely structured; order
could not be maintained for long since quarrels or complaints would
soon interfere. Broken windows were a common occurrence. Other

activities, greatly frowned upon, were drawing and carving on walls
and doors and throwing stones. Equally disapproved was the use of
halls and stairways as improvised play areas by small children.
While this provided the youngsters with protection from the external
turmoil, families without small children resented the traffic impedi-
ment, the excessive noise, and the litter. Two paved sports areas
were equipped for basketball practice; they were completely dominated by a group of older teen-age boys, who kept all others away.
Two additional areas, which had once held swings and other play
fixtures for the very young, had long ago been stripped; only the
skeletons of the equipment remained.

Within the framework of these activities and loose social relationships, there was a small degree of ethnic and racial integration. Among the adults, on a one-to-one basis, a neighborliness--
to the extent that it was practiced at all--existed between white and
Negro tenants. It was rarely carried beyond this level, however,
and there was a guarded attitude on both sides. There was somewhat more tolerance and integration among the young children at
play; however, when serious quarrels arose, realignments took place
along racial lines. Among teen-agers, inter-race relations became
rarer; when these friendships did exist, there was usually intense
parental disapproval, most openly expressed by the whites.

The racial line was sharply drawn, with the separation between the Puerto Ricans and the rest of the population most distinct.
On the one hand, they were targets of discrimination; on the other,
they adopted an aloof attitude that perpetuated the situation and almost made it seem to be of their own choosing. The children were
less comfortable with this accommodation than were the adults, who
were united by language and by memories, customs and habits held
in common. The Puerto Rican children, caught between two cultures, were eager to assimilate but frustrated by discriminatory
practices of the other children. Easily identified by their facial
characteristics, accents, and names, these children hovered on the
fringe of play activities. As a group they were noticeably non-ag-
gressive; a few older youths periodically attempted to break the barriers but had to retreat in the face of taunts and bullying. Conse-

quently these children formed groups among themselves; this was an unsatisfactory situation because their numbers were small and a wide age span separated them. Cultural kinship became a negative bond, arising from their distinctness and accentuating their separateness from the majority group they longed to join.

It can be seen from this description of social interaction among the Farnam Courts residents that there was an acute need for experiences that would promote social skills. In attempting to meet this need through the use of group activities, we defined our goals as follows:

1. Orienting the population to the positive use and enjoyment of leisure time through recreational activities.
2. Effecting socialization above the peer-group level.
3. Acculturating Puerto Ricans and newly arrived southern Negroes.
4. Increasing the integration of ethnic and racial groups.
5. Stimulating creative expression.
6. Educating for increased participation in society.
7. Encouraging and training indigenous leadership.
8. Introducing project residents to the outside world.

These goals made up an ambitious program, and we were by no means successful in achieving them all. Many kinds of activities were tried; some completely failed to attract the people. Those that were considered successful were judged so by staff members, who noted positive changes in participants, and by the community agencies, who were familiar with the housing project and its people. We have chosen to report in detail on seven group work programs, selected because the participants represented key sectors of the treatment population and because the programs answered immediate and pressing needs. Five of the programs were addressed to particular age groups: Pre-school Nursery; Youth Activities; Young Mothers' Club; Adult Arts and Crafts Club; Senior Citizens Club. While some of these programs served the Puerto Ricans, their lack of acculturation called for special handling; therefore, a program addressed to their needs is described separately. The seventh program--the publishing of a neighborhood newspaper--was chosen be-

cause, for the year or so that it flourished, it played a unique role
in the lives of the residents.

Nursery School

In its final form the Nursery School offered a school-readi-
ness program for the culturally deprived child. It began, however,
as a baby-sitting service in conjunction with a daytime program that
we hoped would provide a break in the monotony of housekeeping and
child-tending by arousing interest and encouraging socializing. Only
one woman attended the first meeting, and in her own way she told
us that the real need was for a Nursery School. It was her contention that the women did not need interest programs; as she put it,
"They need relief... period. " We thought our program would provide just that, so we tried a second session. The same woman
again was the only one to appear and this time her words fell on
more receptive ears. Trying hard to interpret the people to the
worker, she pointed out that the young women of Farnam Courts
needed planned, systematic relief from their children before they
could consider programs for themselves. In order to be of help we
had to provide conditions that would relieve and free them; perhaps
then latent imagination and creativity might emerge and there could
be a response to our type of programming.

From these beginnings the Nursery School emerged. Although
it came to have its own philosophy and to serve purposes far removed from those that shaped it, it always served as an important
link to the adult population and as a source of recruitment for subsequent programs. It opened in the fall of 1960 with one afternoon
session a week, but two periods were instituted as soon as additional staff could be recruited. From September, 1961, through June,
1963, the school was in session three days a week--Monday, Wednes-
day, and Friday--from 9:30 to 11:45 a.m. All legal requirements
were fulfilled; pre-enrollment physical examinations were required,
health records were kept, and regular consultations with a nursing
consultant and pediatrician were held.

An intensive, reaching-out approach was required to enroll
a sizable percentage of the eligible children and to realize a fully

integrated group. We first sent personal letters and flyers to the
homes, announcing the program in English and Spanish; then we
made repeated home visits, arranging and expediting physical examinations and providing clinic transportation when necessary. The
Negroes were the first group to respond to the school, the Puerto
Ricans were second, and the whites third.

Once their children were enrolled the parents seemed very
casual, leaving their children without hesitation and not questioning
the staff. The teachers at first interpreted this in a stereotyped
manner as an indication of parental indifference among the lower
class. It soon became apparent, however, that the explanation lay
in the social ineptness of these people. They did not know what to
ask or how to begin. Later, when the barriers were broken, the
questions poured out--in broken sentences, halting speech and two
languages.

The first year, children as young as two-and-a-half were enrolled. When we decided that our goal was preparation for public
school, the minimum age was raised. Top priority was given to
those who would be eligible for school the following September, putting the minimum enrollment age at three years, three months.
Total registration in the two years numbered 54 children, with an
average daily attendance of 42; about 80 percent of our total enrollment were preparing for kindergarten in the fall.

The teachers found among the first group of children rather
unique patterns of behavior, which necessitated a reshaping of the
program. Free play was an aimless, joyless experience for these
youngsters. While the toys and equipment were exciting, they did
not know what to do with them. Some threw them about wildly or
gathered them jealously into big piles; others simply sat about waiting for something to happen. Many were stiff and shy, perhaps as
afraid of doing the wrong thing as were those who cried when they
spilled milk or paint. This may have been related to their dress,
for each was in his best clothes and undoubtedly had been warned at
home to be careful. Simple physical tasks seemed to be beyond
them; they could not hang up their coats or take off their sweaters.
They could not follow simple directions or respond to the spoken

word of either the teacher or other children.   Friendly overtures
often met with guarded responses, and their normal gracefulness
and agility gave way to awkwardness, to jerky, unsure movements
and gestures.   Some of the children would suddenly engage in periods of frantic, blind running, crashing into furniture, other children,
and staff in their speed.

Teaching the children to play, both with the equipment and
with each other, became one of the first objectives.   "Free play"
was given structure; equipped play areas were set up for groups of
about ten children, with a teacher and two volunteers to teach play
skills.   During the initial 30-45 minute period of each nursery session, the teachers worked at socialization and communication among
the children and between staff and children.   School authorities were
asked for estimates of what the children needed in the way of preparation for school; conferences and workshops on the "culturally deprived child" also served as resource material.

The Nursery School had an ambitious set of aims, all designed to ready a child for the "big school" and, hopefully, to lessen the shock of confronting not only a new institution but a new culture.   By helping the child to master new skills and "practical arts"
(such as dressing himself and tying his shoes), confidence and independence could be built; by enhancing his sensory perceptions and
sharpening his responses, creativity would be encouraged.   With improved communication and socialization, experiences could be shared
and the first school lesson--to take turns--learned.   By enlarging
his vocabulary and providing new experiences, the handicap of a restricted environment would hopefully be reduced.   Moreover the organized, structured nursery, with its warm and sympathetic teachers,
would perhaps set up a positive response pattern to schooling that
might carry over to other learning experiences.

The overall program divided broadly into two categories:
child-initiated activities and teacher-organized activities.   Under the
former came such relatively unstructured activities as housekeeping,
dramatic play, construction with blocks, which engaged the children
during the free play period.   As the children responded to play instruction and improved their social skills, they became more imag-

inative and communicative; the free play period was then increased
to allow them more opportunity to exercise their newly-found abilities.

The teacher-organized activities included stories, games and
songs, arts and crafts, plus the usual snack and rest period. Each
session had a period during which small groups of five to six children were engaged in learning practical arts and language arts.
As we have indicated, practical arts consisted of everyday physical
tasks and social graces--hanging up coats, cleaning up work areas,
blowing one's nose, practicing simple table etiquette--necessary for
rudimentary school independence.

Language arts concentrated on recognizing and responding to
language, both spoken and written, in an attempt to develop the children's ability to express themselves. Stories and dramatic play
were used in conjunction with a tape recorder, a phonograph and
records. Rhythms were employed to help in pronunciation, science
experiments (making ice and jello) elicited interested verbal responses, trips were taken that started active discussion. Their
voices were taped and played back to them, slides of their activities were shown to them--even their dramatic play and songs were
recorded and run for their eager ears.

The progress of the children was charted in individual records. With the opening of public school in the fall of 1962, we received our first indication from the "outside" of the school's possible effect. Inquiries were received from elementary school personnel, asking if "something different" were going on in Farnam
Courts. Kindergarten teachers who had known three or four older
siblings were now noticing a difference in the youngest member of
the same family. It was not until we had completed a second year
of the special school-preparatory program that we sought more detailed information from the public schools about the differences that
were being noted. Two kindergarten teachers at the elementary
school that served all Farnam Courts children as well as the larger
Wooster Square area were contacted. Each was given a long list of
names and told only that the NIP social worker wanted her assessment of the children's responses to the new learning situation.

Those children on the list who had been in the NIP Nursery School
had caught the teacher's attention within two days of school opening.
The teachers noted their eagerness to learn, their quick acceptance
of and positive relationship to the teacher, and their longer attention spans. Self-reliant, they participated well and showed mastery
of a variety of tasks. With their friendly, outgoing attitude, ability
to verbalize, and predisposition to learn, they were described by
the teachers as radically different from the other neighborhood children, obviously of the same socio-economic class. The teachers
were unacquainted with the NIP program, for they had been reas-
signed from other areas; they had, however, become aware that
these children had been exposed to "something," from a comment
the youngsters frequently made: "We learned that in our school."

Work with Parents of Nursery School Children

More time was required to involve the parents in the nursery
program than would have been necessary with middle-class parents.
The Nursery School had no meaning to the lower-class mother until
she could see its impact in concrete terms. When the child brought
drawings home and asked for paper to make more, taught his siblings songs and games, and was able to amuse himself for much
longer periods of time, the mother saw meaning and value in the
program, her curiosity was aroused, and she began to respond.

Most of these people had never enjoyed positive school experiences; formal education had never been directly related to their
daily lives. Although they verbalized a desire for their children to
learn, they were completely unaware of their own role and responsibility in the educational process. They had no idea that their children were considered understimulated or that they started school under a handicap.

To reach the mother who was ready to show interest in the
school, we set up an Open House, luring her with a party atmosphere. The refreshments and the pupil art exhibit, the informality
of the proceedings helped many overcome their self-consciousness.
Each was sought out by the staff and told something about her child
that reflected positively upon parental handling. Over refreshments,

brief comments on group discipline and needs of children at this
age were made. One teacher mentioned the ways in which the
school supplements the home and discussed the carry-over from
nursery to kindergarten. The parents listened with interest but
could not bring themselves to ask questions during the formal question period. Instead, they sought the teachers out and asked questions afterwards. Obviously we could not lecture to the group; it
was necessary to take a great deal of time, to talk slowly, and
above all to project warm acceptance. Mrs. S., for instance, had
an older daughter in public school and had attended a P.T.A. meeting. When asked by the staff about her conversation with the teacher, she said, "Oh, she talked a lot...she talked so fast I couldn't
hear her...she said that Donna pouts..she didn't give me a chance
to ask any questions...then she said, 'Come and visit any time'...
I didn't get much out of it...."

A report from our nursery parent-teacher meeting provides
contrast: "Mrs. S. talked to the teachers and was told about her
child's progress. The report was based on the positive aspects of
the little girl's development. The child had made a good adjustment and a great deal of progress in the time we have had her.
Mrs. S. had to be pushed out the door along with the other mothers
at the end of the evening because she had such a pleasant time.
She and a teacher and another mother tried to do the children's puz-
zles and all agreed that they were too difficult for adults! The
teachers liked the mothers and let them know it."

Parent-teacher meetings of this kind were held about four
times during the year. The idea of a mother-child program, i.e.,
mothers involved in helping with the nursery, was abandoned when
it became evident that the women needed free time rather than another chance to be with children. Several attempts were made to
establish a morning activity, such as a craft class, but there was
no interest; for a time it was felt that this was conclusive evidence
that the women wanted to stay home in the morning.

When a Homemaker was appointed to the Housing Authority
after the Nursery School had been in operation for a year, we made
another attempt to hold morning classes. The first class was in

chair re-covering and twelve women and men participated, all with
children in the nursery. A successful mending class followed, succeeded by a cooking class. Morning meetings with the visiting
nurse, dealing with the health needs and concerns of the child at
age three or four, drew a response of eight women.

We found that it took almost two years for families to in-
corporate the nursery program into their way of life, and to be able
to plan their liberated time usefully. The most popular topics of
the morning programs were sex education, first aid, diseases of
childhood, and snacks for children. The most popular homemaking
programs were chair covering, which interested men as well as women, and cooking, which emphasized inexpensive, easy-to-prepare
casserole dishes. The daytime program, even in its best year, was
poorly attended.

Young Mothers' Club

When early attempts to attract women to a daytime program
failed, we realized we were projecting our own ideas of program.
Our view of what they most needed--classes designed to improve
their functioning as mothers and homemakers--did not correspond
with their own desires. When we matched the purpose and type of
program to their need by organizing a Young Mothers' Club, twenty-five to thirty young women with children in Nursery School began
attending. Since they wanted, above all else, a night out, the group
met in the evening; this provided an opportunity to get away from
home, even though it was only as far away as the Social Hall in the
Administration Building. Young, upwardly striving Negro women
were attracted to the club, which met weekly; it remained segregated until the last year, when a few white women joined.

Many of the early members exhibited intolerance toward themselves as well as toward each other. The first meetings were
lengthy bull sessions about life in Farnam Courts. The women
blamed themselves for their children's problems and they showed
little, if any, pride in their own culture and background. Nearly
all of these women had husbands in the home; on the whole, they
showed a negative, hostile, superior attitude toward their partners.

Most of the members had married young and had quickly begun
bearing children. Few had experienced the young adult state, and
they seemed to have much "unfinished business" left over from their
youth. At least this was the impression gained from watching these
young women, all of whom had several children (two had eight
apiece), bringing their records, dancing and laughing together after
meetings, much in the manner of adolescent girls. Involved so
early in parenthood and responsibility, they seemed to have never
finished their own developmental processes. Before we were fully
aware of this, the amount of marital discord that was voiced moved
the worker to suggest that some joint husband and wife sessions
should be held. The women indicated that they wanted no part of
this idea. Emphatic statements such as, "That's what we came
here to get away from," summed up the general attitude.

Difficulties in maintaining peer relationships were manifest
from the first meeting. One woman spoke for all when she said,
"We don't want any officers." Another added, "We've heard (of) it
before; when you have officers, you have trouble. Somebody acts
like boss and you have fights; we don't want our club to break up
like that." They operated with a number of small committees, usually composed of three women; although they all worked hard and
well on their assignments, they remained dependent upon the group
leader. In the early stages many decisions were left to her, but
this responsibility tapered off as the group became more harmoni-
ous and close-knit. The women never reached the point where they
could fully accept peer leadership; they remained adamantly against
electing officers and being independent throughout the two-and-a-half
years of club existence.

As time went on, changes in behavior were noted. There
gradually developed a pattern of dressing up for regular meetings.
Housedresses gave way to prettier clothes, the women wore high
heels and make-up. The sessions ceased to be dominated by one
woman, of commanding voice and figure, with many aggressive tales
to tell. Discussions were balanced between pleasant and serious
topics; sometimes we brought in speakers on specific topics of
group interest.

From the beginning there had been indications that these young women were deeply concerned about their children and their relationships with them. A talk by the Guidance Counsellor of the local elementary school, on the subject of "Reading Readiness," provided an opportunity for airing their problems. In the discussion that followed, it became evident that many carried strong guilt feelings; "Is it wrong to dislike your children sometimes?" one of the women asked. Living in isolation from ideas and people, most of them believed that their difficulties in rearing their children were unique. They were astounded to hear that such problems were universal. Many had no idea that reading readiness applied to all school children, not just their own.

In two other sessions where mother-child relationships were discussed, the characteristic shyness gave way to a frank disclosure by a number of women of their own unhappy childhood experiences. It was evident that these women were desperately sincere when they expressed a desire for their own children to "have it better," to escape the ignorance and the trial and error learning of their own lives.

The most popular activities the first year were those of a social and entertaining nature--supper parties, birthday celebrations, occasional evenings of card playing. The second year saw a shift to an interest in giving service--as the women put it, "doing something for others." Deciding to raise money for "a needy family" and for nursery school equipment, they ran a bingo night to benefit these two causes.

A most significant program was a talk given by an outstanding Negro woman lawyer, Miss Pauli Murray, who was studying at Yale University for a doctorate in international jurisprudence. Born in the South, raised in poverty by a grandmother who had been a slave, she had become a law partner in a well-known New York firm. Her career had included a position on the Women's Commission of the United Nations, and she had spent over a year in Ghana helping to draft its constitution and laws.

She had been invited to our meeting to show pictures of life in Ghana and to talk about her African experiences. But her grasp

of social and economic forces and her understanding of poverty and
deprivation caused her to relate sensitively to the group. Paying
these women a rare tribute, she praised them for continuing, in
spite of poverty and misfortune, to take responsibility for the care
of their homes and families. Aware of society's low opinion of
them, these wives and mothers knew their inadequacies well but
were unaware of their own strengths.

This key experience was followed by others indicative of
widening horizons. The club members were inspired by Civil Rights
speakers to organize a benefit dance to raise money for the NAACP;
they contributed to a nearby settlement house during its building
drive, and held special benefit sales for C.O.R.E.

Dr. Albert Solnit, a psychiatrist on the faculty of Yale University's Child Study Center, who worked with the group, built on
the spirit of pride that Miss Murray kindled. He gave support, encouragement and guidance. In sessions with Dr. Solnit, the women
were able to reveal their anxieties freely. Sex was a particularly
difficult area, and in discussing sex education, the extent of their
basic fears came to light. Many had difficulty talking about sex to
their children because of their own harsh and brutal childhood experiences.

Dr. Solnit gave them advice, a chance to talk, and recognition for their many strengths. These women were often the only
stabilizing force in a large family, and it may have been this unconscious knowledge that led them to restrict the club to females.
Discussion about their rights and responsibilities as women inevita-
bly led to talk about their husbands. Some began to understand that
their husbands' failures were not all due to personal inadequacy.
As a more positive attitude toward men developed, Dr. Solnit again
raised the question of joint husband-wife meetings. This was again
vetoed, with the suggestion this time that the men meet with the
doctor alone. Such a session actually did take place.

The annual highlight of the Young Mothers Club program was
a fashion show put on in Farnam Courts by New Haven's leading
department store, with club members as models. It was held each
June for the three years of NIP action. The mothers were required

to visit the store to try on the clothes they were to wear; many of
them had never been there before, no one had ever been in a fashion show, and few had seen one. The young store employee who
arranged the show and was its commentator showed tact and sensitivity, which helped make the experience an ego-builder for the
models and an occasion of pride for the observers.

For evaluation of the club program, it is helpful to use the
framework of Helen Northern, who has laid out three main areas
in which the social group worker can evaluate change in individuals
as a result of a group work experience. These areas are changes
in attitude, changes in relationships, and changes in other behavior;
i.e., does the individual dress differently, is he more or less destructive, does his behavior conform to socially accepted norms,
and has his pathological behavior changed?[15] As she points out,

> ...the general goal of all social group work is to effect
> changes or adaptations in an individual's attitudes, rela-
> tionships, and behavior, to the end that he may develop
> greater personal adequacy and improved social adjust-
> ment.[16]

To evaluate group change is more difficult, but some attempts can be made to relate individual development to group development through an analysis of intra-group behavior. Using the
Young Mothers' Club as an example the following sets of observations, though not meriting the designation of research, yielded some
indicants about the group's development:

(1) Changes in Attitudes

We saw increased pride in self, an increasing confidence in
attempting activities, and freer self-expression. There was evidence of awakening cultural and racial identity, of some lessened
hostility toward family members. The members became able to express pity for their parents' hard lives. There was more insight
into the inter-relationship of their parents' deprivation, their parents'
behavior, and their own life situations. We saw a lessening of expressed hostility to Puerto Ricans and more toleration for the behavior patterns of others. This was accompanied by a new interest
in the ideas of others, most pronounced in the areas of civil rights
and family psychodynamics. Perhaps the second most important

change (after the rise in self-esteem) was a more benign and accurate view of their husbands as social victims rather than aggressors.

(2) Changes in Relationships

The most pronounced change came within the club, where the women gradually began to be more open, friendly, and supportive. Relationships with their children seemed somewhat easier; they evidenced greater sympathy with their youngster's developmental stages and tasks, stemming from their own increased knowledge. Concern was reflected in their anxiety lest the children "catch the culture." A general distrust of all authority figures became more selective. There was some transfer to teachers of the positive relationship developed with the social workers. A more realistic appraisal of each other, their husbands, and people around them was in evidence. They could tolerate frustration and even failure better. In general, expression of feeling came easier and was less emotionally charged. They assumed that they were "among friends" and their discussions were frank but friendly.

(3) Changes in Behavior

The most visible change was the way the women began to dress up for the meetings. From tales of "doom and gloom," discussions became a balanced mixture of pleasant and serious matters.

No one woman changed in every area, nor did every woman need to. There were, however, two general changes recorded and observed: in the pragmatic realm, new skills were acquired through organizing and participating in club routines and money-raising projects; in the psychological realm, a heightened sense of self-esteem engendered a motivation for change.

Membership in NIP's Young Mothers' Club helped to prepare this group of upwardly striving young women, with few previous outlets, to improve and expand their social relationships, and enabled them to begin to view themselves, their families, and culture more positively.

Youth Activities

There was no need to institute intensive reaching-out efforts to bring the children of Farnam Courts into our group program, for their response was overwhelming. In October, 1959, Mr. William DeGeorge, Director of Farnam Neighborhood House, began a recreational program on the premises of the housing project, with a staff of two assistants and four college student helpers. Picking three boys who knew him from attending camp, Mr. DeGeorge asked that word be spread about a program to start in the Courts the next week. "Yeh? I'll bet!" responded one youngster, and this overt disbelief made one wonder if this recruiting approach would work. The boys were evidently effective messengers, for on the appointed day approximately one hundred children were waiting to greet the staff in front of the Administration Building. The younger ones were gathered from the vestibules and stairways, and registration began.

This enthusiasm created a problem of its own--that of managing and controlling a large number of active, restless children with no prior experience in structured group activities other than the classroom. Programming for twelve to fourteen groups, a total of 175 children, was a challenge. Action games, sports and contests were introduced to meet their need for almost constant movement; however, an appreciable number could not be drawn into this kind of activity in the beginning. For many months leaders were forced to offer a variety of simultaneous activities within each group. An observer would be confronted with the following indoor scene typifying a girls' group during this period: five or six children would be playing a game the leader had taught them; two friends, off in another corner, would be playing catch-ball; two or three loners would be drawing, painting, or cutting paper; another loner or two might be running around, making up dance steps or whirling silently. Any attempt to draw the entire group together invariably lost a considerable number who were not yet ready for such an experience. Superficially it seemed easier to draw the boys together in a group game, but here too, the general behavior characteristics interfered. Essential skills had to be taught, often on an individual basis; frequent disputes had to be mediated; poor losers and the quickly discouraged had to be handled tactfully or they would disappear; and a very wide choice of activities had to be available in order to hold interest and reduce frustration.

The children's almost desperate hunger for program was matched by the extreme patience and flexibility shown by the staff. By June, 1961, social skills were well advanced and groups more in conformance with traditional social work practice were coming into being. This process took eighteen months, during which an expansion of staff permitted the involvement of over 250 children (65 percent of the children in the Courts).

Considerable change had taken place during this period. By offering a wide choice of activities, the leaders were able to become acquainted with and find something of interest for the loners; gradually several of these were drawn together and finally all members were engaged in a common activity. From a widespread inability to relate either to peers or adults, or to accept limits and structured activity, the children became knitted into peer clubs; the members felt a group allegiance and pride meaningful enough to exert a check on negative behavior and individual self-interest. There was evidence that some incorporation of the leaders' values and modes of behavior had taken place. There was more fair dealing, more offers to help the less skilled; there was a reduction in scapegoating, fighting, malicious mischief, and the destruction of property; there was more acceptance of minorities. The resigned acceptance of the narrow insularity of Courts life gave way to curiosity and interest in the wider community. Numerous trips and excursions were made as soon as the establishment of group control allowed.

Several other important changes had taken place, which had implications for future program. There seemed to be a diminished need for constant action and motion. Children could sit still for longer periods of time, their attention span was lengthened, and they could tolerate discussion periods during group sessions. Many boys made a significant shift that can only be appreciated when viewed in the context of their cultural milieu: emulating leaders they respected and liked, they began to respond to creative arts projects--painting, sculpting, collage making. Such activity would have previously earned a boy the taunt of "sissy" and would have been avoided at all cost.

The arts and crafts program was introduced after the groups were fairly well molded; it was an attempt to expand the children's horizons by exposing them to new experiences. Aside from teaching skills and providing an opportunity to cooperate, we hoped it would stimulate the use of imagination and encourage uninhibited expression, at the same time creating a sense of accomplishment and mastery in a non-competitive fashion. Such a high degree of sustained interest was shown in this program that it became a part of all group sessions; in addition, regular weekly classes were instituted.

A newspaper was set up to encourage creative writing. In contrast to the art work, which was offered in school and therefore familiar (but previously uninteresting), creative writing was a totally new experience. A majority of the more than fifty children who became regular contributors to the Farnam Courts Junior News were elementary school pupils handicapped by poor reading and writing abilities. They were, nevertheless, encouraged to write and became so eager to do so that they dictated their stories to staff leaders. The point of view and style of the poems, articles, and "thoughts" were given no editorial treatment, and their originality soon stirred community-wide interest. The newspaper became a model for other groups and outside requests for copies increased circulation to over 200 in the greater New Haven area and in other Connecticut communities.

Out of the group work program appeared indigenous teen-age leaders, both boys and girls, giving rise to an NIP Leadership Training Program. The earliest signs of leadership were noted by the staff, who began identifying individuals who acted as effective peacemakers and who imitated their leaders by patiently giving instruction to less skilled club members. These emerging leaders were found to be grouping, supervising, and instructing younger children in a variety of games and sports during evenings and weekends, after the regular staff had dispersed. While these young residents were to some extent imitating the NIP staff, they were also improvising in a distinct and creative manner of their own. Since they exhibited such natural capabilities, increasing responsibility was

given them while they were being tutored in programming and principles of supervision.   As they demonstrated increasing skill, they
were assigned groups of their own; following a year of apprentice-
ship they were promoted to junior leader positions and given a salary.   This small corps of ten tested indigenous leaders was the
backbone of a much diminished but experienced staff that was able
to run a program during the summers of 1963 and 1964; once trained,
these leaders applied themselves to their work around the clock, in
the evenings, on weekends, and even on holidays.

The Leadership Program served two original NIP goals: (1)
to establish a bridge between the Courts population and the wider
community, and (2) to effect some continuity of service following
the termination of NIP.   Neither goal, in our opinion, could be realized unless the community agencies with which the population
would be connected would take into account certain factors.   First
in importance was the fact that the majority of youngsters in Farnam Courts, although exhibiting great interest in the NIP group work
program, were still not able to independently seek such programs
off the premises.   In addition, it seemed important that community
personnel should become acquainted with the behavioral characteristics of the population, so as to reduce the chance of a cultural clash
that might undermine a workable relationship.   Concerned about the
future, we sought organizations that were willing to offer some continuity of approach during a period of transition, when NIP would be
terminated and the population would still need special services on
the premises.   The Y. M. C. A. at that time was in the process of
instituting an expanded, decentralized "neighborhood" type of program.   Utilizing the indigenous teen-age leadership group in Farnam
Courts, the "Y" professional staff and the NIP Director of Youth Activities set up an exchange-of-staff training plan.   A number of the
Junior NIP Leaders became part of the "Y" staff and continued to
work in Farnam Courts after NIP terminated.

The Boy Scouts of America seemed to offer another opportunity for continuity, if we could bring them into the housing project.
By concerted effort we formed a troop; it was to become our only
exhibit--completely unanticipated--of having effected some fundamen-

tal institutional modifications. The history of Troop 105 showed
how changes in regulations and modes of operation could be made
with a studied regard for the behavior and characteristics of the
population to be served.

The Boy Scouts' outdoor program, with its demands for physical work, movement, and task variation, seemed particularly suited
to the restless, action-oriented, lower-class boy. Many of the requirements for the establishment and maintenance of a troop, however, presented these serious obstacles:

1. Leadership--in traditional troops this is furnished by
   fathers. In deprived homes, there is a high percentage
   of missing fathers. Furthermore, the idea of sharing activities and finding companionship with one's son was foreign to Farnam Courts fathers.

2. Natural peer groupings--this would result in completely
   segregated troops, formed along racial and ethnic lines.

3. Skill requirements--the need for reading ability in order
   to learn the rules would eliminate those who were most in
   need of the program.

4. Financing--purchasing their own uniforms and raising
   money for camping equipment would be too difficult for
   this population group.

We were able to secure college students as part-time group
leaders, since liaison had been established with the local universi-
ties at the time of NIP's activation. We asked the schools for help
when it became evident that we would have to find outside troop
leadership. Alpha Phi Omega, a national service fraternity chapter
at Yale University, quickly responded; a large number of members
had scouting experience and they were interested in the challenge
presented by Farnam Courts. After a number of briefing sessions,
during which the NIP Youth Director described the neighborhood and
its youth, the fraternity men gave invaluable help in detailing the
modifications of the traditional scouting format that would be necessary. They also aided in selling the idea to the local and national
councils.

All eligible boys in Farnam Courts, forty-three in all, were

invited to become scouts. More than half, probably attracted by
curiosity, came to the first meeting; it was typical that they initially expressed scorn at the idea of becoming scouts. The fraternity
supplied a whole company of Scoutmasters; twelve to fourteen enthusiastic young men held interest high at that first meeting by instituting vigorously competitive games, while advertising outdoor fun
and adventure on a camping trip in the very near future. In succeeding weeks the boys came back with friends, so that in a short
time almost every eligible Farnam Courts boy was a member.

An article in the March, 1963 issue of the Boy Scouts' magazine, Scouting, told of our "flexible but standard" scouting program;
part of it is reprinted below.

> Initial patrol organization did not follow the natural boy-
> gang pattern that would have created separate Puerto Rican,
> Negro, and Italian groups and avoided solution of several
> related problems. The boys were assigned to patrols with
> a calculated distribution of potential leaders and potential
> troublemakers. Until boy leadership could be developed,
> an assistant Scoutmaster was assigned to guide each patrol.
>
> More than a dozen Alpha Phi Omegas serve as Scoutmaster,
> assistants, and committeemen. An unusual amount of adult
> help was necessary to give individual training in Scouting
> skills and understanding of the rules of the Scouting game.
> Because of language differences or inadequate schooling,
> some boys could not read the Boy Scout Handbook. Where
> interpretation was needed, a Spanish-speaking leader worked
> with Puerto Rican boys outside troop meetings. The Scout
> Oath and Law were printed on large placards and prominent-
> ly displayed. In early meetings much time was spent help-
> ing boys individually to understand these ideals in terms of
> their daily lives. Thus we devised methods to meet the
> group's special problems as they arose.
>
> Two things at the outset were considered essential for Troop
> 105's success--uniforms and a full outdoor program. Uni-
> forms and camping equipment cost money, and that was one
> thing that neither our Scouts nor their families nor the spon-
> sor had to spare...
>
> Conventional financial support from parents or neighborhood
> projects was unavailable to this troop, at least in the begin-
> ning. We set up a general treasury for both group and indi-
> vidual expenses and built it up by an extensive sale of ball-
> point pens in more prosperous areas of the city. This and
> other money-earning projects were carefully organized and
> carried out under close supervision. All Scouts were re-

quired to participate in the earning in order to share in the treasury. This procedure proved an overwhelming success, financially and otherwise. The boys learned to work for a common cause. One with a long record of thefts proved he could handle money honestly.

A used-uniform collection on the Yale campus provided a stock of uniforms. Boys earned these uniforms at a nominal cost when they became Tenderfoot Scouts. Two silk-screen artists produced a special troop neckerchief at cost. A congressman donated an American flag that had flown over the national capitol. Within a few months a well-outfitted troop began to emerge.

Camping equipment required flexibility and ingenuity. Most of the cooking was done in tin cans or aluminum foil. Army ponchos costing $1.00 apiece were buttoned together and pitched as tents. Horseshoe packs lashed with binder twine were used instead of store-bought packs. Our strong camping program began with a minimum cost for gear.

With the first court of honor the patrol leaders' council insisted on having a family spaghetti supper--despite some hesitancy on the part of adult leaders. Fully half of the parents attended, and many mothers shared in the preparations.

Older teen-agers waited on tables. What began as a dubious project turned into a full-scale neighborhood endeavor. When an Easter egg hunt was held for youngsters in the housing project, uniformed Scouts served as guides to keep spectators within bounds. Their authority was respected by adults and older boys and girls.

Troop 105, a little over a year old (in March, 1963), lacks the full test of time, but the impact of Scouting on the lives of these boys and upon their neighborhood is already visible. The greatest thrill is the response of the boys themselves. Several of them spontaneously coached other boys for an hour a day on the Tenderfoot requirements. For the first time in their lives more than one handled money honestly, and also for the first time gained some recognition for a positive accomplishment. [17]

The enthusiasm, interest, and zeal shown by the service fraternity leaders had some unexpected results. All of the members became self-appointed agents for their pet project, launching individual campaigns to stimulate interest in similar undertakings in their home communities. One member made a documentary film showing Troop 105 in development and action, including "before" footage of the impact of redevelopment on the neighborhood. This

film aroused such interest at the National Scout Headquarters that
an Urban Relationships Workshop was set up at Mendham, New Jersey, for the professional staff and Scouting executives from eastern
cities; similar workshops were held in Chicago and Los Angeles.
Nationwide interest was further stimulated by a letter[18] from the
Commissioner of Public Housing Administration, Marie C. McGuire,
to all local Public Housing Authorities in the country, calling attention to the Scouting article and encouraging them to initiate similar
endeavors in their housing projects.

The two NIP goals--building a bridge between the population
and the larger community, and insuring some continuity of services
beyond the life of the project--were further served by a program developed cooperatively with the state leaders of the 4-H Clubs. This
organization was eager to extend its services to youth in the inner
city, and after joint planning with the NIP staff, it undertood a varied program for the boys and girls of Farnam Courts during 1962-
63. Forty to fifty youngsters attended classes on cooking, science,
woodworking, bicycle repair and dog care. While not all the programs were successful (cooking and science were the most popular),
the response encouraged the 4-H Club leaders to extend their operations. Guided by the Youth Program Director of NIP, in the summer of 1963 4-H sponsored a Busy Beaver Club for boys 12 to 15
years old. The following were the objectives of the club, as listed
by the 4-H Club assistant leader:

1. Establishing a sense of community pride and responsibility through Community Service projects.
2. Learning about the democratic process through practice
   and club meetings.
3. Developing a broadened outlook on people and places,
   through trips and tours.
4. Disclosing some of the projects and activities that 4-H
   can sponsor in an inner city area.[19]

The club began its service activities at the Farnam Courts
basketball courts and the tiny tots' play area. After a thorough
cleaning, equipment was repaired, extensive painting was done in
cheerful bright colors, broken or missing equipment parts were ob-

tained and installed. The positive effects of these activities were quite evident. The Housing Authority staff, which had given permission for the club's operation on its property but was less than confident that any projects would be carried out, made a commitment to replace equipment in the future and to provide labor for heavy chores. The tenants responded by encouraging their children to maintain the grounds in better order. Both the staff and tenants were lavish in their praise and support of club activities.

As in the case of the Boy Scouts, the 4-H Clubs found that they were able to engage this population by making some necessary modifications in their traditional approach. These changes included suspending the practice of democratic procedures and exerting strong leadership for a lengthy indoctrination period; relying on more action and trips, fewer talking sessions; making substitutions for parental leadership and accepting the reality of limited active parental involvement.

Senior Citizens

In no group is the problem of loneliness more acute than among the elderly poor. Their objective problems are intensified by the feeling of being unwanted, and physical frailties due to age and poor health make for a house-bound existence. These factors, coupled with a self-imposed isolation, made the aged of Farnam Courts virtually invisible. The poverty of their social relations and their distress due to loneliness, uncovered by our social participation study in the fall of 1961, gave rise to a special program aimed at the residents sixty-five years of age and over.

Recruiting for the Senior Citizens Club was difficult. Letters, fliers, and notices netted only three people for the first meeting. Home visits followed; in a few instances attendance was dependent upon the group leader personally escorting members to the meeting and helping with first introductions. Many expressed such vehement initial rejection that great skill was required to determine whether or not this was a reversible attitude. Of the 105 elderly who were approached, about 7 percent remained aloof from Farnam Courts life, both informal and organized. When interviewed, they replied: "I'm not interested in mixing or going out. I live a quiet life.

That's the way I am; that's all.   I'm not interested." Approximately another 30 percent were first generation Italians who spoke almost no English; only two women were recruited from among this
group.   Another third of this population was very restricted in
movement, being either bedridden, invalids, or very feeble.   The
fifteen to twenty elderly persons who joined the club were all frail,
so we set up an agenda of activities that were fairly passive while
being potentially pleasurable.   The emphasis was on comfort and
support rather than challenge.   Initially dividing along racial lines,
the club members quickly found that the companionship afforded
within the club was more valuable to them than their prejudices.
They moved from a polite, formal, and tentative relationship with
each other to a warm, relaxed, and supportive one.   In these meetings they talked together about their lives, past and present, and
shared treasured snapshots; the worker reported a degree of rapport and acceptance probably unique in each of their lives.

Planning and sharing a luncheon was one of the earliest activities facilitating socialization.   The menu was simple--hot soup,
crackers, dessert and coffee.   Several individuals saw this as a
rare treat, because the ingredients for home-cooked soup were too
expensive, and the cooking too laborious for a person living alone.
The program included birthday parties and excursions; slides, mov-
ies, travelogues and musicales; and community service of various
sorts.

The members' frailties and lack of social participation had
so limited their horizons that they could offer no suggestions for
destinations when trips were discussed.   They could only say,
"Away from here, anywhere," and they were relieved when the worker suggested a surprise trip.   These excursions brought them into
contact with the world at large; one trip in particular served to alleviate a major worry--that of being "put away in a poor farm" if
they became unable to care for themselves.   The city institution for
New Haven's elderly indigent, Springside Home, had recently been
moved to a beautiful new building boasting a hospital, recreation
facilties, new lounges, and, most important of all, a trained, experienced director.   Under his leadership the home had become a

cheerful place, without the sense of defeat and failure that had previously characterized it.   The NIP Senior Citizens Club visited there
several times, bringing gifts of candy to the residents.   These visits, supposedly to cheer the residents, did in fact cheer their own
club members, who expressed relief about the change in the Home
and also, indirectly, about their own future prospects.

We found that the elderly residents as a group were of all
tenants the most content with their living conditions in Farnam
Courts.   Grateful for their good housing, they often verbalized appreciation for being warm in the winter.   They knew their only alternatives were expensive private apartments or inadequate tenements; they showed their appreciation by keeping their halls and
stairs the cleanest in the project.   One woman cleaned the brass
mailboxes, while another had a little "greenhouse" outside her door.
The complaints about noisy children and quarrelsome neighbors were
apparently not to be taken seriously.   If a NIP worker replied to
complaints by suggesting a move to a different area of the project,
the reply might very well be, "But this is my home! I ain't gonna
move again until I die!"

Members of the club showed clearly that they suffered from
a feeling of uselessness, both to their families and the larger community.   As Bertha Reynolds expressed it in her book:

> The most bitter experience of all is to feel left over from
> a former world... to live an unwanted tenant of a new world
> in which everyone's ideas and interests are incomprehensible
> so that one has nothing to give.[20]

To answer the need to be useful, hospital service (rolling bandages,
cutting gauze dressings, packaging swabs, etc.) immediately suggested itself.   Many of the elderly had poor eyesight and coordination, and they tired easily.   The hospital, however, recognized their
need to give service and felt that it was important to provide as
much work as possible, even though they would have preferred it
done on their own premises.

Club members felt that this was their most significant program, and we could never get enough work to satisfy them.   Seeing
the hospital supplies spread out when they entered the room, they
would say such things as "Good, good!," "I hope you have a lot

for us to do," or "I am always so happy when we do something for
others and help--it makes you feel good to help someone who needs
it." This was the first time in many years that many of these
people had an opportunity to feel useful.

It was occasionally possible to bring in the outside world.
A congressman attended one club meeting and later made several
home visits to individual members. It was a time when everyone
was interested in Medicare; the members eagerly told him about
themselves, their lives, and their medical problems. It made them
feel that they had not been forgotten, to know that someone in Washington was interested in what they thought about policies and politics.

Club members did not always know what type of program
they wanted, but they let us know in no uncertain terms when something did not suit them. At one time, we had thought it preferable
to have the club use the Senior Center facilities at the new Community School nearby. The members were taken there on a trip; later,
arrangements were made for them to do there the hospital work they
liked so much. But the strange worker who supervised the hospital work at the Community School awed them. The attendance sheet
told the tale: average attendance for hospital work at Farnam
Courts, 10-12; average attendance at the three sessions at the
school, 3-4; average attendance for hospital work back at Farnam
Courts, 10-12. Their attendance let us know which programs were
to their liking and which were not. They also boycotted the one or
two occasions when we attempted to introduce them to simple handi-
crafts and creative painting, which they felt suitable only for children.

The drop-outs in this program were caused either by illness
or death--both of which occurred with great frequency. During
NIP's action period, from September, 1960, to August, 1963, there
were ten deaths among the thirty-odd members of the Senior Citizens Club.

Mass Activities

Although a number of successful interest groups were operating, the majority of residents did not attend. To draw these people

out, mass programs were periodically offered, requiring nothing
from the individual other than his presence as listener-observer.
These programs, reaching a large number of adults who had remained aloof, served to establish a tie between them and the outside world and succeeded in fostering some feelings of neighborhood
pride.

Musical variety shows, presented by local professional
groups and individuals, were extremely popular. By including popular, semi-classical, and operatic Italian selections, an audience of
middle-aged and elderly Italian persons was built. Such programs
attracted people who had previously never come together. After
coming to a few mass programs, some of the elderly, especially
those who spoke little English, began to come to Open House parties
sponsored by the Senior Citizens Club. Their pleasure at being
hosts and helping to entertain as many as 100 people from other
clubs on their own grounds was evident. The entertainers who sang
at these and other functions returned the enjoyment and affection;
many of them appeared repeatedly, bringing their own friends and
relatives to meet the Farnam Courts people.

The Christmas season provided an ideal time to involve the
tenants in activities. It had long been a custom to give toys and
candy to the children. In our first year we, too, collected toys;
these were given out by the staff to parents on a first come, first
served basis. In the second and third years, however, the toys
were turned over to the Mothers' Club, which in turn sold them at
very low prices to the parents. The fact that people could choose
which toys they wanted to buy brought a different feeling to the whole
process. The Mothers' Club was able to do a service and make a
small profit for their treasury, while the people did not feel that
they were the objects of charity.

Decorating and displaying a huge Christmas tree became an
annual joint endeavor that united the youth and the adults. The women's and children's crafts classes provided ingenious decorations
representing the handiwork of many individuals, who enjoyed the spirit of cooperative accomplishment and neighborhood pride that resulted. The Social Hall of the Administration Building became an

exhibit hall for the season and the New Haven Chorale came to sing Christmas songs, with refreshments provided for all. The staff was somewhat apprehensive over the people's response to the chorale, since the music would undoubtedly include classical numbers as well as seasonal and popular tunes. Afraid at first of having no audience, we found ourselves with an overflowing crowd, whose enjoyment was loudly expressed.

A staff error led to an unusual program--better than the planned one--in 1962. The New Haven Chorale arrived for its yearly program, but no audience came. Committee people appeared, took their stations, and waited for the rush. As time went by and wonder increased, it was discovered that the fliers announcing the program had not been delivered. We suggested to the members of the Chorale that they go out and serenade in the open air; we might pick up an audience as well as give pleasure to some shut-ins. Carrying candles, the group and the staff walked through the project singing while teen-agers passed out the fliers. The group sang in front of buildings where there were sick or old people. Windows popped open, greetings were exchanged, and the carolling group swelled as residents joined the procession. The singers returned to the hall with an audience and the program was completed indoors.

The gaiety shown at this and other mass programs led to expressions of pleasure that such events were happening at Farnam Courts. People could be heard saying, "Doesn't this old building look beautiful?" or "I can't believe this is happening here!"

Arts and Crafts Class

The reader may recall a small band of six women who had been the key "doers" in the Tenants Council, alienating tenants and helping bring about its demise. We mentioned earlier that they were a force with which we had to reckon in early attempts at setting up programs. Their boundless energy was almost unbelievable. Every meeting or activity brought forth their desire to dominate. When the Mothers' Club was being organized, they were all ready to join. We were able to prevent this by restricting membership to young mothers, ages eighteen to thirty-five--a defensive ruling that later proved logical too.

The only way we could contain them, keep them from dominating and thereby spoiling other groups, was to provide them with an activity exclusively their own. This measure, born of sheer desperation, would also prevent them from driving away other potential participants. As quickly as we could we opened an Arts and Crafts Class restricted to the six, and the battle to neutralize them was on its way to being won.

The crafts teacher quickly realized that these women needed to be kept very busy, for when they were hard at work, their negative and hostile talk diminished, their attitudes towards each other improved, and they willingly cooperated with one another. She also perceived their very deep need for meaningful accomplishment. They lived a very active life but evidently had little of a concrete nature to show for it.

The teacher, therefore, introduced crafts that would produce useful items, things to be used in the home or to be worn; the pace was set so that each item could be finished in one class session. Materials were simple and inexpensive--often free--and readily available. At first the women were amused and even embarrassed at the everyday items used as raw material. Their creative imagination had never been stimulated; they were very inhibited about experimenting; they could not believe that ordinary objects could be transformed into beautiful ones. But as the teacher turned the cardboard rolls from paper towels into Christmas angels, and the tops of tin cans into twinkling stars, they began saving homely discards and brought them to class with pride. The conversion of everyday items soon became just as popular as enameling, ceramics, or jewelry making.

This successful teacher bore out our contention that professional training is not essential in working with people of the lower class. Her maturity and good sense enabled her to assess the women and to fit the program to their most obvious needs. She realized that they had a short attention span and set up short demonstration periods, teaching but a few steps at a time. She was flexible in pacing the schedule and, aware of their low frustration tolerance,

provided an extraordinary amount of individual guidance. On the
other hand, she was careful to remain considerate and impartial,
for these women were hypersensitive to slights and signs of favorit-
ism. Often called upon to arbitrate complaints, she handled herself so well that the women came to realize that her desire to be
fair was sincere. When she disliked their behavior, she did not
hesitate to tell them so in plain terms. She could say, "Boy, Mrs.
X., you sure are a pain in the neck tonight." This directness relieved much of the strain and anxiety that a less clear or more con-
trolled expression of feeling would have produced. In lower-class
culture this frankness can be appreciated and--if unaccompanied by
malice or rejection--can lead to the development of self-awareness.
The women in the crafts class accepted the teacher's criticism without taking offense and this directness helped curb their negative behavior.

This teacher knew her own limitations. She never attempted
to do counselling or amateur casework. But many changes took
place as time passed. The women began bringing their teen-age
daughters, with whom they had rather poor relationships. As all
became involved in the work, a mutuality of interest and a common
sharing of pleasure developed and some of the tensions seemed to
ease. In the second year the women were able to sit down together,
have coffee, and talk amicably--no longer dependent on their work
to siphon off aggression. They also began to recruit new class
members from among their acquaintances. Outsiders, shy isolates
for the most part, began to attend. The same women who had previously aroused so much resentment now could attract new members.

An incident in the spring of 1962, involving two charter members, illustrates the modification of behavior that was effected in
the crafts class. The two women began to feud, their hostilities
based upon old family antagonisms. Soon seven women and their
teen-age children were involved. Our efforts to mediate the dis-
pute, which threatened the continuity of the program, were not successful. The women, highly verbal, carried on their fight in pub-
lic--in the halls, on the grounds, at the bingo tables. But one of
them seemed to become suddenly aware of the consequences. Mrs.

T. confessed privately to the leader that she could not control her temper, and that to avoid hurting the club or the teacher she would stay away for a while.   This resolve contrasted markedly with her behavior on the old Tenants' Council, where her tenacious hold and acid tongue had effectively dissolved the organization.   The other women followed her example to some extent.   Although they some-times looked for sympathy from the NIP staff, they seemed to un-derstand the necessity for a neutral stand.   And it is significant that their class should have become so important to them that they took steps to protect it from themselves.

An Open House and Craft Demonstration in the spring of 1962 created a great deal of interest, and the following season we were required to offer two craft classes.   Our core group of women took great pride in this expansion; their self-esteem was further boosted when the Christmas tree-trimming event became an annual program and last year's ornaments, saved over the summer, were unpacked and used again.   The Arts and Crafts Class, started as a defensive measure, had become one of the popular NIP interest groups.

The Farnam Courts Newspaper

Our unsuccessful attempt at tenant organization, described earlier in this book, showed us that we were starting at too high a level of organization.   A study of the literature supported our con-clusion that Class V of the population has little interest in formal organizations of any kind.   The NIP staff was not optimistic about the possibilities for a successful tenants' council in the future, and yet hope was never completely abandoned.   Distrustful of each other and unable to accept peer leadership, the people had to be thorough-ly prepared before community action could become a reality.   We therefore set about providing cooperative social and work experi-ences tied to a variety of purposes and interests, hoping that this would improve the social climate.

In the spring of 1961, after clubs, classes, and mass activi-ties had been in operation for two years and many residents had shown an ability to cooperate with each other in these programs, another attempt at tenant organization was made.   We established a

Farnam Courts newspaper, hoping to draw both active and passive individuals together, stimulate expression, and encourage the examination of local problems. If the people responded to the newspaper, it might then be used to reestablish a tenants' council.

While we fully expected the newspaper to give rise to social protest we did not anticipate the negative reactions that came from the Establishment. Our newspaper sponsorship unleashed a volume of protest, drew a hostile response from the wider community, and demonstrated our own inability to mediate successfully.

The initial organizing of the newspaper was done by the NIP Director of Adult Activities, a woman well known and respected in the housing project. Choosing the editor was a crucial and delicate task. Indigenous leaders were scarce; what few there were had been connected with the previous ill-fated council and its long-smoldering animosities. Using the NIP social participation study of 1961, she chose as editor one of the three men most often mentioned by tenants as possessing leadership qualities, the only one of the three not previously involved in tenant organization. A Negro with considerable prestige among the Negro tenants, it was felt that he could work closely with the identifiable Italian leaders.

The editor and the NIP advisor waged an active campaign to recruit a reporter from each of the fifteen buildings. It was difficult to convince people that they had something to say and that the way in which they said it would be acceptable. The staff advisor worked hard at breaking both barriers. One woman came in and dictated her column. Another, after rewriting a story three times, had to be visited at home before she would free her article for publication. One shy young woman, a volunteer typist, became so interested she wrote three items for one issue. Calls began coming into the office and little news items were left for publication. At first the tone of the majority of columns and letters was negative, complaining and critical. Yet the very act of writing was positive, for it represented for nearly every resident the only action he had ever taken on subjects of general community concern.

The key members of the News staff formed a power coalition, for the two men who joined the editor were from the Italian group

and had vied for the position of leader for many years. With the
NIP staff acting as conciliatory agents, these men called a truce in
their private wars and worked together for the good of the community for a period of nearly a year and a half. This was a considerable achievement for these aggressive and hostile individuals.

This triumvirate was possible, in large part, because of the
efforts of the NIP advisor, who convinced the men that much more
could be gained, for which each could receive recognition, if they
would band together rather than agitate against each other. Although
the two white men distrusted the editor, they eventually realized
that his leadership did not undermine their positions and they began
working wholeheartedly for the paper. Each had different motives
for participating--and NIP had motives of its own, too. Each man
brought a group of dedicated followers into the coalition. All were
keenly aware of these differences; in individual discussions the worker frankly admitted to the men that all had different reasons for becoming involved. But she insisted that once committed to the endeavor, the job became the important thing. If one man impugned
the motives of another, she refused to either defend or prosecute;
instead she pointed out how much each needed the other. She admitted the differences of motive, temperament, and background instead of attempting to impose a togetherness that did not exist. She
acted as a catalyst and go-between; the men could relate to each
other through her if the need arose. She encouraged each to work
in areas particularly suited to his skills and experience. The political boss took over the tasks requiring direct contact, since he was
thoroughly accustomed to knocking on doors and talking to everyone.
He was the source of insight and information about the Establishment
and ways of influencing it. The second man was disabled, but his
network of friends and relatives kept him the best informed resident
in the Courts. Besides supplying news, he put the paper together
and sent it out, working in his apartment.

The editor was intelligent, articulate, talented, and hostile;
he put out a newspaper that was bitter, negative, and quite outspoken. He was an angry man, with little patience for opposing
arguments, but his temperament did not obscure his perception of

what was wrong. His perceptions, even his distortions, were funda-
mentally those of the average Farnam Courts tenant. Like them,
he viewed the world as hostile and threatening. Of course, for
them the world was just that.

The newspaper reflected this assessment of the world, and
it caused reactions that at first surprised us. Nearly every issue
brought a number of telephone calls--from community officials, social workers, housing authority personnel--requesting us to "stop
him from making his accusations" in such a negative and hostile
manner. Forced to examine the newspaper and our relationship to
it, we decided on a policy of non-interference. The editor would be
asked to alter his wording or approach only when there was a legal
violation. The worker was to offer help only when she could assist
him in making his point more effectively; she was there to enable
editor and staff to put out a paper reflecting their own thinking, not
that of the NIP personnel. Without our protection, we believe, only
"acceptable" social protest could have come from the housing project. The fact that free expression drew such opposition from the
community at large and from professional social workers caused us
to wonder what such people really meant when they talked of community organization. Our experiences led us to conclude, sadly,
that many think of community organization as community manipula-
tion.

The first topic of general concern that the newspaper featured
was the obvious one of redevelopment and its impact on Farnam
Courts. Breathtaking changes were taking place in the neighborhood
surrounding the housing project. Although NIP had sponsored meetings with a redevelopment staff member, the tenants had been unable
to visualize the end results of the program. Relief was the first
reaction when surrounding slum areas were torn down. But soon
the only drugstore closed, as did the small grocery convenient for
purchasing bread and milk in the evening. In the only store still
open at night, reputed to be a bookmaking establishment, a can of
evaporated milk cost 18¢, twice the usual price. There was widespread dismay when the people began to realize the extent of their
future isolation.

The News editor hammered away in his editorials at both the city and the tenants, the first for its lack of concern and the latter for their apathy and indifference. After the first such editorial, the NIP staff was concerned lest the Redevelopment Agency fail to meet even the minimal tenant demands, for this would cause the collapse of tenant initiative, now perhaps about to develop. These fears led to a consultation between the newspaper advisor and the city agency, prior to a scheduled meeting between tenants and the city, at which a positive attitude toward meeting some of the tenant demands was expressed. At the public meeting, with twenty-five residents in attendance, spirited discussion evoked a sympathetic response from the Redevelopment Agency representative. Optimism prevailed after this show of concern by what appeared to be a thoughtful, dedicated public servant. But as time went on, the promised revisions failed to materialize--New Haven's plans for the Wooster Square Redevelopment Area were already too far advanced to be changed to meet the needs of the Farnam Courts residents.

The early optimism faded. In February, 1962, two months after the agency's show of concern, a petition bearing three hundred signatures was sent to the mayor. Tenants ran the campaign and obtained the signatures for the petition, which requested the city to (1) reestablish a neighborhood grocery and a drug store; (2) build a playfield and park near the Courts, in a traffic-free zone; (3) create separate play areas for children under ten; (4) establish safety barriers between the railroad and the apartment buildings to replace the existing fences, which were full of holes; (5) widen streets and provide adjacent parking facilities; (6) allow access to an important city artery, State Street, which had been cut off; (7) improve lighting in areas where demolition work was close to living units, to discourage arson and vandalism.

Eight months later, in October, 1962, an answer was received from the Redevelopment Agency. The letter, printed in the News, was interpreted by the people as an evasion of their request for changes. The following answers were given to the specific requests listed above:

1. The Agency is encouraging all grocers and druggists in

the area to relocate and/or stay. Land is being sold for
a delicatessen near Farnam Courts.

2. Conte School (not in the immediate area) will have a ball
   field and playground facilities for children ten years and
   over.

3. The Redevelopment Agency is designing a play area for
   children under ten, to be built in space fronting the housing project when the last condemned buildings go down.

4. The Interstate Highway will provide fencing to the west.
   When industrial land is sold on Hamilton Street, there will
   be fencing to the east.

5. When the Interstate Highway is built, the two adjoining
   streets will be dead-end and parking will be permitted
   there.

6. Access to State Street will be provided.

7. New lights have been installed along Hamilton Street.
   When the Interstate Highway is built, lighting will be improved along Franklin Street.

In the months before this official reply was received, the
newspaper flourished. Consequently, we decided to take the next
step toward establishing a Tenants' Council. We started an effort
to get reporters from the two buildings in the project that were
without such representation, for we thought that all the reporters
plus the three leaders could serve as the nucleus for the new council. One year remained for NIP to exercise an enabling advisory
role before the social-action project terminated.

At this point, the editor was found to have too high an income and, according to Housing Authority rules, he was required
to move from the project. He was followed in a few months by one
of the Italian leaders, and the other was also slated to move. So
the newspaper lost its tenant voice and spirit, although we did our
best to keep it going. In this unsophisticated community, where
people rallied around leaders rather than issues, the loss of these
three dominant personalities within a few months dealt the paper an
irreparable blow. This draining off of indigenous leadership occurred regularly in Farnam Courts, for the more competent eventu-

ally qualified for better jobs and higher pay, making them ineligible for low-income housing. Unfortunately, the loss of these men supported the lower-class attitude of fear. "Don't stick your neck out," the people would say, "If you do, something will happen to you." Soon rumor had it that the leaders were investigated and forced to move because of their outspoken stand in the newspaper. Thus the general belief in withdrawal as a safety measure was reinforced.

In this manner our last attempt at community organization failed. We were unsuccessful in locating new leaders and so the newspaper was discontinued. During its short life the newspaper had contributed to individual movement as well as to community cohesion. People initially involved themselves in the paper's campaigns for selfish reasons or for the purpose of sheer survival. Soon, however, it seemed to us that they began to experience the kind of satisfaction that comes from joint endeavor on behalf of the larger community. As they worked on stories and planned issues, they began to exhibit sympathy for the life situations of their neighbors, an emotion that had been absent before. And the fact that the newspaper staff was successfully integrated indicated the ability of these people to form cooperative relationships that ran counter to their most deeply ingrained survival patterns.

Notes

1. Margaret E. Hartford, ed. Working Papers Toward a Frame of Reference for Social Group Work. (New York, National Association of Social Workers, 1963), p. 4.

2. Robert D. Vinter. "Social Group Work." Encyclopedia of Social Work. (New York, National Association of Social Workers, 1965), pp. 715-724.

3. Ibid., pp. 716-717.

4. Ibid., p. 716.

5. Ibid., p. 717.

6. Joyce Watson, Jane Krisberg, and Ludwig Geismar. "Farnam Courts Social Participation Study." (Unpublished study, Neighborhood Improvement Project, New Haven, 1962). The study was based on interviews with a 33 per-

cent random sample of Farnam Courts women (N=97) on
formal and 14 percent random sample (N=41) on informal
participation.

7.   Women's Formal Participation

Age Range	N's	% Participation in Total Activities	% Participation in Activities Exclud- ing NIP
21-28	(20)	45	25
29-35	(19)	42	37
36-58	(39)	31	13
59-80	(19)	26	0

8. 40 percent of women with husbands as against 27 percent
   without.

9. The percentages are 39 and 25 respectively.

10. 56 percent Negro and 21 percent white participation in
    activity. With NIP activities excluded the percentages
    were 31 and 9.

11. Scores based on mean number of contacts per week.

12. Mean informal participation scores for the sample (N=
    41) were as follows: planned 4.58, casual 8.46, telephon-
    ing 5.56. The telephoning score for women who had
    phones in their apartments was 9.12, making this the most
    common method of informal participation.

13. Informal participation scores were 22 for women with
    husbands in the home and 27 for women living without
    husbands.

14. The participation scores were 26 and 20 respectively.

15. Helen Northern. "Evaluating Movement of Individuals
    in Social Group Work." Group Work Papers, National
    Conference on Social Work, 1957.

16. Ibid., p. 29.

17. Richard B. Couser. "The Odds Were Against Us."
    Scouting, March 1963.

18. Public Housing Administration, Housing and Home Fi-
    nance Agency, Washington, Circular, dated 4-17-63.

19. John DeBerardinis. "Report on Inner City 4-H Work,
    City of New Haven, Connecticut, Farnam Courts Housing
    Project," 1963 (mimeographed).

20. Bertha Reynolds. Social Work and Social Living. New
York, Citadel Press, 1951, pp. 23-24.

American policy toward its minorities tends to fluctuate between two polar positions--the concept of the melting pot on one hand and cultural pluralism on the other. The former theory holds that minority problems will be solved by a free merging of the races and ethnic groups; the latter, postulating a pre-established harmony of cultures, sees the free and democratic expression of culture groups that retain their identity as the best means of developing a healthy society. Since the great immigrations before and after World War I, social theorists in this country have come to lean increasingly toward cultural pluralism. At the same time, it is safe to say, social policy has been guided predominantly by the melting pot theory.

Our treatment of the Puerto Ricans is a case in point. Their position is complicated by the fact that they are American citizens. Unlike foreign immigrant groups, for whom we design programs of Americanization and who are on occasion the beneficiaries of special welfare programs (the Hungarians and Cubans, for example), the Puerto Ricans are expected to show behavior consonant with their citizenship.

We confess that the NIP staff shared in some of this thinking. Although aware of the distinctive language and behavior patterns of the Puerto Ricans in Farnam Courts, we assumed that a sensitive, individualized approach would be the major requisite for improving their social functioning. Our casework experience with these families cast doubt on this assumption. Our group service efforts to integrate them taught us that the special needs of this population called for a special approach, which would take into account their culturally and socially marginal position in American society. The present chapter describes our work with the Puerto

Rican minority, which comprised roughly 10 percent of the Farnam
Courts population.

Our first contacts revealed that over half the adults and
many of the younger children spoke no English. In the first year
of NIP operation the need to establish program priorities addressed
to the total population did not permit us to direct a major effort toward this small minority. One of the few concessions we were able
to make during this period was that of translating all letters, fliers
and posters into Spanish. The Puerto Rican school-age children
flocked to the group activities provided for the general youth population, but the pre-schoolers and adults did not attend the programs
designed for them. The few who did come were noticeably frustrated by their language handicap and they did not continue to participate. Although problems of staff and budget limited our efforts,
we did institute special programs; over a two-year period we were
able to help a few adults and an appreciable number of children in
activities especially adapted to meet their needs.

There were four such programs: (1) Family-centered casework; (2) Pre-school nursery; (3) Adult English class; (4) Group
work with youth. Because of their positive results, these programs
would seem to have implications for attempts by others to meet the
needs of similar groups.

During the first year that the Farnam Courts casework service was made available, the few Puerto Rican clients who came for
help knew enough English to pose no serious treatment problem. In
the second year, applications began to come from families where
neither adult spoke English. Concerned neighbors and staff members brought a few more such cases to our attention. Our problem
was to find a Spanish-speaking caseworker. Only one community
group had such a person, and the demands upon her were so heavy
that we could not share her services. For one year we attempted
to give treatment by hiring interpreters to work with the caseworker. In this way we hoped to alleviate the most pressing needs,
those in the areas of public assistance and medical care. This
emergency measure was far from satisfactory.

In the fall of 1960, when an increasing number of these families were coming to our attention, NIP hired an Administrative Assistant who, we found, was fluent in Spanish. More in desperation than by design, she was increasingly called upon to act as interpretor. Familiar with the network of social services and community institutions, she quickly demonstrated a capacity for the skillful handling of complex family situations. In addition to her other duties, she gradually became the caseworker for a total of ten non-English-speaking families, working under close supervision for the remaining two years of NIP activity.

In the total Courts population during the period of NIP operation, the number of families native to Puerto Rico ranged from thirty to thirty-four, or 10 to 11.3 percent. Over the three-year period that the casework service was available, nineteen of these families were treated--aside from the Puerto Ricans in the experimental multi-problem family group. This gives a treatment percentage of 60, in contrast to a 43.2 percentage for other families. One can speculate that the ratio of need declines as the degree of acculturation rises. Although direct information on this was not available to us, indirect supporting evidence is provided further on in this chapter by data showing a longer treatment period for the exclusively Spanish-speaking Puerto Ricans than for those who also spoke English.

Possible evidence of less disorganization in Puerto Rican families than in the general Farnam Courts population was found in statistics showing 15 percent broken families and 12.5 percent multi-problem families among the Puerto Ricans, as against non-Puerto Rican percentages of 33 and 18.4 respectively.

Nine of the nineteen families treated were fluent in English; their functioning was commensurate with that of the total population and they required, for the most part, minimal service for short-term problems. In the remaining ten families, constituting over half of those treated and almost one-third of all the Puerto Rican families living in the housing project, neither adult spoke English. These families, like other deprived lower-class members of society, did not make use of community services; the language barrier made the problem more acute.

Although the basic difficulties encountered by these ten families were similar to those of the larger population, the complications created by language caused enough differences to warrant a
separate tabulation, given in Table 13.

Table 13
Problems Confronting the 10 Puerto Rican Families
That Spoke No English

Problem	Number of Instances
Financial	10
Health	8
Unemployment	6
Debts	4
Marital	3
Personality problems--adult	3
Child	2
Behavior problems--child	2
Parent-child relationships	2
Physical abuse	2
Drinking	1
Fraud	1

The implications of the data in Table 13 become more meaningful when examined together with data on the community resources
with which the worker made contact during treatment, because the
latter, shown in Table 14, highlight the intensity of problems in
certain areas.

From the combined data in Tables 13 and 14 we can see
that financial problems were particularly severe, even though each
household was headed by an able-bodied man. These men had no
illnesses or physical limitations, and we were able to verify that
the majority performed satisfactorily when work was available. We
also had evidence substantiating their claims that they earnestly and
repeatedly looked for a steady job. Although they were chronically
unemployed, we could find no confirmation of the conclusion that
they were "last hired, first fired." Some of these men were long-
time employees in good standing, so that their layoffs seemed to

Table 14
Community Resources Used in Treatment of the 10
Puerto Rican Families

Type of Resource	Number of Instances Worker Initiated Contact
Department of Welfare	10
Hospitals	7
Employer	6
Housing Authority	5
Credit Bureaus	4
Visiting Nurse	4
Lawyer	3
Doctor	2
School	2

demonstrate their extreme vulnerability to economic fluctuations because of the kinds of jobs they held.

In all of these cases, the layoffs were sudden and of short
duration, just long enough to create a variety of complications. Until welfare applications could be processed, the families had to borrow rent money and buy food on credit. Often the man would be
called back to work just when eligibility was established; while assistance would cover the family until payday, there would be no
compensation for the debts that had been acquired. For those who
could not earn enough to support large families, supplementary assistance was necessary. This became a chaotic affair, since wages
fluctuated in their seasonal and factory work; the supplementary
grants, needing continuous adjustment, never kept up with need.

These families found it extremely difficult to deal with social
agencies, to establish eligibility and maintain a relationship with a
worker, because of their language handicap. Polite and passive,
they usually acquiesced when asked whether they understood what was
being said. Fooled by the few English words they knew and used
again and again, the agency judged them as dull and uncooperative
when in truth they could not communicate.

Even during periods of full employment their marginal earnings caused severe management problems. Following the general

neighborhood pattern, household appliances and clothing were status symbols; they were given high budget priority and were often obtained on credit. A week or two of unemployment could create serious difficulties. The basic food and rent allowance from Welfare did not cover credit payments. Faced with the loss of possessions, families paid these debts by misusing their assistance allotments. These families felt trapped by an unreliable labor market, inflexible creditors, and sub-marginal welfare allotments.

Tables 13 and 14 show that health problems were second only to finances, but medical care was usually sought only in cases of extreme necessity. Many of the families already had outstanding hospital bills, some for substantial amounts of $400 to $900. This made it very difficult to persuade them to get current medical care. Even when the debt deterrent was not operating and a worker-translator was giving them every type of support, there still existed an inability far greater than that found in the population at large to return for repeated clinic visits or to continue the use of medication. This may be due to cultural differences, to level of education, and/ or fear and superstition. [1]

Problems related to the Housing Authority are subsumed under several headings such as financial, debts, etc. in Table 13, but are revealed in Table 14. In these cases the worker acted as mediator, negotiating an interim plan to stave off rent penalties. Contacts with employers were made more often for this group than for the general population. The worker was often required to gather information regarding possible re-employment, and to establish average earnings for welfare eligibility as well as creditor negotiations. In both areas, housing and employment, language problems were particularly handicapping.

The mean length of time that the non-English-speaking cases were open is shown in Table 15 below. It differs from that of both the English-speaking Puerto Rican families and the non-Puerto Rican families treated. In this group the mean length of treatment was 8.5 months; for the English-speaking Puerto Rican clients it was 4.5 months, much closer to the 3.5 figure for the general population served. In one sense language difficulties made chronic clients

Table 15
Length of Treatment for Non-English-Speaking
Puerto Rican Families

Number of Cases	Length of Treatment
1	1 month
2	3 months
2	5 months
2	8 months
1	12 months
1	16 months
1	24 months

of these people; although a certain process might be demonstrated and learned once, they still needed an interpreter the next time. As a result, the worker had to be extremely flexible, available much of the time on a demand basis should intermittent need arise. Regular ongoing contacts in the traditional manner were set up where needed, but they were not commonly maintained. The more characteristic pattern was that of a period of activity related to a crisis often calling for daily contact; then, when need had diminished, less frequent but regular contact was maintained until the worker judged that order had been restored.

Treatment commonly consisted of giving advice and information, performing a vast array of tangible services, coordinating community aid, and, in addition, interpreting and translating all manner of documents and correspondence. Counselling was given in eight cases, but it was not feasible to continue each case for as long a period as was diagnostically indicated because of serious worker time limitations. As a result, it was necessary to establish a priority list, giving counselling for extended periods ranging from twelve to twenty-four months to the three families we judged most in need of continuing treatment.

As was common in the total treatment population, the Puerto Rican residents of Farnam Courts were reluctant if not unable to face problems quickly; they were equally timid about applying for help. They also needed an open-door, reaching-out, family-centered approach; ready accessibility to service; worker initiative in assigning priorities, structuring the problem-solving process, and serving as a demonstration model in bewildering assignments. The additional difficulties these people faced were related to their lack of fluency in English. This was extremely crippling when they had to deal with the community. In addition, their habit of politely agreeing with outsiders, which seemed to be culturally determined, was misleading to agency personnel who were attempting to help them.

The language barrier made it impossible to pursue any major goals with four Puerto Rican youngsters in the Nursery School during 1961. The children knew no English and the staff knew no Spanish. This disappointment led us to institute a new program, aimed at fifteen similarly handicapped children who would be entering public school the following autumn. To meet their special needs a weekly session was established, with a young, bilingual Puerto Rican woman as teacher. Because theirs was a male-dominated culture, it was thought that a man's presence would add security and facilitate their acceptance of authority. Accordingly a male university student, who had volunteered for the job, was assigned to assist the teacher.

Starting off the class in Spanish, the teacher began speaking English after three sessions; by this time all but two of the children were ready to follow her lead. She relied heavily upon visual material, using picture cards to tell a story first in Spanish, then gradually substituting more and more English words. The children loved these story games, calling out the words along the way; they also enjoyed the recitation periods when they told their own versions of these tales, learning to express themselves freely and using their rapidly expanding vocabularies.

The children--like other Courts children--also had to be taught how to play games and use the equipment. This was demonstrated step by step, first in Spanish and subsequently in English.

The Nursery Director worked closely with the Spanish-speaking teacher. As the children progressed there was an exchange of personnel with the regular Nursery in order to help them make the

transition to the general pre-school program. Although it was possible at the end of three months to integrate these children into the
regular Nursery School, we continued their special sessions. Although the Spanish-speaking teacher used more and more English,
and eventually stopped speaking Spanish, her continued presence gave
security to the child who happened to lapse into his native tongue.

Although uninhibited at home, the children were withdrawn
in the presence of strangers. Though they shared a common language with the teacher, it was necessary to use the same methods
for putting them at ease and drawing them out as were used with the
children of the larger population. This seemed to indicate that even
after the language problem was overcome, class distinctions still
operated to inhibit their dealings with middle-class personnel.

Of the fifteen children who attended the special program for
nine months and the regular Nursery for six months, thirteen made
noticeable progress. Once their shyness was overcome, their natural exuberance and volubility created quite another problem, and it
became necessary to help them find a permissive mode of behavior
suitable for the classroom and the fostering of peer relationships.

The parents as a group gave a great deal of support to the
program, showing evidence of putting a high priority on education.
Many of the parents, including some fathers, escorted the children
to school regularly, asking about their children's progress and how
they could supplement the program at home. Their active encouragement was most helpful in the one year we were able to run this
program. Because of the manageable size of the treatment universe,
it was possible to reduce the cultural and language barriers hamper-
ing these Puerto Rican children and, at the same time, give them a
positive orientation to education.

If we were to help the adults as we did the children, it
seemed obvious that English lessons were the answer. But canvass-
ing revealed only moderate interest, more from the men than the
women. This brought up again the issue of perceived need versus
felt need. Our lack of Spanish-speaking personnel kept us from
picking up clues to program desires. Our one part-time interpretor
was excluded because of class difference, just as we had been ex-

cluded in the early days of the project. Moreover, the Puerto
Rican people would not give program preferences when directly
asked; we could not determine whether this excessive politeness to
strangers was a cultural phenomenon or the adaptive mechanism that
prompts lower-class people to give the answer they think the outsider expects.

Since we could not determine felt need and time was short,
we decided to establish English classes. We held discussions with
persons experienced in work with the Puerto Ricans and explored
several language-teaching experiments. We decided to set up our
classes on the project grounds, guided by the following principles
recommended by the Puerto Rican Labor Department:

1. The instructor should be conversant in Spanish.
2. A sitter should be provided in the building, since Puerto
   Rican people take their children wherever they go.
3. Functional English should be stressed rather than English
   grammar. The course content should be related to the
   needs of daily living. Extensive use of props such as
   telephones, pictures, etc. should be made. Role playing should be included.
4. Instructors geared to meeting the requirements of various
   accomplishment levels should be provided.
5. Home visiting should be done before and during the program.

To aid recruitment we contacted those who had dropped out
of an Americanization class (this was the only adult English class
conducted by the city and it presumed lack of citizenship) as well as
residents of the project. Although many Puerto Rican men had enrolled in the Americanization course, very few ever completed it.
After studying the situation, we decided that these people, who were
citizens, probably resented being forced to attend citizenship classes
in order to learn the language. Our class was limited to language,
and it was run by a volunteer from Yale University and two assistants. With them came a young woman who baby-sat, so that both
parents were free to attend class.

The young teacher spoke excellent colloquial Spanish and exhibited a positive attitude; he had previously worked with a group in East Harlem. One of the men accompanying him was a Puerto Rican who was studying English literature at the university and the other was majoring in Spanish; with their help, individualized instruction could be given. For six months in 1961 six people attended regularly, and another five came intermittently. One couple brought their three children for four months to the class, which met three times a week. Home visiting, carried on at varying periods, seemed to have a positive influence on class morale and attendance.

Four people learned enough English to carry on a conversation. Therefore we looked forward to repeating the class in the fall of 1962. The chief instructor had left for study abroad so we asked the Puerto Rican student to continue in his place, on a salaried basis. New members had to be recruited--perhaps the most highly motivated felt they knew enough English from the few months' instruction. The teacher visited the homes of the new students and found many men particularly interested. We had high expectations because the teacher shared the students' ethnic background and had a year of experience in the program. But the class never established itself. People drifted in and out, and only four women attended regularly. We attempted to remedy the situation by consulting with the Director of the Department of Education of the Puerto Rican Labor Department, by visiting the homes, by changing study materials, but to no avail. The class never drew more regular students. We were told later that the loss of the baby-sitter was significant, as the men did not want to leave their wives alone in the building with a male teacher. Our channels of communication were so restricted that we were unaware of this deterrent at the time.

Other factors were undoubtedly operating to the detriment of this second class. The first teacher was able to build a warm and relaxed relationship, structured enough so that learning could proceed. His personality, plus the presence of three assistants, gave vitality and excitement to the program. Since the second class was so small, only the teacher was in attendance; he was often alone in the building at night with three or four students. When we realized that the very quietness might have an adverse effect, we tried to schedule other activities the same evening but our intervention came too late. In all probability, however, our greatest oversight was the failure to provide an acceptable female chaperone in the form of a baby-sitter.

The fourth and last special program for the Puerto Rican minority in the Courts was set up to help integrate sixteen pre-teen and teen-age boys into the existing pattern of youth activities. As we mentioned earlier in describing the people (Chapter 2), the Puerto Rican boys were noticeably isolated; the girls, on the other hand, met no such peer barriers. The reasons for this difference escaped us. True, the girls were more closely guarded and kept from mass activities such as dances, a fact which restricted their peer contacts and possibly served to avoid problems; however, they were usually allowed to attend club groups, where no acceptance problem was noted. The boys were allowed freedom to socialize outside the home; they followed the neighborhood pattern of confining their activities to the housing project area and their difficulties were very visible.

All of these boys came from homes where only Spanish was spoken. Their limited knowledge of English hampered them both at school and at home. Our plan was to teach them the procedures and skills necessary for participation in the wider youth culture and to expose them to a variety of experiences that they had missed because of their isolation, both imposed and voluntary. We hoped this would result in an improved self-image and increased confidence and would give the boys the background necessary for acceptance by their peers.

One of our most experienced and popular leaders was put in charge of the group, which convened three times as frequently as the other clubs. The wide age span (from 10 to 16) was initially compensated for by the homogeneity of background, language, and lack of game skills. The boys felt comfortable with one another; the group atmosphere was relaxed, and there was great freedom of expression.

They were greatly motivated to share in the majority culture.

"What's a peabody?" they shouted at the leader at one of the first group sessions. It took some time for the leader, surrounded by voluble and excited boys, to unscramble the puzzle, for the "peabody" they had heard of in the neighborhood was the name of a museum. Many of the clubs had visited there; when this was explained to the Puerto Rican boys, they decided a trip to the Peabody Museum of Natural History was the activity they wanted most. In this fashion they developed a knowledge of places and institutions in the city, and also worked hard to improve their game and sport skills.

Joint activities were held with other groups; within a year the boys had entered the regular youth clubs. When eight Puerto Rican boys joined the Boy Scout troop, the language problem again became acute. A Spanish-speaking leader was assigned to interpret the handbook to them; after six months they were able to participate in the Scouting program without special help.

In the last six months of NIP work, a new group came into being. This was Pablo's Club, named after the university student who served as leader. By this time the boys were accepted in the regular youth program. Why then another special group? Its purpose was to develop in these boys, who had few memories of life outside the mainland, a sense of pride in their heritage. One of the program highlights was a sightseeing trip to New York City, where they visited an exhibit of Puerto Rican paintings and artifacts and were impressed by the number of Puerto Rican people they saw while traveling around the city. This may in some small way have helped to alleviate their negative feelings about minority status.

Acculturation is probably an easier process for youth than for adults, and in many cases children can become integrated into the wider community with a little outside help. The more positive response from the youngsters in our Puerto Rican program may simply indicate that our efforts were in line with the natural process by which children adapt to new and strange customs and experiences.

Notes

1. We have been told by Puerto Rican social workers that the availability of free medical service on the Island most likely accounts for the resistance to medical

care on the mainland, where, although minimal at times, some financial responsibility is usually required.

Chapter 12
Work with the Community

The Status of Projects

In an age when social action projects are sprouting all over the nation, the field of social welfare may not be showing enough concern for the precise meaning of the term "project" or for the institutional consequence of such endeavors for community organization. It appears that the notions of experimentation and innovation, which are after all the raisons d'etre of most limited-tenure endeavors, have in the past, with some exceptions, been applied to findings on direct service to client populations and to method in the narrow sense, i.e. techniques of intervention and evaluation of the effect of intervention on the target population.

This state of affairs is hardly accidental. Projects are not born in a vacuum. They are promoted, launched, and operated by people who are part of an existing structure, and the projects operate close to that structure. These people often represent points of view that favor the existing structure or alternatives of their choosing. Research-action projects, in particular, generally contain a mandate for change or at least for the advocacy of change. Federal granting agencies and large private foundations, which give financial backing to projects, are usually quite explicit regarding the possible change implications of the efforts they support. Yet the contracts between grantor and grantee cannot possibly spell out any obligations for instituting structural change, since the projects are designed only to establish whether change is appropriate and what kinds of changes are indicated.

It would be unfair to assume that local organizations associated with projects are not aware of their change implications. But our experience in New Haven and several other communities leads us to conclude that local bodies perceive potential change more in

278

terms of specific services than in modifications of structure.
Structural alterations involve not only complex and sensitive issues
but they deny, on occasion, the very roles played by project participants, namely those of innovator and change agent.

It would be an oversimplification to state that all project participants view structural change without reservations. One might,
first of all, differentiate between the project staff and the members
of sponsoring organizations. Staff has a relatively smaller investment in the existing situation than the well established local professionals and leading citizens who serve as agency executives, board
members, etc. Professional staff may be here today, gone tomorrow. Heads of agencies and members of boards have a continuing
responsibility for maintaining services, and they are likely to pre-
fer an existing structure to the uncertainty of a future one.

This is not to say that all executives or board members advocate the status quo. Their views may range from "hold on to the
old system" to "shake down the whole structure." But by the nature
of the relationship between role and orientation, the modal attitude
tends to favor existing agency structure.

The most recent wave of community action projects, anticipating and following in the wake of the Economic Opportunities Act
of 1964, addresses itself to issues broader than direct service to
clients; indeed, some of the projects have a clear-cut community
organization focus. Yet it appears that the greater the emphasis on
the discovery of ways for modifying existing service patterns--in
contrast to specific service techniques--the more likely it is that
such projects will operate independently of established agency structure. This type of operation generally means that the sponsors believe that the existing structure has failed to meet the specific needs
of the community and its population. At the same time, the projects are being developed with little or no thought being given to the
ways in which their establishment will effect present service patterns. In this sense projects outside of agency structure, as much
as those which are superimposed upon it, leave unanswered the question of how a desired outcome might lead to integration into the
structure of services.

A possible clue to the future implications of an action project may be found in the manner in which a project defines its role during its tenure of operation. An action-research project such as NIP might be viewed as a kind of professional experiment with a minimum of local commitment--especially if its value is more in the realm of theory than in local practice--toward which the community reserves judgment. An opposite view holds an action-research project to be an important community investment and a blueprint for the future operation of services. Between these views may be found intermediate positions combining elements of both. Furthermore, conceptions of projects are likely to change in time, as we shall illustrate from the experience of the Neighborhood Improvement Project.

The Community's Early Conception of the Neighborhood Improvement Project

When we speak of the community's early conception of the project, we mean the way in which NIP was viewed before it started its service operation. The word community is to be understood in its more restricted meaning, applying to the small group of professional and lay planners who had taken it upon themselves to organize the project. Their thoughts and expectations, as gleaned from minutes of meetings, were reported in Chapter 3 and can be summarized as follows: NIP was created as a community endeavor, which was to break new ground and at the same time coordinate the work of various agencies concerned with Farnam Courts in general and multi-problem families in particular.

Clearly, the planners did not intend to create a new agency, and there appeared to be little justification for doing so. New Haven was being served by a network of agencies, whose services extended into Farnam Courts. To set up a temporary agency would have been self-defeating, for at the end of the project period the neighborhood would be left without the newly instituted services. At the same time the planners of NIP were keenly aware of the fact that the needs of the people of Farnam Courts were not being met. This was an obvious conclusion, inferred from the observed economic and social deprivation, family disorganization, juvenile delinquency, and lack of social participation. The proposed project was expected to accomplish three things: to develop appropriate programs for the people who were not being served; to develop techniques of reaching people who may have failed to respond to earlier efforts at giving services; to extend existing services, such as the Farnam Neighborhood House recreational program and health and counseling services, more fully to the residents of the Courts.

The chief emphasis of the proposed program was on developing new content and techniques of service. But the overall design of NIP also included an attempt to create administrative service patterns that would allow existing agencies to coordinate their work and reduce duplication of effort. This administrative arrangement was to be an alliance of agencies, patterned along the lines of the Family-Centered Project in St. Paul, Minnesota.

The advantages of an agency alliance were twofold: first, project experience would be shared with the agencies and would strengthen their practice, and second, agency participation would guarantee the continuity of improved patterns of service resulting from the project. The importance of a specific formulation of interagency collaboration was one of the lessons we were to learn as the Neighborhood Improvement Project developed.

This essentially rational model of inter-agency organization was more implicit than explicit in the deliberations of the planners of NIP. Their first concern was, of course, with the problems of the Farnam Courts area, particularly juvenile delinquency, and they anticipated a joint effort of community agencies directed toward problem prevention and control. At the same time, the favorable response of private and public agencies in the planning and advisory committees as well as in the original NIP social work team, lent support to the expectation that the community's concern with multiproblem families and deviant behavior would serve as a firm foundation for an ongoing inter-agency endeavor. The project planners clearly hoped that as a result of the pilot project, agencies would be sparked to participate fully and would eventually extend their participation into a commitment for ongoing service after the termination of the project.

Such an assumption disregarded the differing service orientations and service priorities of local agencies. A rational model of community organization rests upon the contention that the actions of agencies are guided by such objective considerations as needs of the population, urgency of problems requiring a solution, community-wide availability of alternate treatment resources, etc. In actuality, the behavior of agencies, like that of human beings, is determined by a variety of forces both rational and non-rational; any community organizational planning effort must take into account the existence and relative importance of these forces.

The New Haven social agencies that were associated with NIP in the planning process, in the advisory process, and in the actual operation represented a considerable variety of interests and experiences. All were ongoing concerns that had developed over the years, were part of a statewide and/or national organization or professional association, and served a specific clientele. The respective professional roles of the agencies' executive, supervisory, and direct service personnel were devoted primarily to organizational continuity, along lines determined by broader organizational policy. More leeway was provided in the policies of voluntary organizations such as the Family Service Association of America than in those of public agencies such as federal or state bureaus of public assistance. The latter, in contrast to the former, provided its member agencies or branch offices with fairly specific directives on whom to serve and how to serve. Although all local programs, even state and federal ones, leave some room for local initiative and maneuvering, the mandates and charges of the national or state organizations are major determinants of the actions of the agencies and the behavior of their executives.

The Neighborhood Improvement Project was counting heavily upon the inclination and ability of local agency executives to make use of whatever latitude their position offered for committing agency time and resources to the experimental project. Several executives followed the logic of their own thinking, which favored a climate of experimentation and innovation; in response to strong leadership by the Community Council of Greater New Haven, they joined hands in forming the alliance of agencies called NIP. This alliance was not formalized by written contracts; it rested upon a tacit agreement, between the Community Council of Greater New Haven and the agencies associated with NIP, on project objectives and on the nature of agency participation. The agreements were summarized in the minutes of meetings and were generally followed by letters specifying the agencies' contributions of worker time or, in two instances, the monetary compensation by the Council for the time of workers contributed by the agencies. Voluntary agreements may reflect a climate of opinion in which change is feasible. Unfortunately they do not provide a structure in which change can be guaranteed; they carry no sanctions against withdrawal from participation, nor do they provide a mechanism for continuous re-examination of project objectives and method.

The Changing Structure of NIP

At the start of the action phase in January, 1960, the Neighborhood Improvement Project had brought together six agencies, two public and four private, that had agreed to participate in the demonstration project. The agencies had committed themselves to contribute workers, to serve on the policy-making NIP Advisory Committee, to participate in the Supervisors' Committee, to encourage feedback from the project to agency service, and to give general moral support to what was seen as an experimental undertaking. The Community Council of Greater New Haven, which had been the prime mover in the development of NIP (see Chapter 3), continued to assume major responsibility for the administrative and financial aspects.

The six agencies contributed worker time for both direct service and supervision. Three casework agencies each made a half-time worker available, which meant that a caseworker devoted two and a half days a week to the treatment of NIP cases. Two casework agencies each provided a fifth-time worker, the equivalent of one day's service per week by one caseworker. The group work agency, Farnam Neighborhood House, supplied the project with services by the executive, his assistants, and several part-time group

workers.   The Neighborhood Improvement Project, with the aid of
funds from the New Haven Foundation, compensated two private
casework agencies and the group work agency for their professional
services to the project, which was the equivalent of roughly half a
worker's salary.   This financial subsidy for services was seen as
justified and necessary in view of the limited budgets of these agencies.

The interaction between project staff and casework agencies
was closer at the worker level than at the supervisory or administrative level.   A closer relationship was maintained, however, between the executive of Farnam Neighborhood House and NIP project
personnel.   The shared concern between the project and the agencies was treatment of clients or groups of clients.   Attention was
given to specifics of techniques, use of diagnostic and research
tools, problems of financing services.   There was comparatively
little dialogue on community organization and broad service policy.
Agency participation in NIP during the first year of service was, of
course, far from uniform.   It ranged from close involvement and
shared programming through low involvement to indifference.   The
modal stance was in the direction of minimal involvement.   The atmosphere at meetings was friendly and free of overt conflict or controversy, but generally lacking in enthusiasm.   Some executives
failed to attend most of the Advisory Committee meetings.

The writers of this study are in no position to give an objective analysis of the multiple factors that contributed to the low level
of agency involvement, since we were engaged in the action process.
Yet we do believe that our expectations about the workability of an
alliance of agencies rested upon the false assumption that there existed a natural mutuality of goals that would soon give rise to a
mutuality of roles.   Such an assumption made it seemingly unnecessary to firm up the alliance with contracts and to develop a system
of sanctions and rewards for assuring continued participation.   The
goal of serving a seriously deprived minority was a remote one in
1959 and it was in direct conflict with the primary obligation of
most of the participating agencies, which was to serve their own
clients, whether these were motivated middle-class families or per-

sons falling into given categories of service eligibility.

The attitude of the six social agencies originally associated with NIP could best be described as disengagement. Two more agencies, both public, joined the project in the fall of 1960, one of them under the condition that its worker be paid out of project funds. One agency withdrew after only eight weeks of participation, two withdrew after one year and one after a year and a half. Two agencies stayed in the project for two years, and one stayed for two and a half years. Only one agency, Family Service of New Haven, remained with NIP for the full four-year period of service. Its participation, which had been subsidized throughout from project funds, was increased during the last year of operations from one to three half-time workers.

The agencies gave varying reasons for withdrawal. The most frequent reason was a shortage of workers. This argument was advanced when the project did not subsidize the service of the agency. Some agencies cited lack of workers only at the time their participating worker left the agency. Worker turnover, however, was no larger among NIP-affiliated workers than among social workers in the community as a whole. One agency gave internal reorganization as the reason for leaving the project and did, indeed, have a serious organizational problem that kept it from functioning at capacity for many months. Two cases of agency drop-out could best be described as a parting of the ways by mutual consent. One of these was caused by personality factors, the other represented an instance of non-compatible priorities of service.

The latter case, which involved the Farnam Neighborhood House, dramatically illustrates what is probably the overriding issue standing between a project geared to innovation of service and an agency whose major concern is maintenance of service. Farnam Neighborhood House, located a few blocks from the Farnam Courts housing project, in an area of lower middle-class and stable working-class homes, had served only a handful of project children in 1959. During the first two years of project operations the executive of the Neighborhood House collaborated closely with the NIP staff in planning and rendering appropriate services for the children

from the Courts. As a result, social participation of Farnam
Courts youngsters in the activities of Neighborhood House rose sharply. The growing response of Farnam Courts youth to diversified
programming made it desirable and necessary to have activities held
in the Courts themselves. Quarters provided by the Housing Authority made this extension possible.

As activities for Farnam Courts children mushroomed and
came to be increasingly centered in the housing project, the issues
dividing NIP and the Farnam Neighborhood House became apparent.
The two organizations served different populations, which did not
have compatible needs. The more conventional recreational programming done by the Neighborhood House was meeting the needs of
conforming youngsters from stable homes. Farnam Courts boys and
girls had to be given activities geared to the special requirements
of children who showed considerable aggressiveness, a low span of
attention (especially at younger ages), and a need for identification
with a strong leader. Farnam Courts youngsters, above all, needed
a full schedule of diversified activities to occupy the many hours not
claimed by school or family. Their need was especially great during the summer, when boys and girls of less deprived families, such
as those who were attending Farnam Neighborhood House, were busy
with camp and family vacation activities.

The facilities of the Neighborhood House became too limited
once the boys and girls of Farnam Courts began to join NIP activities in large numbers. The program that had been developed in the
Courts proper was quite different from that offered at the Neighborhood House. To step up Neighborhood House activities for the housing project children would have meant displacing the previously existing services.

When in the fall of 1961 the Neighborhood Improvement Project and the Farnam Courts Neighborhood House agreed to run their
respective recreational and group work programs separately, the decision merely reflected the realization of policy makers in both organizations that their goal priorities were not compatible.

Divergent goal priorities were equally at stake when a casework agency decided to withdraw from NIP. While executives and

boards of the various participating agencies were intellectually
aware of the issues of social and economic deprivation and multi-
problem behavior, and had expressed willingness to support action
to deal with the issues, they invariably viewed participation vis-a-
vis their commitments to serve the specific clientele for which
their agencies had assumed primary responsibility.

Faced with the wholesale withdrawal of participating agencies, the policy makers and staff of NIP were confronted with the
choice of sharply reducing services or changing NIP into a direct
service agency rather than an agency alliance. We chose the latter
course even though it meant surrendering one of our original objectives, a full sharing with the affiliated agencies of a service and
research program for multi-problem families and a seriously deprived neighborhood. Desirable as this objective was, our overriding concerns had to be the needs of the Farnam Courts population and the necessity to test the effectiveness of new approaches.

A substantial grant from the National Institute of Mental
Health in September, 1960, when added to the financial support giv-
en by the New Haven Foundation, made it possible to pay the salaries of direct service workers as well as the administrative, supervisory, and research staff. Additional financial contributions from
the Housing Authority, miscellaneous organizations, and private individuals permitted a consolidated operation centered in Farnam
Courts. As stated earlier, only Family Service of New Haven remained a partner in NIP to the end. The Board of Education provided the one-fifth-time services of one worker until one year before the termination of the service operation. The State Department
of Welfare collaborated with NIP in research by making cases available for an experimental-control evaluation study (see Chapter 15).

One result of agency withdrawal was a simplification of
structure. Supervision of casework and group work services became
the sole responsibility of the project Director, except for the supervision of the three caseworkers on the staff of Family Service.
That task was shared on an informal basis with the supervisor of
that agency. The centralized supervision enhanced flexibility in two
ways: it brought caseworkers and group workers into closer con-

tact and it enabled them to carry on joint service planning on the basis of shared experience.   It gave the project Director a free hand
to modify program on short notice without having to obtain agency
approval.   In this last period of functioning, covering approximately one-half of the action phase, NIP was a centralized, neighbor-
hood-focused operation with minimal integration into the larger community welfare structure.   The NIP Advisory Committee and the
Community Council of Greater New Haven continued to serve as
sponsors and parent bodies, providing an important link with the
community.   On a direct service level, NIP worked toward maximum use of community resources by the population of Farnam
Courts.   The project Director also played an active role as teacher
of in-service training and lecturer at professional conferences, insti-
tutes, organizational meetings, college forums, etc.   From an experimental and demonstration project whose operation was to be of
functional significance for local service planning and community organization, NIP had remodeled itself into an imposing entity on the
local welfare scene.

The Implications of Non-Integration

If the centralized operation sketched above sounds like an ad-
ministrator's paradise, let us look at some of the implications of
the self-contained structure of NIP or, for that matter, any short-
tenure community project.   Projects, as stated earlier, are not only
experimental endeavors but often, as in the case of NIP, prototypes
for institutional change.

The question of institutional change becomes most salient
when a project undertakes to render services that will meet urgent
but previously unmet needs.   Such is likely to be the case when
services are being rendered to a socially and economically deprived
population.   These experimental services are more than an alternative, more than new and more desirable patterns of community welfare operation.   They are, above all, a support to the socially handicapped, whose mode of life may be greatly affected by their establishment.

Maximal integration of a project into a community service

pattern can be seen as providing a high potential for service continuity. Non-integration puts the continuance of services into jeopardy. The planners of NIP had these considerations in mind. They saw a project resting upon an alliance of agencies as the best guarantee for the preservation of successfully tested programs and methods. The gradual disbanding of the agency partnerships confronted the Neighborhood Improvement Project and the community with the problem of what to do at the point of project termination.

Unfortunately this problem was not unique to NIP. The nationwide tide of demonstration and research projects made possible by the ready availability of grants has created a number of situations where the discontinuance of services means hardship for the population served. Our thesis here, based upon our New Haven experience, is clear. The discontinuance of much-needed services is a more irresponsible act than the failure to establish such services. The degree of deprivation and frustration becomes magnified when we increase the gap between people's expectations and the actual situation with which they will have to live. The wholesale response of people to services and activities newly created for them usually signifies the existence of prior need for such services. The termination of such services is a form of mass desertion that negates the previously shown concern.

The original citizens' group that planned the establishment of NIP called itself the Temporary Committee on Neighborhood Saturation. It may be that the choice of terminology was not an entirely happy one from the point of view of professional goals. The concept of neighborhood saturation, nevertheless, reflected the committee's awareness that areas like Farnam Courts are service barrens. They are marked by an absence of social, educational, recreational, and health services, except for compulsory schooling, public assistance, and emergency medical care. Even these last three generally leave much to be desired. The Farnam Courts neighborhood was in dire need of a wide range of services and facilities, everything from a pre-school nursery to activities for lonely senior citizens.

The network of services and activities established during the four years of operation did not wipe out want and destitution.

The services did, however, give aid to many in distress or faced
by problems; they increased social participation greatly in all age
groups; they provided socializing, educational, and recreational experiences for many, especially the young; they created ties with
community institutions and a few national organizations; and finally,
they enabled some individuals and families to reshape their self-image in a positive direction.   Our research could evaluate only a few
of the changes introduced by the project--more dramatic evidence of
the impact upon the population was provided by a tenants' petition
to the Mayor asking for the continuation of NIP.

The change in structure and mode of organization during the
course of operation gave rise to a situation where, at the beginning
of the final year of services, no provision had been made for the
continuation even of those services deemed most essential.   The
agency partnership, had it not been dissolved, would have served
as the logical authority for evolving the means by which the project
might have been converted into an ongoing pattern of services.   As
it turned out, the community of New Haven and the project staff itself were left to grapple with the problem of service continuity.

By a combination of social developments and fortuitous circumstances, including a large grant from the Ford Foundation, the
larger community was launching a series of programs in the summer of 1963--when the action phase of NIP was slated to end--
through the medium of a new organization, Community Progress,
Incorporated (CPI), aimed at social rehabilitation of the deprived
population.   Farnam Courts, as one of the deprived neighborhoods
of the city, was included in the plans.   Although the program was
still in its early stages, NIP staff and the Advisory Committee were
able to enter into negotiations with CPI for the continuation of services and activities in Farnam Courts.

Community Progress, Incorporated was not the product of a
faltering agency alliance such as had originally supported NIP.
CPI was a community-wide endeavor, not restricted to the welfare
community; it drew support from a variety of systems including the
Office of the Mayor, Urban Renewal Authority, Yale University,
management and labor, etc.   The Community Council of Greater

New Haven was, of course, instrumental in sparking and supporting the program. The Neighborhood Improvement Project was examined by the planning group and used as a model for community-wide programming. However, the bulk of social agencies that had joined hands to launch NIP were not involved in this broader program of social rehabilitation, whose roots went back to Mayor Lee's Citizens' Action Committee and other efforts aimed at broadening the city's concept of urban renewal to include social renewal. Ideas for community-wide programming to alleviate poverty were pushed by a few leading citizens, both within and outside the welfare system. When the program came to fruition in the form of CPI, it was essentially the product of a coalition of forces in which social welfare was represented but played, in the beginning at least, a relatively minor part.

Frank Harris, the Executive Director of the New Haven Council of Social Agencies and one of the prime movers in the establishment of NIP and CPI, held that "the Council should be a partner in joint planning with the economic, educational, physical, and political planners," adding that "the Council has an essential contribution to make but it is not the organization under whose banner all planning should or will take place."[1]

Harris' model of community planning reflected to a large extent the New Haven experience. It is questionable whether it can be used as a blueprint for all communities, since there are considerable differences from community to community in the strength and orientation of the respective systems concerned with planning. Council participation in community planning in New Haven is largely a function of the staff's vigorous leadership and initiative. Harris and his associates, after becoming aware that local welfare agencies lacked an interest in community organization and had no change orientation, turned to the larger community for the planning of social renewal. In the process that culminated in the CPI, the Council made what was a major contribution, but it did so without much support, at least in the initial stages, from its member agencies.

The threatened demise of NIP was viewed with concern by the Council staff and CPI, whereas the agencies, which had helped to bring the project into existence, considered the Farnam Courts operation as marginal, and outside their own field of professional functioning.

The joint efforts of the NIP staff, the Community Council of Greater New Haven, and CPI succeeded in preventing a discontinuance of services to the Farnam Courts population in the fall of 1963. What happened could best be described as a retrenchment of services. The significant occurrence for the future of Farnam Courts was its inclusion in a community-wide plan for the rehabilitation of deprived neighborhoods. Farnam Courts became in effect part of the Wooster Square area project, which was served by a community school and center and by neighborhood workers.

Without discussing the details of the Farnam Courts post-NIP program, which cannot be evaluated at this early stage, it is possible to give a general characterization of the program, keeping in mind that community-wide social renewal of deprived neighborhoods in New Haven is a program "becoming," not "in being." Some areas of the city were earmarked for the kind of intensive services rendered by NIP, but Farnam Courts was not included. Several voluntary organizations, such as the Boy Scouts, the 4-H Club, the YMCA and the Yale Service Fraternity (A.P.O.), which were brought into the housing project under NIP auspices, carried on without NIP supervision. A few educational and social work services were continued, others were dropped. Those that continued did so without the guidance of professionals who had learned to adapt services to a lower-class, socially handicapped culture. Waiting lists suddenly appeared, and a middle-class type of programming became more prevalent. Farnam Courts, although it did not revert back to its former status as a forgotten neighborhood, became an area of diminished concern. The stepped-up war on poverty will, hopefully, once again focus attention upon the needs of the people of Farnam Courts, but that had not begun to happen when these lines were being written.

In summary, the Neighborhood Improvement Project, because of the wider community's concern, did not become a case of experimentation ending in neglect. Examples of such happenings, however, are not rare in the annals of welfare projects in the United States. The failure of NIP to become institutionalized as an ongoing program of services can be attributed to the failure of sound community organization. Our rational model for inter-agency collaboration turned out to be an unworkable one.

Our experience in NIP, and in other projects with less happy endings, leads us to recommend strongly that there be an end to experimental action projects that culminate in the discontinuance of needed services. A nationwide network of anti-poverty projects, financed largely but only temporarily by federal grants, poses the danger of post-project social neglect that can exceed in magnitude the neglect inherent in our affluent society's toleration of poverty. Until the time that joint action by federal, state, and local government will assure the socially handicapped an income and services above the poverty line, all communities, agencies, and institutions have the irrevocable responsibility of planning their projects for human renewal with continuous, unceasing concern for those chosen to be helped, for as long as their need exists.

Notes

1. Frank W. Harris. "A Modern Council Point of View,"
   Social Work, Vol. 9, No. 4, October 1964, pp. 34-41.

Chapter 13
Trained Versus Untrained Workers in Services
to Individuals and Families

In its operations the Neighborhood Improvement Project faced
a problem that has plagued the field of social welfare ever since it
became professionalized[1]--a shortage of trained manpower. NIP
group work services, not dissimilar to those given by the field as a
whole, utilized untrained personnel and volunteers to render direct
service. Supervision of the overall group work program was provided by the Director of the total project, a trained and experienced
social worker, but supervision of specific adult and youth activities
was in the hands of individuals who did not possess professional social work degrees. The adult program supervisor had one year of
graduate training in social work; the youth program supervisor held
a degree in the field of recreation.

For the program of services to individuals and families,
every effort was made to recruit candidates with a graduate degree
in social work. However, in the initial stages of the project the
shortage of trained workers precluded the filling of all positions with
those holding graduate degrees. Later, as our casework services
were expanded, budget limitations raised a further obstacle to the
hiring of full-fledged professionals. Eliminating a few workers,
mostly untrained, whose participation in NIP was of very short duration, we find that the project employed five untrained workers[2] and
eleven trained social workers. Of the former, four had a general
caseload that included a few multi-problem families; one carried a
caseload of multi-problem families only. All of the trained workers
participated in the program of intensive services to multi-problem
families.

The distribution of the two categories of workers left limited
room for an objective comparison of outcome. The one untrained
worker serving multi-problem families was also the only social

294

worker in the service to multi-problem families who carried a full
caseload.   The overall movement of her families did not differ significantly from that of the cases carried by the trained professionals.   This result may seem surprising, but it is not out of line
with findings in the St. Paul Family-Centered Project and two studies that have not yet appeared in the literature.[3]

What are the reasons for the absence of a difference in the
effectiveness of treatment, at least as measured by currently available criteria of outcome?   Are we justified in stating that training
is not a significant factor in treatment outcomes?   In the present
discussion we must confine ourselves to observations made in the
Neighborhood Improvement Project, whose unique features suggest
that caution must be exercised in extending our conclusions to the
field as a whole.

Before comparing some of the specific traits of trained and
untrained workers and their respective reactions to the services,
two qualifications must be made: (1) When we talk about training
or formal education in social work we mean past experience.   Only
two of the workers were recent graduates; the others had attended
graduate schools of social work a number of years ago.   Keeping
in mind the changing nature of education in general and social work
practice in particular, we must remember that we are looking at
the appropriateness of training given at an earlier period being applied to present-day practice.   (2) Hiring practices were not identical for the two groups.   The trained workers were mostly persons
assigned to NIP by their parent agencies, and the project had to accept, within limits, those who were given this assignment.   Those
without formal training were selected from a pool of applicants for
casework positions and thus were carefully screened before acceptance.

Obviously, the unique and preferred equipment of the trained
worker came in good part from his special education, through which
he acquired a theoretical framework; interviewing, diagnostic and
treatment skills; and practice in making objective and disciplined
judgments.   His training has emphasized the relationship between
personality factors and malfunctioning; the need for client motiva-

tion; the importance and use of relationship, usually on a one-to-one basis.   Psychoanalytic theory exerts great influence on social work education and practice;[4] generally, one of its effects upon the trained worker is to make him view inadequate functioning as being related primarily to inadequate personality.   In training, client motivation is given particular stress.   It then follows that in treatment the client is helped to examine how he functions in relation to his problems and his part in resolving them.   While some recognition is given to economic, social, and cultural deprivation as factors in malfunctioning, their importance is underplayed, especially by workers who received their professional education in the psychiatrically oriented schools of social work.

We have seen that the deprivation of multi-problem families is first and foremost of a material nature.   They lack adequate income, shelter, clothing, food, medical care.   The trained worker, more so than the untrained one, is apt to overlook this deprivation, using the inadequate personality concept as the explanation for family malfunctioning.   On first contact he observes that the multi-problem family is usually beset by a long list of seemingly individual inabilities: to find and hold a job; to achieve or adjust in school; to abide by legal regulations; to use available resources appropriately, etc.   And then there loom client apathy, hopelessness, indifference, resignation, coupled with the all too common "It's not my fault."   The worker is appalled that the client wants someone to do things for him and wants them done immediately, that he even wants the worker to make decisions on his behalf.   His training has not sufficiently prepared this social worker to deal with the totally unmotivated, immobilized client with whom he is now expected to form a relationship.   He starts with a feeling of hopelessness and right at the onset questions his ability to effect movement.

The situation is further complicated by the client's lack of verbal skill or his inexperience in communication.   His speech is as random and scattered as are his thoughts, and he is sometimes described as "incoherent."   Lack of education and limited exposure to diverse social situations account for a good deal of the client's inability to organize and articulate his thoughts.   The well-educated

worker, not conditioned to expect this kind of verbal exchange, has
difficulty understanding it. As a result the trained worker has to
do some "unlearning": he must set aside the sophisticated casework
approach he has been taught or else he must glean from it whatever
can be adapted to fit this unfamiliar situation. The worker comes
to learn that his non-verbal client often gives clues, but does not
make direct requests. He indirectly says, "Do something for me,"
because he cannot do for himself at this point in time.

Although the trained worker has been taught to appreciate the
value of "supportive" treatment, he comes to feel strongly that making decisions for the client or acting on the client's behalf makes
him an authority figure. This, the worker feels, is an inappropriate role that contradicts the principle of client self-determination
he has been taught. In those situations where the trained worker
clearly sees the client's helplessness, he accepts with mixed feelings the need to take the initiative. The degree of dependency evidenced at the outset almost overwhelms the worker; he fears that
it will grow unmanageable when he begins to act for the client.
The discrepancy between what the worker perceives or senses and
what he has theoretically learned renders him temporarily indecisive
in the presence of a client that wants, above all else, to be shown
a clear and decisive course.

Most of the untrained workers in NIP had a background in
public welfare. This experience, aside from indoctrinating them in
agency policies, regulations, and procedures, helped them acquire
interviewing skills in dealing with clients, the ability to sort out
problems and establish priorities and treatment goals, and a knowledge of resources and how to use them appropriately. The more
mature worker had also acquired from his life experience a body of
knowledge about such matters as individual behavior, family life,
child rearing, and household practices, which could be used to good
advantage in the work situation.

One source of knowledge open to the untrained worker has
been overlooked, and that is the accessibility of psychological theory.
Today a variety of media fosters exposure to the psychological factors governing human behavior. A degree of sophistication with re-

spect to psychological concepts is held by today's college-educated individual, regardless of his field of study. Many of our untrained workers had such knowledge and were able to draw on it in a treatment situation.

We observed that an untrained worker confronted with a multi-problem client tended to do what seemed right and sensible at the moment--answering the most immediate need of the client. He did this in a direct, uncomplicated manner by responding to the most conspicuous aspect of client deprivation, invariably material problems. He was prone to view the client as an underdog rather than a product of personality defect, and he did not seriously question the idea that the meeting of tangible needs would result in an improvement of client functioning.

The untrained worker, then, tends to take literally the client's first expressions, which are usually half-articulated requests for information, advice, direction, or decisions. He does not seek underlying motives or disguised meanings, but assumes that the client genuinely wants an answer. This unsophisticated approach seems to work more often than not. This type of client cannot discuss feelings, seek to understand the why of behavior, or weigh a given course of action. He learns best through demonstration, and by imitation of a model who can structure a course of action and introduce him to a more effective method. After the client has experienced a degree of success, he may be termed ready for the more sophisticated process of looking for the underlying factors in previous failures. Only then can he learn procedures for the future, applying the lessons learned in his new, successful experience.

It is readily apparent that such an approach depends upon the worker setting the pace and direction, taking the initiative by "doing something" to relieve the situation quickly. The untrained worker, rarely troubled by the question of whether it was appropriate for him to make decisions for the client, did so as a matter of course and was comfortable, even pleased, with the client's dependency.

As mentioned earlier, the trained worker felt strongly that such decision-making for the client cast him in a role contradictory to the principle of self-determination that he had been taught. When

the demands of some clients made them appear "insatiable," the
trained worker's reaction was one of misgiving, and he suspected
the client of being "manipulative." He lost sight of the fact that the
reality of need might well take precedence over attempts to understand the client's behavior.

The untrained worker, more action oriented, was eager from
the very beginning to "do for and with" the client, for he had not
yet thought beyond a rather primitive step-by-step approach to tangible unmet needs. While this may be regarded as naive, it had
two definite advantages: the worker was not overwhelmed by worry
over a badly deteriorated situation, nor was he immediately awed by
the task of trying to meet contemplated long-range goals. Thus the
untrained worker was aided by an early momentum that worked very
effectively, to the point where a positive relationship was established and the client replaced his former attitudes with trust, hope,
and some motivation for change.

It is essential for all caseworkers to realize job satisfaction,
i.e., movement in treatment, but it is of particular importance
when one is dealing with seriously deprived families because progress can be slow and difficult to achieve. The uncomplicated approach that the untrained worker used had the effect of offering job
satisfaction early in contact.

The turmoil that characterized much of the NIP home visiting, especially in the early stages of contact, was accepted by the
untrained worker as part of the job. If he had had work experience, it frequently involved visiting clients in similar living situations. He was, therefore, neither so oriented to the office interview routine nor so dependent upon it as was the trained worker.
Although he lacked the diagnostic skills of the trained professional,
the untrained worker was an astute observer of the home scene.
Wherever possible he made maximum use of the confusion to note
the quality of interpersonal relationships between parents and children, among siblings, and between family members and outsiders.
He also absorbed significant details about household practices and
standards.

Whether or not they are so indoctrinated during academic

training, trained workers tend to relegate work in the environmental
or instrumental areas to a position of lesser importance than work
in the area of interpersonal problems.   They are at first apt to
concentrate on reducing the turmoil in the home rather than making
use of it for the insights it may offer into family functioning.   Furthermore, the trained worker, especially if newly exposed to the
home life of lower-class society and severely deprived people, tends
to experience "cultural shock."   Even when theoretically prepared
for the gap between himself and the treatment population, reality
strikes him in such a manner that he requires a period of adjustment.   It is during this period that he finds it difficult to view the
client's behavior as anything but deviant.   Only gradually does he
realize that the treatment families can not be fitted into his psychological frame of reference and that their behavior may have to be
viewed in a different cultural context.

This is illustrated by the confusion centering around appointment hours in the NIP program.   Our worker, having informed the
client of the time of the weekly home visit, would arrive to find the
house full of children and neighbors, with the radio or television
blaring.   The client would be "surprised" at the worker's presence
and greet him with a remark about his unexpected appearance.   The
trained worker's usual assessment was that the client was resistive
and probably hostile.   If the appointment had been remembered the
client appeared to have set up diversions or "protection" to keep
from talking with the worker.   It is possible that something quite
different was involved, and that the client had truly forgotten the
appointment.   Strict adherence to time is not an important principle
to the client.   Appointments she has had--with clinics, welfare departments, the school, or court--have rarely been kept strictly on
time; furthermore, she doesn't function on a close time schedule in
her home management or personal life.   Usually tied to the home,
having no particular commitments, operating on a routine with little
variation, these clients see the casual dropping-in of neighbors as
a welcome diversion.   The blaring television set or radio is also
common throughout the neighborhood.   Thus what may be viewed as
hostility toward the interview may be in reality only a different cul-

tural response.

The untrained worker might be regarded as too little tutored in the exploration and handling of feelings. He particularly tends to avoid the direct handling of hostility. Although he usually allows ventilation of such feelings and reacts with sympathy, he does not deliberately encourage such expression. By contrast, the trained worker is all too aware of the relation between functioning and latent or repressed hostility. Whenever possible his inclination is to approach treatment by giving early attention to hostility, encouraging its expression and attempting to relate it to client behavior. However, in the case of a multi-problem family, he is dealing with individuals who do not as a rule verbalize their feelings. Since it is quite some time before this kind of client is sufficiently easy or trusting to personalize his feelings directly or to examine his hostility, the client is distinctly more comfortable with a worker who is not urging self-examination. From our own experience and from accounts given by other workers, we have concluded that the client tolerates--and indeed for some initial period requires--the verbalization of his feelings by the worker. Since the client's emotions and attitudes are so thinly disguised, it is possible for the sensitive untrained worker to diagnose them with considerable accuracy from the client's limited statements or facial expressions.

Another factor in the make-up of an effective caseworker is the personality of the worker and the way he is able to use himself in the work situation. His success depends upon his ability to establish a relationship with the client. The multi-problem family, surrounding itself with a strong wall of suspiciousness, exhibits seeming defiance or indifference; in effect, it is serving notice that proof will be required before it can be convinced that help is really being offered. This kind of family, conditioned to expect rejection, is further sensitized by an awareness of the differences in values, customs, level of education and standards that separate it from the worker. The feeling of apartness, differentness, and alienation must be reduced; the family must begin to hope, to feel that effort is worthwhile and that accomplishment is attainable. It has by now become a truism that the worker must take the initiative with this type of family.

While training can help develop the ability to express warmth
and genuine concern, not all workers have the capacity to project
these in such a way as to elicit a positive response from a super-
sensitive client.   The Director of NIP, with prior experience in
treating over 300 multi-problem families, was strongly concerned
about this ability.   When given a choice, she would by-pass a worker with training and considerable experience who was cool, aloof,
and detached, and select a discernibly warm, friendly, out-going inexperienced worker.   Justification for her choices can be found in
NIP records, which reflect in the client's own words and reactions
the significance of a worker's capacity to project sincere warmth
and acceptance.   Further support can be found in cases where a
comparison was possible because a collateral agency worker was involved or referrals were attempted but were not successful.   In
both types of situations, clients emphasized that the "other worker"
could have been of definite help but was "so cold;" "so unfriendly;"
"made me feel dumb;" "looked down on me. "   One of the saddest
and most frequent statements was: "I was so scared I didn't even
understand what he was saying to me;" this would be followed by,
"I'm not going back there; he made me feel like a beggar; I
couldn't talk to him. "[5]

To sum up, there is no clear-cut basis for deciding whether
trained or untrained but experienced workers should be given preference in work with multi-problem families.   The unexpected finding
that trained workers did not perform better than untrained ones has
led us into an examination of possible causes.   Bias in the NIP selection process in favor of those who were untrained might account
in part for the results.   A more far-reaching conclusion might be
that formal academic training frequently fails to prepare practitioners for service to lower-class, seriously disorganized families.   If
this is indeed the case, social work education is faced with a major
issue in curriculum policy.

Within the limits of our own data, we can state that some
untrained workers with previous experience in public welfare can
become able practitioners in the treatment of multi-problem fami-

lies. Their lack of sophistication in diagnostic and treatment techniques, while a deficit in treating motivated clients, may be an advantage in dealing with a lower subculture. Good supervision and
in-service training then become the principal instruments of worker
learning. It would appear that supervision and training, coupled
with an active experience in the field, represent a kind of learning
that does not come into conflict with knowledge and skills previously acquired. The trained worker, especially if trained in traditionally oriented programs, has to reorganize his thinking and reformu-
late his concepts to fit his new experience. This readjustment, demanding as it is on client, worker, and supervisor, is likely to be
only second best to a program of formal training that from its inception is geared to work with the multi-problem family.

Notes

1. It is difficult to set an exact date for professionaliza-
   tion, partly because the concept is based on a number
   of attributes that social work acquired only gradually
   over a period of time. If we are satisfied to focus
   on two of the most central attributes, the following
   quote from the Encyclopedia of Social Work can serve
   to approximately locate the onset of professionalism:
   AASW (American Association of Social Workers) did
   not emerge full-blown as the organized representative of social work as a profession. Though founded
   in 1921, it was 1929, for instance, before a membership criterion calling for education in a recognized school of social work was adopted, and even
   this was not fully implemented until 1933.
   David G. French, "Professional Organization," in
   Harry Lurie (editor), Encyclopedia of Social Work
   (New York, National Association of Social Workers,
   1965), pp. 574-578.

2. These were women holding bachelor's degrees in the liberal arts field, which generally included some social
   science courses; in one case, the worker had taken
   several undergraduate social work courses.

3. Study of family service agencies done at the Buffalo, N.Y.,
   School of Social Work; Chemung County (N.Y.) Research
   Action Project with multi-problem families.

4. This generalization, though less true at the time this
   book was being written, was quite valid when NIP was
   recruiting its staff.

5. Lillian Ripple, in her study involving 178 clients (re:
   motivation for treatment), found that "the most important single variable" as far as client continuation
   in treatment was concerned "did not have to do with
   the worker's skill in specific activities," but rather
   concerned "the amount of encouragement given the client during and immediately after the initial interview."
   Lillian Ripple, <u>Motivation, Capacity, and Opportunity
   Studies in Casework Theory and Practice,</u> Social Service Administration, The University of Chicago, 1964,
   p. 199.   Further on she states that "there was a high
   association (almost complete in the cases of clients
   with external problems) between continuance and 'strong
   encouragement,' characterized by early positive
   (worker) effect, efforts to relieve discomfort, assurance that the situation could at least be improved, and
   a plan to begin work on the problems in the next interview." One characteristic mode of discouragement
   was a "bland, seemingly uninvolved eliciting and appraisal of the client's situation, in which the worker
   appeared neutral in effect, left the client's discomfort
   untouched, and offered no basis for hope that the situation could be improved." Same, p. 203.

Chapter 14

Studying Casework Method Systematically

Problem and Method

One of the research objectives of the Neighborhood Improvement Project was a systematic study of the casework method. Systematic research on treatment was seen as important for two reasons:
(1) We needed to know whether we actually carried out our plan of
intervention, in other words did we practice what we preached? (2)
We wished to determine whether it was possible to isolate any of
the techniques and skills involved in our plan as being particularly
correlated with treatment outcome.

Casework rather than total neighborhood intervention became
the subject of systematic study because the former was carried out
by one worker, or at least one worker at a time--a circumstance
that enabled us to get standardized information from a single source.
Our other forms of intervention were in the hands of a number of
workers, professional as well as volunteer, who operated within a
looser structure and found it more difficult to supply standardized information about their work. Moreover casework, as the main component of the movement study (reported in Chapter 15), was the most
logical factor for analysis.

The study of casework method differed from other types of
research reported here in that it was not only undertaken without the
benefit of a prior design but was conceived largely as a methodological contribution rather than a substantive investigation. We had
hoped initially that the methodology of the research effort could be
worked out in time for its utilization in a study of the components of
the casework method. That hope remained largely unfilled because
too much project time was occupied with efforts to cope with the
problem of methodology.[1] These efforts are reported here, as well
as a preliminary analysis of data on the nature of treatment. Of

necessity, the latter aspect of the study is merely a feasibility report, whose findings are suggestive of further research.

A systematic study of casework method must necessarily rely
upon a technique for documenting it. The Profile of Family Functioning used in the movement study covers only one side of the
treatment process--the psycho-social functioning of the client. The
other side, the efforts of the worker, are not documented methodol-
ogically but only reported in summary fashion under the heading
"The Family's Relationship to the Social Worker." In an experimental project such as NIP we felt the need for a reliable account
not merely of what happened to the client but also of what the worker did.

No profession is more careful to document the activities of
its practitioners than is social casework. The casework student is
taught in school to report carefully in writing on every phase of the
client-worker interaction and to spell out fully his every idea, plan
and action. This reporting, known as case recording, takes many
forms, with variations in the order of subject presentation, the
amount of detail reported and, of course, the theoretical and conceptual mold in which the reporting is cast. Students and beginning
practitioners are encouraged to use process recording, which means
relating the client-worker interaction chronologically in complete detail and reporting verbatim on verbal exchanges in the treatment
situation. At the other end of the spectrum is brief summary recording, whose greatest virtue is economy in professional and cleri-
cal time. Many agencies, intent upon maximizing the professional
time spent in direct service to the client, have chosen summary recording as the preferred mode of reporting on treatment. Most recording in the social work field represents a summarization of the
treatment process, with elaboration of those aspects that are focal
points in the work of the agency.

How adequate are the common techniques of recording for
purposes of documenting systematically the method of worker intervention? The concensus seems to be that traditional recording techniques do not meet the requirements of social work research.[2] The
requirements of research are generally specific and call for a large

measure of standardization and reliability in documentation. The variables that the researcher may be looking for in the case record are infinite in number and do not necessarily coincide with the information that is important for supervision.

Needing an instrument specifically designed for documenting casework treatment method, we devised a semi-structured schedule that we called a Treatment Log.

While there is no dearth of social casework conceptualization we have not come across any formulations that lend themselves readily to being operationally defined.[3] Our schedule, which lacks the conceptual underpinning of a sensitive research instrument, is a first attempt to document systematically the activities that are part of the casework method. A more sophisticated effort would have required a separate study, beyond the scope of the research assignment in the Neighborhood Improvement Project.

The limited task we set ourselves was that of answering the following questions: Which members of the client families were seen? Where and how often were they seen? What subjects were discussed? Who initiated the discussions? What collateral contacts did the worker make?[4]

The project researchers had posed some additional questions relative to client attitudes toward the worker and the subject discussed and to the treatment techniques used by the worker. Information under these headings lacked the reliability necessary for analysis. The question of treatment techniques in particular posed serious research problems. The techniques identified in the casework literature and listed in the Treatment Log were found to be devoid of operational definitions (the instructions for use of the Log cited the definitions most common in the literature) and did not adequately cover the range of techniques used by the caseworker.

The items in the Treatment Log that were finally selected for analysis were those dealing with concrete, factual matters in the client-worker relationship, such as the persons and the subjects dealt with by the social worker. A collection and analysis of conceptual information would have required prior studies to remove the methodological barriers.

The Treatment Log study, launched about a year after the start of the Neighborhood Improvement Project, covered twelve multi-problem families. Only one-fourth of the families in intensive treatment were included in the study, for several reasons: worker resistance to a new report form; the difficulty of enforcing the use of a new form while some agency supervisors continued to demand conventional case recording; worker turnover that produced delays in processing the new schedules.[5]

In actuality all workers had a try at treatment logging sometime during their stint at NIP. However, only three of them used it consistently for a sufficiently long time to justify data analysis. One of these workers, A, completed Treatment Logs for six families; a second worker, B, did so for four families; and a third worker, C,[6] carried two cases. All three workers were professionally trained and had previous work experience. The cases that are the subject of the present analysis were carried from thirteen to twenty-five months.

In spite of sample limitations arising from the above cited difficulties, an analysis of the Treatment Log data appears justified for they provide (1) a first systematic account on a few dimensions of family-centered treatment and (2) a preliminary test of the Log as an instrument, however rudimentary, for the study of casework method.

Findings

In the twelve cases for which we gathered data about the activities of the caseworker there were 932 face-to-face interviews, or an average of 77.7 interviews per family. The mean monthly frequency of interviews was 4.4, indicating that the caseworkers maintained close contact with their client families.

Of these 932 interviews, 579 (62.1 percent) were held at the clients' homes. The percentage of interviews held in the home ranged from 56 percent for the worker with cases active the longest period of time, to 65.9 percent for the worker with families in treatment over an intermediate period of time, to 84.9 percent for the worker having the shortest cases. Even on a case by case basis, families with a shorter period of treatment tended to have a

higher percentage of home interviews. Although the data were not
analyzed in detail it seems reasonable to suppose that all workers
began service with a high percentage of home interviews and then
gradually switched some of the interviews to the office. This would
indicate that as their rapport with the family increased they were
able to motivate the client to seek out the worker for at least some
of the interviews.

Of the 932 interviews, 244 (26.2 percent) included the father,
either alone or jointly with the mother. A more accurate picture of
the extent of worker contact with fathers was obtained by examining only the six cases in which the father was part of the family
picture throughout the treatment period. In these six families there
were 541 interviews, of which 239 (44.2 percent) included the father.
Clearly, the caseworker managed to make the father a partner in
the treatment process.

The Treatment Log showed that in the course of 932 interviews, 2,226 subjects were covered--an average of 2.4 per interview and 10.5 per month for each case. Subject is here defined as
discussion content coded in terms of the twenty-six subcategories of
the Family Profile. The figures give no indication of the length of
time the subjects were discussed nor the number of repetitions.
There was only minor variation among the three workers in the
mean number of subjects that constituted the content of case discussions per month, the range being from 8.7 to 11.4. The client took
the initiative in bringing up a subject most of the time. Only one
of the three workers showed a tendency to increase the proportion
of client-initiated discussion from one treatment period to the next
(68 percent were client initiated during the first six months' period,
85 percent during the last period). Treatment Logs of the other
two workers revealed fluctuating trends (slightly above or below 50
percent) on client-initiated subjects for interviews.

The caseworkers maintained 763 collateral contacts (service
contacts by visit or telephone with persons other than the client) for
the twelve families, nearly one contact (.82 contacts) for each interview. There were, however, sharp differences among the workers.
Worker C, with two cases, listed an average of 122 collaterals per

case, or 5.1 per case per month.   Worker A, with six cases,
showed an average of 62.7 collaterals per case (2.9 per case per
month), and Worker B, with four cases, showed an average of only
35.8 per case (2.43 per case per month).

With whom were these collateral contacts made?   The agency
contacted the most was, as might be expected, the State Welfare
Department, with 119 contacts; Juvenile Court and its probation officers were next, with 88 contacts.   The schools accounted for the
largest block of contacts--64 contacts with school guidance counsel-
ors, 53 with teachers or principals, 32 with school social workers,
9 with the school psychiatrist, and 6 with school nurses, a total of
164 contacts.   Child placement institutions were contacted 60 times.
The preponderance of collateral contacts with agencies concerned
with problems of children reflected our method of selecting families,
which limited the treatment group to those having children in clear
and present danger.

Health agencies constituted the next largest block of collater-
als--114 contacts spread among hospitals, doctors, dental clinics,
the Visiting Nurse Association, and the city Health Department.   The
balance of the collateral contacts were with a wide variety of agen-
cies--40 connected with correctional and legal matters, such as police, court officers, attorneys, etc.; 55 with recreation or camp
facilities for children; and many others with ministers or priests,
Family Service, the relocation office, the Salvation Army, etc.
Only four calls were made to the employment office, two to an employer, and two to the Vocational Rehabilitation Office.   This is an
indication that there was little room in treatment for economic rehabilitation due to the fact that many multi-problem families in Farnam Courts were headed by women or handicapped fathers.

In attempting to relate the information in the Treatment Logs
to the nature of family functioning and movement, the analysis must
be restricted to the eighteen-month period covered by the movement
study (see Chapter 15).   Late starts by some workers in logging the
treatment process restricted the number of months covered by Treatment Logs to 9.45 months per case on the average.   Treatment
Logs covered only about one-half the treatment period in which

change was measured by means of the Profile of Family Functioning, reducing the sensitivity of measurement of change.

During the mean treatment period of nine and one-half months
for which we have Treatment Logs, 493 face-to-face interviews
were recorded, in which 1,195 subjects were discussed. The number of interviews per month ranged from 6.4 to 3.1 and the number
of subjects discussed per month ranged from 20.2 to 7.4. The total movement per case ranged from +12 to -5.[7] No correlation was
found between either the number of interviews per month or the number of subjects discussed per month and the total movement per
case. (Spearman rank correlations were -.06 and -.07 respectively.)

The Treatment Log yields specific information on what subjects were discussed and the frequency with which they were discussed. Two questions might be posed: (1) Is there a relationship
between the frequency with which subjects were put on the treatment
agenda and the extent of malfunctioning in any particular area? (2)
Is the frequency of discussion of certain subjects related to movement in a given area? Since all three dimensions of measurement
utilized the same categories or areas of family functioning, the associations can be easily tested.

The subject discussed most frequently in the treatment of the
twelve families studied was Health Conditions and Practices, followed by Individual Behavior and Adjustment, and Family Relationships and Unity. Social Activities was lowest in frequency among
the subjects discussed, after Child Care and Training. For the
same twelve families, Individual Behavior and Adjustment ranked
first among the problematic areas of family functioning, followed by
Family Relationships and Unity and Economic Practices. Home and
Household Practices rated lowest in "problemicity," and Social Activities represented the next most adequate area of social functioning. The rank order correlation between "problemicity" in given
areas and subjects discussed was +.65, revealing a substantial association between what the worker saw as the major problem and
what either he or the client selected as the subject for discussion.
This is what we would have expected on the basis of our supposition

that by and large the worker addresses himself to those areas of
behavior that are of concern to the family and/or the community.

Movement or change in family functioning was greatest for
the twelve families[8] in Relationship to the Caseworker, followed by
Health Conditions and Practices, and Use of Community Resources.
Movement was lowest in Home and Household Practices and only
slightly greater in Care and Training of Children. The rank order
correlation of movement per category and frequency of discussion of
that category was +.58, a moderately close association.

It is possible that the degree of relationship between subjects
discussed and movement in given areas is to a large extent a function of the amount of verbal inter-action between client and worker.
It can be assumed that for the non-verbal Farnam Courts population
discussion may not be as effective a technique for modifying social
functioning as demonstration or "doing with." For instance, in the
six cases carried by a single worker, highest movement was shown
in both Family Relationships and Use of Community Resources. The
worker indicated frequent discussion of Family Relationships but
very little discussion of Use of Community Resources. However,
this worker had used community resources for these families and
had demonstrated the advantages that the family could gain by increasing their use. She brought the families into direct contact with
the resources by taking members to clinics, recreational services,
etc., and by occasionally bringing resources to their homes. The
families learned by "seeing" and "doing" rather than by "hearing
about," or discussion. This approach resulted in a substantially
better use of community resources, as indicated by the change in
social functioning score.

Summary and Interpretation

The study reported here was designed chiefly to document
some aspects of the casework process in service to multi-problem
families. Lacking a standardized instrument for the systematic
study of casework process, we developed our own Treatment Log.
At its present stage of development this Log is but a first attempt
to identify some of the readily measurable dimensions of casework

treatment. Because the Treatment Log was introduced into the project after the launching of casework services it was not possible to
attain full participation of the workers in the experiment. Data collected from three workers on twelve cases covering 932 interviews
and 763 collateral contacts provide us, nonetheless, with a more objective picture of the practice of family-centered casework in the
Neighborhood Improvement Project than we have had previously. A
comparison with findings from an earlier study of treatment done in
the St. Paul Family-Centered Project[9] does add perspective to our
present findings. The St. Paul treatment study did not use a log or
special worker schedule but was done by means of content analysis
of a sample of case records.

The average monthly interview count of more than four face-
to-face contacts is very much in line with the NIP aims, which were
primarily concerned with transmitting continuing concern for the welfare of the families by frequent and regular visits. The frequency
of contacts was double that in the St. Paul Project,[10] a fact that can
be explained in part by the larger caseload carried by St. Paul
workers (twenty versus twelve in New Haven) and by the wider geographic dispersion of St. Paul multi-problem families.

The proportion of interviews held in the home was similar in
both projects (62.1 percent in New Haven, 64.3 percent in St. Paul).[11]
The reaching-out nature of family-centered casework was further revealed in the fact that in nearly half the interviews where the father
was in the home the father was also seen by the worker (New Haven)
and fathers were involved early in the casework process (St. Paul).[12]
Children likewise, the St. Paul data indicated, were involved in interviews in about one-fourth of the contacts studied.[13]

Treatment in the New Haven and St. Paul projects was also
comparable in the near 1 to 1 ratio of face-to-face and collateral
contacts.[14] We are led to conclude that casework with multi-problem families typically calls for extensive worker activity aimed at
bringing the family into contact with community resources or at working out problems that have arisen by the client's use of such resources, particularly schools, welfare departments, and correctional
agencies and health services.

The subjects discussed and the frequency with which they were discussed reflected (1) the subjective aspect of the client situation, namely those conditions which the client defines as problematic and (2) the worker's and/or the community's perception of what is problematic in the family's life. The two do not always coincide, although social casework will rarely fail to concern itself with matters that trouble the client. The fact that the majority of subjects discussed in the interviews were introduced by the client rather than the worker supports this particular thesis.

We listed earlier the relative frequency of subjects in the casework discussions. A comparison of NIP with St. Paul data[15] showed similarities and differences expressed by a (Spearman) rank order correlation of +.48. The greatest discrepancy was shown in the area of Health Problems and Practices, which ranked first in frequency in New Haven and sixth in St. Paul. Inadequate health resources for the economically deprived made the question of health care an important focus of treatment in New Haven.

Although Relationship to the Caseworker was not among the top-ranking items of discussion in either project, the subject was covered relatively more often in NIP (fifth in rank) than in the St. Paul project (ninth or last in rank). One possible explanation is that the three professionally trained NIP workers who used the Log may have patterned their treatment more closely after the spycho-therapeutic model than the Family-Centered Project workers, whose ranks included some without professional training.

Urban multi-problem families are characterized by common patterns of malfunctioning, as we have been able to show elsewhere.[16] Differences in the saliency of problems do exist, but the similarities seem to outweigh the differences. Whatever differences there are, together with the variations in treatment method, produce differences in the rank order of subjects discussed. The remarkable aspect of the finding of a +.48 correlation in the frequency of subjects discussed is the similarity rather than the difference in content of treatment in two communities over a thousand miles apart.

Both the New Haven and St. Paul[17] projects yielded comparable evidence that the frequency with which subjects were covered in casework discussion is related both to problem function at the beginning of service and movement during treatment. This triangular relationship is marked by low but consistent correlations among (1) the problems a client manifests, (2) the kind of subjects the caseworker discusses, and (3) the areas of functioning in which movement occurs.[18] Here, as in the previous analysis, a regularity of process is apparent in which treatment method and treatment outcome are tied to the social functioning of the multi-problem family.

Such regularities in the treatment process provide promising leads to research in greater depth on the nature of social work method. The Treatment Log analysis has enabled us to look at the behavioral side of casework method and compare it with the goals guiding this method. For lack of good conceptualization we have been able to examine only a few dimensions of casework treatment, but this effort has provided a beginning paradigm for the study of social work intervention. The small size of the sample set serious limitations on any attempt to achieve substantive conclusions on such significant variables as worker's training, length of experience, ratio of time spent in face-to-face interviews, etc.

This study yielded some impressive evidence that casework treatment in the Neighborhood Improvement Project was more than a bundle of good intentions, that the social workers took pains to address themselves to the problems that were burdening the families. Comparisons between two experimental multi-problem family projects in different regions of the country revealed striking similarities,[19] not merely in philosophy but in the way in which workers carried out their assignments and in the consequences of their intervention. The continuing gathering of evidence, transcending single settings, on similarity and difference in method is, we believe, nothing less than a cornerstone in the development of a science-based practice of social work.

Notes

1. For a more advanced treatment of the subject by means

of an improved Treatment Log, see Bruce W. Lagay
and Ludwig L. Geismar "The Treatment Log--A Recording Procedure for Casework Practice and Research." (New Brunswick, N. J. , Graduate School of Social
Work, Rutgers, The State University.) (Mimeographed)

2. Leonard S. Kogan and B.H. Brown. "A Two-Year
   Study of Case Record Uses," Social Casework, XXXV,
   6, June 1954, pp. 252-257. Leonard S. Kogan, "The
   Electrical Recording of Social Casework Interviews,"
   Social Casework, XXXI, 9, November 1950, pp. 371-
   378. John Frings, "Experimental Systems of Recording," Social Casework, XXXVIII, 2, February 1957,
   pp. 55-63, p. 56. Leonard S. Kogan, "The Short-
   Term Case in a Family Agency, Part I, The Study
   Plan," Social Casework, XXXVIII, 5, May 1957, pp.
   231-238.

3. This statement is not meant to detract from Lillian
   Ripple's pioneer study of the casework process in family agencies.   For our purposes the Ripple technique,
   based upon the coding of available case records, was
   inappropriate for two reasons: her theoretical framework was largely geared to the motivated rather than
   the hard-to-reach client; it highlighted intra- and inter-
   psychic functioning but was non-specific in the area of
   environmental functioning. See Lillian Ripple, Motivation, Capacity and Opportunity. (Chicago, The School of
   Social Service Administration, University of Chicago,
   1964).

4. The schedule we developed for obtaining answers to these
   questions can be obtained from the Graduate School of
   Social Work, Rutgers University, New Brunswick, N. J.

5. The failure of NIP to make more extensive use of the
   Treatment Log might be ascribed to administrative
   reasons rather than to any shortcomings of the tool itself. The Chemung County Multi-Problem Family Project used a slightly modified version of this Log in work
   with 150 families. (Unpublished interim report. Summary of Treatment Logs, January 1965) The Rutgers
   Family Life Improvement Project is now utilizing a re-
   vised form of the Log in the treatment of 230 young
   families.

6. Actually, C represents the work of two workers, since social worker C resigned and was replaced by another
   worker during the last third of the treatment period.
   Because of the limitations of the total sample we shall
   not differentiate in this analysis between the two workers.

7. For the meaning of scores see Chapter 15.

8. This rank order is similar to but not identical with movement for the total thirty cases in the experimental control study.   See Chapter 15.

9. L. L. Geismar and Beverly Ayres. Patterns of Change in Problem Families. (St. Paul, Minn., Family-Centered Project, 1959), pp. 23-28.

10. Ibid., p. 24.

11. Ibid., p. 24.

12. Ibid., p. 24.

13. Ibid., p. 24.

14. Ibid., p. 25.

15. Ibid., p. 24.

16. L. L. Geismar and Michael A. La Sorte. Understanding the Multi-Problem Family. (New York, Association Press, 1964.), p. 88.

17. Ibid., pp. 26-27.

18. For the twelve families under consideration the Spearman rank order correlations were as follows: Frequency of subjects discussed and problems in beginning situation +.65; frequency of subjects discussed and movement +.58; family functioning (or malfunctioning, which can be equated with having problems) in the beginning situation and movement -.37.

19. NIP was initially patterned after the St. Paul Family-Centered Project and it used the Overton-Tinker Casework Notebook produced in the Family-Centered Project as a text for instructing workers.

Chapter 15
Did the Multi-Problem Family Change
As a Result of Treatment?

The Why and What of Evaluation

As a publicly sponsored undertaking, NIP must invariably
address itself to the effectiveness of the experimental services instituted with federal and community funds. Of course the question
of outcome cannot be overlooked either in services that are not publicly supported. The helping professions, such as medicine, psychiatry, social work, clinical psychology, nursing, etc., by their
very nature are accountable to themselves and to their clients for
the utility and the effectiveness of the services they render. Yet a
project such as ours, receiving wide publicity because of its experimental nature and eliciting support on the strength of its claim to
test new methods of dealing with socially handicapped people, faces
a special challenge in evaluating its efforts.

The most important prerequisite for reaching conclusions on
the effectiveness of a service or method of intervention is the availability of a criterion by which outcome can be evaluated. But first
let us review the history of NIP. An early community concern with
juvenile delinquency later shifted to the multi-problem family, seen
as a seedbed for the deviant behavior of juveniles. The first direct
service phase of NIP comprised casework to forty-five Farnam
Courts families identified as being multi-problem. This considerable investment in casework services provided the greatest challenge
for systematic evaluation. [1] The program was multi-faceted, going
far beyond work with the most disorganized families. Services to
the whole neighborhood were seen as a necessary extension of effective treatment to the multi-problem families. Yet casework to these
families represented the most concentrated and clearly focused effort of the Neighborhood Improvement Project, and the undertaking

whose efficacy might be most subject to question. The utility of
reaching-out casework continues to be one of the untested assumptions of modern American social work; this form of intervention
calls for a substantial retooling of the social service apparatus of
most communities. In the New Haven experience, the establishment
of intensive casework services on an experimental basis to roughly
15 percent of the Farnam Court households put the burden of proof
about the value of this service on the project staff and on the participating social agencies.

In stating that the multi-problem family in Farnam Courts
had become a major focus of concern and the object of planned action, we have not yet specified the precise criterion by which the
effectiveness of such intervention can be measured. Assuming that
multi-problem behavior is a source of family and neighborhood disorganization, what kind of modification in these families can be
reasonably expected? Our social work service, which included
treatment of the most disorganized families as well as group work
and community organization work in the neighborhood, had as one
important goal the modification of the social functioning of the multi-
problem families.

Social functioning of the family or family functioning, a concept discussed in great detail elsewhere,[2] denotes all behavior of
family members, individually and collectively, that pertains to the
welfare of the family group. Family functioning is made up of the
diverse, socially expected roles of family members, which may contribute to the well-being of the family or threaten its existence.
The planners of NIP, in setting up treatment for multi-problem families, hoped to improve the social functioning of these families. As
a realistic goal the directors, supervisors, and workers looked for
changes in family behavior in such areas as family relations, child-
rearing, social activities, economic and health practices, etc. The
St. Paul Scale of Family Functioning, used by NIP to measure the
results of its intervention, contains a total of nine areas and twenty-
six sub-areas, which will be shown below. Change was measured
by means of a seven-point Level of Functioning Scheme,[3] ranging
from Inadequate (1) to Adequate (7) on the basis of the following

criteria: Is family functioning in line with the community's laws
and mores? Is family functioning conducive to the family's well-
being? Is it conducive to the welfare of the community? Is the social functioning of the family in line with the expectations of the social group to which the family belongs? Is the behavior of individual family members personally satisfying and in keeping with their
physical and intellectual potential?

The question of reliability and validity has been taken up in
considerable detail in the manual Measuring Family Functioning and
some subsequent publications[4] and will not be discussed here. NIP
built upon the methodological findings of earlier research, but undertook an independent assessment of the reliability of the measuring
instrument.

The reliability test reported here covers the first set of interviews with thirty experimental cases. Three independent judges
rated the level of family functioning before the beginning of treatment. Agreement was defined as occurring when, on any of the
nine main categories of the scale, all three judges marked the same
position or two marked the same position and one checked an adjacent one. Disagreement occurred when the raters checked positions
more than one scale step apart. The results of this reliability test
were as follows:

Three judges agreed	28.9%	of main categories
Two judges agreed, one checked adjacent position	58.5%	of main categories
Two judges agreed, one checked position two scale steps away	2.2%	of main categories
Each judge checked a differ-ent position	10.4%	of main categories
	100.0%	

The scale values used in the analysis were the positions on
which there was inter-rater consensus and those on which two raters
had expressed agreement while the third had checked an adjacent
position. In the 12.6 percent of cases where independent ratings
failed to produce reasonable agreement, the conference method of
evaluating level of social functioning was used. All subsequent
evaluations of the treatment group and the assessment of the control

group were handled in the same way. Movement evaluation, which
built upon an agreed-on beginning position, resulted in a higher level of reliability, as is shown below in the first movement evaluation
of the thirty treatment cases.

Three judges agreed	54. 4% of main categories
Two judges agreed, one checked adjacent position	43. 0% of main categories
Two judges agreed, one checked position two scale steps away	1. 5% of main categories
Each judge checked a different position	1. 1% of main categories
	100. 0%

It might well be asked why our method of evaluation did not
confine itself to the more conspicuous forms of behavior, such as
delinquency, neglect, adult crime, etc. The answer has to do with
the nature of malfunctioning of the multi-problem family. Although
deviant behavior is more prevalent among the multi-problem than
among the more "normal families," most multi-problem families,
as is shown elsewhere in this book, are not recorded officially as
law violators. Thus the relatively low frequency of adjudicated deviant behavior limits its usefulness as an index of change. Moreover,
law-violating behavior known to the authorities probably constitutes
only a small part of all deviant behavior. Students of juvenile delinquency are well aware that many factors other than the misdeed
itself determine whether the police and the courts become involved.

A further argument against undue reliance upon official statistics for assessing problem behavior is that deviant behavior known
to the community is merely a symptom of the more basic problems
faced by the family. There is no comprehensive diagnostic framework that can fully reveal the many-faceted character of multi-problem behavior. Our approach was a step in the direction of characterizing family behavior and measuring changes in an objective manner.

The question of how to evaluate a program of intervention can
also be viewed within the context of the tough-minded versus the
tender-minded approach to evaluation. [5] In the words of Kogan and
Shyne: "The advocates of 'environmental mastery' criteria have

been characterized as the tough-minded evaluators... (while) one
would describe as 'tender-minded' those evaluators whose considerations include subjective states and intra-psychic factors."[6] Our own
method of evaluation could be said to lean toward the tender-minded
approach.

The Study Design

It was clear from the outset that our plan to study change in
the families as a result of treatment would have to be able to show
that change was due to NIP intervention. It is extremely difficult
to demonstrate a causal connection between observed changes and
the means employed to create them. The traditional way of demon-
strating this relationship is by utilizing the experimental control design. In the applied behavioral sciences, especially clinical psychology, psychiatry and social work, the use of experimental techniques is usually avoided; its absence is justified on the grounds of
excessive cost, difficulty in matching cases, or problems of finding
control groups that are not subject to the contagious influence of
treatment applied elsewhere.

These are cogent arguments, but they do not provide an answer to the question of whether there are reasonable grounds for at-
tributing change to the means used for bringing it about. Use of an
untreated control group remains the most satisfactory device for
eliminating factors other than the planned intervention as causes of
change. The untreated control group, which is part of the experimental-control design, is composed of subjects matched with those
in the treatment or experimental group. If the latter shows changes
during the action phase that are not apparent in the control group,
then we have grounds for claiming that intervention was responsible
for the changes.

Our own study posed a number of problems in the building of
a design that would follow the logic of the above model. While the
nature of the experimental group was dictated by the decision to extend reaching-out services and neighborhood-wide group work services to forty-five families in Farnam Courts, the action program,
established prior to this research, made no provision for a matched

control group. It became the responsibility of the research staff to
find a control group that would be as similar to the experimental group
as possible in the characteristics that were likely to influence the
course of intervention, such as social class, housing, living conditions, levels of family functioning, etc.

Farnam Courts was automatically excluded as a source of a
control group because the entire housing project had become an area
of social work intervention. Consideration was therefore given four
other similar low-cost housing projects in New Haven--Quinnipiac,
Rockview, Elm Haven, and Elm Haven Extension. Although these
housing developments differed in age [7] and had diverse ethnic com-
positions (the proportion of Negroes was over 80 percent in the two
Elm Havens and ranged from 10 to 40 percent in the other projects),
they had a good deal in common. All were mass developments
composed of rental apartments for low-income families. The New
Haven Housing Authority assigned the tenants and managed the projects, which were multi-story dwellings built around or surrounded
by courtyards and playgrounds. While the physical structures were
in reasonably good condition, the neighborhoods appeared run-down
and neglected because of dumped waste, broken playground equipment, and poorly kept lawns. The families, with few exceptions,
belonged to the lower socio-economic class; the median family income placed them all in the low-income category, as shown in
Table 16 below.

A more critical consideration in the establishment of a control group was the comparability of the families with regard to the
variable to be measured. Since we were interested in studying
movement or change in family functioning, the experimental and control families had to be similar in functioning at the point at which
the experimental factor was introduced.

How similar must the two groups of families be? We cannot answer this with much authority. However, it seems reasonable
to assume that the results of treatment are directly related to the
need for treatment. Non-problem families do not need sustained social work service, and if they receive it anyway, they should not be
expected to show much movement since their initial functioning was

Table 16
Size and Income of Families in Housing Projects (1963)

Housing Project	No. of Housing Units	Mean Family Size	Median Income per Family
Farnam Courts	300	3.84	$ 2,643
Quinnipiac	200	3.12	2,811
Rockview	248	4.87	3,213
Elm Haven	487	3.24	2,576
Elm Haven Extension	368	4.71	3,231

satisfactory. It is clear, therefore, that research on movement requires the use of families that are problematic or, in our terminology, malfunctioning.

Our research employed a scale of values that permitted numerical comparisons on family malfunctioning. Experimenters would agree that it is desirable to have treatment and control groups as similar as possible, but whether they must be exactly alike to satisfy the conditions of the experiment is open to question. The St. Paul movement study did not show a decisive relationship between the degree of malfunctioning of families before treatment and the amount of movement registered after treatment.[8]

Although we were intent upon locating a control group of families who not only lived under similar social conditions as the treatment group but also revealed similar patterns of problematic functioning, the limited research evidence available suggested that some variation in the malfunctioning pattern would not violate the conditions of the experiment.

Having decided to select the control families from the four other low-cost housing developments in New Haven, we were faced with the task of selection. The technique of locating the most problematic families in Farnam Courts was described in Chapter 4. A similar, but hopefully less time-consuming approach, would have to be employed to select control group families.

To avoid having to read the records of all project residents

known to any community agency--an expensive and lengthy procedure
--we decided to work through the agency with the largest caseload
of socially handicapped families in the four housing projects, the
State Department of Welfare. This department administered the
categorical assistance program in New Haven as well as in the rest
of Connecticut. Their Aid to Families with Dependent Children program contained the families that in age and composition were most
like our treatment families; the AFDC families had dependent children, were economically deprived, and had multiple unmet needs
that had brought them to the attention of several social agencies.
As a group, they could not be termed multi-problem, but among
their ranks were some that fit into the malfunctioning category.[9]
It became the researcher's task to locate from among the AFDC
cases in the four housing projects those families whose social functioning was similar to that of the families in the experimental group.

Two reservations could be made regarding the use of AFDC
families as controls. One is that they were not a true control
group with reference to the experimental variable, treatment. AFDC
families receive a public assistance grant, which may or may not
be accompanied by services. If such services are given, they are
of a short-term nature because the public assistance agency has
neither the time nor the professional workers necessary for rendering more extensive services. Yet the dispensation of financial aid
and some service makes the AFDC families a comparison group
rather than a pure control group.[10] Comparison groups offer an alternative to genuine controls in behavioral science experiments
where it is impossible to completely refuse services to persons in
need. In our own experiment the use of AFDC families would appear justified on the grounds that we were comparing a special
method of intervention with conventional techniques available to multi-problem residents of low-income housing projects.

The second reservation about the control group pertains to
the high incidence of absent fathers. In our experimental group only 43 percent of the fathers were regularly in the home, and two-
thirds of the families were or had been clients in the AFDC program. A smaller proportion of fathers in the home among the con-

trols did not seem to be loading the dice in favor of the experimental group, since the evidence from the St. Paul project points to the same or greater amount of movement in fatherless families.[11]

Because of the difficulty involved in finding control families that would match the treatment cases, it was decided to resort to frequency distribution rather than precision matching. The latter method, one of the most precise in experimental design, requires that each experimental case be paired with a control case. This method calls for large samples since it frequently results in high attrition rates, the loss of one case meaning the loss of a pair. Our small sample made frequency distribution matching more advisable. Under that system, treatment and control groups are selected in such a way that they are comparable in measures that are applied to the group as a whole.

At this point our design was based upon a treatment group of forty-five families, with the control group yet to be selected. In constituting treatment and control groups it was necessary to allow for some shrinkage because intervention was planned for about a two-year period, the time span seen as necessary, judging by the St. Paul and other experiences, for bringing about a modification in the social functioning of the treated families.

To set up the control group, our research staff read all records of AFDC families living in the four low-income housing projects other than Farnam Courts.[12] The seventy most problematic cases, i.e. families experiencing difficulties in interpersonal relationships and in the management of health, economic, and/or household tasks, were chosen for the control group. These seventy families were then interviewed to establish a quantitative measure of their social functioning.

Data for evaluating change in social functioning on the treatment families were collected by the workers carrying the case. For the control families the corresponding information was procured by the AFDC worker serving each one. Because public welfare workers see their clients only once or twice a year, mainly for purposes of establishing eligibility, it was necessary for the AFDC workers to schedule extended home visits in the course of which information on the families' social functioning could be collected. Both treatment worker and AFDC worker entered the required information in the Schedule of Family Functioning. Interviewing of control cases, by request of the State Department of Welfare, was done initially only by the AFDC worker carrying the case. After the first wave of interviews, the agency, in order to expedite the pace, agreed to having workers interview cases other than their own and even to employing interviewers hired by our research project. Twenty-seven percent of the control interviews were done by persons not employed by the Department of Welfare.

Deadlines for completion of the research phase of the project and a gradual sample attrition made it necessary to set the time for measuring the effects of intervention at eighteen months. The main reasons for the loss of families are given in Table 17 below.

Table 17
Reasons for Sample Attrition

Reason for Loss of Families	Number of Families Lost
Treatment Group	
Diagnosis revealed that family was not truly multi-problem	8
Lack of treatment continuity because of worker turnover	3
Dissolution of family or radical change in family constellation	2
Family rejected services	2
	15
Control Group	
Insufficient data for rating family functioning because of staff turnover or other reasons	10
Assignment of families to intensive treatment	5
Dissolution of family or radical change in family constellation	3
Family moved out of town	1
	19

At the end of the eighteen-month period we were left with an experimental group of thirty families and a control group of fifty-one families. We had gathered information on family functioning at six-month intervals for the experimental group and nine-month intervals for the control group, thereby utilizing what is also referred to as the panel technique in experimental research design. [13] Evaluation of changes in functioning using recurrent data collection and measurement provides a more concise picture of movement than evaluation based simply on before and after measurement. Recurrent data collection minimizes the chances of omitting relevant information, which may not be registered when there is a big time gap between the measurements. Multiple measurement has the additional advantage of showing the movement trend, which permits a more accurate assessment of the relationship between intervention and change than before and after measurement. Moreover, knowledge about the rhythm and timing of movement is of great value to the development of social work method. The nine-month interval for securing information on the control families was decided on for two reasons: as an economy measure, and to reduce the so-called "Hawthorne," or treatment, effect likely to be produced by recurrent research interviews.

To recapitulate briefly, a control or comparison group for the Farnam Courts treatment families was set up by selecting families from four low-cost housing projects resembling Farnam Courts in size and layout. In order to identify the problem families with dependent children, case records of all families in the AFDC program administered by the State Department of Welfare were read and those cases judged to be most malfunctioning were selected. The end result of this process was a group of fifty-one families whose social functioning had been evaluated over an eighteen-month period, the minimal treatment period for the experimental group cases.

Comparisons of the experimental and control groups on selected demographic variables and on level of family functioning at the beginning of treatment intervention are shown in Tables 18 and 19 respectively.

The array of data in Table 18 reveals that we achieved only
limited success in matching a control group to the treatment families. There was little question regarding the comparability of the
two groups on residence and social status; income and family size
likewise revealed no dramatic differences. As we had expected,
the proportion of fatherless families was higher for the control than
for the experimental group, although the difference of nineteen percentage points was not striking. Fifty-seven percent of fathers out
of the home was within the expected range for multi-problem cases.[16]
The control group's proportion of families headed by men was about
the same as the national average for welfare cases.[17]

The ethnic composition of the two groups reveals the most
striking difference. While the proportion of Negroes in the treatment group comes close to the number for Farnam Courts as a
whole, the Negroes are greatly overrepresented in the control group
(see Table 18). This reflects the higher proportion of Negroes in
two of the housing projects, Elm Haven and Elm Haven Extension.[18]

Table 18

Treatment and Control Groups Compared on
Selected Characteristics

Comparison Factors	Treatment Group (N = 30)	Control Group (N = 51)
Residing in low cost housing project	100%	100%
Class V on Hollingshead's Index of Social Position[14]	97%[15]	100%
Whites	57%	18%
Negroes	37%	78%
Puerto Ricans	6%	4%
Families with fathers out of the home	57%	76%
Mean number of children	4.3	4.8
Mean per capita yearly income in dollars (1963)	649	615

A further difference between the two groups is shown in the
main dependent variable, family functioning. The reader will recall

that it was in relation to this factor that we had made the most far-reaching efforts to locate control families that would be similar to the treatment families. Measurement by means of the St. Paul Scale of Family Functioning showed a mean difference of slightly more than one scale step between experimental and control groups. In Family Relationship and Unity, Care and Training of Children, and Individual Behavior and Adjustment the treatment families functioned at a below marginal level, while the control group functioned between the marginal and above marginal positions in the beginning situation. The two Profiles showed a similar shape, with the control cases being more adequate in functioning than the treatment families.

Table 19

Treatment and Control Groups Compared on
Family Functioning

Areas of Family Functioning	Treatment Group (N = 30)	Control Group (N = 51)
Mean Score at beginning of treatment	3.85	4.97
A. Family Relationships and Unity	3.10	4.76
B. Individual Behavior and Adjustment	3.10	4.35
C. Care and Training of Children	3.33	4.78
D. Social Activities	4.43	5.06
E. Economic Practices	3.50	4.55
F. Home and Household Practices	5.03	5.71
G. Health Practices	3.80	5.22
H. Relationship to Social Worker	4.10	5.18
I. Use of Community Resources	4.27	5.14

Two possible explanations come to mind for our failure to match the controls more closely to the experimental group. One, the universe of AFDC cases contained only a small fraction of truly multi-problem families. This observation was partly borne out by a study in New Jersey,[19] in which the AFDC families, with some exceptions, were found to be a group that conforms rather well to societal laws and mores. If this holds for New Haven AFDC cases, it might be said that the universe of families was simply not large enough to select thirty or more truly multi-problem cases. We did, nevertheless, find four families whose mean family functioning was marginal or below, corresponding closely to the average functioning pattern of the treatment families.

A second possible explanation for the differential in functioning level lies in the nature of data collection. The control families were interviewed for the most part by AFDC workers, who maintained limited contact with the family, mostly in the form of annual or semi-annual eligibility reviews. Data on family functioning required for measurement were collected in a specially scheduled home interview. Such diagnostic information, based on one extended interview plus some additional interviews spaced several months apart, probably lacked the depth of information secured in the course of treatment. Also, the families may have withheld unfavorable information from the worker that held the purse strings, lest their answers affect their eligibility. On the other hand, the public assistance worker would in all likelihood be informed about deviant behavior coming to the attention of the authorities, such as crime and delinquency, neglect, school truancy, treatment for mental illness. Thus severe pathology in family life would undoubtedly be included in the data.

The interview material secured from the control families was comparable to that obtained from the experimental group in breadth of information and in descriptive detail on family life. The second and third interviews with the control families revealed up-and-down fluctuations in functioning, evidence of the potential in the evaluative approach for registering changes in family functioning. Hence, whatever the shortcomings of data collection in the control sample, they did not result in a blunting of the technique of measurement. On the strength of this evidence, which is shown in the movement data on the control group, we would argue that the possible omission of data would equally effect the three interviews, spaced nine months apart, thus would not tend to bias the findings on movement.

As a final consideration in judging the adequacy of the control group, let us examine to what extent differences in character-

istics between treatment and control groups might have introduced
a bias. The question may be posed as follows: Do those properties that are more characteristic of the control group than of the
experimental group tend to limit the control group's chances of registering movement? This can be answered by comparing the movement scores of control families showing traits characteristic of the
treatment group with the scores of the control families whose traits
typify the control group.

A few ground rules are necessary before deciding whether
fluctuations in family functioning within the subgroup might be considered change that was significantly related to the properties of the
subgroup. In the absence of precise parametric tests of measurement that would permit an inference of significance from the degree
of change in functioning, we have to resort to more arbitrary criteria in determining the meaning of change in subgroups.

Two experimental projects employing identical means of
measurement, the Family-Centered Project of St. Paul (using no
control group) and the Neighborhood Improvement Project, found the
mean degree of movement per family to be 3. 4[20] and 6. 9 scale
steps respectively. The changes were statistically significant in
both groups. It seems reasonable to assume that changes of less
than one scale step per family on the average are not significant.
Empirically such small net changes represent a narrow balancing of
plus and minus movement rather than clear-cut overall change in
any direction.

Let us now examine those characteristics for which treatment
and control groups show substantial differences, to find whether
those differences introduced a bias into the experimental control design. The control group contained more Negroes, more families
with fathers out of the home, and a higher level of family functioning in the beginning situation than did the experimental group. We
had to determine whether families in the control group having these
characteristics showed movement scores different from families not
having these characteristics. The results are shown in Table 20.

The evidence in Table 20 strongly suggests that the presence
of traits differentiating between experimental and control group had

Table 20

Mean Movement Scores of Control Families

Types of Families	Mean Movement Score Per Family
Negro families	+.50
White families	-.01
Families with father out of the home	+.31
Families with father in the home	+.21
27 Families with the highest functioning score (5.1 or more) in the beginning situation	-.04
24 Families with the lowest functioning score (5.0 or less) in the beginning situation	+.54

little effect upon the movement pattern of control families. None of the subgroup sets manifested differences of more than 0.6 of a scale step of movement per family. If being Negro were a biasing factor, it would tend to militate against the treatment group. Having a father in the home appeared to have little effect upon change in functioning in the untreated cases. Higher functioning in the beginning situation--in contrast to the evidence from the treatment group in the St. Paul study[21]--seemed to have a slightly adverse effect upon movement but the difference here is only slightly more than half a scale step.[22]

Our efforts to constitute a control group that would match the existing experimental group of families were only partially successful, when we use the similarity of groups on seemingly relevant variables as the criterion of success. However, an analysis aimed at showing the influence of those matching variables on which experimental and control groups differed revealed that these variables had a negligible effect upon movement.

Results of Experimental Control Study

Let us now look at the differences in family functioning before and after treatment in the experimental and control groups. It will be recalled that during the eighteen-month period of research the treatment families were interviewed four times, whereas the

control group was subjected to three interviews. This procedure
yielded sets of three and four family functioning scores respectively, which revealed the trend in family functioning over the total
period rather than just the net change.

Before considering the dynamics of change in family functioning, let us compare the overall change in the groups to establish
what changes, if any, occurred during the experimental period.
This comparison is shown in Table 21.

Table 21

Movement in Experimental and Control Groups
During Treatment Period

	Mean Total Family Function- ing Score		Net Change
	Before Situation	After Situation	
Experimental Group	34.67	41.60	+6.93
Control Group	44.75	45.00	+.25
	Mean Family Functioning Score Per Category		
Experimental Group	3.85	4.62	+.77
Control Group	4.97	5.00	+.03

Table 21 shows that the average family in the experimental
group gained almost seven scale steps in family functioning, while
the control families gained less than one scale step on the average.
When these total movement scores were translated into category
mean scores, the amount of change for the treatment families was
just over three-quarters of a scale step, while the families in the
control group revealed movement of only 3/100 of a scale step.

The chi square test, which relates membership in experimental or control group to the number of scale steps families
moved, yielded a coeffficient of X^2 = 26.16 (3 d.f.)--significant beyond the .1 percent level. A comparable non-parametric test, the
median test, resulted in a coefficient of X^2 = 25.96 (3 d.f.), whose
statistical significance also exceeds .001. These data lead us to
conclude that it is highly improbable that the differences in movement between treatment and control group occurred by chance.[23]

The nature of the experimental design for this study enables us to draw also the hopeful conclusion that changes were the result of social work intervention. We make this assertion with a degree of caution, since the statistical findings provided no conclusive evidence. The chi square of the difference in movement scores and the resultant confidence level merely indicated that differences such as were found between experimental and control group did not occur by chance. If not by chance, what else but intervention can explain their occurrence?

Treatment, in the form of casework services and a variety of group work and recreational services for children and adults, was extended only to the multi-problem families in Farnam Courts, not to any of the control families in the other housing projects. We had postulated that the impact of the services would be reflected in higher social functioning scores of the experimental families. Social work research does not at this stage supply knowledge on the cumulative effect of intervention upon family functioning. Our hypothesis on movement was non-specific, postulating only positive change in the experimental group during the treatment period. This might mean substantial improvement in functioning during the first evaluation period (six months) with a leveling-off during the two subsequent periods; or it might mean cumulative improvement at a non-specific rate throughout the three periods. Significant positive movement precludes both change that is no greater than that found in the control group and fluctuating rates of functioning, which would signify improvement of an unstable kind at best or random changes of an extreme nature at worst.

A comparison of levels of family functioning at the beginning situation and at subsequent points of evaluation for the experimental and control groups is shown in Table 22.

The treatment group manifested positive mean change per family amounting to nearly three scale steps during the first six months of treatment; it continued at the rate of approximately two steps during the next two periods of evaluation. The control group revealed an improvement in family functioning of one scale step per family for the first nine months, then registered negative movement of three-quarters of a scale step.

Table 22

Movement in Experimental and Control Groups at
Each Point of Evaluation

	Beginning Situation	Move-ment I (6 mos.)	Move-ment II (12 mos.)	Move-ment III (18 mos.)
Experimental Group				
Mean Total Family Functioning Score	34.67	37.60	39.47	41.60
Net Change	---	+2.93	+1.87	+2.13

	Beginning Situation	Move-ment I (9 mos.)	Move-ment II (18 mos.)
Control Group			
Mean Total Family Functioning Score	44.75	45.76	45.00
Net Change	---	+1.01	-.76

The two groups showed opposite change patterns. Movement for the control group took the form of an up-and-down fluctuation, while the treatment families showed cumulative gains throughout the eighteen-month period of research and action. This observation lends strength to the argument that movement in families in the experimental sample was due to treatment intervention and was not the result of random fluctuations.

The Components of Movement

Since these significant differences in movement between the two groups during the treatment period tend to support the assumption of a causal nexus between social work intervention and movement in the treatment group, a closer look at the nature of such movement is warranted. Four aspects will be considered: (1) Granted an average of almost seven scale steps of movement per family, how representative was this figure for the total treatment group? (2) Did movement occur in all areas or some areas, in some more than others? (3) How did the timing of overall movement correlate with the timing of change in the nine categories of family functioning? (4) What were the principal correlates of movement?

With reference to the first aspect, we observe that among the thirty families in the experimental group, three (10 percent) showed negative movement or deterioration in family functioning. For two families this amounted to a net minus movement of one scale step, while a third family registered a net loss of five scale steps. This latter family, which we shall call the Y family, showed increasing malfunctioning in Individual Behavior and Adjustment (two scale steps) and in Family Relationship and Unity, Child Care and Training, and Social Activities (one step each). The Y family heads, prior to the onset of treatment, had engaged in unlawful behavior, which was discovered while the family was being served by NIP. The resulting court action proved disorganizing to the family and made them immune to social work intervention.

Only one family (3 percent) showed no overall change in social functioning. This family improved in Home and Household Practices by two scale steps, but the gain was balanced by losses of one scale step each in Individual Behavior and Adjustment, and Social Activities.

The remaining twenty-six families (87 percent) in the treatment group showed various degrees of improvement in social functioning. Table 23 shows in detail the changes in social functioning of all thirty families in the experimental group.

The median and modal movement patterns were eight scale steps. Two-thirds, or twenty-one of the families around the median, showed positive change of between two and eleven scale steps. The A family showed an atypical movement pattern amounting to a spectacular gain of twenty-two scale steps, spread nearly equally over all areas of family functioning. Movement in this family could best be characterized as acculturation to living in an American urban community, with the "acculturater" a Spanish-speaking NIP worker. In helping the A family make connections with diverse community agencies, she also went a long way toward solving many problems rooted in their ignorance about the local way of life. Equally important, of course, was the intervention of the NIP worker with school, health, and welfare agencies on behalf of this family.

Table 23

Changes in Social Functioning of the
Experimental Group Families

Type of Change	Number of Families
Negative change of 5 scale steps	1
Negative change of 1 scale step	2
No change	1
Positive change of 2 scale steps	2
Positive change of 3 scale steps	3
Positive change of 4 scale steps	2
Positive change of 5 scale steps	2
Positive change of 7 scale steps	1
Positive change of 8 scale steps	4
Positive change of 9 scale steps	2
Positive change of 10 scale steps	2
Positive change of 11 scale steps	3
Positive change of 12 scale steps	2
Positive change of 14 scale steps	2
Positive change of 22 scale steps	1
	30

The answer to question number 2, did movement take place in all areas, is a qualified "yes." The mean movement score of 6.93 per family was the sum of at least some positive change in every area of family functioning. But the degree of change was unequal, with the greatest movement category showing four times more change than the smallest movement category. The movement profile is shown in Table 24.

We had hypothesized that there would be significantly more movement in the treatment group. However, the research staff did not specify in what areas movement would occur. It was hoped that the social work services in general and the casework services in particular would produce results in those areas where the project invested most of its efforts and skills. On the basis of this formulation, we might have predicted that the areas of family relationships and the use of community resources would reflect the most movement.

The results, as shown in Table 24, were not too far from

Table 24

Movement by Area of Family Functioning

Area of Family Functioning	Proportion of Scale Step
Health Conditions and Practices	1.10
Relationship to Social Worker	.97
Use of Community Resources	.96
Family Relationships and Unity	.93
Individual Behavior and Adjustment	.83
Economic Practices	.70
Care and Training of Children	.67
Social Activities	.50
Home and Household Practices	.27

this retrospective prediction.   A better use of community resources was reflected in the three leading movement categories.   The striking improvement in Health Practices showed what energetic intervention could do to combat the inadequacies of a system in which the medically indigent must weigh the disadvantages of no treatment against the indignities of long queues and frequent displays of rude and primitive attitudes.   The project acted as a mediator between our clients and the medical system, bringing about a more frequent use of hospital and outpatient clinic services as well as a greater readiness to use health resources.   There was also a reduction in health problems among the treatment families, as shown in Table 25.

Table 25 shows an improved relationship to the social worker; this of course is the sine qua non of good social work, while from the client's point of view better worker-client relations denote one instance of better use of community resources.   Project families, particularly the children, also used recreational facilities to an increasing extent during the treatment period, whereas relatively less change was evident in the families' relationship to the schools (see Table 25).

A movement of between four-fifths of a scale step and a full scale step on the average was registered in Family Relationships and Unity, and in Individual Behavior and Adjustment.   Both of these areas of social functioning, because of their problematic status

in disorganized families, were major focuses of the worker's intervention. Improvement in the sub-categories of parent-child relationships, marital relationships, and family solidarity was quite pronounced, while few gains were registered in sibling relationships
(Table 25). The effort to bring about a modification of family roles
was most successful with the mothers and had some effect upon the
fathers in the family picture, but brought only limited results with

Table 25

Movement by Sub-Categories of Family Functioning

Area[24] and Sub-Category of Family Functioning	Proportion of Scale Step
Health Conditions and Practices	
Health Problems	.70
Health Practices	1.13
Relationship to Social Worker	
Attitude toward Worker	1.03
Use of Worker	1.00
Use of Community Resources[25]	
School	.33
Health Resources	1.10
Social Agencies	.60
Recreational Agencies	.66
Family Relationships and Unity	
Marital Relationship	.65
Relationship between Parents and Children	.73
Relationship among Children	.20
Family Solidarity	.63
Individual Behavior and Adjustment	
Father	.48
Mother	.93
Children 10 years and over	.27
Children under 10 years	.14
Economic Practices	
Source and Amount of Family Income	.47
Job Situation	.17
Use of Money	.50
Care and Training of Children	
Physical Care	.43
Training Methods and Emotional Care	.53
Social Activities	
Informal Associations	.40
Formal Associations	.17
Home and Household Practices	
Physical Facilities	.27
Housekeeping Standards	.28

the children.   The very small gain in social functioning of the
younger children (under ten years of age) can be explained by their
greater adequacy in the beginning situation.

The Neighborhood Improvement Project appeared to have had
some impact also upon the economic functioning of the families.
The movement was primarily due to improved money management
and an increase in the amount of income available to the family,
often the result of intervention with public assistance agencies.   The
insignificant gains in job situation reflected the widespread absence
of gainful employment in our families as well as the project's inability to influence the employment situation in the community.

Child Care and Training, including both physical and emotional care, improved to a comparable degree (see Table 25) during the time of the project; the overall change was two-thirds of a
scale step.   Social activities showed movement of one-half step, a
gain accounted for largely by enhanced informal social participation.

The area of smallest gain in family functioning (slightly
more than one-quarter of a scale step) was Home and Household Practices, for obvious reasons.   The multi-problem families in Farnam
Courts and the other low-income housing projects were not living in
substandard housing, at least not by physical housing standards.
Home and Household Practices was the area of relatively most adequate functioning before the start of treatment and therefore was
least in need of professional intervention.   Beyond that, the existing housing provisions left only limited room for change, since the
project's social work program was aimed at services within the
housing project and precluded moving clients to other housing.

Question 3 under the heading "The Components of Movement"
dealt with the relationship between the timing of overall movement
and the timing of change in the nine areas of family functioning.
We observed earlier that all three six-month movement periods
were marked by positive changes in family functioning.   However,
the cumulative change for the eighteen months was not distributed
equally over all three periods.   The first six months showed an
average gain of 2. 93 scale steps per family, while the second and
third periods were marked by changes of 1. 87 and 2. 13 scale steps,

respectively.   Were these changes distributed in similar proportions
among the nine areas of family functioning?   Table 26 provides the
answer.

Inspecting the rankings of the percentages of movement in
each period, we find that the first treatment period, with the largest
amount of total positive change, showed the greatest proportion of
change in four areas.   In four more areas the first treatment period either yielded a split first rank with the third period or ranked
second.   Only Home and Household Practices, the area of least
overall movement, ranked third, which in this case meant no change
in family functioning.   The third period, showing the second largest
amount of total movement, was characterized by percentage changes
that yielded a first or second rank in six areas.   The second period,
with the smallest amount of total movement, ranked third in six
areas and higher in three areas.   Social Activities was the area of
greatest movement during this treatment period.

Table 26 shows that the relative amount of overall movement
in each period was clearly correlated with the percentage of movement in each area.   This relative uniformity in the pattern of change
suggested the presence of factors that might account for the differential in movement in the three treatment periods.   However the
complexity of the nature of intervention made it difficult to pinpoint
the specific factors responsible for the variations in the pattern of
change.   Our experience in supervising the social workers suggested
an explanation based more on the worker's reaction to the client than
on the client's behavior.   It does not seem far-fetched to assume
that the workers' perception of and feeling about their clients were
major determinants in the social functioning of the latter.

The workers, after an initial strong reaction to the negative,
problem-laden data of the screening-in summaries, found entry less
difficult than anticipated.   As a result they tended to consider the
families less resistant and less pathological than they had at first
believed them to be.   While they saw the clients as apathetic, or
pessimistic about their ability to "do for" themselves, the workers
also began to appreciate the difficulties that beset such families in
their ineffectual attempts to cope with the delivery system of serv-

Table 26

Movement in Treatment Families by Mean Score and Percentage of Change
Occurring in Treatment Period

Movement Categories	Score Change by Scale Step	Change During Treatment Periods						
		1st Period		2nd Period		3rd Period		Total
		%	(Rank)	%	(Rank)	%	(Rank)	%
Overall Movement in Nine Areas (Scale Step)	6.93	2.93		1.87		2.13		
Percentage of Overall Movement		42.3†		26.9†		30.8†		100.0
Category of Overall Family Functioning								
Family Relationships and Unity	.93	42.9	(1)	25.0	(3)	32.1	(2)	100.0
Individual Behavior and Adjustment	.83	36.0	(1.5)	28.0	(3)	36.0	(1.5)	100.0
Care and Training of Children	.67	30.0	(2)	25.0	(3)	45.0	(1)	100.0
Social Activities	.50	26.7	(2)	60.0	(1)	13.3	(3)	100.0
Economic Practices	.70	42.9	(1.5)	14.2	(3)	42.9	(1.5)	100.0
Home and Household Practices	.27	0	(3)	50.0	(1.5)	50.0	(1.5)	100.0
Health Practices	1.10	60.6	(1)	18.2	(3)	21.2	(2)	100.0
Relationship to Social Worker	.97	48.3	(1)	31.0	(2)	20.7	(3)	100.0
Use of Community Resources	.96	48.3	(1)	20.7	(3)	31.0	(2)	100.0

† These percentages are based on the movement in each period as a proportion of the movement for the total treatment period. These percentages differ slightly from the mean of column percentages (not shown) because the various categories did not contribute equally to overall movement.

ices. The workers began to take considerable initiative in easing
the way and effecting some alleviation of stress, with a noticeably
positive response on the part of the clients. This assessment of
the treatment experience is reflected in the fact that the greatest
movement occurred in the first six-month measurement period, particularly in those areas of family functioning where the worker initiated action in response to an urgent need. Building a relationship
with the client was a first order of business for the worker, so
movement in the area of Relationship to Social Worker was particularly pronounced during the first half-year of treatment.

As the families began to trust the social worker they assumed a less guarded attitude and revealed heretofore hidden or repressed behavior that was a barrier to continued movement. They
also were somewhat more likely to act out their problems, particularly in the areas of individual behavior and relationship. It was
during this second six-month treatment period that the initial ad-
vances in family functioning slowed down.

The third measurement period reflected both the workers'
increased skill and the family's capacity to use counselling in a way
that moved them beyond the point of using workers as "doers" and
enablers. During this period the clients developed some capacity
for self-examination and autonomous action.

The fourth question we raised earlier pertained to the correlates of movement. We have shown (Table 23) how the mean movement per family of almost seven scale points was distributed over
the thirty families in the treatment group. We also have presented
data on the nature and timing of change in family functioning, and
have pointed to some factors in the client-worker relationship that
might help explain the particular rhythm of the movement registered.
What other factors, both in client and in worker, can help explain
the differential in movement among the thirty treatment families?

In an earlier study using the St. Paul Scale of Family Functioning, we had postulated a negative relationship between social
functioning and movement. In other words, we had thought that
families with more serious problems at the onset of treatment would
tend to show greater change in family functioning as a result of

worker intervention. The results of this study of 150 families provided slight support for our hypothesis.[26] We found a -.31 relationship (Gamma) between the mean social functioning of families
when they became part of the experimental project and the total
movement during the eighteen-month treatment period. Looking at
the change pattern in terms of movement by area for the total experimental group, we may ask whether more movement was registered in those areas where social functioning was relatively inadequate in the beginning than in areas where functioning was more
adequate. The Spearman rank order correlation between mean family functioning per area and mean movement was -.27,[27] which
corresponds rather closely to the results obtained from correlating
beginning family functioning and movement for each family. Neither
coefficient was statistically significant. In short, there was some
tendency for families with more problematic functioning to register
more movement during treatment than families characterized by
more adequate functioning. This was not surprising, as one would
expect to find the most determined effort by workers to improve
families' functioning in those areas where functioning is least adequate.

A number of other family characteristics revealed an association with movement. We shall cite only those factors whose
Gamma coefficient of association was in excess of plus or minus
.50. The number of cases used in each test of association will be
listed in brackets, preceded by the Gamma coefficient. The number of cases is less than thirty in those instances where information was missing or where not all cases in the experimental group
were relevant to the cross-tabulation.

The age difference between husband and wife at time of marriage revealed a high negative relationship with movement (-.60,
N=28). This paralleled the findings reported in an earlier study,[28]
which showed a direct relationship between age discrepancy and
family malfunctioning in a group of seventy-five low-income families. Age discrepancy, which results when a woman marries a
man older than herself, exceeded nine years in 25 percent of our
sample.

It should be noted that age discrepancy at marriage does not coincide with age differences between husband and wife at the time the study was done.   In nine families for whom there were data on age discrepancy, the husbands had left the home and had lost contact with the family; six more absent husbands continued to be in contact with wife and children.   The three types of status were equally related to age discrepancy, i. e. the continuity of marriage was unrelated to differences in age between the partners at marriage.   Considering only situations where the husband was in the home or in contact with the family, a negative relationship between age discrepancy and movement of -. 45 (N=19) was found.

These cross-tabulations suggested that age discrepancy at marriage was a factor that influenced movement in treatment regardless of whether the husband happened to be around at the time the family was being treated.   The age discrepancy factor loomed even larger when the husband had been out of the home (Gamma -. 80 (N=9).   So variables other than the interactional aspect of age discrepancy between husband and wife had to be sought to explain the negative correlation between age discrepancy and movement.

These variables were largely in the realm of conjecture--our research provided no study in depth of personality factors that might conceivably supply a link between the marriage of a woman to an older man and the inability at a later period to respond positively to a treatment program.   We considered whether age discrepancy at marriage tended to be diagnostic of situations where a socially inadequate woman married an older man who may have failed in earlier attempts at finding a mate or remaining married.   The low negative correlations we found between age discrepancy and movement of mother (-. 21) and between age discrepancy and change in relationship (involving chiefly mother's role) to the social worker (-. 23) supplied some evidence that age discrepancy might have reflected the woman's ability or inability to respond to the treatment process.

Among the personal characteristics that we examined, the amount of education of the husband, but not of the wife, was positively related to movement (+. 75, N=17; this number refers to the men in the home or in contact with the home for whom we had educational data).[29] It would be easy to exaggerate the significance of a relationship based upon only seventeen cases. In the absence of more exhaustive information on the personality of the fathers, we speculated that perhaps more extensive education (in this case beyond the eighth grade) enabled them (in response to intervention) to contribute positively to improved family functioning. Prior to the onset of treatment, a low negative association (-.37) was found between formal education of the husband and the family's social functioning. This inverse correlation may have served as a predisposing factor in bringing about movement during treatment. Education of the wife, which had been found unrelated to movement, also showed no relationship to the beginning situation.

Some factors that we had expected to be related to treatment outcome yielded no discernable positive or negative relationship. These were mental retardation of parents (present in one or both parents in eleven families), drinking problem of parents (present in thirteen families), presence or absence of father in the home, number of children in the home, and forced marriage of parents (involving sixteen cases). The race of the parents did not influence the amount of movement in treatment, nor was race related to the family's beginning level of social functioning.

The data analysis did, however, isolate two additional variables that showed a clear-cut relationship to movement. One was the father's employment situation. Families with employed fathers responded more positively to the worker's intervention (+.54, N= 17; fathers out of contact with the home are omitted), probably because the father's relatively stable job situation made it possible to concentrate on other areas of family functioning. The other variable, number of children over age 10 in the home, was found to be negatively related to movement (-.55, N=30). That is, movement tended to be greater in families with fewer or no children older than ten. Correlations in the same direction, but of a low magnitude, were found between movement and number of all children in the home (-.25) and between movement and number of children known to the Juvenile Court (-.28).

The converging evidence indicated that children, particularly those over 10, tended to retard movement, presumably because of a proclivity toward acting-out behavior. This behavior appeared to have an adverse effect on the family equilibrium and the functioning of the parents during treatment. The number of children older than 10 in any one family had no effect upon the change in social functioning of these children. As a group they showed more movement during treatment than the younger children, but less than the mother and father. The number of children manifesting acting-out behavior decreased from eighteen to ten over the total treatment period. There was a reduction also in the incidence of other forms of child behavior symptomatic of maladjustment--cases of excessive withdrawing went from five to one; cases of enuresis, nightmares, functional maladies, etc. went from fifteen to two. The significant factor to us in the correlation between children over ten and movement was not the children's behavior per se but the increased concern on the part of the parents about the functioning of the children. This concern, by the scale of values governing the NIP research, was viewed as an essential component of both family functioning and change in such functioning.

Our final consideration in the analysis of factors related to movement was whether the family's initial attitude toward treatment was in any way related to treatment outcome. Traditional casework and psychotherapy postulate a direct relationship between the client's motivation and his chances of benefiting from treatment. This association of outcome with the desire for treatment is scarcely surprising in situations where the tenure and effect of treatment are seen as being largely a function of client motivation.

But work with lower-class disorganized families, as pointed out by Overton, Tinker[30] and many other writers, cannot rely on the families' readiness to be helped. The only valid criterion for intervention into the lives of these families is their need for help. This need may be unrelated to their desire for help, at least at the onset of treatment.

In the Neighborhood Improvement Project there was little basis for postulating a close connection between early client motivation and treatment results. Families in urgent need were served regardless of whether they favored being helped. The greater the need, the more concerted the effort to render assistance. In return, the more problematic families, as noted earlier, tended to register somewhat more movement than the less problematic ones.

Our scheme of assessing functioning provided no direct measure of client motivation at the beginning of treatment. However, the category "Relationship to NIP Worker," which covered attitude toward and use of worker, supplied an approximate index of the families' attitude toward professional intervention. The assumption can be safely made that a favorable relationship to the caseworker was highly correlated with motivation to accept help.

The correlation (Gamma) between relationship to NIP worker at the outset of treatment and movement in the course of treatment was -.44. With a sample of thirty, this negative relationship was not of a high magnitude and probably was due to chance.[31] More important than the magnitude of the negative relationship between motivation and treatment outcome was the absence of a positive relationship. This implied that problem families' early receptivity to treatment did not serve as a predictor of treatment outcome. The client's attitude toward being helped may be an important factor in planning the strategy of intervention; but while the mandate for intervention is morally independent of the client's expressed wish to be helped, this study leaves us without a basis for making the rendering of services contingent upon probable results.

Summary

This study, designed to assess the effect of a treatment program upon a group of thirty multi-problem families, yielded evidence that the services rendered by the Neighborhood Improvement Project significantly affected the social functioning of the families. The tentative nature of these findings must be stressed in view of the small number of families (thirty treatment and fifty-one control group families) and the problems of matching experimental control cases. The results nonetheless affirmed our belief that multi-service intervention could effect measurable changes in social functioning.

An analysis of movement patterns showed that changes in
family functioning were cumulative over the eighteen-month treatment period, with the greatest gains being registered during the
first six months. Neither the families' social functioning nor the
clients' relationship to the worker at the beginning of treatment was
significantly related to movement. Thus, this study produced no
evidence to support the widely held notion that the client's behavior
and attitude toward treatment at the onset of services are related
to treatment outcome. This finding weakens the argument of those
who would establish a priority of services, particularly to multi-
problem families, on the basis of client motivation rather than on
client need.

A number of other characteristics, related to the behavior of
the parents and family composition, were found to be associated
with treatment outcome. The link between these characteristics
and movement remains hypothetical, requiring verification by studies
in depth on the personalities of the treatment population.

Notes

1. For a description of services see Chapters 6 and 14.

2. Ludwig L. Geismar and Michael A. La Sorte, Understand-
    ing the Multi-Problem Family: A Conceptual Analysis
    and Exploration in Early Identification. (New York,
    Association Press, 1964), Chapters 1 to 4.

3. Ibid. , p. 73 ff.

4. L. L. Geismar and Beverly Ayres. Measuring Family
    Functioning. A Manual on a Method for Evaluating the
    Social Functioning of Disorganized Families. (St. Paul,
    Minn. , Family Centered Project, 1960).
    L. L. Geismar, Michael A. La Sorte, and Beverly
    Ayres. "Measuring Family Disorganization," Marriage
    and Family Living, Vol. 24, No. 1, February 1962,
    pp. 51-56.
    L. L. Geismar.   "Family Functioning as an Index
    of Need for Welfare Services," Family Process, Vol.
    3, No. 1, March 1964, pp. 91-113.
    The most comprehensive data on scale reliability and
    validity based on ratings of separate teams of judges
    and different movement scales can be found in David
    Wallace and Jesse Smith, The Chemung County Re-
    search Demonstration with Dependent Multi-Problem
    Families. (New York, The State Charities Aid Asso-

ciation, 1965), pp. 46-47.

5. Leonard S. Kogan and Ann W. Shyne. "Tender-Minded and Tough-Minded Approaches in Evaluative Research," Welfare in Review, Vol. 4, No. 2, February 1966, pp. 12-17.

6. Op cit. , p. 15.

7. The years of initial occupancy for the five projects were as follows: Elm Haven, 1940; Quinnipiac, 1941; Far- nam Courts, 1942; Rockview, 1952; Elm Haven Exten- sion, 1955.

8. L. L. Geismar and Beverly Ayres. Patterns of Change in Problem Families. (St. Paul, Minn. , Family-Cen- tered Project, 1959), p. 10.

9. L. L. Geismar. Report on Checklist Survey. (St. Paul, Minn. , Family-Centered Project, 1957 (mimeographed)

10. Margaret Blenkner makes reference to this kind of de- sign, which utilizes instead of untreated controls a group subjected to a different type of treatment. See Margaret Blenkner, "Control Groups and the Placebo Effect in Evaluative Research," Social Work, Vol. 7, No. 1, January 1962, pp. 52-58, p. 53.

11. L. L. Geismar and Beverly Ayres. Families in Trouble. (St. Paul, Minn. , Family-Centered Project, 1958), p. 137.

12. Several hundred records were gone over in the selective process, but the exact number was not recorded in view of the goal of selecting problem families only.

13. Alfred Kahn. "The Design of Research," in Norman Polansky (editor), Social Work Research. (Chicago, University of Chicago Press, 1960), pp. 48-73, p. 60.

14. Jerome K. Myers and Bertram H. Roberts. Family and Class Dynamics in Mental Illness. (New York, John Wiley and Sons, Inc. , 1959), pp. 40-41.

15. One treatment family was rated at the bottom of Class IV as the husband had had some college education.

16. In a study of 150 New York multi-problem families, 55 percent of the fathers were reported as being deceased or out of the home. New York City Youth Board, Reaching the Unreached, New York, 1958, p. 17. In a study of 150 St. Paul multi-problem families the percentage of absent fathers was 45. L. L. Geismar

and Beverly Ayres. Patterns of Change in Problem
Families. (St. Paul, Minn. , Family-Centered Project, 1959), p. 2.

17. According to a national survey in 1961, 67. 2 percent of
fathers were reported absent from the home and 7. 7
percent were reported deceased. Robert H. Mugge,
"Aid to Families with Dependent Children: Initial
Findings of the 1961 Report on the Characteristics of
Recipients," Social Security Bulletin, March 1963, p.
9.

18. Thirty-five out of the fifty-one control cases were residents of these projects, which were over 80 percent
Negro.

19. Ludwig L. Geismar. "The Social Functioning of the
AFDC Family," The Welfare Reporter, Vol. XIV,
No. 3, July 1963, pp. 43-54.

20. L. L. Geismar and Beverly Ayres. Patterns of Change
in Problem Families. (St. Paul, Minn. , Family-Centered Project, 1959), p. 8.

21. Ibid. , p. 10

22. The evidence pointing to the possible biasing effect resulting from initial differences in family functioning
between experimental and control group is not incontro-
vertible. St. Paul and control group data suggest that
level of family functioning has a negligible effect upon
movement. In the experimental group of the present
study a statistically not significant Gamma correlation
of -. 31 was found between the beginning situation and
movement during treatment. These inconclusive findings, nonetheless, raise questions about the association between the level of social functioning and movement. Is there an inverse relationship between these
two factors only in a population of clearly malfunctioning families whose mean level of functioning is marginal (4) or below? Is an inverse correlation only a function of treatment intervention? The correlation in the
control group between beginning functioning and movement during the study period was only Gamma -. 15.)
If the latter is true, the possibility of bias resulting
from differing levels of functioning prior to treatment
would be ruled out. An affirmative answer to the first
question would mean that differences in experimental
and control samples served to stack the cards in favor
of the former.

23. This conclusion is based upon the assumption that the

samples of multi-problem experimental and control families, though not selected randomly from a specific universe of multi-problem families, are yet representative of disorganized families in urban communities. The chi squares obtained in the two tests indicate that in successive samples drawn from a universe of urban multi-problem families we would expect to find differences similar to those obtained here between families receiving special treatment and those getting only conventional services; we would expect to find such differences in more than 999 out of one thousand trials.

24. The amount of movement in the areas or main categories of Family Functioning is not the arithmetic mean of the sub-categories. Area movement scores represent composite values based on a weighing of sub-category scores for each family rated.

25. Church attendance was omitted because of its low power for discriminating between well functioning and malfunctioning lower-class families. See L. L. Geismar and M. La Sorte, Understanding the Multi-Problem Family, op. cit., pp. 117-118.

26. L. L. Geismar and Beverly Ayres. Patterns of Change in Problem Families. (St. Paul, Minn., Family-Centered Project, 1959), p. 10.

27. The corresponding coefficient in the St. Paul study was -22. Ibid., p. 10.

28. L. L. Geismar and Michael A. La Sorte. Understanding the Multi-Problem Family. (New York, Association Press, 1964), pp. 153-155.

29. For ten men, most of whom were out of contact with the family, we had no information on education. For three more men, also out of the home, data on education were available. Including them in the above crosstabulation reduces the Gamma coefficient slightly to +.69.

30. Alice Overton and Katherine H. Tinker. Casework Notebook. (St. Paul, Minn., Family-Centered Project, 1959). See especially Chapters 2 and 10.

31. The nature of our sample limits the use of inferential statistics. Assuming a representative sample, we would have to conclude from the cross-tabulation on which the correlation is based, that similar results could at best be expected in 70 to 80 out of 100 samples ($X^1 = 1.62$, 1 d.f. p. = $<.30$).

Chapter 16
The Quest for Indices of Neighborhood Change

The Neighborhood Improvement Project, under a community mandate to provide reaching-out services to delinquent and delinquency-prone youngsters and their multi-problem families, came early to the realization that neither the children nor their families could be studied or treated independently of their neighborhood. The decision to extend services to the whole neighborhood was the logical result of this modified approach, aimed at coping with social deprivation and deviancy.

Services in Farnam Courts were characterized by different degrees of breadth and intensity, the most concentrated services going to the families identified as multi-problem. The vast majority of the youth and a goodly number of the adults were involved in one or another activity or helping service. Some families and some non-family households were not included in the NIP program, either because the people chose to remain aloof or because the project offered no appropriate service.

We thought it important to evaluate the changes resulting from intervention in the total neighborhood. We were handicapped by the absence of sensitive indices or of a scale that would provide a reliable and valid measure of change in neighborhood functioning. The reduced level of intensity in neighborhood-wide intervention as compared with family-centered intervention made sensitive instruments of measurement especially necessary.

Yet we did not consider the results of our multi-service intervention in Farnam Courts unmeasurable. We had been guided by the theoretical consideration that our program would reduce the tenants' social isolation and personal anomie, would fill certain voids in their lives, and would help them achieve a more favorable image of their neighborhood.

354

Our efforts to implement these expectations were rewarded not only by the positive response of the population to the program, but by spontaneous requests at the end of the project to have the program continued. This social participation and continued interest in activities and services represented to us evidence of positive change from a prior state of observed apathy and non-involvement. Since our research did not possess appropriate tools of measurement and was not geared to assess changes in the areas of tenants' morale, social isolation, or attitudes toward the neighborhood, etc., no efforts were made in this direction. The community had, however, raised the question of whether the type of social work intervention we had carried out should not be reflected in change in types of social and economic behavior that are readily subject to measurement. The reference was primarily to crime, juvenile delinquency, and economic dependency, which were perceived by the community as problems of serious concern in two respects: they constituted non-conforming behavior, and they were costly to the total community.

The question that concerned us was not whether delinquency and economic dependency were indeed the chief community problems but rather whether statistics on these problems constituted valid indices of the social health (or illness) of a neighborhood and could be used to measure changes in that condition. Juvenile and adult delinquency, one might agree, represent norm-violating behavior that has a disorganizing effect upon community and family life. Economic dependency is also norm-violating and often socially disorganizing, but the norms that are being violated are middle-class rather than lower-class norms. The lower class, with its great vulnerability to unemployment and loss of income, must invariably take a view of public assistance different from that of the middle class. The lower class is likely to view economic dependency as inevitable and thus more acceptable, without the stigma that the middle class attaches to it.

But even if the lower-class could adopt the middle-class disdain for economic dependency, would their desire to be economically independent decisively influence their ability to achieve such a condition? A further consideration involves the effectiveness of the project's intervention in the area of the tenants' economic behavior. Unlike some community development projects in the federal anti-poverty program, NIP was not in a position to make modifications in the community's economic system to benefit the treatment population.

A final issue in the use of statistics on delinquency and economic dependency for documenting changes in behavior has to do with the validity of such data. The susceptibility of official statistics to influences other than the variables being measured is great, as we saw from our own data.

Despite our many reservations regarding the value of such data, an effort was made to collect and analyze official data on deviant behavior. We saw this as a methodological problem in the study of human behavior, and a convenient opportunity to throw additional light on what continues to be an area of controversy.

Method of Data Collection

In order to obtain evidence of changes in neighborhood functioning resulting from the program of social work intervention, the research team of NIP decided to look at four indices of malfunctioning, comparing those for Farnam Courts with two other city low-income projects, Rockview and Quinnipiac. Comparisons were made for a six-year period; this would give us a broader perspective and enable us to take account of factors other than treatment. The analysis covered two years prior to the establishment of the Neighborhood Improvement Project, Periods I and II (May 1, 1957 - April 30, 1959); the year during which NIP was organized, Period III (May 1, 1959 - April 30, 1960); and three years of NIP action program, Periods IV, V, and VI (May 1, 1960 - April 30, 1963).[1]

The indices of neighborhood functioning that we selected are listed below. We sought at first to include figures on school truancy, but data on this were not uniformly available in the New Haven school system.

Indices of Neighborhood Functioning

(1) Appearances before the Juvenile Youth Bureau (pre-

delinquency).

(2) Referrals to the Juvenile Court, both by number and percent of individuals involved and by number of referrals.

(3) Adult arrests by number and percent of adults arrested and by number of arrests made.

(4) Financial assistance received from the Connecticut State Welfare Department program of Aid to Families with Dependent Children (AFDC) and from the New Haven Department of Welfare.

In the last two years of the study, a new State program came into being, Temporary Aid to Families with Dependent Children (TAFDC). For purposes of the study, this was combined with City Welfare, the welfare program it most resembled in eligibility requirements.

The housing projects that served as controls, Quinnipiac and Rockview, comprised 200 and 248 dwelling units, respectively. The percentage of occupants under age 21 was roughly comparable in all three housing projects. In family size and income, the three also did not differ greatly. But the racial composition of one of the two control neighborhoods, Quinnipiac, was only 10 percent Negro in 1963, while the populations of the other two housing projects were about evenly divided between Negroes and whites.

Findings

(1) Appearances before the Juvenile Youth Bureau (generally children under ten) never exceeded twelve in any of the projects during any one year (see Table 27). That number was too small to justify the calculation of rates or proportions. Except for Rockview, which showed a conspicuous rise in 1962/3, the trends in the experimental and control projects showed more similarities than differences. Any fluctuations were within a narrow range of small numbers, on whose significance it would be idle to speculate.

(2) Referrals to the Juvenile Court for children between the ages of ten and fifteen showed substantially higher numbers and rates for Farnam Courts than for the control projects (see Tables 28 and 29). This reflected the greater prevalence of officially reported juvenile delinquency in the experimental project as compared

to the two control projects.   The discrepancy was especially large
in number of referrals (in contrast to number of children referred),
indicating that a number of children in the Courts accounted for
multiple referrals.

Table 27

Number of Children Referred to Juvenile Youth Bureau
(No adjustment made for size of population)

	Farnam Courts	Rockview	Quinnipiac
Period I 1957-58	10	10	9
Period II 1958-59	10	6	2
Period III 1959-60	12	4	6
Period IV 1960-61	3	1	0
Period V 1961-62	4	4	1
Period VI 1962-63	1	12	2

Table 28

Total Number of Juvenile Court Referrals
(No adjustment made for size of population)

	Farnam Courts	Rockview	Quinnipiac
Period I 1957-58	38	7	20
Period II 1958-59	38	20	15
Period III 1959-60	42	22	22
Period IV 1960-61	49	18	6
Period V 1961-62	47	15	9
Period VI 1962-63	39	26	13

Table 29

Number and Percentage of Juveniles Referred
to Juvenile Court
(Percentages based on the juvenile populations,
10 to 15, in May, 1960.)

	Farnam Courts (N=182)		Rockview (N=183)		Quinnipiac (N=133)	
	N	%	N	%	N	%
Period I 1957-58	26	14.3	7	3.8	17	12.8
Period II 1958-59	29	15.9	17	9.3	14	10.5
Period III 1959-60	20	11.0	16	8.7	20	15.0
Period IV 1960-61	33	18.1	14	7.7	6	4.5
Period V 1961-62	36	19.8	14	7.7	6	4.5
Period VI 1962-63	31	17.0	20	10.9	11	8.3

Like the figures for appearances before the Juvenile Youth
Bureau, the trend for juvenile court referrals showed no pattern
that lent itself to an interpretation in keeping with our experimental
design.   Fluctuations from year to year were wide, seemingly subject to influences other than the NIP program of intervention.   The
idiosyncratic character--from the standpoint of delinquency theory--
of factors accounting for changes in the incidence of court referrals
was illustrated by an event that happened one day in Period IV, the
first full year of NIP operations.   The police had discovered a
group of children throwing rocks near the railroad tracks and charged
ten of them with an "act of mischief."   All ten were dismissed with
a warning, but their behavior became recorded as court referrals.
These ten cases made up 20 percent of the referrals for the year
1960-61.   Similarly, in Period II two incidents were responsible for
24 percent of the year's total, and in Period VI three events produced 39 percent of the referrals for the whole year.

(3) Adult arrests also failed to present a coherent trend for
the six-year period under study (Tables 30 and 31).   All three pro-

Table 30

Number of Adult Arrests
(No adjustment made for size of population)

	Farnam Courts	Rockview	Quinnipiac
Period I 1957-58	89	92	23
Period II 1958-59	88	42	18
Period III 1959-60	103	69	26
Period IV 1960-61	93	79	35
Period V 1961-62	97	42	56
Period VI 1962-63	109	77	50

Table 31

Number and Percentage of Adults Arrested
(Percentages based on the populations over age 15
in May, 1960)

	Farnam Courts (N=599)		Rockview (N=353)		Quinnipiac (N=469)	
	N	%	N	%	N	%
Period I 1957-58	58	9.7	52	14.7	16	3.4
Period II 1958-59	61	10.2	31	8.8	17	3.6
Period III 1959-60	63	10.5	46	13.0	24	5.1
Period IV 1960-61	63	10.5	53	15.0	21	4.5
Period V 1961-62	58	9.7	28	7.9	24	5.1
Period VI 1962-63	70	11.7	59	16.7	28	6.0

jects registered a slight upward trend, with Rockview alone showing sharp fluctuations in the arrest curves. Farnam Courts ranked at

the top in the number of adults apprehended but was similar to
Rockview in the percentage of arrests made.   The influence of the
neighborhood program was not reflected in the crime statistics any
more than in the juvenile delinquency data.   The bulk of arrests in
1962-63 were for minor offenses such as motor vehicle law viola-
tions (38 percent), intoxication (22 percent), and breach of peace
(18 percent).   The remaining 22 percent covered all other law vio-
lations, such as resisting, abusing, or interfering with an officer,
trespassing, gaming, lascivious carriage, non-support, fraud, theft,
rape, assault, etc.   The incidence of major crimes in all projects
was so small as to preclude a qualitative trend analysis.

        (4) Financial assistance received from the State of Connecti-
cut and the city of New Haven might be viewed as a better index
of change than delinquent behavior, since the readily available information on frequency and quantity of assistance payments could hopefully reflect degrees of need.   The asset of data reliability was,
however, counterbalanced by the problem of the relevancy of the
change index within the framework of social work intervention.   The
project, to be sure, attempted to transmit in its program a concern
for adequate economic functioning, including self-support and responsibility for dependents.   This was stressed in casework with the
families, yet the social situation of the Farnam Courts tenants frequently precluded any changes in source of income.   This was especially true of the cases receiving AFDC, Aid to Families with Dependent Children.   A mother with six children could be expected to
need state aid until at least some of the children were grown, even
if casework resulted in improvement in family functioning.   The
Federal-State program of Aid to Families with Dependent Children
had been created for the precise purpose of providing deprived families with an economic base that would enable them to live a normal
family life.   So in many instances intervention by NIP was not
aimed at removing the family from dependent status, at least not in
the immediate future.   As might be expected, then, the AFDC picture did not show any differential trends among the three projects
(Tables 32 and 33); the number of families receiving such aid remained fairly constant in Rockview, showed some decline in Farnam

Table 32

Number and Percentage of Families Receiving AFDC

	Farnam Courts (N=300)		Rockview (N=200)		Quinnipiac (N=248)	
	N	%	N	%	N	%
Period I 1957-58	82	27.3	64	32.0	69	27.8
Period II 1958-59	82	27.3	72	36.0	69	27.8
Period III 1959-60	86	28.7	65	32.5	64	25.8
Period IV 1960-61	86	28.7	57	28.5	63	25.4
Period V 1961-62	79	26.3	59	29.5	57	23.0
Period VI 1962-63	73	24.3	61	30.5	46	18.5

Courts, and more decline in Quinnipiac. Expressed in percentage terms (number of families receiving AFDC divided by the number of units in the project), Rockview moved from 32 percent in the first period to 30.5 percent in the sixth, Farnam Courts from 27.3 percent in the first period to 24.3 percent in the sixth, and Quinnipiac from 27.8 percent in the first period to 18.5 percent in the sixth. This might have been a reflection of changes in the composition of families in Quinnipiac, for the average number of persons per family there decreased from 3.72 in 1958 to 3.12 in 1963, while Farnam Courts was rising from 3.68. The average amount of assistance received per family on the AFDC program went up in all three projects but most sharply in Quinnipiac, rising from $1,158 in the first period to $1,613 in the sixth period. By the sixth period Farnam Courts had the lowest average amount of assistance per AFDC family ($1,581), even though its average family size was considerably larger than Quinnipiac's.

City Welfare, covering temporary emergency needs, is the index that might most reasonably be expected to vary as a result of intervention of the NIP type. To the extent that social work in-

Table 33

Total AFDC Amounts and Mean AFDC Payment Per Family

	Farnam Courts		Rockview		Quinnipiac	
	Total Amount	Mean Payments	Total Amount	Mean Payments	Total Amount	Mean Payments
Period I 1957-58	$ 108,006	$ 1,317	$ 91,828	$ 1,435	$ 79,885	$ 1,158
Period II 1958-59	112,238	1,369	121,232	1,684	91,036	1,319
Period III 1959-60	113,824	1,324	109,634	1,687	86,589	1,353
Period IV 1960-61	116,606	1,356	98,161	1,722	78,475	1,246
Period V 1961-62	116,764	1,478	97,359	1,650	78,335	1,374
Period VI 1962-63	115,410	1,581	104,317	1,710	74,191	1,613

tervention may be seen as seeking the reduction of economic dependency in the present or near future, we are more likely to be
working toward the removal of clients from the general assistance
roles than from one of the categorical assistance (including AFDC)
programs.   This statement is based upon the supposition that general assistance families, having suffered less severe psycho-social
and physical handicaps (loss of father, blindness, old age, physical
disability) than the AFDC families, have a substantial potential for
economic rehabilitation.   This theoretical differentiation rests on the
assumption that the two types of clients differ in their capacity for
economic rehabilitation as a result of the NIP type intervention.   In
actuality the distinction is likely to be less clear-cut, because a
great many general assistance families suffer from handicaps that
may not fall into one of the federal categories but which are no less
severe.   The amounts of welfare received are greatly affected by the
administrative policies and decisions of the department, and the
changes in a municipal department may well exceed those in state
and federal programs.   During the six years of the study the New
Haven Welfare Department went through many changes in personnel,
policy, and budget.   We assumed, however, that these changes were
uniformly reflected throughout the three housing projects selected
for comparison, so that differential changes among them could be
ascribed to factors other than administration.

There was a surprising degree of variation in the amount of
City Welfare received during the six years of the study,[2] as shown
in Tables 34, 35 and 36.   A comparison of the year preceding NIP
(Period III) with the last year of NIP's operation (Period VI) revealed a reduction of almost 19 percent in total City Welfare in
Farnam Courts, compared with an increase of almost 12 percent in
Quinnipiac and an increase of over 63 percent in Rockview.   Similarly, the average city welfare per family increased only 4 percent
in Farnam Courts, whereas it went up 46 percent in Quinnipiac and
over 100 percent in Rockview.   The number of families receiving
welfare went down in all three projects.   There was a reduction of
21.7 percent in Farnam Courts, 23.5 percent in Quinnipiac, and
18.6 percent in Rockview.

Table 34

Number and Percentage of Families Receiving City Welfare
(TAFDC included in Periods V and VI.)

	Farnam Courts (N=300)		Rockview (N=200)		Quinnipiac (N=248)	
	N	%	N	%	N	%
Period I 1957-58	75	25.0	48	24.0	22	8.9
Period II 1958-59	91	30.3	47	23.5	29	11.7
Period III 1959-60	92	30.7	43	21.5	34	13.7
Period IV 1960-61	89	29.7	33	16.5	40	16.1
Period V 1961-62	74	24.7	40	20.0	36	14.5
Period VI 1962-63	72	24.0	35	17.5	26	10.5

Table 35

Total Amounts of City Relief Received
(TAFDC included in periods V and VI)

(No adjustment made for size of population)

	Farnam Courts	Rockview	Quinnipiac
Period I 1957-58	29,246	20,013	16,736
Period II 1958-59	47,425	22,176	15,966
Period III 1959-60	45,610	18,132	13,958
Period IV 1960-61	39,316	12,808	15,222
Period V 1961-62	38,757	18,639	19,904
Period VI 1962-63	37,076	29,646	15,606

Table 36

Number of Families Receiving City Relief and
Mean Payment per Family

(TAFDC included in Periods V and VI.)

	Farnam Courts		Rockview		Quinnipiac	
	No. of Fami- lies	Mean Pay- ments	No. of Fami- lies	Mean Pay- ments	No. of Fami- lies	Mean Pay- ments
Period I 1957-58	75	$ 390	48	$ 417	22	$ 761
Period II 1958-59	91	521	47	472	29	551
Period III 1959-60	92	496	43	422	34	411
Period IV 1960-61	89	442	33	388	40	381
Period V 1961-62	74	524	40	466	36	553
Period VI 1962-63	72	515	35	847	26	600

We would like to think that NIP was responsible for lowering
the dependency on City Welfare in Farnam Courts, but unfortunately such a statement cannot be backed up. By selecting other years
it is possible to show similar changes in any three-year period for
any of the three communities. For instance, Rockview between Period I and Period IV showed a decrease of almost 37 percent in total
city welfare, and a decrease of over 31 percent in number of families receiving welfare. What caused this reduction? We know of
no special project operating in Rockview during that period. Why
did Rockview, from that low point, then show an increase of over
131 percent by the last year of the study, Period VI? The number
of families did not increase sharply, moving only from 33 to 35,
but the average yearly relief payment per family zoomed from $388
to $847 in that interval. Perhaps this was a result of the new
State TAFDC program, which provided more adequate funds for
larger families. The effect on Rockview, with its high average size
of family, would be greater than on either of the other two projects.

Why was the average city welfare per family so high in

Quinnipiac at the start of the study? Why was the welfare total for
Farnam Courts so low at the start of the study? What caused the
sharp rise (62 percent) in total city welfare in Farnam Courts between Period I and Period II, while Rockview showed a slight increase and Quinnipiac a slight decrease? We do not know the
causes of the great variations, and a special study covering administrative as well as social and economic aspects of the welfare system would be required to answer the questions posed. The simple
statistics on the dispensing of public assistance to the population of
three housing projects provided an index too crude for the many-
faceted program that represented our attempts to manifest economic need in Farnam Courts. The complex nature of this transaction,
which was affected by economic conditions in the community, changes
in the composition of the population, changes in welfare budgets,
eligibility requirements, other administrative provisions, etc., made
it practically impossible to assess the effect of our service project
by noting the amounts of relief given in the neighborhood.

Comment

It may be argued that our conclusions regarding the utility of
indices on delinquency and economic dependency were clearly a case
of post hoc reasoning. It may be said that the absence of any
trends toward reduced deviant behavior and economic dependency in
the neighborhood where NIP was operating denoted a failure of the
experimental project to have an impact upon the population, not just
the assumed inadequacy of the indices of measurement. The question may even be raised why, considering our skeptical attitude toward that type of data, we invested a substantial amount of time
and effort in its collection and analysis.

The answer to this question can be found in the charge given
to NIP by its sponsors, the Community Council of Greater New
Haven, Inc. and the NIP Advisory Committee, to carry out research
in the project. The mandate for research called for an outcome
evaluation that would show the effects of intervention on delinquency
and on economic dependency. The researchers' doubts about the
adequacy of available data were not backed up by any empirical evi-

dence. They launched their study in order to secure more knowledge about the nature of local trends in officially reported delinquency and dependency. Perhaps one of the most important observations arising from this effort was the seemingly idiosyncratic--at
least with reference to variables for which we could account--char-
acter of the trends in geographically restricted areas. In other
words, the indices selected were not sensitive to the kind of intervention sought by the project. The NIP program was chiefly directed toward improving the functioning of the family and neighborhood. The official indices of deviant behavior and economic dependency, although to some extent a mirror of family and neighborhood
functioning, mainly reflected the operation of the larger systems--
the agencies of social control and the economy and welfare apparatus. The NIP program was not geared to effect changes in these
larger systems, but even the most effective intervention in family
and neighborhood would have had only a limited effect upon the exchanges between the family and the large social systems that dominate the nature of such interaction.

The researcher interested in the influence of social work intervention upon officially reported delinquent behavior and economic
dependency must look for an interrelationship between these indices
and the program of intervention. This should be done when at least
one of two conditions have been met: there must be a good theoretical base for postulating that the intervention will clearly affect
the interaction between the research subjects and the systems that
influence their deviant and economic behavior; and the researchers
must be able to control the variables that account for changes in the
behavior of the larger systems. Such changes include modifications
in police methods of apprehending delinquents, in legal procedure
and correctional approaches, in the employment situation, welfare
budget, eligibility requirements, administrative agency processes,
staff competence, etc. Where these conditions for measurement
can not be met, researchers are charged with the responsibility for
selecting such indices as are theoretically relevant and methodologi-
cally controllable within the framework of their design for outcome
research.

Notes

1. The action program ended on August 31, 1963.

2. In the fifth and sixth periods, the State TAFDC program was added to the city amounts because the eligibility rules were practically identical. Therefore, to omit TAFDC payments would make the fifth and sixth period City Welfare figures not comparable with the earlier years.

Chapter 17
Implications for Programs of Intervention

Recapitulation and Some Afterthoughts

These lines are being written thirty months after the phasing out of the NIP action program and twenty months after the official declaration of the War on Poverty. This is a time when the social work profession is asking itself searching questions about its role in social change, while a changing need for services and an increasingly serious manpower shortage are leading those engaged in social work education to take a critical look at curriculum. It is the writers' hope that the experience of the Neighborhood Improvement Project will contribute to this reevaluation of the role of social work, as well as to anti-poverty programming.

The Neighborhood Improvement Project constituted a community's effort to cope with a contemporary social problem. The success of such an undertaking depends, at the outset, upon defining the problem and determining its nature. As any observer of the American welfare scene will note, difficulties inherent in the social situation that are defined as problems are usually those that have been so perceived and so characterized by individuals with the authority to express an opinion about the ills of society. In other words, problems are not necessarily considered such because of their impact on certain segments of the population. The fact that some leading individual or group is interested in particular kinds of problem-solving activities may be equally or more important.

During the early 1950's juvenile delinquency was seen by the social welfare community as a concern of national importance, while during the late fifties the multi-problem family held center stage and tended to be viewed as the major cause of delinquency. In the first three years of the 1960's mental health and mental retardation received the major attention of professionals and lay persons in the fields of health and welfare, but in 1964 interest and the initiative

370

for social action moved toward anti-poverty programming. Throughout the 1950's and early 60's the civil rights struggle gathered momentum but seems to have lost some of its vigor in the mid-sixties as national interest became centered upon U.S. involvement in Vietnam. No one would claim that each problem reached its climax during these particular time periods, being relatively quiescent in the immediately preceding and following years. Clearly, each problem came into the spotlight as a result of the definitions and emphasis given to it by the community and its leaders. For instance, social issues such as mental health and retardation, and the War on Poverty owed much of their prominence to the leadership of the late President Kennedy and of President Johnson.

The problems of New Haven in the late fifties were typical of those of a medium-sized American city. They included a decline of downtown commercial enterprises, migration of the more affluent population to the suburbs, the influx of deprived minority groups and low-income populations into neighborhoods previously occupied by higher status groups, a concomitant increase in unemployment, juvenile delinquency and poverty. These do not exhaust the list of problems. Mental illness, tuberculosis, and a host of other diseases correlated with deprived living might be added. New Haven, one of the leading communities in urban renewal, decided in the latter part of the 1950's to attack the problem of juvenile delinquency, one of the more dramatic manifestations of social disorganization. Since it is a threat to the property and, in some instances, the lives of members of the community, it has been relatively easy in New Haven and elsewhere to enlist community support for such a fight.

New Haven chose juvenile delinquency as the target of its first action program in the field of urban social renewal. The problem was not narrowly conceived nor confined merely within the context of social control; every effort was made to see it within a framework of cause and effect relationships. The planners of NIP considered family life an important causative factor in the deviant behavior of juveniles. Deficiencies in neighborhood life were also singled out as a contributory cause. Therefore the initial action

formulation called for intensive casework with multi-problem families, plus group work, recreational activities, and community organization in the entire target area.

The professional staff employed to implement the Neighborhood Improvement Project, with a clear community mandate for its
work, was entrusted with the task of translating the mandate into a
program. In the process the staff was bound to modify to some ex-
tent--and the planners surely would not have wished it otherwise--
the original formulations. Some changes were guided by theoretical
considerations; others flowed from the prior experience of staff
members. But most of the modifications came about as a result of
lessons learned in the course of carrying out the program.

While the stimulus was juvenile delinquency, the issue to
which the project directed itself came to be much broader. Such a
trend was already implicit in the choice of the name Neighborhood
Improvement Project. But several months of operation drove home
two points, which though long understood had not guided our planning: (1) juvenile delinquency is closely interwoven with other conditions and problems, many of which are in the long run as harmful or more harmful to the target population as well as to the total
community, and (2) successful coping with juvenile delinquency requires coming to grips with the many other problems related to it.

As NIP moved into the action phase, practitioners and researchers alike addressed themselves to an attempt to ameliorate
conditions of serious family disorganization and neighborhood-wide
social deprivation. No comprehensive theoretical formulation guided
the overall effort. Nor are we even at this point aware of any consensus among scholars and researchers on what constitutes a satisfactory set of theoretical guidelines for a program of social intervention.

Perhaps the most serious obstacle to freedom of programming was the limited economic resources at our disposal. Theory
on opportunity structure,[1] for example, sounded plausible enough,
but the project's resources for modifying that structure were strictly limited. We had no jobs to offer to the unemployed or under-
employed, no power to effect a raise in wages, no funds to augment

inadequate public assistance allotments, and no authority to modify
an educational system that was not attuned to the needs of the poor.
Our assets consisted of our experience and skill in working with the
socially handicapped and our ideas for extending to the people of
Farnam Courts certain services and resources, which we hoped
would bring about some modification in the opportunity structure,
particularly for children.   Our plans for neighborhood intervention
were to bring about whatever modification could be made in existing
resources, to guide the population toward a better use of resources,
and to supplement these when necessary with such new programs
and services as seemed to better meet the needs of the population.

A superficial acquaintance with the housing project and its
people convinced us that service to the Farnam Courts neighborhood
could not await completion of a comprehensive diagnosis of the social situation.   There was an urgent need to offer programs on the
basis of perceived need, even if this had to be done on a trial and
error basis.   In carrying out this programming, the treatment and
research staff applied their knowledge about lower-class urban populations in the United States, knowledge gained from readings in the
sociological literature.   This background aided in the programming,
for it provided a more or less balanced perspective on the strengths
as well as the weaknesses in the lower-class life pattern.   A recent
monograph by Catherine S. Chilman articulated a point of view that
summarizes the philosophy underlying our own intervention programs: Lower-class life patterns may represent adaptive behavior
in the light of existing environmental conditions.   This should lead
us "to recognize that a number of these patterns tend to operate to
the disadvantage of many of. . . (the very poor)."[2]

The most crucial question is how lower-class behavior relates to the actual goals and/or the intended goals of the people.
Some characteristic kinds of lower-class attitudes--such as lack of
goal commitment, lack of belief in long-range success,[3] and fear
and distrust of the school system[4]--may be functional to a program
of intervention that emphasizes increased social security without upward social mobility.   Such attitudes, however, are clearly dysfunc-
tional to a program stressing high social, educational, and occupa-

tional horizons.

The NIP program, in keeping with its mandate and structure,
was a neighborhood-centered operation that emphasized the reduction
of conflict and tensions among the various groups, an improvement
in needed services, protection of tenants' basic civil rights, and en-
richment of life through recreational and cultural activities; it also
attempted modification of seriously problematic behavior.   Higher
horizon activities were largely confined to the children and adoles-
cents.   Whatever the shortcomings of such a restricted approach,
its merit lay in avoiding the risk of trying to change knowledge,
skills, and orientation without a concomitant improvement in the opportunity structure.   This discrepancy in higher horizon programming appears to be one of the greatest weaknesses in the national
War on Poverty, but for better or worse it was not an issue confronting the Neighborhood Improvement Project.   We felt that our
program of education and socialization for the young would defer the
likely conflict between aspirations and opportunity to a time when
conditions might be more conducive to social mobility than they were
in Farnam Courts in the late fifties and early sixties.

Indices of Success and Failure

The community's expectation that a new and fairly expensive
social action project should be evaluated was reasonable enough.
While the project staff fully agreed that an assessment of its work
was desirable, it was skeptical about our ability to evaluate it by
scientific means--a skepticism that came from knowing how ill prepared, how unready social science is to utilize evaluative research.

The problem was the "what" as well as the "how" of evaluation, for the first must be answered before the second can be dealt
with meaningfully.   While the project sponsors and participants were
in agreement on general objectives, there was no consensus on the
specific goals deemed both worthy and realistically attainable.   The
original aim of combatting juvenile delinquency was never abandoned;
however as time went on it became subordinated to other objectives,
all of them related to the social rehabilitation of the neighborhood.
Which of these objectives, or what combinations of them, were to

be evaluated?

Reducing economic dependency was the objective very much
on the minds of some lay members of the NIP Advisory Committee.
But the project staff believed that reduction of economic dependency,
although desirable, was not a realistic goal within the framework of
NIP intervention.   Economic dependency is viewed by some groups
in our society, particularly the more conservative elements, as evidence of individual or family failure.   Psycho-social rehabilitation,
it is argued, must address itself to coping with such failures in order to bring about greater economic independence.   There is no
denying that ignorance, poor motivation, and personal maladjustment
contribute to economic dependency, but it is highly questionable
whether one can assert that they are its major causes in a population characterized by low social position, lack of education, minority group status, fatherless families, and lack of employment opportunities.   Given these multiple handicaps it would seem that the most
immediate objective should be greater, not reduced, economic dependency, for in the absence of changes in the other handicapping
environmental factors, increased financial assistance is the only
means of lessening economic deprivation.

Another NIP objective was the involvement of the population,
particularly the youth, in constructive recreational, social, and educational activities.   It was hoped this would avert much of the law-
violating behavior that resulted from aimless drifting around the
neighborhood.   There is some evidence that anti-social activities
drop where aggression finds constructive outlets,[5] an observation
which was seen as being most relevant to the young people of Farnam Courts.   For the adult population organized activities were
viewed as an escape from humdrum routine and boredom or even
from social isolation.   Formal social participation was seen as an
index of the attainment of the above objectives.

For the multi-problem families in Farnam Courts, changes in
the level of family functioning were the criterion of successful intervention.   There were two reasons why we confined this form of
measurement to the multi-problem families: (1) These families,
because of their inadequate social functioning, were the focus of a

concerted family-centered treatment effort; raising their level of
functioning thus became a major goal.   (2) Since the measurement
of movement or change in functioning called for the collection of
family data over an extended period, available resources for research made it necessary to confine such data collection to the
treatment and control groups.

Our conclusion, that the statistically significant movement
among the NIP treatment families was due to our program of intervention, is defendable but not entirely beyond challenge.   The multi-
faceted nature of the service program left several important questions unanswered: Which among the various programs of service
and treatment accounted for the change?   If all of them contributed,
what was their proportionate share?   Were we entitled to assume
that the more extensive movement in NIP when compared with the
St. Paul Family-Centered Project, which utilized the same method
of evaluation, was due to the group work and neighborhood services
that were not offered in St. Paul?   Too many uncontrolled variables
in both projects preclude such a conclusion.   The hypothesis that
NIP's multi-faceted intervention is more effective than mere family-
centered reaching-out services merits testing.

The chapter on "The Quest for Indices of Neighborhood
Change" presented some of the problems inherent in the use of the
so-called "hard indices" in evaluation research.   Whatever the merits or demerits of the criteria of change selected by the community,
i.e. deviant behavior and economic dependency in Farnam Courts,
they failed to reveal a clear trend as a result of project intervention.   Social participation, by contrast, as shown in the chapters
"From Physical to Social Renewal" and "Work with Groups," rose
from a minimal level to a very high level in the young age groups
and to a moderate level among mothers and senior citizens.

It may be argued that greatly enhanced social participation
is a means, not an end in the process of intervention.   This is essentially true.   We do not hold that organized social participation
is inherently superior to non-participation.   But since we planned
our program of intervention with the assumption that increased formal participation in recreational, social and educational activities

would constitute desirable change, we viewed the augmentation of
formal social participation as an index of success.

The composite statistical picture of changes as a result of
NIP programming was a mixed one. Results of the movement study
were very encouraging, especially against the background of evaluation research such as the Cambridge-Somerville Study, [6] Girls at
Vocational High, [7] and the Chemung County Research Demonstration, [8]
all of which failed to show any positive effect from treatment. Findings from the research using neighborhood-wide indices of deviant
behavior were inconclusive, largely because the indices were too
crude for a sensitive measurement of behavioral change. The
change in social participation, especially in the younger age groups,
was striking and might be seen as a positive index of change.

NIP's attempts to involve the local population in neighborhood programming were not uniformly successful. Our group work
and recreational programs failed, with a few notable exceptions, to
reach adult men below retirement age. This meant, among other
things, that we failed to attract indigenous leaders, leaving NIP essentially an operation directed by outsiders.

The reader will recall that during the early stages of the
project Frank Harris, then Director of Group Work and Recreation
for the Community Council of Greater New Haven, tried to identify
and work with some of the socially more active and vocal members
of the Farnam Courts community. That effort, which centered in
the Tenants Council, was continued by the NIP staff until it became
clear that the Council members had little community support and
were engaging in activities that were splitting rather than uniting the
people. A house-to-house survey, asking Farnam Courts tenants to
name residents who could serve as spokesmen and representatives
of the community, resulted in a wide variety of names, with almost
no duplications. The persons named were neighbors or acquaintances, rather than individuals prominent in the community. The
men who had composed the active nucleus of the Tenants Council did
not receive any endorsement in this survey.

But whether or not local leaders could be identified and thus
involved in planning, sponsors and staff of the project were deter-

mined to move ahead with the program because of the great unmet needs in Farnam Courts.   Although NIP never succeeded in cultivating a group of indigenous leaders to become partners in the project, a few individuals, of both sexes and of different age groups, came to take a responsible part in various aspects of NIP activities. They did not function spontaneously as representatives of the local population, but acted under the direction of the professional intervenors.

The program of intervention in NIP could, therefore, be characterized as the introduction by professionals--or by untrained workers operating under professional supervision--of services and activities designed to benefit the local population.   Tenant participation in activities was considered a key objective and a criterion of success, but the possibility of involving the residents in planning became increasingly remote as the project moved toward its concluding phase.

The decision to extend services to meet need and to neglect the issue of local initiative and power was based upon a set of priorities adhered to by the NIP staff.   Other community organizers, in keeping with Saul Alinsky,[9] might have reached an early conclusion that the absence of social and political leadership and power was the most critical aspect and therefore should become the primary focus of outside intervention.   While not wishing to minimize the importance of indigenous power, we would ask whether the issue does not have to be weighed against the total constellation of needs in the target area.   In each situation, the decision to intervene and the form that intervention will take must be based upon total need analysis and an assessment of the urgency of the various needs. One can readily agree that the slum dwellers need indigenous power, but that need may rank only third or fourth, after their needs for food, clothing and medical care, decent housing, and improved educational and recreational facilities.

There was yet another consideration in the failure of NIP to develop local leadership and power.   Action toward this end must necessarily focus upon those issues that are of greatest concern to broad groups of the population; effective indigenous leadership should preferably be developed around efforts to resolve these issues, whether by collaborative or contest strategies.[10] As the staff of NIP became increasingly involved with the situation in Farnam Courts, these major issues could be identified: lack of employment, poor medical services, inadequate relief payments, restrictive Housing Authority policies, and an urban renewal program that almost completely ignored the tenants.

In attempts to modify offending practices by utilizing local power, a protracted struggle with the power structure very often occurs. Contest strategies appeared to be the least appropriate technique of change we could use in Farnam Courts. In 1965 some communities supported by funds from the Office of Economic Opportunity--an organization with a potential for operating outside the local power structures--were beginning to use such techniques as the road to social change.[2] Six years earlier this approach was not on our agenda, largely because NIP operated under the direct auspices of the social welfare community. We viewed intervention mainly and expediently as setting up services and activities that we could control, while bending and stretching existing resources and policies for whatever improvement might be gained for the target population.

Research Demonstration Projects, Anti-Poverty Programming and Institutional Change

In this era of anti-poverty planning and programming, the social work profession is constantly being challenged to depart from its tradition of concentrating on the treatment of individuals and families. Social scientists are exhorting social workers to direct their professional concern to what they perceive to be the essential issues in poverty: the flaws in the economic and social systems of American society.

The popular view that American social work has its roots in concern for individual behavior is, of course, far from the truth. Professional social work, whose growth is closely associated with the names of Mary Richmond and Jane Addams, arose out of a broad concern for the welfare of the poor and from a spirit of social reform. The ascendancy of the psychiatric approach to human

and social problems characterized the philosophy and services of
but one epoch, albeit a recent one, in the development of the profession. Yet even while a psychoanalytically oriented pattern of
casework dominated the social work scene, group work and community organization emerged, disciplines concerned with the problems
inherent in the broader social environment. Still, from the Depression until the mid-fifties, American social work was preoccupied
with the problems of individuals and families.

The Neighborhood Improvement Project, initiated and sponsored by a Community Council representing local health and welfare
agencies and staffed by social work professionals, was--not surpris-
ingly--guided largely by plans representing the mainstream philosophy of social work. That philosophy is subject to criticism, not so
much in terms of its validity as a way of helping people but in
terms of the relative emphasis given to casework and group work,
i. e. direct service intervention, as ways of improving the lot of socially and economically handicapped citizens. There is more at
stake here than whether activities like counseling mothers, helping
families improve homemaking, placing children in nursery school,
etc., are helpful. The value of the NIP approach hinges on a
broader question: What is social work's responsibility relative to
the responsibility of the larger society? If this can be answered
satisfactorily it then will be possible to assess social work action
within the limits of a clear mandate.

Answers to the question of the responsibility for dealing with
such issues as poverty, individual maladjustments, and social disorganization must necessarily be translatable into roles or ideal
roles for social work in society. Not only do writers on this subject emerge with different answers, the type of answer put forth
varies from time to time. The variations found among writers at
any point in time reflect their divergent philosophies, while changes
over time in the modal patterns for defining social work roles tend
to mirror changes in professional thinking, generally influenced by
the attitudes of opinion makers in the fields of social and behavioral science, government and politics.

Wilensky and Lebeaux wrote in 1958 that "contemporary definitions of welfare are fuzzy because cultural values regarding the social responsibility of government, business, and the individual are now in flux."[12] This observation is just as true in 1966. The flux is greater than ever now, but the modal position of welfare leaders has shifted. The residual approach, which holds "that social welfare institutions should come into play only when the normal structures of supply, the family and the market, break down,"[13] has been losing ground. The institutional formulation, which "sees the welfare services as normal 'first line' functions of modern industrial ascendancy,"[14] is gaining.

The genesis of the Neighborhood Improvement Project was a community philosophy and structure approximating the residual pattern. As in most communities in the United States, the Council of Social Agencies of Greater New Haven (later called the Community Council) viewed itself as an organization devoted largely to working in the traditional spheres of health, welfare, and recreation. The dawn of the new era of community-wide mobilization against delinquency and poverty raised the horizons of the Council but did not cast it into an "institutional" role until the closing days of the NIP operation. When the Community Council extended its concern to the broader aspects of social welfare, it was instrumental in bringing to life a new organization, Community Progress, Incorporated, which served to bridge the gap between traditional social welfare and the job market, housing and education.

Mayor Lee's Citizens Action Committee provided much of the impetus for later developments in social urban renewal. This early push and the generous support of the Ford Foundation enabled New Haven to enter the War on Poverty much better equipped than most other cities in the United States. In all these developments social welfare, public as well as private, played a residual role, i. e. it functioned as an accessory rather than a leader or coordinator in the movement toward institutional change.

This general course of developments explains to a large extent why NIP was neither conceived nor operated as an experiment in fundamental social change, but was seen rather as an innovation in the traditional area of social welfare. The community's mandate

for the project contained some unrealistic expectations regarding the
effects of the NIP program of intervention on a deprived population's
way of life.   NIP staff members were generally aware of the limitations inherent in the project's approach; yet we were guided by
the belief that between the polar points of total social reconstruc-
tion and the status quo of wholesale societal neglect, lay a potentially fertile area of social action.   We also believed that within the
framework of delayed institutional change there was room for inno-
vative local activity that might point the way toward nationwide
measures for social change.   Such activity could take the form of
new or improved services, provision of resources, neighborhood organization, and the like.

It should be noted that this line of reasoning, which may be
justified when applied to a small local action project, loses much of
its strength when it guides the planning of a nationwide effort such
as the War on Poverty.   The advocates and planners of the anti-
poverty program have stated loudly that traditional welfare approaches
have been found wanting and that a new policy of economic, social
and educational opportunities is needed.   Yet the budget and new
programs under the auspices of the Office of Economic Opportunity
and related bodies are clearly inadequate.   Once more we are wit-
nessing a plethora of halfway measures, experimental projects and
programs for special groups instead of a broadside attack on poverty.

The mitigating circumstances cited for the slowness of implementing an effective welfare policy are the same in Washington as
they were in New Haven.   The people, i.e. the nation or the community, are said to be not yet ready to support a significant program.   The terms "people," "nation," and "community" can only be
interpreted to mean those persons who, as a result of election, appointment or influence, are in a position to speak on behalf of the
larger population.   In the late 1950's New Haven was willing to take
action on the issues of juvenile delinquency and multi-problem family functioning--especially since the projects would receive a federal
subsidy--because both problems could easily be put into the category
of "social dynamite," a potential threat to the welfare of the whole
community and a definite drain on its financial resources.

In a similar vein the Congress of the United States finds it
easiest to endorse programs for school drop-outs, urban slum
dwellers (particularly Negroes), and the aged. While the urgency
in helping the first two groups can be explained, at least in part,
in terms of their explosive potential, the deprived aged represent an
ever-growing block of disgruntled voters. Why, it might be asked,
should this nation provide Medicare only for the aged or indigent?
Why are there not medical programs for children? Why not for
everybody, particularly people in the productive years when serious
illness may constitute not only personal suffering and financial deprivation but also a loss of manpower to the nation? Why, we might
ask at this point, has this country chosen research and demonstration projects as one of the important means of dealing with domestic social problems of our day?

Research and demonstration projects such as the one in New
Haven have sprung up throughout the country because they have a
two-fold appeal. They are designed to produce scientific evidence
indicating that new approaches or techniques are helpful. Positive
results, in a scientifically oriented culture, are seen as the necessary prelude to change in existing methods. Secondly, they put a
convenient moratorium on the much more difficult and complex task
of immediate institutional change. Those opposed to the program
can buy time by awaiting the results, which may be either negative
or years away. Those who favor the program can ease their conscience by having effected a compromise with their opponents or by
falling back on the consolation of having put their faith in the findings of science.

There is yet another parallel between the New Haven and the
national approaches to tackling basic welfare issues. Those in a
position to set policy tend to favor limited programs focusing on
changes in behavior or on the modification of small systems. The
New Haven community was eager to reform the behavior of juvenile
delinquents and multi-problem families. The local sponsors of the
Neighborhood Improvement Project anticipated changes in neighborhood organization, in police practices of dealing with delinquents
and pre-delinquents, in the schools' methods of helping seriously

deprived youngsters, and the like; but there were practically no expectations regarding revisions of basic policy in public housing, public welfare, employment, and education.

The Economic Opportunity Act of 1964 puts a premium on
the training and work experience of certain groups, particularly
children and youth, who are undersocialized and undereducated, unskilled, unemployed or sporadically employed. The Act proposes
local and regional action by urban and rural community organizations to combat poverty by means of a variety of education, health
and welfare programs. Neither the anti-poverty bill nor any concurrent legislation is aimed at measures of economic reform that
would attempt to provide full employment, revise our regressive
system of taxation for social security, revamp the inadequate system of public welfare, and so forth.

Therefore, it would be fair to say that the Economic Opportunity Act represents a continuation on a national scale of the policy
of federally financed research and demonstration projects such as
NIP. These projects operate on the tacit assumption that this country's basic economic and social systems are sound and bear no responsibility for the problems of poverty, social deviance, etc. The
New Haven project was in no position to challenge the role of the
local economy in neighborhood rehabilitation. Nor were the community's basic institutions of health and welfare seen as handicapping the process of helping a socially deprived population. The community perceived the role of NIP as one of building services and activities on top of the existing structure; it did not anticipate any
modification of structure, except perhaps minor changes involved in
coordinating welfare services and introducing more professional
techniques.

The Economic Opportunity Act likewise evades the question
of whether the national economy as presently constituted can come
to grips with the problem of poverty. By and large, government
economists put their faith in a continuing rise of the gross national
product and in a limited regulation of the economy by varying taxes
and interest rates. Unemployment rates ranging between 3. 5 and
4. 0 percent, considered high by European standards, are seen as

normal and perhaps even desirable--except in time of war, when manpower is at a premium--because some economists equate a low unemployment rate with a sluggish manpower pool. Superimposed on this economy and its affiliated health and welfare institutions is a patchwork of education, training, work experience and action programs, loan and assistance provisions, designed to help various categories of the poor. Local, regional, and state authorities are called upon to help in the implementation of these programs. Even the most loyal of Administration backers would readily concede that the one to one-and-a-half billion dollar welfare budget per year, curtailed periodically in favor of military needs, is not going to make a substantial dent in American poverty. However the emphasis at this stage of the anti-poverty war, as in the research and demonstration projects, is on experimentation and innovation. The main difference between the old and the new approach lies in the latter's political emphasis and its more forceful attempt to involve some of the target population.

In addition to experimentation the programs of the Office of Economic Opportunity, particularly the Community Action Programs, emphasize administrative decentralization. By following the American tradition of local responsibility and initiative, they run counter to an overall trend toward Federal planning and programming in such fields as business, industry, banking, transportation, health and welfare. "Curiously, then," write Rein and Riessman, "social welfare remains the last bastion of laissez-faire and free enterprise. Social planning has not been able to reconcile its advocacy of directive policy with its faith in the vitality of an undirected, individualistic, market-oriented society."[15] It may be that the paucity of the resources of the War on Poverty dictates this strategy of shared Federal and local responsibility, both for the sake of distributing the financial burden and for sharing the blame should the enterprise prove a failure.

The Neighborhood Improvement Project and similar experimental projects throughout the country have helped put the problem of the socially handicapped into a clearer perspective and have provided some pointers of aid for setting up a nationwide program of

intervention aimed at combatting poverty and deprivation. These
programs have also brought to the national consciousness increasing evidence that change is possible and perhaps within reach. The
extension of this approach has begun to convince the leaders of the
political and welfare systems that change is feasible, but it has already convinced the poor. However their conviction has assumed
some unanticipated and--from the point of view of the Administra-
tion--undesirable forms. The poor have become demanding, vocal,
sometimes violent. Like the civil rights movement, which gathered
strength and forcefully stated its case for the complete emancipa-
tion of the Negro only in the wake of Federal action, the cause of
the poor appears to have received most of its impetus from the
limited action taken by the Government. We do not wish to imply
a simple cause and effect relationship between official action and
activity by the underprivileged, but the two can be seen to interact.
A given need or non-articulated demand gives rise to official action,
which in turn tends to strengthen the demand and leads to activity
by the underprivileged group.

Poor self-images and feelings of powerlessness on the part
of the underprivileged tend to act as major barriers to self-initi-
ated action; an official declaration that the socially handicapped are
not to be blamed for their lot would help promote self-respect and
encourage constructive activity. By stressing opportunity as a major factor in rehabilitation the Economic Opportunity Act of 1964 has
indeed shifted some of the onus of poverty from the poor to the nation as a whole. The programs under the respective Titles, however, fail to carry this thinking to its logical conclusion. The Economic Opportunity Act skirts the issue of meeting basic immediate
needs of the American poor. Education and job training may be a
long-term solution to unemployability, but they bypass the problem
of finding jobs now for the country's able-bodied workers. [16] Health
programs for the old and those proposed for children ignore the
fact that a large segment of our population has no health insurance
or has only inadequate coverage. Also, the special grants and
loans and various other kinds of assistance do little to bring about
a life of security and dignity for those who must maintain them-

selves on social security and/or public assistance.

Finally, the anti-poverty program, like the Neighborhood Improvement Project and other demonstration programs, is set up explicitly to serve the poor and the socially handicapped. Undertakings of this kind identify the poor, label the poor, and help ghettoize the poor. Psychologically, programs that advertise themselves as of low status start out on the wrong foot. Limited to low-income neighborhoods and problematic populations, these projects in their operations tend to inhibit upward social mobility. Programs destined for the poor, the socially handicapped, multi-problem families, delinquents, etc., could be presented as general national or community programs for families, youths, senior citizens, residents of the inner city, workers, farmers, small businessmen, and so forth, thereby avoiding stigmatizing the specific target groups.

The anti-poverty program is, or should be, a program for all the people, at least a very large segment of them. An effective assault on the problem of poverty should take the form of laws, provisions, programs, and institutions that can bridge the gap between our view of the Great Society and the present reality. The choice of measures for bridging the gap would automatically guarantee that those most in need would be served, but that service would be rendered to Americans as a right accompanying their citizenship, not as a favor to the handicapped or deviant or poor.

Another problem inherent in the establishment of separate programs for the poor is that it tends to create what Martin Rein has called the Dual-Delivery-System, [17] separate but generally unequal programs for the poor. Rein concludes that the alternative to such a system is

> ...a policy...to achieve institutional reform designed to produce basic changes in education, job training and placement, medical care, etc. so that these institutions do not serve to perpetuate the advantages of those who already have, but that they become instruments for the redistribution of privileges and opportunity to those who have been excluded from the system. [18]

Does the foregoing strategy of coping with poverty mean the end of action-research programs like the Neighborhood Improvement

Project? The authors of the present volume do not draw this conclusion. We believe that a clear distinction must be made between
the meeting of basic unmet needs and action demonstration--with or
without research--in areas where the needs to be met are clearly
outside the realm of physical and social survival. Research-demon-
stration projects are especially appropriate where they involve inno-
vative action or alternative courses of action for meeting needs that
are not satisfied by the ethos of society or that have not been clearly identified.

Demonstration projects are hardly an adequate response to
basic survival needs. With the tools of economic, sociological,
psychological, and social work research that are at our disposal,
there is no problem in documenting basic survival need. The tech-
nology for coping with this need is also within our grasp. And if
our experience in comprehensive welfare planning is limited, the
programs of some of the Scandinavian and western European nations
can be useful models. Unfortunately, the chief obstacles to the introduction of a satisfactory welfare program lie in the political
realm, not in economic or technological factors.

A research demonstration project such as NIP has a particularly useful function when it operates in a setting where the urgent instrumental needs of the people are reasonably satisfied.
This means family incomes meeting the minimum levels recommended by home economists; insurance against unemployment, illness, disability, and loss of wage earner; and equal opportunity in
education for the young. A program of intervention in such a setting could address itself to aspects of living that are above the
floor level of survival needs, and the problems of the people could
be dealt with more effectively outside the context of economic and
social security.

When the design of the Neighborhood Improvement Project
was drawn up, we were aware of the intricate interrelationship between the economic and social deprivation of the Farnam Courts
population and the multi-problem behavior pattern manifested by a
considerable number of the families. But limitations in project
scope and resources resulted in a program of intervention that

could deal with only some of the needs identified.   Certain social
and psychological needs could be dealt with directly; economic
needs had to be disregarded or treated in a marginal manner.   In
the light of the staff assumption that economic, social, and psychological needs are intertwined, this design for intervention had
some built-in theoretical weaknesses.   The actual impact of the
program of intervention could hardly be expected to exceed our theoretical expectations.   A well designed project, according to this
line of reasoning, would have a program of intervention aimed at
specific needs likely to be satisfied by that form of intervention,
whose satisfaction will not be blocked by other unmet needs.

The growing demands of a complex urban society and the
increasing affluence of that society make it mandatory to provide in-
situtions and services for meeting the needs of the socially and economically deprived segment of our population; the establishment of
these institutions and services calls for multiple strategies on the
part of social planners in general and the social work profession in
particular.   We have tried in this book to convey our position that
intervention in adjustment and recreational services at the neighborhood level is not enough.   An effective program must address itself to all levels of human need, and the measures for meeting this
need should be part of an interlocking system of action carried out
at the Federal, state, and local levels.

What value is there then in the type of neighborhood program
represented by NIP?   The chief strength of NIP was its ability to
work closely with the people, in their homes and in the neighborhood, on problems of social relationships, adjustment, social and
cultural participation, leisure time and recreation, and use of community resources.   Key measures for accomplishing these goals included locating the offices in the housing project proper; having
volunteer and paid group workers, case workers, and the project
director keep close contact with the tenants and visit them in their
homes; and maintaining a full schedule of activities, including evenings and school vacations.   The close and continuous contact with
the tenants helped us understand them and their needs and enabled
the population to make contact with the larger community.   The es-

tablishment of a Boy Scout troop and of 4-H activities in Farnam
Courts and the use by Farnam Courts youth of various outside educational, recreational, and cultural institutions--previously beyond
their reach--were signs that a bridge between the neighborhood and
the larger society had been built.

In conclusion, we submit that the NIP type of program, far
from being superfluous, is of particular value in satisfying needs
that are not met by existing economic, health, and education programs, in situations where the basic survival needs of the population have already been cared for. A neighborhood program under
these circumstances could hardly fail to address itself to problems
of individual and family adjustment, socialization of the young, education and recreation and community integration. Efforts to bridge
the gap between neighborhood and community would have as their
aim the reduction of the alienation so characteristic of lower-class
America.

Alienation is, of course, closely related to lack of opportunity and social deprivation. Measures to relieve these conditions
are widely regarded as being instrumental in reducing alienation,
but the connection may not be so uncomplicated. After years of
societal neglect, alienation becomes an orientation and state of mind
that does not respond to simple reconditioning. The people in Farnam Courts and similar settings desperately need better opportunities, economic aid, and countless services; but the multi-problem
families, the socially isolated aged, the mothers on public assistance, the aggressive teenagers, also need to be assured that they
can become part of American society. That assurance requires
more than financial aid and a better opportunity structure. It needs
to be conveyed directly to the residents of the neighborhood, by professionals and volunteers with the motivation, knowledge, and skill
for improving the lot of the socially handicapped.

Notes

1. Richard A. Cloward and Lloyd Ohlin. Delinquency and
   Opportunity. (New York, The Free Press, 1960).

2. Catherine S. Chilman. Child Rearing Monograph. (unpublished manuscripted dated June 3, 1965), pp. 98-99.

3. Ibid. , p. 38.

4. Ibid. , p. 53.

5. Frederick Solomon, Walter L. Walker, et al. "Civil Rights Activities and Reduction in Crime Among Negroes," Arch. Gen. Psychiatry, March 1965, 12, pp. 227-236.

6. Edwin Powers. "An Experiment in Prevention of Delinquency," in Matilda White Riley, Sociological Research (New York, Harcourt, Brace and World, Inc., 1963) pp. 572-580.

7. Henry J. Meyer, Edgar F. Borgatta and Wyatt C. Jones. Girls at Vocational High. (New York, Russell Sage Foundation, 1965).

8. David Wallace and Jesse Smith. The Chemung County Research Demonstration with Dependent Multi-Problem Families. (New York, The State Charities Aid Association, 1965). (mimeographed)

9. Saul D. Alinsky. "The War on Poverty--Political Pornography," in The Journal of Social Issues, Vol. XXI, No. 1, January 1965, pp. 41-47.

10. Roland L. Warren. Types of Purposive Social Change at the Community Level. (Waltham, Mass., The Florence Heller Graduate School for Advanced Studies in Social Welfare, Brandeis University, 1965), p. 17.

11. The reasons for apparent failure, evident in 1967, of some of these programs may be inherent in the paradox of a design that provides Federal financing for action programs aimed at uprooting the very institutions that are the source of government power and authority.

12. Harold L. Wilensky and Charles N. Lebeaux. Industrial Society and Social Welfare. (New York, Russell Sage Foundation, 1958), p. 139.

13. Ibid., p. 138.

14. Ibid., p. 138.

15. Martin Rein and Frank Riessman. "A Strategy for Community Action Programs," Social Work, Vol. 11, No. 2, April 1966, pp. 3-12, p. 6.

16. Vis-a-vis the argument that the American economy no longer has room for the low skilled and under-educated, one can only point out that the steel mills and

automobile plants of western Europe are able to make good use of the even less skilled and less educated Moroccan, Spanish and southern Italian migrant laborers.

17. Martin Rein. "The Dual-Delivery-System," <u>Social and Educational Analysis and Policy, Informal Notes.</u> No. 1, April 1966, pp. 2-4 (mimeographed).

18. <u>Ibid.</u>, p. 4.

Index

393

National Institute of Mental Health 87-8, 287
Neighborhood functioning study of change in 354-69
Neighborhood Improvement Project (see NIP)
Neighborhood saturation 60, 62, 64
New Haven, Connecticut description 51
community councilof 58, 64, 68, 282-3, 288, 290-2, 381
planning commission of 51
New Haven Foundation 64, 68, 284, 287
New York City Youth Board 99, 100, 108, 160
Nichols, John 58-9, 66
NIP (Neighborhood Improvement Project)
advisory committee 69, 375
as a project title 10
changing structure of 283-8
design 88-95
early concept of 280-3
launching of 68
seminars 75
Northern, Helen 237, 262
Nursery school
aims of 229
early behavior of enrollees 228-9
program of 229-30
progress of enrollees 230-1
work with parents of enrollees in 231-3

Ohlin, Lloyd 390
Opportunity structure theory 372, 390
Overton, Alice 96, 160, 348, 353

Philp, A. F. 195, 204
Polansky, Norman 351
Poverty
official thinking re 10
programs to combat 11
war on 10, 370-1
Powers, Edwin 391
Profile of Family Functioning 74, 92-4
on E. case (illustration): beginning of treatment 111

first year of treatment 132-5
second year of treatment 147-9
third year of treatment 154-5
Puerto Rican population
and relations with social agencies 268
casework with 113, 175, 270-1
characteristics of 225
English classes for 272-5
nursery school for children of 271-2
percentage of in Farnam Courts 23
social integration program for youth of 275-6
treatment needs of 265

Redlich, Frederick C. 24, 32, 33, 102, 109
Rein, Martin 387, 391
Research
and demonstration projects 278-80, 289, 379, 383
early design of NIP 87
evaluating change, 92-4, 318-69
expansion of NIP 87-8
tough vs. tender-minded evaluation 321-2
Reynolds, Bertha 249, 263
Richmond, Mary 379
Riessman, Frank 391
Ripple, Lillian 304, 316
Roberts, Bertram H. 24, 47, 351
Rotival, Maurice E. 51

St. Paul Family Centered Project 68, 75, 87, 91, 93, 99, 281, 313-4, 319, 332, 344
St. Paul Scale of Family Functioning 73, 74, 89, 111, 330
Sarason, Seymour B. 109
Scherz, Frances H. 160
Schneiderman, Leonard 110
Screening-In Report 74
on the E. family 117-122
Senior Citizens' Club 247-50
Shyne, Ann W. 321, 351
Smith, Jesse 391
Social change
agents of 53, 55